Keep It
Together

DATE DUE

Keep It Together

RANDOM HOUSE REFERENCE

New York

Toronto

London

Sydney

Auckland

200+ tips, tricks, lists, and solutions for everyday life

Kirsten M. Lagatree

646.7
LAGA

Please address inquiries about electronic licensing of any products for use on a network, in software or on CD-ROM to the Subsidiary Rights Department, Random House Information Group, fax 212-572-6003.

This book is available at special discounts for bulk purchases for sales promotions or premiums. Special editions, including personalized covers, excerpts of existing books, and corporate imprints, can be created in large quantities for special needs. For more information, write to Random House, Inc., Special Markets/Premium Sales, 1745 Broadway, MD 6-2, New York, NY 10019 or e-mail specialmarkets@ randomhouse.com.

Library of Congress Cataloging-in-Publication Data is available.
Visit the Random House Reference Web site: www.randomwords.com

Design by Nora Rosansky

ISBN-10: 0-375-72179-7
ISBN-13: 978-0-375-72179-3

Printed in the United States of America

10 9 8 7 6 5 4 3 2 1

In Memory of

Helen Crane
(June 25, 1913–February 21, 2004)

Who gave birth to Mary and Joseph
but raised a dozen more children

and kept the memory of the old Bronx
alive for a grateful new generation

◆◆◆

Table of Contents

▮▮▮▮▮ [III   Community

▮▮▮▮▮ [IV   Correspondence

▮▮▮▮▮ [V   Social Life

[X House and Home

[XI Housework and Other Emergencies

[XII Flowers and Plants

XX Death and Grieving

Acknowledgments

I'm fortunate to have a village full of people who helped me with this book in a variety of ways. It's daunting to attempt to thank each one, but it's sure worth a try.

First, absolutely, on my gratitude list is my friend and companion in writing and reading, Rita DiMatteo. Without Rita's fine mind—a veritable fireworks fountain of inspired ideas—this book would be less complete. And without Rita's friendship, so would my life.

Thanks to Richard Schlesinger, friend to all creatures great and small, for his assistance with research and writing.

I'm grateful for professional advice from: Caryl Heaton, D.O., Associate Professor and Vice Chair of Family Medicine at UMDNJ–New Jersey Medical School; Ron Owens, M.A., Hospice of New Jersey; Mary E. WanderPolo, J.D., founding member of the New York State Bar Association's Elder Law Section and the National Academy of Elder Law Attorneys. Real estate professionals Barbara and Leon Shoag of Remax Realty in Long Beach, California, and Adriana O'Toole and Barbara Rudy of Montclair Realty in Montclair, New Jersey.

A bundle of gratitude to pals Alice Bredin, Kerry Donahue, Page Edmunds, Pam Satran, and Lisa Vitale, whose personal experience of being new moms contributed richly to this book. Thank you and awe to the amazing Karen Weaver for cosmopolitan savvy and great list ideas and tips.

I am grateful for the contributions of Katherine Tallmadge, author of *Diet Simple*, and Washington, DC nutritionist who makes the movers and shakers in Washington move and drink shakes; event planner Carol Beaugard, founder and president of Affairs of Distinction (*www.affairsofdistinction.com*), who could show Ms. Stewart a thing or two about throwing an elegant wedding; and organizer Deborah Gussoff of In Order, Inc.

(*www.inorder.com*), who has shown me a thing or two about getting and staying organized.

My thanks to Lance Ness, L.C.S.W., behavior health-care administrator, for his insight and advice on a wide range of issues, and also to Michelle Lepak, L.C.S.W., for lending moral support and insight on several areas of the book. Thank you to consummate professional Marion Lagatree, for coaching me on legal and crime prevention tips, and to Catherine Carlisle, Kitty Felde, John Galligan, Richard Koonce, Marian McDonald, Meg Mc-Sweeney, Annie Paine, Frank Paine, Suzanne Paine, Reverend Victor R. Peterson, and Jon (H. G.) Randel for their great ideas and wholehearted support.

Special thanks to Steve Adamczyk for technical assistance and waffles.

Much love and deepest appreciation to my friend Epp Raun, who literally flew to my side whenever I needed help of any kind.

Many thanks to my talented agent Jonathan Peckarsky of The William Morris Agency, and a veritable blizzard of gratitude to my meticulous, marvelous, and patient editor, Paula Consolo. I also want to recognize Jena Pincott, late of Random House and last heard from somewhere near the Himalayas, who was a great champion of this book from its earliest days.

Special thanks to Elinor Lipman, my friend, guardian angel, and favorite author.

As always, my love and gratitude to Bruce, Marion, Donald, and my favorite person on the planet, Leo T. Lagatree.

Introduction

Remember when you were a kid and you thought adults knew everything? You figured by the time you grew up you would know everything, too. Then you hit that magic age; maybe for you it was twenty-one. If you could be served in a bar, surely all the important facts and answers you'd ever need would soon begin to congregate in your head. But no, not quite, not yet.

If you're in your twenties or thirties right now, you may still hold out hope that at some point the answers to all life's questions will be right on the tip of your tongue. Don't hold your breath. If you're already forty, the cat's probably out of the bag by now. You're resigned to the fact that getting older doesn't mean having all the answers.

The plain truth, as it turns out, is that adulthood descends, experience accumulates, and still we stumble into situations that baffle us. No matter how many birthdays have scampered by, none of us is ever quite ready for all of life's challenges.

Raise your hand if you've ever thought: "Oh jeez, shouldn't I know this already?" Or worse: "Yikes, how do I deal with *this*?" Hey, it happens. Eventually, even the coolest and most confident person will have an "oh jeez" or "yikes" moment. No one can know everything, and why bother to try? As Albert Einstein very sensibly asked, "Why should I memorize anything if I can just look it up?" He had an excellent point. And you now have *Keep It Together,* the very book where you can "just look it up."

There are so many practical skills we need to master as adults. We learn some from our parents, and occasionally we soak up useful information at school, but wouldn't it be great to be offered a class called "On Your Own for the First Time 101," when you find yourself on your own, whether you are twenty-one, forty-one, or sixty-one? This book serves as that class, covering down-and-dirty, hands-on topics, such as how to:

- *Do the laundry without doing it any harm.*
- *Choose and use a credit card without ruining your credit.*
- *Rent an apartment you will enjoy living in.*
- *Shop and cook for yourself in a reasonably civilized manner.*
- *Manage monthly bills so they don't sneak up on you when you're broke.*

Eventually those ordinary tasks become old hat, but life changes quickly and, before you know it, you are stepping into unknown territory once again. Perhaps you're facing a sensitive or sorrowful situation that would be a challenge for anyone, no matter what their age or experience. *Keep It Together* can help with those less concrete, but no less critical, how-tos:

- *Help a friend who's dealing with grief or a serious illness.*
- *Work any room and be the perfect guest—or host.*
- *Find ways to connect with your community.*
- *Apologize graciously or mend a rift with a friend.*
- *Negotiate with anyone.*

For those carefree moments in life, *Keep It Together* can guide you with the frivolous, but no less compelling, questions of how to:

- *Choose an exotic vacation.*
- *Write the perfect on-line dating profile.*
- *Choose a feng shui practitioner.*
- *Pick out the perfect present.*
- *Shop for airfare and hotel deals on the Internet.*
- *Tip with confidence and style wherever you go.*

Whether you're just starting out in life or on your own for the first time in a long while, *Keep It Together* will become your new best friend, your dependable reference for life in the world today.

Keep It Together will help you get it together, too.

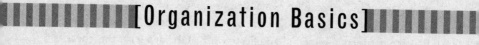

[Organization Basics]

Write an Effective Daily To-Do List

Note to self: People forget. I am a person; therefore . . .
what was I writing about? Oh, yes, to-do lists.

A good daily to-do list gets short-term tasks out of your brain, where they can float into dark crevices and be lost forever, and puts them in an easily retrievable location, physical or virtual. Writing any to-do list brings an immediate sense of virtue and accomplishment. Writing an effective to-do list increases your chances of actually getting some essential tasks done. There's a subtle difference between any list and an effective list, and that's what this checklist is about.

1. **Make it real.** Your daily to-do list is not your life plan. It's a list of things you need to do today. Lose weight doesn't belong on it; buy toilet paper does.

2. **Make it simple.** If a task needs an explanation, it doesn't belong on this to-do list. Items on this list should be self-explanatory and consist of a single action.

3. **Distinguish between a task and a project.** A project is "plan the Thanksgiving party"; a task is "buy the turkey." Projects don't belong on daily to-do lists; they're too big and daunting (see "Keep a Master List" below). Break projects down into discrete, doable tasks.

4. **Be specific.** Don't write "touch base with Joe"; write "call Joe." Don't write "dinner"; write "buy hot dogs, potato chips, apple pie, and ice cream."

5. **Stick to "next actions."** A to-do list is a commitment to short-term tasks, not long-term goals. Limit your entries to the next thing you need to do to move a project along. If this is the Monday of Thanksgiving week, "buy turkey" should be on your to-do list, but "determine the seating plan" should not. The seating plan may appear on Thursday's list, but it's not the next thing you need to do today.

6. **Prioritize.** The lack of prioritizing is often the bane of an effective to-do list. Start with the items that will give you the biggest payoff in terms of accomplishment. Rank lower the tasks you'd like to get done but that

will have less impact on your overall productivity, such as sorting junk mail.

7. **Give yourself enough, but not too much, to do.** The longer the list, the more daunting it may seem, and you are less likely to take it seriously enough to act on it. On the other hand, putting a few more items on the list than you think you can achieve might be a good motivator, lending a sense of urgency to your progress throughout the day.

8. **Banish or subdue the repeat offender.** If the same item appears on your list day after day without your acting on it, it should be reconsidered or eliminated. For example, if "call Joe" has been on your lists for the past two weeks, you need to consider why you are not calling him. Once you identify the reason for your inaction, you should decide whether you can overcome the issue and make the call or if you should simply eliminate "call Joe" from your list.

9. **Keep your list in one place.** Decide where your to-do list will reside: on your paper day planner, on your wall calendar, in a separate pocket notebook, in your personal digital assistant (PDA), or on your computer. If you write your list on whatever piece of paper is handy, you're sending yourself a message that this is a grab-as-grab-can list, not a serious commitment to necessary tasks. Note to technophiles: If you love electronic gizmos, choose one for your to-do list, but only one. If some items live on your computer and others in your PDA, some will get done and others won't. If you're really more comfortable with paper and pencil, stick to that method.

Organize Files and Records

There are at least as many ways to organize files and records as there are to organize books. You can sort files by color and size, by category, or by date, but if you ever want to find a document again, you'll have to devise a more sensible system. Here are some suggestions to get you started.

1. **Choose a good file cabinet.** Don't skimp here. Choose a cabinet that's big enough for your files with plenty of extra room for the files you'll accumulate in the next few years. The cabinet should have drawers that ✳

STREAMLINE YOUR DAY

One reason for keeping an effective to-do list is to help you stop wasting time on trivialities, at least until the most important tasks are done. Here are a few more tricks to help you streamline your day.

Create your to-do list the night before. You'll sleep better knowing you've laid out the day ahead, and you'll be able to spend that day taking action on your list rather than trying to decide what should go on it.

Do the quick things up front. If your list includes items that typically take very little time, such as making a dentist appointment or backing up computer files, get those out of the way first. This will boost your self-esteem while paring your list quickly.

Eat the worm first. Which is to say, schedule the most unpleasant thing you have to do as early in the day as possible. Having something unpleasant hanging over your head makes the whole day drag and encourages procrastination.

Shop during off hours. Avoid the mall and supermarket between 11 A.M. and 1 P.M. and between 5 P.M. and 7 P.M., the busiest times.

Plan a circular route. Plan your errands so that they take you in a circle that ends back at your home. This saves gas and time.

Zap distractions. Turn off your e-mail notification and turn on your answering machine. The fewer distractions you have while doing important tasks, the faster they'll get done. Recent studies suggest that multitasking actually reduces efficiency. Set aside particular times of the day to check e-mail, listen to messages, and return phone calls.

Plan long-term. People often plan their days one at a time, which is a time-wasting mistake. When writing your to-do list and planning your schedule, think in terms of at least a week; even better, think two weeks ahead. Planning is always more efficient than reacting (see "Keep a Master List" below).

Leave some wiggle room. If you plan your day down to the last quarter hour, your entire schedule will fall apart when something unexpected comes up. Leaving time for inevitable interruptions increases the chances that you will stay on schedule.

KEEP A MASTER LIST

Limiting your daily to-do list to items you can reasonably expect to accomplish in one day keeps your day focused, but you also need to plan ahead. That's where the master list comes in. Typically, a master list is a group of projects that you would like to complete in a week's time (although you can keep a monthly or bimonthly master list if you prefer). This list is very much a working document that you use to keep track of the larger projects from which your daily tasks evolve. It should also be the central repository for any quick ideas, bits of information, and any new or leftover to-dos that accumulate as the week goes on. Your master list gives you one place to look for everything you should be doing all week long. It takes the place of those multiple sticky notes that once dotted your computer monitor and desk top.

pull out all the way so that you can easily access all files. It should also be solid enough that it doesn't threaten to tip over when the top drawer is fully extended. If you have enough room, legal size is a better choice than letter size, even if you don't have a lot of legal papers. The larger file size can accommodate catalogs, magazine-size papers, and instruction books without excessive folding. Lateral file cabinets, which hold files from left to right rather than from front to back, may be a better choice for you, depending on the configuration of your space.

2. **Choose a good location for your cabinet.** Lateral or standard, put your file cabinet in a convenient, easily accessible spot. If you have to crawl behind the couch to get to it, you'll defeat the whole purpose of having it and revert to the thoroughly discredited "file by pile" method.

3. **File alphabetically.** Files certainly can be organized by subject or category, but the simplest method is to arrange them alphabetically. Professional organizer Barbara Hemphill, author of *Taming the Paper Tiger,* argues persuasively for alphabetizing because it eliminates gray areas, when an item might easily fit more than one category. Still, you need to make rational decisions. For example, you should have a file labeled "Car" in which you keep maintenance records, warranty documents, and the title for your car, but correspondence concerning your car insurance should go in the "Insurance" folder, which should contain all of your insurance information: health, home, car, disability, liability, and any other kind you have.

4. **Create subfiles.** Placing files within files will help you find specific papers quickly. For example, in your insurance folder, you should have a subfolder for each type of insurance. You can do this by putting individual manila folders into larger hanging folders that have plastic label holders. But there are limits to how much you can fit into a single hanging file. If the category is large—and insurance papers can easily grow beyond the confines of a single hanging file—simply use a series of these files, each labeled "Insurance," along with a subcategory: "Insurance: Health," "Insurance: Car," "Insurance: Household," and so on. And don't hesitate to create subfiles within subfiles. There should be a separate folder for each family member under "Insurance: Health," for example. This makes filing and retrieving information fast and foolproof.

5. **Do it now.** Filing postponed is filing abandoned. Resist the temptation to just take a peek at your mail. If you open it, deal with it. Once the piles grow, they become daunting, and a simple task becomes a day's project. When you buy the new digital camera, file the receipt immediately. If you need to produce proof-of-purchase because it fails six months down the road, you'll be glad you didn't let that flimsy cash-register receipt languish under piles of mail on your desk, only to disappear entirely in a fit of spring cleaning.

6. **Keep a "tickler" file.** This is a special file, separate from your filing cabinet, that has a pocket for each day of the month. Here's where you should keep time-sensitive mail, including bills, filed according to when you need to act on them. If a bill is due on the 29th, for instance, put it in the slot marked the 22nd, so you can mail it in plenty of time. Just don't forget to check your tickler file each day. Transfer items from the tickler file

either to the garbage or to a permanent file, depending on whether or not you'll ever need them again.

7. **Throw away old files.** Don't clutter your filing system with useless paper. Each time you file something, glance at what else is in the folder and discard what you no longer need. Insurance companies tend to send new policies every year; you don't need last year's once the new one arrives. Discard warranties and instruction booklets for items you no longer own. Don't keep paperwork on a car you sold months ago unless you need it for tax purposes. Just be careful with what you throw in the garbage; if it has personal information, shred it.

Make Your Workspace Work

Your personal record for time wasted may be more or less than the norm, but experts say that a person who works at a messy desk wastes about an hour and a half every day. Productive time seeps away when you're forced to search for what you need or are distracted by irrelevant items constantly drifting into your field of concentration. If you are a victim of clutter, don't despair. Just follow these steps to put your work area in order. Remember, you're in charge of the paperwork; it should not be in charge of you!

1. **Purge the piles.** Doing this takes time, but the payoff is big. Every piece of paper that sits around on your desk represents a postponed decision and drains your focus. Start sorting your accumulated mess into three piles: action, file, and toss. If you can't face this job all at once, schedule at least half an hour every day to do it.

2. **Decide to decide.** Sort your action pile into tasks that can be postponed and those that can be dealt with quickly. For the latter, just do them. You'll be surprised how much you can get done inside twenty minutes once you simply get going. Next, work through the list of postponed tasks and either delegate them to someone else or schedule a time to do each one.

3. **File the pile.** As you sort through each piece of paper to file, ask yourself the following questions: Do I *really* need to keep this? If so, the next ques-

tions are: Why? and Where will I look for it when I need it? If the document really belongs in a file, see "Organize Files and Records" (page 3) for tips on creating an easy-to-use filing system.

4. **Use two trash bins.** This trick helps you let go of papers you're unsure about. The first trash can is for papers you can easily toss, shred, or recycle. Paperwork you're unsure about goes into your second trash can, one that you empty only every couple of weeks. This gives you time to go back and retrieve something if you decide that you need it. Meanwhile, it's out of the way and off your mind.

5. **Be fussy about your desk top.** Reserve the surface of your desk for items you use daily. These items include your computer, of course, your Rolodex or PDA, a message and note-taking pad, your calendar, and anything else you reach for several times a day. Items that don't need to be within immediate arm's reach should go elsewhere. Yes, you can keep a picture of your spouse, child, or pet on your desk, but don't get carried away with multiple photos or "good luck" tchotchkes.

6. **Organize desk drawers.** Pens, stapler, paper clips, cellophane tape, and similar supplies belong in desk drawers. Other items and backup supplies should be placed in a cabinet, credenza, or storage closet. Remember, you don't need to fill your desk drawers to the brim to be using them efficiently.

7. **Keep reference material nearby.** Hang a shelf over or close to your desk to hold your dictionary, thesaurus, project notebooks, manuals, or other books or bound items you refer to frequently. This way they're handy but not constantly in your way.

8. **Keep up the good work.** Conduct weekly cleaning rituals when you sort, file, and toss the paperwork that accumulates. This is the only way to maintain the organization you worked so hard to create. Be faithful in doing this, and you'll not only continue to be productive, but you'll also never have to repeat the daunting task you began at the top of this list!

TIP: Productivity expert Donald E. Wetmore (*The Productivity Handbook,* Random House Reference, 2005) recommends that you keep no more than three or four items on your desk to handle right away.

Organize Photos

◆◆◆

Photos are a lot like mail. The arrival of both is greeted with a wave of excitement and anticipation, followed by some disappointment (the bills, the out-of-focus shots of your shoes) and some happy surprises (the check you've been waiting for, the perfect moment caught for posterity), and, inevitably, both can end up in oblivion. But one day you will need to find that particular letter in the now enormous pile on your desk or that special photo sitting somewhere in a shoe box, but which shoe box? Digital photos make the need to organize more imperative. If you don't adopt a rational plan early, you'll likely wind up with nameless files scattered haphazardly among countless gigabytes, effectively lost and irretrievable. The solution: Organize early, organize often, and organize rationally, so you and your posterity can enjoy your photos for years to come.

For Traditional Photos

1. **Choose the right albums.** Choose albums that are comfortable to handle, fit easily on a bookshelf, and don't get lost among the books and other objects. They should be made with archival materials, including acid-free paper and acid-free protective plastic sheets. These albums are more expensive than nonarchival albums, but your photos will last much longer in them.

2. **Choose the right boxes.** Like photo albums, photo boxes should be acid free and a convenient size. Take your photos out of the envelope they come in and put them in acid-free envelopes. Put the negatives in special negative sleeves and put these in an acid-free envelope, too. Make sure to keep the two envelopes together and label the outside of each with the date and the subject of the photos.

3. **Do it now.** When you get a roll of film developed, organize and store the photos as soon as you bring them home. If you wait for a more convenient time, chances are the photos will remain in the envelope you picked them up in and the envelope will wind up at the back of a drawer until you move.

4. **Sort them by subject.** Don't file photos by date; instead, create categories—family celebrations and holidays, vacations, pets, children, home

life—and keep like with like. Put all the vacation photos in one album, the birthday and other celebration photos in another, and so on.

5. **Identify each photo.** You can write lightly on the back of a photo with an acid-free pen (available in art-supply stores), or you can attach a separate label under the photo in an album. Either way, write the date and subject of each photo, even if it seems obvious. You may know Uncle Al and cousin Larry, but sixty years from now, your great-grandchildren won't unless you leave them a hint.

6. **Include longer descriptions.** You can put a pocket divider between major sections of an album in which you can keep a sheet that describes the pages that follow. This gives you much more room than small labels provide, and allows you to write something that gives meaning and dimension to the photos that follow. This can also be a good place to keep the negatives. Cut the negatives up and store them in sleeves if you don't use a separate box system.

7. **Think in terms of story.** Some subjects lend themselves to a story-like system of organization. For instance, you might organize photos of children by starting with pictures taken in the hospital when they were born. Birthdays form natural chapters, as do milestones such as the first day of school, the first season at sleep-away camp, and weddings.

For Digital Photos

1. **Use quality inks and paper.** If you print out copies of digital photos, use a printer with so-called archival inks as well as archival paper. Exactly how long these inks last is debatable, especially those used in nonprofessional printers, but digital prints made with archival inks on quality paper may last as long, if not longer, than chemically processed photo prints.

2. **Treat digital prints like regular photos.** Put digital prints in albums or boxes with archival paper and plastic, keep them out of strong light, and handle them with care.

3. **Take advantage of digital organizers.** Because they take up no actual space, digital photos can pile up on your hard drive. Keep them there long enough, and your collection will devolve into a useless mélange of unnamed, unseen images. Programs to store and organize digital pictures are extremely effective, easy to use, and either free or inexpensive. Among the best is Apple's iPhoto, part of the company's iLife series, which comes

free with every new Mac. Other options are Adobe's Photoshop Album (Windows), ACDSee (for Windows and Mac), and iView Media (for Windows and Mac). Many digital cameras ship with free photo-organizing software for Macs and PCs.

4. **Label and sort.** Digital cameras assign numbers to each photo. These numbers are totally useless unless you're an idiot-savant, so as soon as you upload images to the computer, give each file a descriptive name and assign it to a folder. The folder hierarchy you design should make it easy to find pictures by theme or date. At the top of the hierarchy, make a folder for photos; within that folder you can make as many subfolders as you like. Photo-management software always includes a field where you can describe the picture. Don't mince words. The more precise you are, the better the chances of finding the photo years later by doing a search on any of the words you've used. Again, programs like iPhoto make the filing system much easier than trying to do it ad-hoc.

5. **Back up.** Be sure to make at least two back-up copies of important digital photos. The easiest way to do this is to burn them onto a CD or copy them onto an external hard drive. For safety's sake, keep a copy in a place other than your primary residence. This could be a safe-deposit box, a second home, or the home of a friend or relative.

> **TIP:** If you can add pages to the albums you choose, be sure to buy extras. You'll be using these albums for a long time, possibly longer than the manufacturer stays in business.

Organize Your Clothes Closet

◆◆◆

Imagine facing your closet in the morning with the feeling of pleasant anticipation that comes from knowing you can quickly and confidently pull together an outfit. Can't quite conjure up that image? Don't despair. Figuring out what to wear will be a snap after you devote a few hours to the following process.

1. **Rip through it ruthlessly.** Your first order of business is to remove any items that aren't wardrobe related. If you've been using your clothes closet to store miscellaneous household objects, banish them now. Buy a plastic container for those rolls of gift-wrapping paper and slide it under the bed. Move, donate, or throw out anything else that's cluttering your wardrobe storage area.

2. **Cull favorites, toss fashion errors.** We've all purchased clothing that somehow looked like a foreign object after we got it home. Keeping the patchwork skirt or the purple shoes that you'll never wear doesn't bring back the money you accidentally spent on them. Put these items aside and donate them to a thrift store.

3. **Try on clothing you haven't worn in a year.** This job is tedious at best and can be demoralizing at worst. It might be helpful to have a friend help you make decisions about what to keep and what to toss. As a bonus, you'll have someone to laugh with as you part with items that no longer—or never did—flatter you.

4. **Put like items together.** Now that you're working with only the clothes you'll actually wear, sort them by type of garment—skirts, dresses, pants, and so on. Next, sort each category by color. This will help you see what goes with what. It has the additional benefit of letting you quickly spot which colors you have lots of and which you may be missing. If you have only one or two items in a particular color and nothing much that blends with them, these items may belong in the "donate" pile.

5. **Move out-of-season items out of the way.** If you have a spare closet, use it to store seasonal items that you won't be wearing for a few months. If you don't have a separate closet, place seasonal clothing farther back in the closet so you won't be reaching past it to get what you need.

6. **Line up your shoes.** Ideally, put your shoes on a shoe rack or, if you're tall enough, on the shelf above the hanger pole. If you can, avoid having a jumble of shoes on the closet floor. If you have nowhere else to stash your shoes, upend a couple of crates on the floor of your closet and place your shoes in and on top of the crates. If you've watched too many episodes of *Sex and the City* and have cornered the market on shoes, store them in shoe boxes with their color and style written outside in marking

pen. Consider taking a snapshot of each pair and taping the photo to the end of the box.

7. **Hang sweaters gently.** Purchase some padded hangers for your sweaters and knit items. They will thank you by holding their shape for years to come.

8. **Avoid wire hangers!** Wire hangers should be used only by dry cleaners to return clothes to customers. They aren't suitable for long-term storage of any garment. Treat yourself to plastic, wooden, or padded hangers. Your dry cleaner will be happy to take back the wire hangers next time you drop off your cleaning.

9. **Access accessories easily.** Purchase an assortment of hangers designed especially for ties, belts, and scarves. With these items in plain sight, it will be a breeze to coordinate your look as you plan the basics of your outfit.

TIP: If space in your closet and bedroom is at a premium, fold any clothing that doesn't need to be hung and that you don't wear frequently. Put these items in a wicker basket or other attractive container and make it double as a bedside table.

Eliminate Unwanted Mail and Phone Calls

If you look forward to the ring of the phone as you sit down to dinner, if you can't wait to sort through the catalogs and circulars the postal worker brings each day, read no further. But if you prefer to eat dinner without interruptions and have some feelings for our forests, there are steps you can take to reduce, if not completely eliminate, unwanted phone calls and junk mail. (To reduce electronic junk mail, see "Eliminate Spam," page 42).

1. **Sign up to be on the federal government's Do-not-call Registry.** The simplest way to cut down on telemarketing calls is to put all of your phone

numbers—home, fax, mobile—on the federal Do-not-call Registry. You can do this online at *www.donotcall.gov*, or you can call 888–382–1222 from the phone you wish to register. This registry is not foolproof. Phone calls from outside the country, such as those from Canada, can often get through, and signing up on the registry won't take you off many lists, such as those of companies you do business with, nonprofit groups, and political parties, but being on the Do-not-call Registry will certainly reduce calls from companies pushing the latest in ab-firming devices.

2. **Get off the Direct Marketing Association (DMA) members' lists.** You can eliminate a great deal of unsolicited mail by asking to be removed from the DMA's members' lists. Write: Mail Preference Service, Direct Marketing Association, P.O. Box 643, Carmel, NY 10512. This can also be done online for a $5 fee; go to *www.dmaconsumers.org*. While at that site, you should also register with the DMA's Telephone Preference Service to be taken off members' telemarketing lists. None of these services will eliminate all unsolicited mail and phone calls—you might still receive communications from local merchants, professional and alumni associations, political candidates, officeholders, and companies that don't subscribe to the DMA—but all of these services will cut down on mail and calls you don't want to get.

3. **Get off the lists of other major marketing associations.** Other direct marketing firms and associations maintain lists of people who don't want to be contacted. They include: Metromail Corporation, Name Removal, 901 West Bond St., Lincoln, NE 68521, 800–228–4571, ext. 4633; Donnelly Marketing, Inc., Database Operations, 1235 N Ave., Nevada, IA 50201–1419, 888–633–4402; R. L. Polk & Co. Opt Out File, 26955 Northwestern Highway, Southfield, MI 48034, 800–873–7655.

4. **Don't send in warranty cards.** Warranty cards are used for marketing purposes. Why else would a company want to know your sex and how many children and animals live with you? You're covered under all warranties whether you return the card or not. The only things you won't receive are product recall notices, but when have you actually received one of these? If you've already returned the card for your answering machine or nonstick cookware, you can get off the warranty marketing lists by writing or calling National Demographics & Lifestyles, Customer Service Department, 1621 18th St., #300, Denver, CO 80202, 800–525–3533.

5. **Cut coupon clutter.** To eliminate most unwanted coupons, ads, and free samples, write ADVO Inc., Delivery Services, 1001 W. Walnut St., Compton CA 90220–5191.

6. **Check (or don't check) the right boxes.** Many companies provide a check-off box on membership or order forms so you can request that your name and address not be shared with other companies. Read these forms carefully and do the right thing: Sometimes checking the box means you want the company to share your name, sometimes it means you don't want the company to share your name.

7. **Be careful when filling out forms online.** Again, when you order on-line or even download programs, there's often a box to be checked that gives or withholds permission to share your name. Read it carefully and check the box, or don't, depending on how it's worded.

8. **Call or write the major credit reporting agencies.** Each of the three major credit reporting agencies is required by law to abide by your directives about sharing your name and address with others. Call or write to each of the three: Experian (formerly TRW), Opt Out, P.O. Box 919, Allen, TX 75013, 800–353–0809; Trans Union Corporation, Name Removal Option, P.O. Box 97328, Jackson, MS 39288–7328, 888–567–8688; Equifax Options, P.O. Box 740123, Atlanta, GA 30374–0123, 800–556–4711.

Open a Safe-Deposit Box

A desk drawer may be the perfect place for current bills, and a cigar box—does anyone still smoke cigars?—may be ideal for last year's holiday cards, but when it comes to storing the really important stuff, you'll need someplace secure, someplace you know will be there even after a bout of spring cleaning fever. That's why safe-deposit boxes were invented.

1. **Select a bank.** The usual choice is the branch where you do your banking. Banks usually give first dibs and discounts on their often scarce boxes to regular customers. Just make sure you can easily get to the branch from your home and/or office and that its hours are convenient.

2. **Decide on what size box you need.** Safe-deposit boxes come in various shapes and sizes, from long and narrow to wide and deep. If you're going to use your box only for documents you can fold, you might get away with the smallest size, but most people keep jewelry, documents they don't want to fold (such as diplomas), and other larger items in their boxes, so it is worthwhile to at least consider larger sizes. If you want to include CDs with copies of irreplaceable photos and DVDs of home video in your box, make sure it is big enough to accommodate them.

3. **Make sure someone else has access to your box.** If you are the only one with access to your box, and you find yourself out-of-town or incapacitated but needing something in that box, you will be out of luck. And if—heaven forbid—you should pass away, family members will have a hard time retrieving the items in your box. You can jointly rent a safe-deposit box with a spouse, partner, child, other close relative, or anyone else. Both of you have to sign the rental agreement in person at the bank. You can also appoint a deputy or agent who will be authorized to gain access to the box if you can't. The deputy must be appointed in the presence of the box renter(s) and a bank employee. A person holding power of attorney for you may not be granted access to your box, because the bank may not be able to verify either the identity of the person or the validity of the power-of-attorney agreement.

4. **Keep the keys in a safe place.** Two different keys will be required to open your safe-deposit box. One key remains with the bank. You are given two copies of your key. The bank does not retain a copy of your key, so if you don't have it, there's no way to open the box without breaking the lock, which requires the service of a locksmith. If you lose your key, the bank will charge you for the locksmith and a replacement lock and keys. That's why they give you two copies of your key, and that's why you should be sure to keep them in safe places—plural— places you'll remember. It doesn't help to have two keys and forget where you put them.

5. **Pay the fee on time.** If you fail to pay the rental fee, you might lose access to your box. If you fail to pay for a certain period of time, which varies by state, the contents of the box may be considered to be abandoned, in which case the contents revert to the state. Banks have to make

reasonable efforts to locate you and warn you, but you'd be surprised how often safe-deposit boxes are simply abandoned or forgotten. Make sure you're not the only one who knows about a safe-deposit box you rent, lest it be abandoned in the event of your death.

6. **Decide what to keep in the box.** There are two questions that can help determine what things should be in your safe-deposit box: Would I be in deep trouble without this item, and would I be heartbroken if it were gone forever? As for the first question, make sure you don't put something in the box that you might need when the bank is closed, such as your passport. Also, check with your attorney about whether to store originals or copies of such important documents as wills and powers of attorney in your box. (See the sidebar, "What to Keep in a Safe-Deposit Box and What Not to," for suggestions of things to keep in the box and things to keep at home.)

7. **Consider purchasing vault insurance.** Items in a safe-deposit box are not automatically insured by the Federal Deposit Insurance Corporation, the body that insures bank deposits up to a certain amount. Your homeowner's policy might insure the contents up to a set amount, but don't count on it. If you keep jewelry or other valuables in the box, talk to your insurance agent about vault insurance, which is quite inexpensive and usually covers jewelry stored in the box even if it's lost or stolen when it's temporarily out of the box. And while bank vaults are pretty safe places, they're not immune to fires, floods, or terrorist attacks. If the bank can be proved to be negligent in preventing a loss, their liability insurance will kick in; if not, you're on your own.

8. **Know what's in your box.** Keep a detailed list of everything you have in your safe-deposit box. Include serial numbers of stocks, bonds, and certificates of deposit.

WHAT TO KEEP— AND NOT KEEP—
IN A SAFE-DEPOSIT BOX

YOUR SAFE-DEPOSIT BOX IS A GOOD PLACE TO KEEP:

Copies of or original estate-planning documents. Examples of such documents are wills, trusts, and powers of attorney. The originals should be kept in the box only under the advice of your attorney. If you live in a state where a box is sealed upon the death of one of the renters, the originals should be kept elsewhere, such as at your lawyer's; if your state allows access to co-renters when one renter dies, the originals may be kept in the box.

Deeds, titles, and property documents. Keep deeds and titles to your house, vacation house, vehicles, and burial plots in your box.

Other legal papers. This category includes patents, contracts, partnership agreements, notes, and loan agreements.

Stocks, bonds, and certificates of deposit

Family documents. These important papers include birth, marriage, divorce, and death certificates; military records; adoption papers; citizenship papers.

Diplomas and transcripts. You might want to keep copies of these at home as well.

Complete home inventory. This should include all appraisals of jewelry and fine art and antiques as well as pictures of what's inside and outside your house. Include pictures of vacation property and all vehicles.

Jewelry

Heirlooms

Photographs. Copy irreplaceable photographs and videos onto CDs and DVDs and keep a copy in the box.

Records and Documents You Need at Home

◆◆◆

Keeping certain important papers and items at home has advantages. The alternative is to keep them in the safe-deposit box, but getting to the bank, waiting for the vault attendant to retrieve your box (assuming you haven't lost the little key), the trip to the cubbyhole of a room, and waiting for the vault attendant to return the box can be a drag. Here are some items that can be kept at home (see also, "Take Reasonable Precautions," page 182).

1. **Insurance policies.** Keep your insurance policies in one place and review them annually. Toss out old policies, and just keep current ones. These include homeowners, automobile, and health policies.

2. **Health-care records.** Keep a separate file for each member of the household. Ask your doctor for copies of lab reports, so you won't have to repeat them or translate results if you need to see another physician. It's helpful to have copies of x-rays and MRIs, especially if the condition for which they were taken is chronic. Also, don't forget about your pets' health records; a copy may help avoid expensive repeats of tests.

3. **Education records.** These include diplomas and certificates, licenses, and professional association memberships. If your diploma has sentimental value, you might want to put the original in a safe-deposit box, because replacement copies would lack the original seal. Otherwise, it's fine to keep diplomas at home.

4. **Employment records.** If your company issues a press release about you or work you've done, save a copy. Also keep any documentation of per-

formance, announcements of promotions, and letters of commendation. Save old résumés; they often list early accomplishments that may someday become relevant again, for example, should you decide you want to change your career.

5. **Will and living will.** Consult your attorney about just where to keep these. Your attorney or your executor might want the original or a copy. Leaving the only copy of a will in a bank vault can prove problematic if the vault is sealed after death. You and your physician, as well as next of kin or the person who holds your health-care proxy, should have a copy of your living will. Keep a copy of a durable power of attorney at home but give the original either to the person you've designated to hold the power or to your attorney.

6. **Passports.** Keep your family's passports at home just in case you need them for an emergency trip when the bank is not open. Keep a copy of the numbers of each passport either in your safe-deposit box or with a friend or relative.

7. **Tax and investment records.** The IRS has three years to audit returns, so you should keep the returns and supporting evidence of deductions for at least that time. If the IRS suspects fraud, it has six years to prosecute, so if you're a suspicious character, play it safe and keep everything for six years (although if you're a suspicious character, you probably have more to worry about than record keeping). Keep investment records as long as an account is open, and at least three years beyond that.

8. **Household inventory.** Keep a copy of your household inventory at home or with a trusted relative or friend. This should include all appraisals of jewelry and fine art and antiques as well as pictures of what's inside and outside your house. Include pictures of vacation property and all vehicles. The original copy of this inventory should be in your safe-deposit box. (See also, "Take Reasonable Precautions," page 182, and "Take a Home Inventory," page 312.)

9. **List of everything in your wallet.** Include credit card numbers, license numbers, even short descriptions of the pictures you carry. If you lose your wallet or it's stolen, you'll save time and heartache if you know exactly whom to contact and what to replace.

10. **Safe-deposit box contents.** Keep an inventory of everything in your safe-deposit box, including copies of documents.

11. **Receipts for warrantied purchases.** You should have a file for receipts of purchases that carry a warranty, including appliances, electronics, and computer equipment. Keep receipts for major purchases even after warranties expire if the item is tax-deductible and is being amortized. It's also wise to keep these receipts for insurance purposes, in case you ever need to file a claim for loss or theft.

12. **Receipts for all home improvements.** If you sell your home you can deduct the cost of capital improvements from profits for tax purposes. Keep home-improvement receipts for at least three years after a home sale in case the IRS decides to audit you.

13. **Instruction manuals.** Keep these in one place, so when you need to re-program the cordless phone you won't harm any household members in your frustration.

MAKING IT SECURE

Not everything you keep at home needs to be in a secure place. Anything you can duplicate and relatively uncritical things, such as instruction manuals, should be kept in a file cabinet. Some things, however, are best kept either in a bank vault or in a home safe. Home safes, which start at less than $50, while not as secure as bank vaults, can protect important and irreplaceable items from most threats. Just make sure the safe has at least a one-hour fire rating. For extra security, get a safe that can be bolted to the floor. Be sure to put the safe in a logical place. If you're in a flood zone, don't put it in the basement; your safe may be waterproof, but that won't do you much good if you need to get to important papers while the safe is under four feet of flood water.

Hire a Pro: Choose a Professional Organizer

If your idea of organization is the classic Theory of Piles, you could find yourself frantic when the piles don't yield the papers you're looking for. If you're daunted by the prospect of taming the feral papers or segregating the client information from your children's homework, a professional organizer can be helpful. Here's how to organize yourself enough to find a pro.

1. **Decide what kind of help you need.** Take a moment before beginning the search to decide if organization is a general problem in your life or if it's confined to just one part of it, such as your home or office. Some organizers are generalists, others work only in homes or offices. Any pro you talk to will first want to know the parameters of the problem, so begin by defining it for yourself as best you can. Keep in mind that part of disorganization syndrome is not quite being able to define what organization is.

2. **Begin the search with friends, neighbors, and colleagues.** A personal referral from someone you trust is always the best place to start a search for any professional. Just make sure your source doesn't take three days to find the phone number; that's a sure indication whatever pro was hired had minimal effect.

3. **Check the National Association of Professional Organizers.** This organization's well-organized Website, *www.napo.net*, has a "find an organizer" link. If you can't find the computer under all the papers but you still know where the phone is, call them at 847–375–4746. Also check out the Professional Organizers Web Ring at *www.organizerswebring.com*.

4. **Ask key questions.** If you live in or near a major city, you'll probably come up with a number of names. In addition to the standard questions you'd ask any person you're thinking of hiring—how long have you been doing this? Are you insured? Do you specialize in a particular area?—there are specific questions a professional organizer should answer.

   - *How long is a typical session and what results can I expect?* Some organizers work by the day, others by the hour. Often, a pro will want to do an assessment (for which there may or may not be a charge) before scheduling a standard session. If you've done step one properly and assessed your needs, he or she might be able to give you an idea over the phone of what you can expect after the first session.

- *How much will this cost me?* Before you ask this question, ask one of yourself: How much do I want to pay? OK, the honest answer is $10. Now ask yourself how much you're actually willing to pay. Most organizers charge by the hour, with a national range between $50 and $200 per hour, although some charge by the project. Tell the organizer what you had in mind. If the figure is reasonable, the individual might well be willing to tailor the services to your budget.

- *Do you belong to the National Association of Professional Organizers (NAPO)?* Although this is not a guarantee of quality, membership does suggest commitment to the profession and to continuing education. NAPO holds an annual conference as well as continuing education teleconferences. Another plus: Members of NAPO pledge to adhere to a professional code of ethics.

- *Will you assure me of absolute confidentiality?* An organizer will be privy to personal information. NAPO members are bound by their code of ethics to maintain absolute confidentiality. You might, however, want to get this in writing.

- *Do you have references I can check?* Just as you would when considering a contractor, ask an organizer for references—and then check them.

5. **Make sure you and the organizer click.** Once you've narrowed your choices to one or two, choose the organizer you feel most comfortable with. You're going to be spending time with this person on what can be an emotionally charged project. He or she will become pretty familiar with your daily routine, your business and personal life, perhaps your finances, and even your family and friends. If you don't hit it off, keep looking.

[Electronic Servants]

Choose an Internet Service Provider

◆◆◆

The World Wide Web offers an almost unlimited number of choices in many areas, but the first choice you need to make may be the most difficult: how to access it. There are basically two types of Internet connections—dial-up and broadband. Dial-up, done through the phone lines, is slow but relatively inexpensive. Much faster (but more expensive) broadband connections include DSL (digital subscriber line), cable, and satellite. Choosing an Internet service provider (ISP) is a matter of what you do on the Web, where you live, and how much you're willing to pay.

1. **Think about what you do on the Web.** If all you want to do is send an occasional e-mail and check a headline or two, your best choice might be a dial-up account. If, however, you frequently use the Web to download large files, such as upgrades to computer programs, photographs, music, and video, you definitely need broadband. If you intend to have a personal Website, broadband is the only practical choice.

2. **Decide if speed and a continuous connection matter.** Most computers come equipped with a 56k modem that you plug into your phone line for a **dial-up** connection. Each time you want to access the Web or send e-mail, you tell your computer to dial the number provided by your ISP. If you're lucky, you'll connect after a ring or two, but you may get a busy signal and your computer will have to redial. Small companies sometimes have too few access lines, resulting in frequent busy signals. When you're connected to the Web, you won't be able to use your phone or fax machine unless you have a separate phone line installed for your computer, an option that will cost you more. **Cable TV companies** in most major cities and many suburbs offer fast broadband connections via the same cable that delivers television to your house. A cable modem offers such fast connections—from five to thirty times faster than dial-up—that you can download large files without waiting literally hours, as you would with a dial-up connection. Furthermore, cable connections are always on; if your computer is on and your browser or e-mail program is open, you're connected. One caveat: The advertised speed may be misleading. Companies generally state their best-case scenario. Since everyone in your immediate area who uses your cable provider uses essentially the same bandwidth,

connection time will slow when your neighbors are all using the Web. Even then, however, your connection will be much faster than dial-up. (Cable use, by the way, will have no effect on your TV reception.) The company will provide a modem that connects to your computer's Ethernet outlet. In some cases, you can do the installation yourself, in others the cable company will do it for you. Cable isn't your only choice for a fast connection. **DSL** may be offered by your local phone company, but unlike dial-up, it doesn't monopolize your phone line, and it is five to ten times faster than dial-up. Because it uses a separate digital line, DSL allows you to connect to the Internet and make regular phone calls at the same time. And, like cable, a DSL connection is always on. DSL is available at varying speeds; the consumer version tends to be slower than cable, but often not by much. And if your cable company hasn't invested enough in nodes to handle the traffic in your immediate area, you might find that DSL is actually faster than cable. The only way to find out is to ask your neighbors about their experience. If you live in a rural or suburban area that offers neither cable nor DSL service, **satellite** is your only broadband option. Satellite service is in its early stages as of this writing, and some people think it isn't ready for prime time. Satellite Internet connections are neither faster nor better than DSL or cable connections, and they can be twice as expensive. What's more, they are subject to the same weather-related reliability issues as satellite television reception. If it's your only choice for broadband, it can be worthwhile, but if you can get cable or DSL service, those remain the better choices. Satellite offers relatively fast connection speeds when downloading material, but sending large files may be slower (that's true of cable and DSL, but satellite is even slower). With satellite, as with cable and DSL, you are always connected, but your connection will be affected by weather conditions.

3. **Find out what's available.** Your choices will depend on where you live. In some rural communities, dial-up and satellite are the only options, but cities and most suburbs also offer cable and DSL connections. Cable is available anywhere cable TV is offered. DSL, provided by the local phone company through a separate digital line, is available only to those who live a certain distance from the telephone company's switching office; people residing beyond that distance are out of luck.

4. **Determine the cost.** For low monthly cost, **dial-up** wins, but you'll pay a steep price in slow connection speed. Also, if you don't want to tie up

your phone line while you work on the computer, you will need to pay extra for a second phone line. When choosing a dial-up ISP, make sure the company provides either a toll-free or local access line; otherwise, you'll be hit with long-distance charges each time you connect. And if you travel, make sure your ISP has toll-free or local numbers you can use in the places you travel. If you choose to get broadband through your **cable TV** provider, you will likely pay more than dial-up. Although the situation may change in the future, at present, there is only one cable TV provider in each geographic area, which means prices are driven up by the lack of competition. Generally, cable companies charge from $40 to $50 per month for broadband, with some discounts offered with package deals. **DSL,** another option for broadband, tends to be cheaper than cable by about $10 per month, but it may or may not be available where you live. Check with your local phone company to find out. The last-resort option for broadband is **satellite,** which costs about $70 per month and is a lot less reliable than either cable or DSL.

5. **Ask for a package deal.** Cable providers and phone companies usually offer package deals that discount the cost of individual services. If you already subscribe to cable TV, the charge for a cable modem connection is usually less than if you don't. Similarly, phone companies will often bundle DSL service with land-line or cell phone service at a discount.

Set Up a Web Page or Blog

The White House has one, and so does Disneyland. The folks who bring you the news at night and your cereal in the morning have one. Even your teenager has a Web page, and when she isn't adding pictures from last night's mosh-pit disaster, she's contributing this morning's regrets to her blog. A Web page can be useful for professionals, artists, and the self-employed, as well as for those who want to share pictures with family and friends. A blog—Web-speak for a diary maintained on the Web—is a place for those so inclined to share their diary entries, essays, and random thoughts with others. If you are thinking about having a Website or blog of your own, read on.

1. **Decide if you need a professional.** If you need a professional Website, you probably shouldn't be creating it yourself, unless you happen to be a graphics professional with expertise in Web design. Sure, anyone can design a Website, but leave the professional work to the professionals and save yourself the time and expense of mastering a Web-design program. Your time is probably better spent building your business, and a professional Web designer should create a better site than you ever could.

2. **Take the easy route.** The easiest and fastest way to set up a Web page is to use the free home page service provided by your Internet service provider (ISP). Most ISPs, especially broadband providers, will give you a free home page—sometimes several, so each member of the household can have one. ISPs provide a template, and you simply fill in the blanks to create a personalized site where others can go to download pictures and messages you post. There is usually a limit on the amount of material you can upload, but unless you want to include lots of video or an inordinate number of digital images, you shouldn't bump up against it. If you do need more room, most ISPs let you purchase additional storage for a small fee. Note that the name of the site will include the provider's address and won't start with your name.

3. **If you're a Mac user, get a .mac account.** A .mac account, which costs about $100 per year, offers a number of handy services for Mac users, including a free home page with many customizable templates. You can easily upload pictures, text, and video to your site, which can then be accessed by anyone to whom you give the address. A subscription includes 1 gigabyte of storage; if that's not enough, you can purchase up to twice that amount for an additional fee. The address will start with homepage .mac.com, followed by your user name.

4. **Do-it-yourself: Register a name and find a host company.** If you prefer greater design flexibility and a more personalized Web address, you can go the do-it-yourself route. The first step is to choose and register a Web address, known as a domain name, such as mycompany.com. You'll also need a company to host your site. Search for Web host providers online. When comparing companies to host your site, ask about broadband capacity and what the monthly limit on traffic is. Unless you're running a mail-order business this shouldn't be a concern. That said, you should not accept anything less than a one-gigabyte-per-month limit. When some-

one logs onto your site, their request is automatically routed to the computer at your host company, which is connected to the Web via a very high-capacity broadband connection that can handle multiple requests at a time and that can download the information on your site quickly. Generally, the company you choose to host your site can also take care of registering your domain name for you. Expect to pay about $35 per year for the name registration; hosting costs vary, depending on the amount of traffic you expect at your site, but costs generally run in the neighborhood of $10 to $15 per month for low-traffic sites.

5. **Do-it-yourself: Design and maintain content.** Many of the programs you probably already use, such as Microsoft Word, can save pages in Web language, known as HTML. You can post these directly to your Website, but if you want anything fancier, with links to other pages or sites, you'll have to use a special Web-design program, such as Macromedia's Dreamweaver or Adobe's GoLive. These programs are expensive and entail a pretty steep learning curve. Many Web-hosting companies offer site design and maintenance for an additional fee, and if you choose one of the company's templates, you won't pay too much. This is a more practical choice than trying to maintain the site yourself.

6. **Hire a pro to keep you active.** If you have a business that requires an interactive Web presence, or if you simply want a professional-looking Website with all the bells and whistles, such as animated graphics, hire a pro to design and maintain it. A professional Web designer will not only design a spectacular Website but will also be able to recommend the most reliable host service, which is important if your business depends on interactive sales or help-desk features.

7. **Choose a blog host and start writing.** Like Websites, blogs can be accessed by anyone with an Internet connection. Blog hosts make the whole process easy. Blogger, for instance, now a unit of Google, provides free hosting and walks you through the whole process. There's even a free plug-in (a mini-program that works with other programs) that allows you to post directly from Microsoft Word. An alternative to Blogger is Live Journal, which provides free, powerful blogging software and lets you host your blog on its site. There are also specialized blog programs that allow you to customize your blog, but they usually require some programming skills and a separate Web-hosting service. If you maintain a customized

Website, you might want to go to the trouble and expense of using a customized blog program. Otherwise, take the simple route: Choose a blog host, such as Blogger, and start writing.

Organize E-Mail

E-mail programs make organizing your e-mail so simple it's a wonder that so many people just let everything accumulate in the in-box. Why bother organizing your messages? If you stuff all your e-mail into your in-box it will be just a matter of days before you won't be able to find the important mail amid the junk. If you don't want to look through countless jokes forwarded by friends, recipes from your mother, or invitations to enlarge critical body parts while trying to find the details your boss sent about tomorrow's meeting, you'd better adopt a good system for organizing e-mail.

1. **Determine the categories you need.** The first step is to set up categories for your mail. As with any filing system, the trick is to find the balance between categories that are so broad as to be useless and those that are so narrow that each contains a single item. Think first in terms of general areas: work, family, friends, newsletters. Then break these down further, as necessary: work, for instance, might be further divided into personnel, projects, budget, and so on. Freelancers and small business people might have a separate category for each client and another for old business. Exactly what categories you set up depends to a large extent on how you use e-mail.

2. **Make a separate folder for each category.** E-mail programs, whether for PCs or Macs, tend to set up windows in three parts: a list of folders—the defaults are usually "In-box," "Sent," "Deleted," and, often Junk"—a list of new messages, and an area where the message can be opened to read. Adding additional folders is usually just a matter of clicking "New" in the folder area. Name the new folder, and continue the process until you've created folders for each category.

3. **Set up rules to send messages to the appropriate folders.** Every e-mail program has a place, usually located under "Tools" on the toolbar at the top

of the screen, where you can set up rules that govern how incoming messages are handled. Take, for example, Outlook Express, one of the more popular mail programs. To set up a rule that sends friends' e-mail to a "Friends" folder, click "Tools" at the top of the window and choose "Message Rules," and then "Mail," from the drop-down menu. Now, click on "New." In the next window select "Where the From line contains people" as well as "Move it to the specified folder." Then click on the highlighted "contains people." Type each of your friends' names into the following window, clicking on "Add" after each one. When you're finished, click "OK." This will bring you back to the previous window, where you will click on the word "specified" highlighted in the line "Move it to the specified folder." In the next window click on the "New Folder" option, type in "Friends," and click "OK." Make sure "Friends" is highlighted and click "OK" again. Now all the messages that contain one of the friends you've included in this rule will be routed directly to your "Friends" folder. Follow the same procedure for all of the categories you've established.

4. **Add new senders to the rule.** If you're lucky enough to make a new friend, open the rule named "Friends" and add the new name, just as you did when you set up the rule in the first place. Similarly, if you get a new client, and you've decided to set up a separate folder for each client, create an additional folder and a new rule to send messages from that client to the new folder.

5. **Enable the junk-mail (spam) filter.** Most e-mail programs include a filter that sends what it determines to be junk mail to a "Junk" folder. Typically, you can set the level of sensitivity for the filter or disable it altogether. Some e-mail programs have learning features, in which junk mail that winds up in your in-box can be labeled as junk; messages from that sender will then be forwarded to the "Junk" folder. These are useful features, but they need to be implemented, and you have to be diligent about marking messages as junk, if that's what they are, for the filter to work effectively.

6. **Delete what you don't need.** As you do with regular mail, you should make a habit of deleting mail you no longer need. The leaner your folders, the easier it will be to find what you're looking for.

ORGANIZE AN E-MAIL ADDRESS BOOK

Most e-mail programs include an address book or link to a separate address book program. These are extremely handy, because when it comes to addressing e-mail, all you have to do is begin to type the person's name and the e-mail address will automatically appear in the "To" line. (Just be careful: If you have three people named Sue, make sure you've chosen the right one.)

Sort by categories. You can usually assign a category to each entry, which makes it easy to sort addresses in any number of ways, limited only by the number and precision of the categories you use. As with establishing folders, you're not limited to the program's built-in categories. If you often need to find all the e-mail addresses at a certain company, for instance, you can establish a distinct category for that company.

Create groups. Your address book allows you to create groups, which is an extremely handy way of sending the same message to a group of people. Just set up the group, following the program's instructions, and the next time you want to send an e-mail to all the members, type the group name, rather than an individual name, in the "To" line. The program will automatically forward the message to every member in the group. When setting up groups, there is usually an option that lets you hide addresses. Click this option if you don't want people to see the e-mail addresses of other members.

Practice E-Mail Etiquette

◆◆◆

In today's casual and disposable culture, e-mail may seem as formal as a tailgate party and as permanent as last summer's sandcastle, but it is quickly replacing paper and stamps for personal and business correspondence. That's why it's so important to observe the basic rules of e-mail etiquette. That missive you tossed so casually into the ether may return one day as a missile aimed right at your personal reputation.

1. **Press "Send" only when you're sure.** Remember: there's no turning back once you press "Send." It is just like dropping a letter in the mailbox, except the mailbox is down the street, and "Send" is just a keystroke away. Make a habit of never sending an e-mail before you double-check where it's going and what you've written. Most e-mail programs are linked to an address book and automatically fill in the address as you start to type it. If you type "An," your message may fly to Andrew instead of Anna, and that could make all the difference, especially if they know each other.

2. **Never send an e-mail when you're angry.** Don't fire off an e-mail in the heat of anger (or any other passion, for that matter). As a corollary to rule 1, think three times before sending an e-mail: before you write it, after you write it, and before you press "Send." Things said in the heat of an argument may be forgotten; e-mail gets printed out or stuck in hard drives where it can surface again days, months, even years later.

3. **Don't shout.** Make sure the "caps lock" button isn't pressed. Writing in all caps is like shouting: rarely appropriate, never appreciated.

4. **Don't be informal, unless you really mean to be.** If you don't know the person you are e-mailing, use a respectful form of address, "Edward" not "Eddie," and titles, if appropriate. Don't use slang, even if you might in a conversation, unless you're writing to a friend. Spelling and grammar count.

5. **Use a descriptive subject line.** "Hi!" won't do. It's really annoying to get a ton of e-mail and not know what's in any of it. Don't summarize your philosophy of life, but try to describe the purpose of your message in a few words.

6. **Reply in a timely manner.** If you give someone your e-mail address, they assume you read your mail. Check it every day and reply promptly. One of the chief advantages of e-mail is its speed—they don't call the old-fashioned way snail mail for nothing—so if you wait to reply, your delay is especially noticeable and could be seen as rude.

7. **Keep it brief.** It's harder to read material on a screen than in print, so try not to tax your reader with more text than is necessary. Of course, there

are times when the material being sent simply can't be shortened, but it's usually not a good idea to send copies of long articles or lengthy disquisitions in e-mail. The do unto others rule applies: If you'd rather not squint through pages and pages of e-mailed rhetoric, don't send it.

8. **Eschew emoticons.** These groups of punctuation marks that form smiling and frowning faces are loved by tweens and teens across the world. If you're over 20, stick to words like the rest of the adults. Also avoid all those cyberspace abbreviations, such as LOL and BTW, which every high-schooler knows but your colleagues may not. (LOL means laugh or laughing out loud; BTW is short for "by the way.")

9. **Forward frugally.** When you get that e-mail promising that the next 100 people to reply receive a year's supply of jalapeño popcorn, don't forward it to all your friends. If it seems too good to be true—or too ridiculous—it probably is. Same with worthy causes. The petitions to save the rain forest or rescue wrens are almost always hoaxes, and it's not as though your friends don't get enough spam of their own. Even when these appeals are truly worthy, the simple volume of them becomes a nuisance to those who carry on most of their business or personal communication via e-mail.

10. **Forward considerately.** Before you forward an e-mail, strip out the previous sender's e-mail address and message. This protects the privacy of those who send you e-mail and also pares away the bulk and distractions within the forwarded mail.

11. **Don't broadcast.** If you want the world to get your message, put it in a blog (see "Set up a Web Page or Blog," page 27). Resist the temptation to send e-mails to your entire address book, and always use the "cc" and "bcc" parts of the address field judiciously. Generally speaking, reserve "cc," a wildly outdated acronym that stands for carbon copy, for recipients who need take no action. If action is required on the part of the recipients, include them in the "To" field. As for "bcc" (blind copy, which means other recipients don't see that you're sending it to this person), it always carries a whiff of the unethical. There might be times when "bcc" is appropriate, but use it sparingly. And be sure you know the difference between the "reply" and the "reply all" buttons. The first sends a message back to the sender; the latter sends one to everyone who received the message. If you and the other 100 people in your department get a message reminding you of the company picnic next week, and

each of you writes "see you then" and hits "reply all," it will generate 10,000 messages.

12. **Assume your boss will read your e-mail.** That's because, if you're using a company computer or e-mail address, she can and might. A company can legally monitor employees' e-mail when it is sent from company computers. Observe the rule: Don't send anything from a company computer that you wouldn't be comfortable having your boss or your boss's boss read.

13. **Never assume your e-mail has been deleted.** You may have hit the delete button, but that doesn't mean an e-mail is really gone. Always assume that e-mail is forever. The folks at Enron wish they had read this list.

WHEN NOT TO E-MAIL

Whether to communicate via e-mail or in a more traditional format is a matter of convenience, time, and etiquette. E-mail certainly wins the convenience test, but it may not always be appropriate, and it's sometimes not reliable.

Don't flaunt convention. There are some things that demand paper and pen. High on the list are condolence cards and invitations to formal events. Birthday and anniversary greetings are also right up there, despite the cute virtual versions of the traditional cards.

Résumés and job applications depend on the circumstance. An e-mail résumé or job application for a summer stint at the mall is fine for high school and college students, but it's not usually appropriate for high-level positions. That's not to say that headhunters won't ask you to e-mail material, but any position more senior than receptionist demands hard copy. *Exceptions:* Many high-tech jobs will actually prefer electronic transmissions, but don't assume that's the case. Ask before e-mailing. Some jobs in creative fields, especially those for graphic design, may also appreciate electronic delivery; just make sure your e-mail reflects your creative talent.

Don't e-mail criticism or bad news. If you have serious criticism for an employee, deliver it face-to-face. The same is generally true of any unwelcome news. Using e-mail suggests expedience has won out over decency and concern.

Avoid prolonged e-mail debates. E-mail is not really suited to complex debates. If the issue requires lots of back and forth, it's much less cumbersome to discuss it in person or on the phone. E-mail also has a way of polarizing people. Perhaps it's because opinions seem stronger and more determined when they're in writing. Issues tend to heat up on-line, and when they do, you should switch to a face-to-face discussion or phone call.

Don't e-mail very private or sensitive information. E-mail is far from secure. When you e-mail to a corporate address, the corporation might well have access to your message, and even e-mail addressed to home computers may not be secure from prying eyes. Who else has access to the computer? Who might be eavesdropping on an unsecured connection? What's more, e-mail has a way of persisting that words on paper don't. Paper can be torn up and burned; e-mail can be deleted, but that doesn't mean it's really gone. Deleting a file from a computer simply means you've deleted the marker that points to its location on the hard drive. There are plenty of ways to recover the file if someone really wants to. Observe the rule: If you don't want anyone but the addressee to see your message, use something other than e-mail to communicate.

Recognize Hoax E-Mail

When your in-box fills up on a daily basis, you will need to sort through the messages as quickly as possible. Recognizing hoaxes will help you get through your e-mail faster.

WHY WORRY ABOUT HOAXES

Hoaxes don't necessarily contain viruses, so antivirus programs won't stop them. If they're not going to infect your computer or erase your hard drive, what's the big deal? Actually, there are good reasons not to pass on hoax mail.

First, it's a tremendous waste of time, money, and bandwidth. If 10 million people take a minute each to read and forward or discard a hoax message (that's just the seventh generation if 10 messages are each sent to 10 people, and so on), and each person costs some company $50 an hour (wages, benefits, overhead, etc.) that comes to a net cost of $8.33 million. Add to that the cost of the bandwidth used, which will be passed on by service providers in price hikes, and you're talking real money. And there's also the cost in speed and convenience as servers slow down to handle the glut of junk.

More importantly, hoaxes can result in fraud (see "Guard against E-Mail Fraud," page 38). Spammers can harvest hoax mail for real e-mail addresses, and those addresses can easily end up in the hands of scam artists.

1. **Beware frantic phrases.** An e-mail that says "forward this to everyone you know" should get your antennae up, whether or not the message is signed by a stranger. Some of your otherwise intelligent friends and family members will pass along hoaxes in all sincerity.

2. **Watch out for "This is NOT a hoax."** In all likelihood it is.

3. **Think about what's missing.** Be suspicious if an e-mail is lacking references to reputable sources or links to Websites.

4. **Don't trust a message that asks for personal information.** See "Guard against E-Mail Fraud," page 38.

5. **Recognize common ploys.** Typical hoaxes warn of a new computer virus or appeal for support for a worthy cause, such as saving the life of a terminally ill tot. Variants may be prayer solicitations or the old chain letter that promises good fortune if you continue the chain and dire consequences, usually personal misfortune or death, if you break it.

6. **Investigate and report.** If you suspect an e-mail is a hoax, go to Snopes .com, a Website dedicated to debunking hoaxes and urban legends.

Guard against E-Mail Fraud

◆◆◆

Despite your best efforts to eliminate spam, e-mails proclaiming "Incredible Money-making Deals!" and other dubious offers may still sneak through occasionally. When dealing with these, practice common sense and an abiding belief in the adage that "if it seems too good to be true, it probably is." The Federal Trade Commission has listed these common schemes you should guard against.

1. **Business opportunities.** Short on details and long on promises, these range from Internet-based ideas ("Get rich selling your castoffs and white elephants on-line!") to franchise offers. Often staggering amounts of money are promised for little or no work. These "business opportunities" are frequently old-fashioned pyramid schemes or empty promises to set you up in business in return for a "small investment."

2. **Bulk e-mail.** These solicitations offer to provide either millions of e-mail addresses or a service to send bulk e-mailings on your behalf. Some offer software to handle the mailings. The addresses are usually hopelessly out-of-date, and the practice of using a false return address, which many automated programs insert, is often illegal. Your Internet service provider may shut you down for issuing mass mailings, and the strategy rarely works as a sales device anyway, which is why few legitimate businesses use it.

3. **Chain letters.** You're asked to send a small amount of money to each of a few names on a list, replace one of the names with your own, and then forward the revised message via bulk e-mail. Despite what the offer may suggest, these schemes are illegal, and you're virtually guaranteed to lose whatever money you send.

4. **Work-at-home schemes.** These are a variation on the business opportunity schemes. Some of these require investment in supplies and equipment that will never pay for themselves; others offer simple manual work, like

stuffing envelopes. The problem arises when it turns out no one actually needs you to stuff envelopes, but for a slight fee you'll receive instructions on how to send your own bulk e-mailings. Either way, you lose.

5. **Health and diet scams.** Health and diet supplements sold on-line are frequently accompanied by testimonials or phrases like "scientific break-through," "secret formula," or the ever-popular, "miracle." However they are billed, these products are being peddled via the Internet just as potions and snake oils were once dispensed from the backs of wagons by traveling healers. The "miracle" products work just about as well as those of old.

6. **Free stuff.** Computers, digital cameras, long-distance phone cards—all for free—except for the small fee you pay to join a club. Then you're told the goods aren't exactly free, they're payment you receive when you get others to join. Most of these are just pyramid schemes in disguise.

7. **Investment opportunities.** The hook with these is an amazing rate of return for absolutely no risk. Some are seeking investors to help form an offshore bank. Others are vague about exactly what the business is. Many are Ponzi schemes—after Charles Ponzi, who organized such a swindle in the United States in 1919–20—in which early investors are paid off with money contributed by later investors, which encourages early investors to solicit new suckers. By definition, Ponzi schemes collapse, leaving all but the promoters with nothing but losses.

8. **Cable descrambler kits.** For a small sum, you can buy a decoder to receive premium cable channels without having to pay a fee. These decoders often don't work, and if they do, you would be receiving cable services illegally, otherwise known as stealing.

9. **Guaranteed loans or credit, always on easy terms.** These may be home-equity loans that require no home equity or unsecured credit cards, regardless of your employment or credit history, all offered for a small, up-front fee. The cards are never delivered, and the home equity loans are just lists of lenders who will turn you down once you apply.

10. **Credit repair.** These schemes offer to erase negative information from your credit history, again for a fee. At best, these are worthless; at worst they offer advice to commit fraud.

11. **Vacation prize promotions.** As with those that arrive in your regular mail, there's always a catch. Perhaps you have to pay a fee to upgrade

your accommodations—from steerage in a tug boat—or to reschedule, say from 3 A.M. next Tuesday to something a bit more convenient.

DON'T LET THEM GO PHISHING

Phishing is the practice of trying to get Internet users to divulge sensitive information, such as credit card or bank account numbers and passwords. Typically, the user receives an e-mail or a pop-up ad that purports to be from a major financial institution or credit card company saying they need to verify certain account information. You might even be referred to a Website that looks completely legitimate, with the institution's brand and logo. Beware: This is a phony site, set up only to steal your data. Never respond to these requests; don't even click on the link. Call your institution directly. If a company really wants to verify information, it can send you the request in writing. Never give out personal information over the Internet.

Keep It Private

One of the key questions posed by the global, connected community is the question of privacy. Justices and pundits may debate the issue of constitutional guarantees or privacy, but for the rest of us on the ground, the real question is: Does privacy even exist anymore? The number-one threat, of course, is technology, and it's not just a matter of personal computer use. Every time you drive and use an EZ-Pass tag to negotiate toll roads, every time you charge something at the mall or swipe that "special members card" at the grocery store, you're giving away information about yourself. The only way to assure real privacy is to unplug and stay home, preferably in a cave. But there are some things you can do to maintain as much privacy as possible without becoming a recluse. (Also see "Prevent Identity Theft," page 326.)

1. **Button your lip.** It's amazing how people tend to violate their own privacy by blabbing about themselves when they don't have to. Don't give out your phone number or your e-mail address to people you don't really know. If a clerk asks for this kind of information, simply say it's unlisted. Sure, there are times when it's really necessary to reveal these details, but if it isn't, don't. If you decide to fill out a warranty card (and the only reason to do this is so that you will be notified in case of a recall), provide only your name, address, and date of purchase. The personal information requested on the card is used only for marketing purposes.

2. **Take privacy policies seriously.** Get to know the privacy policies that businesses are obliged to give you when you sign up to do business with them. That includes business on the Web. Companies need your permission to share information about you with others. Some companies tell you they'll share it only if you authorize them to; others say they assume you want them to share it unless you check a box or specifically tell them you don't. Never allow a company to share personal information, either with its subsidiaries or with outside companies. If they ask if you'd like to receive information about products like the one you've just bought, decline. This is a ruse to allow them to sell your personal information to others.

3. **Don't wait to respond.** You needn't wait to respond to privacy policy inserts in your bills. Take the initiative and write directly to the charities, businesses, and organizations with which you do business and tell them not to sell or give out your name and personal information. If you suspect one of them has already given your name to others, ask the offending organization to give you a list of everyone to whom they've given your information and write each one asking to be placed on their "do not sell" and "do not mail lists."

4. **Beware of doctors, hospitals, and pharmacies.** Despite the Health Insurance Portability and Accountability Act (HIPAA), a copy of which you're asked to sign at every doctor's office, your medical information isn't necessarily very private. Not only may your information be shared with insurance companies and other medical practitioners for legitimate reasons, it may also be shared, without your knowing it, with drug companies for marketing purposes. Hospitals typically list patients in their directories and release that information to anyone who calls unless the

patient specifically instructs the hospital not to. Pharmacies may release patient information to drug companies for marketing and research purposes. Your defense: Take the initiative and instruct all health-care providers and institutions—in writing—not to release any information about you without your express permission.

5. **Tell your child's school to keep records private.** Under the Family Educational Rights and Privacy Act (FERPA) schools may release directory information, including students' names, addresses, phone numbers, date and place of birth, awards, and attendance records, to third parties such as financial aid officers and other academic institutions. Under the act, however, schools must give parents the opportunity to refuse permission for the release. Similarly, the Department of Defense has a right to student information for recruiting purposes unless parents specifically request that information not be released.

Eliminate Spam

The origin and derivation of the word *spam*, as applied to unwanted e-mail, is veiled in mystery. Some attribute it to the Monty Python skit in which Vikings, who loved Hormel's meat in a can, sang the word at ever-increasing volume until nothing else could be heard. Less romantically, it is thought to be an acronym for "simultaneous posting of a message." Wherever the term comes from, it signifies something you don't want. And while actually eliminating spam is, at this point, far beyond even the best efforts of the federal government, and certainly beyond the province of this book, there are steps you can take to limit it.

1. **Read "Eliminate Unwanted Mail and Phone Calls," page 13.** One of the easiest ways for spammers to get your e-mail address is to buy it from a company with which you do business. Follow the procedures outlined in the "Eliminate Unwanted Mail" list to take advantage of the privacy rules and regulations companies have in place to forbid them from disseminating your personal information.

2. **Don't give out your e-mail address unnecessarily.** Just as you shouldn't routinely disclose your home phone number to every cashier who asks for it, don't reveal your e-mail address when you subscribe to a magazine, join a club, donate blood, or do anything else that may request it. Remember, you're free to say "no."

3. **Use a disposable e-mail address.** A number of services allow you to register a temporary e-mail address with them (usually at no cost to you), and they will forward e-mail that comes to this address to your permanent e-mail address. Among the more popular services are spamgourmet, mailinator, and E4ward. You give the temporary address to Websites and on-line stores with which you're not familiar. For new personal contacts, it would be more diplomatic to use an alternate e-mail address (see below), because these disposable addresses often contain some indication that you are using a site designed to weed out unwanted mail. If spam is included in the forwarded messages, you simply stop using that temporary address and choose a new one.

4. **Practice address masking.** Spammers cull addresses from message boards, chat rooms, on-line groups, and other places on the Web where addresses are posted by employing software to automatically harvest them. If the address isn't in a form the software looks for, it won't harvest it. Instead of writing "yourname@Internetserviceprovider.com," spell out the *at* sign and the period: "your name at Internetserviceprovider dot com." You can also disguise your address by writing yourname@inDELET_THISInternetserviceprovider.com. Actual human beings who want to contact you will be smart enough to follow your instructions; spammers using this address will find their messages undeliverable.

5. **Opt out of the free newsletters.** When you order something on-line, you'll often be presented with an option at checkout in the form of a checkbox with text like, "YES, I want to receive notices from third parties—or our corporate partners—about special sales and updates." Don't check the box, or if it's already checked, uncheck it. If you're not careful, your address will soon be circulating among an ever-growing circle of spammers.

6. **Take advantage of spam filters.** Some e-mail services, such as Yahoo Mail, have very effective spam filters, but you have to activate them and in some cases fine-tune them. It's worth the effort. Similarly, many e-mail

programs, such as Apple's Mail and Microsoft's Entourage, offer "learning" spam filters, which route what they consider spam to a special junk folder. You need to enable these filters in the software's preferences and "teach" them by marking any spam they don't filter out as junk. If all goes according to plan, after you've flagged them, messages from those domains will go right to the junk folder.

7. **Use an alternate e-mail address.** Most Internet service providers will allow you more than one e-mail address. Set up a second address that you reserve for on-line purchases and other sites you rarely use. You'll get spam at that address, but since you don't use it all the time, it won't be as bothersome as if it came to your regular mailbox.

8. **Use a firewall.** A hardware firewall, built into your computer or wireless router, can make your computer invisible to spammers, and anyone else for that matter. A software firewall, while less effective, can still help protect against spyware, little software programs that can read personal information from your hard drive and furnish your address to spammers.

9. **Turn on security options.** Web browsers have options that allow you to set security parameters. They may not be terribly effective, but they're still worth using. You can, for instance, disable cookies. Some sites you visit may require that cookies be enabled; if you know and trust the site, enable cookies when you visit that site and disable them again when you leave.

Protect Your Computer from Viruses

◆◆◆

When you purchase your computer it is immunodeficient. Unless you protect it, it will succumb to whatever virus is around this season. Isolation is no guarantee of protection. Even if you never connect to the Internet (as unlikely as that may be), if you install a program or borrow a disk from a friend, your computer will be vulnerable. And, while there's no way to completely protect your computer, there are steps you can take to minimize the chance of a fatal infection.

1. **Use antivirus software.** Many computers come with a free copy of antivirus software. Make sure it's turned on, and make sure it's set to scan

automatically in the background. If for some reason you don't already have an antivirus program installed, buy and install one immediately. Popular choices are available from McAfee and Symantec, among others.

2. **Update your antivirus software regularly.** New viruses appear just about every day, so you need to stay one step ahead of them. All major antivirus software manufacturers offer update services, although some are on a subscription basis. It's worth the price. Just make sure your software is set to update itself automatically.

3. **Scan all drives.** Most antivirus software is set, by default, to scan your C-drive. That's fine as far as it goes, but it doesn't go far enough. Set it to scan *all* of your drives, including temporary drives, such as flash drives, as well as CDs, DVDs, and "virtual drives" that are used to install new programs.

4. **Be skeptical of all e-mail attachments.** Most viruses are spread through e-mail attachments, but if you don't open the attachment, the virus can't infect your computer. Don't assume an attachment is safe just because the e-mail comes from a friend. Your friend, forwarding one of those hilarious cartoons or little movies you simply must see, may inadvertently be passing on a virus that has already infected his machine.

5. **Beware of floppy disks and CDs.** Prior to the rise of the Internet in the mid-nineties, floppy disks were the most common vehicle for transmitting PC viruses. These disks are still dangerous, especially if you don't know where they've been. Even a friend's floppy can be dangerous if your friend's computer is infected. The same is true of CDs. If you use either, make sure your antivirus software scans them first.

6. **Download files only from Websites you absolutely trust.** While files downloaded from reputable sites, such as Microsoft, are safe, there are no guarantees when you're dealing with the sites of smaller companies or personal Websites. If you do download from such sites, make sure your antivirus software can check these files. If you're at all uncertain, download to a floppy or flash drive and check the disc before you open the file.

7. **Don't even think about pirated software.** Bootleg software is widely available for download from rogue Internet sites. Virus writers know how insatiable the appetite for free stuff is, and they take advantage of it. Beware!

8. **Use a firewall.** Just as a firewall can keep your information from leaking out to people who shouldn't have it, a firewall can also keep outside viruses

from seeping in. If you have a hardware firewall built in to a cable connection, great. If not, use a software firewall and make sure it's active (it's built into Windows XP and SP2).

9. **Back up compulsively.** Just as there are no guarantees against hard drive crashes and hurricanes, there's no guaranteed immunity against all viruses. The one sure protection is to back up your important files on external media—CDs, DVDs, or an external drive. That way, if your computer becomes hopelessly infected to the point where the only cure is to completely reformat its hard drive, you'll still have all of your crucial data, ready to reinstall on the cleaned machine.

Organize and Optimize PDAs, iPods, and Cell Phones

◆◆◆

Our electronic gizmos—including personal digital assistants (PDAs), iPods, and cell phones—are supposed to make life easier and more enjoyable. But,

A WORD ABOUT SPYWARE AND ADWARE

It's not just viruses that threaten your computer. Spyware—little programs that surreptitiously monitor your computer and Internet use—and adware, which inundates your computer with unwelcome pop-up ads, also pose real problems. As the name implies, spyware steals your personal information and browsing habits, and both spyware and adware sap bandwidth and slow down your access to the Web.

Use a spyware/adware blocker. Spybot, a free program, does a good job of preventing spyware from infecting your machine, although it doesn't do much to remove spyware that's already on it. Webroot's Spy Sweeper detects and removes spyware, and Panda Software's Platinum Internet Security 2005 is an antivirus program that protects against spyware and adware as well.

Check shareware and freeware for adware. Many shareware programs—programs distributed free on the Web—contain adware; that's how they make money for their designers. If you're willing to pay the price of pop-up ads, fine. If not, do a Google search (check Google Groups, in particular), using the software's name and the word *adware*. Since people tend to complain on blogs and other sites about adware, if nothing comes up, the shareware program is probably free of it.

perversely, they can also be a source of unending frustration. Like puppies, unless carefully disciplined, they can quickly get out of control. And, like puppies, they need to be taken in hand when they're young. An iPod with 4,000 songs and no discernible organization is daunting if you want to listen to "Girls Just Want to Have Fun" or the second movement of Bach's Suite No. 4 for Unaccompanied Cello. And just try to locate the number of the dermatologist you saw six years ago on your PDA if you've filed all your entries by their first names. With a bit of planning and organization, however, in no time at all you'll be humming along to Bach and speedily dialing that dermatologist on your cell phone while driving your car over the embankment.

1. **Establish categories.** Most PDAs allow you to assign a category to your entries. That way, you don't have to search through every one of your

contacts to find the one you need. Set up a category for business, one for health-care professionals, one for your children's friends and their parents, and one for any group that's big enough or important enough to warrant it. On your **iPod** sort music into playlists with names you'll recognize easily, even in the abbreviated form displayed on little screens. For each album and individual song, make sure you include information in all of the fields: artist, type of music, composer, and so on. That way, you'll be able to find all the Beethoven, all the Madonna, all the Beth Orton you want, even if you forget the title of the particular song or album. You can download entire CDs or individual tracks.

2. **Attach a keyword to seldom-used entries.** For each contact on your PDA that you rarely use, type in a key descriptive word in the notes field to help you find the person, should you forget her name. For example, when you enter the plumber's name, attach a note with the single word *plumber*. That way, when a pipe bursts, you can search for *plumber* to find his name—and number—which you've forgotten.

3. **Give yourself a warning.** Enter birthdays, anniversaries, and other forgettable-but-important-dates into your PDA, and use it to remind you of the events by choosing the "repeat" function and, for these, "annually." At the same time, add an annually repeating reminder entry a few days before each event so that you don't forget to get a card, buy a gift, or make a reservation.

4. **Stay in sync.** Synchronize your PDA with your computer on a regular basis, generally once a day, every day. This ensures you have your latest schedule, to-do list, and address book with you at home, at the office, and everywhere in-between. You'll also have the peace of mind that comes from knowing this vital information won't be lost even if your computer crashes or your PDA stays behind in the cab.

5. **Choose devices that communicate with one another.** When your cell phone, PDA, and computer can all communicate with one another, you need to enter addresses and schedules only once. Many common computer-scheduling and address-book programs, such as Microsoft's Entourage, can easily share information with PDAs, such as those made by Palm, and many cell phones can join the party, either by connecting to a computer or by communicating with PDAs via the wireless Bluetooth standard. If your devices don't already take advantage of one of these technologies, take it into consideration the next time you upgrade.

6. **Don't think that just because it can, it should.** Sure, your iPod and your cell phone can hold your daily schedule, and your PDA can play music. But can they do it well? When tiny devices are asked to do more than they were originally designed to do, they usually do the extras about as well as your hairdresser does plastic surgery. Keep your PDA for addresses, schedules, and to-do lists, your iPod for music (and the occasional episode of your favorite TV show, if you can really identify with those tiny little people), and your phone for, well, phoning.

Make On-line Phone Calls (Cheaply)

E-mail is free (so far), but even when a message is packed with emoticons, it lacks the warmth of a voice-to-voice visit. Calling your friend in Japan or Paris can be costly, however, especially if you tend to chat for an hour or two. If you have a computer and a broadband connection to the Web, there's a third way to be in touch: voice-over-the-Internet phone calls. These allow you to make calls for a fraction of what they would otherwise cost, and sometimes for free. What's more, Voice over Internet Protocol (VoIP) lets you choose your area code (within some limits) and take your number with you wherever you may go.

1. **Use your regular phone.** The easiest way to take advantage of Internet-based telephony is to choose one of the major phone-service providers, such as AT&T and Verizon, which supplies you with an adapter to route calls from your regular land phone through your broadband connection (either cable or DSL) over the Internet and to any kind of phone on the other end. A number of other companies, including Vonage, Net2Phone, and Dialpad Communications, provide pretty much the same service. You really won't notice a difference in the quality of the calls made with these providers, but the bill is usually lower. You can make calls directly to any phone, just as you always did. Voice mail is a standard feature of this service, so you can check voice messages on-line from wherever you are (it doesn't work with a standalone answering machine). You can also dial by clicking an entry in your computer address book.

Videophones never took off, despite all the hype around the time of the last World's Fair, but video chats are entirely possible on the Web. In fact, Apple's new iMacs all come equipped with a little camera that lets you send live video over the Web. Most of the major e-mail programs now support video, so you can attach a little movie to your e-mail. Chat programs, including Apple's iChat and AOL Messenger, and Microsoft's MSN Messenger, among others, let you chat and watch live. If you don't have a new iMac, all you need is a webcam, a little video camera that sits on top of your monitor or on your desk, and a software program that encodes and compresses the video so it can be streamed over your Internet connection. The catch is that both parties need to have the software installed on their computers. Logitech is probably the most popular manufacturer of webcams. Don't expect the image to be up to network standards, but it's certainly clear enough to be highly embarrassing.

2. **Call computer-to-computer for free.** Free software, such as Skype (the most popular), MSN Messenger, and Google Talk, lets you call other people who have the same software installed on their computers absolutely free. This is perfect for people who have friends or family overseas. Of course, it only works if both parties are at their computers and the computers are on and connected to the Internet. As of this writing, most of these packages are for PCs only, although Skype is available for Macs as well.

3. **Use Skype to call regular phones at low rates.** In addition to its free computer-to-computer service, Skype offers a service that lets you make calls from your computer to regular phones. The per-minute charge for these calls, whether domestic or international, tends to be much lower than that of traditional phone service.

4. **Don't rely on these services in an emergency.** None of the VoIP services handles 911 calls the same way that regular phone service does. In

some cases, 911 calls may be routed to an emergency center's central number, where it might be answered by someone not specifically trained to handle emergency calls.

5. **Keep a land line for power outages.** In the event of a power outage, none of the above services work. Nor do traditional cordless phones. That means it's important to keep a corded land-line phone, or at least a wireless phone, on hand.

Shop On-line (Safely) at Stores and Auctions

On-line shoppers spent an astounding $30 billion during the 2005 holiday season, a jump of 30 percent over the previous year, according to a report by CNN. On-line shops never close, comparison shopping is a breeze, and there's never a parking problem. It couldn't be easier—for shopaholics, it's too easy—and it can be at least as safe as shopping at a bricks-and-mortar store, so long as you take certain common-sense precautions.

1. **Turn the security feature on.** Most browsers, such as Internet Explorer, Firefox, and Apple's Safari, include a security feature that meets an industry standard known as Secure Sockets Layer (SSL). This scrambles the information you send, allowing the store, but no one else, to read it. Check your settings to make sure the security feature is turned on.

2. **Look for the security symbol.** Before you actually send an order that includes any personal information, you should see a picture of a little locked padlock at the bottom of your screen. If you don't see it, don't click "Send."

3. **Verify that it's a legitimate business.** Anyone can open a virtual storefront today and be gone tomorrow. Legitimate companies have a reputation to protect. If you don't know a business, look to see if it has a physical address, not just a post office box. Try calling for a catalog, and see if the company sports any seals of approval, such as those of the Better Business Bureau. If you're unsure, do business with a company you know.

4. **Check out what others have to say.** If you're unfamiliar with a company, find out what other people say about it. Look it up on any of a

number of sites that rate on-line businesses for reliability, dispute resolution, and timeliness of delivery. Two of the most popular business-rating sites are *www.epinions.com* and *www.bizrate.com*.

5. **Pay by credit card.** If you use your credit card you're protected under the federal Fair Billing Credit Act as well as by the individual card issuer should you have a dispute with the company. The extended warranties and other protections that some cards offer for purchases at stores are valid for on-line purchases, too.

6. **Know the company's privacy policy.** The company should post its privacy policy on its Website. You don't have to read every word, but you should understand what information the company is collecting about you and how it intends to use that information. If the company doesn't post its privacy policy in clear English, don't do business with it. Also make sure the company will not share any information about you. Some companies try to assume that right by having a prechecked box next to a statement that says they'll share some information about you with trusted third parties. If they have, indeed, checked that box, uncheck it. If they haven't, don't be tempted. Those interesting newsletters about related products come at the price of your privacy.

7. **Don't use simple or obvious passwords.** Many e-commerce sites require a password, especially if you want to set up an account. Never use your social security number or anything obvious, such as your birthday. Don't use your name, or the names of your children, spouse, or partner. Try to include numbers as well as letters, and don't use the same password for every site.

8. **Double- and triple-check before you click "Send."** Make sure all the information you are giving is correct and all the particulars of the purchase are agreeable. Pay attention to that final price; it might include shipping charges you hadn't considered or add-ons you had no intention of buying. Also, be certain that the address where the merchandise is to be sent is correct. You don't want to accidentally send it to your billing address if it's meant to be a gift for someone in another state.

9. **Keep a record of every purchase.** Most e-commerce sites suggest that you print out the actual order that you submit. Do it. Most vendors will send you a confirmation of your order by e-mail. Print it out and save it until your order arrives and you're completely satisfied with it.

BUYING AT AUCTION—EBAY

The first step you need to take before you raise your paddle at any auction is to understand the basic rules. The same is true when you bid on eBay. Fortunately, there is a very clear tutorial in eBay's "Help" menu that walks you through the process, from finding items you're interested in, to setting up an account, bidding, and paying for what you've bought. Once you understand the procedures, follow these basic rules.

Before you bid, check the seller's reputation. "User Feedback" provides invaluable information from people who have dealt with this seller, including what the quality of the merchandise is, how fast you can expect to receive it, and how the seller handles complaints.

Use proxy bidding. You don't necessarily have to stay by your computer to keep inching up your bid as the auction heats up. EBay features proxy bidding, in which you set a high bid and eBay automatically begins your bidding at a lower price and increases it as others outbid you until your maximum is reached.

Consider automated sniping. Sniping is the term used when you put in a bid during the last seconds of an auction, at which point no one else has time to outbid you. The problem, of course, is timing. By the time you type and send your final bid, someone else has beat you to it. Sniping software can handle the process much faster than you can. You can find sniping software at *www.ezsniper.com*, *www.auction-sniper.com*, and *www.powersnipe.com*, or do a Google search for "sniper software." An alternative to software is to use a sniping service. These services charge a fee, but they're usually faster and more effective than software, especially when bidding gets really hot. There are many sniping services; one of the most popular is eSnip.

Computer Lingo Tip List

◆◆◆

Some computer lingo is easily translated. *State of the art,* for instance, refers to any computer you can't afford; *obsolete* is the one on your desk. A *disk crash* is computerspeak for "my dog ate my homework," and when it comes to an oxymoron, there's the popular *Microsoft Works.* But some terms need translating. Here are the more common ones.

Hardware

1. **BIOS:** Basic input/output system. This is stored in ROM and tells the computer how to start up and control input and output devices, such as the keyboard and monitor.

2. **Bits, bytes, and kilobytes:** Units of software code. A bit is a single digit, either a 1 or a 0; a byte is 8 bits; a kilobyte (KB) is a thousand bytes; a megabyte (MB) is a million bytes; a gigabyte (GB), a billion bytes; a terabyte (TB), a trillion bytes.

3. **Cache:** Where information is stored for quick access. A cache may be in RAM or on the hard drive.

4. **CD-RW and DVD-RW:** Compact disc, rewritable, and DVD, rewritable. You can erase these and reuse them as many times as you want.

5. **CPU:** Central processing unit; the heart of the computer, the chip that actually does the computing.

6. **Firewall:** Specialized hardware and/or software used to prevent hackers or anyone else from getting into your computer.

7. **Flash drive:** A small device that plugs into a USB port and stores data; it can be written to and erased millions of times.

8. **Hard disk:** The device that stores your files.

9. **LAN:** Local area network; a small group of computers, often in an office, connected to each other and such other devices as a printer so as to share resources and data.

10. **Megahertz:** The speed with which a computer processes information. Higher is faster, all things being equal (which they rarely are).

11. **Modem:** A device that connects the computer to the Internet. A phone modem is used for dial-up connections; a cable modem connects via cable TV service; a DSL modem connects via a special designated phone line.

12. **Motherboard:** The electronic circuit board that connects the various internal components of the computer.

13. **RAM:** Random access memory; the internal memory that's used by programs to perform tasks while the computer is on. This is where the actual work gets done; the results, if you save them, are stored on your hard drive. The more RAM, the better.

14. **ROM:** Read only memory; cannot be written to; used to store miniprograms that have to survive when the computer is turned off, such as the instructions the computer uses to start up.

15. **USB:** Universal serial bus; the means for connecting peripherals, such as printers, scanners, keyboards, and mice to the computer.

16. **WAN:** Wide area network; a network of computers in a large geographical area connected to share resources and data. The Internet is a really big WAN.

The Softer Side

1. **Avatar or AV:** A little picture often used in chat rooms that represents the person in the room.

2. **Cookie:** A small text file stored on your computer by a Website you visit. When you access the site again, the information in the cookie is sent back and is used to customize log-in or registration numbers, online "shopping cart" information, user preferences, and more.

3. **Chat room:** A virtual place—often a Web page—where people gather, all at the same time, to correspond back and forth in real time. To enter a chat room you must have a chat program Web browser.

4. **E-mail program:** The program you use to access and send e-mail. Most manufacturers include one with the computer.

5. **Firewall:** Specialized hardware and/or software used to prevent hackers or anyone else from getting into your computer.

6. **FAQ:** Frequently asked questions.

7. **Forums:** Another term for message boards (see below).

8. **IM:** Instant message. An IM program, often part of a chat program, allows you to chat with a list of friends—people you've included in a personal list of correspondents—without having to participate in a chat room. It works even when you're using other programs. If a friend wants to chat, the program signals you, either with a sound or a flashing indicator on your screen, and you can switch to the IM program and receive and send messages in real time. If your computer isn't on when a friend sends a message, the message is stored, much like e-mail.

9. **Link:** A bit of text, a picture, or a symbol on a Web page that takes you to another Web page when you click on it.

10. **Message boards:** A Website where you can sign on as a member to post questions, comments, announcements, and other text or files or simply to read others' comments. These are often established for communication on a specific topic.

11. **Text messaging:** This is the cell-phone version of IM. It really has nothing to do with computers.

12. **Web browser:** A program that allows you to view pages on the World Wide Web. Virtually all computers come with at least one browser.

COMMON CHAT, E-MAIL, AND MESSAGE BOARD ABBREVIATIONS

ADN: any day now

AFAIK: as far as I know

AFK: away from keyboard

BAK: back at keyboard (I'm back)

BBL: be back later

BRB: be right back

BTW: by the way

CU or cya: See you

ez or EZ: easy

Flame: to insult someone

FWIW: for what it's worth

FYI: for your information

GAL: get a life

GMTA: great minds think alike

HTH: hope that (or this) helps

IMHO: in my humble opinion; some people omit the H

IRL: in real life

JK: just kidding

L8R: later

EMOTICONS

:-(	sad
;-)	wink
(((((person's name)))))	giving the person mentioned a virtual hug
;-)~~~~~~~~	giving someone the raspberries
[_]>	cup of coffee
@@@	cookies
?^	what's up?
^5	high five
<:-|	curious
:~)	cute
:-}	embarrassed
:-/	perplexed, confused
>:-(	angry
:->	grin/mischievous
>:-||	mad/angry
:0)	smiles (w/nose)
:-)))))))	lots of smiles
&-(	crying
!:-)	I have an idea

[Community]

Connect to Your Community

In the groundbreaking book *Bowling Alone: The Collapse and Revival of American Community* (Simon & Schuster, 2000) Robert Putnam reveals how the traditional ties that have woven people into the broader fabric of community are coming undone, at tremendous cost to individuals and society. His research found that over the past 25 years Americans have joined fewer organizations, signed fewer petitions, met fewer of their neighbors, and even had fewer dinners with family and friends. There are ways you can reverse that trend (and reap rich personal rewards) by connecting—or reconnecting—to your community. Here are some suggestions:

1. **Follow your interests, hobbies, or sports.** Whatever you're into, there's a group in your community that shares your passion (I'm not talking about that thing you have for what's-his-name). If it's quilting, check the local crafts store; someone there should be able to connect you with a quilting group. If you prefer to spend your time at sports, join the local gym or find an evening or weekend pickup game (better yet, start your own). Animal lovers can volunteer at a local animal shelter or check local pet stores for information on dog-walking groups or charity events they can participate in with their pet. This is a perfect way to meet others with whom you'll have an immediate bond.

2. **Become involved in civic organizations.** The United Way, YMCA, Chamber of Commerce, Lions Club, NAACP, and LGBT (Lesbian Gay Bisexual Transgender) groups all provide great ways to connect with others, discuss local issues, and become involved in community projects. Joining the Friends committee of your local library, a women's club, or a garden club can also offer good opportunities to meet neighbors, network, and hone skills that you can draw on in other areas of your personal and professional life.

3. **Be active in your local school.** This is a no-brainer for those with children. Children whose parents become involved in school activities are more likely to be engaged in school. But even those who don't have kids in the school system can volunteer—as tutors, readers, chaperones, and more—an excellent way of connecting with others while doing something worthwhile for the entire community.

4. **Enter town hall.** You can attend open meetings of your town council or other government groups where you'll form new ties while advocating for issues you care about. Most local governments also have committees that advise on policy for everything from historic preservation to parking; since these are nonpaying, nonelective positions, anyone willing to put in the time and effort is usually welcome.

5. **Volunteer just about anywhere.** Hospitals, nursing homes, even the local police station, all may welcome volunteers. You can be a docent at a local museum or tourist attraction, sign up as a volunteer firefighter or emergency worker, or become involved with the local Red Cross chapter, helping out with blood drives, shopping for shut-ins, or driving people to doctor appointments.

6. **Get involved in politics.** This can mean anything from running for local office to ringing doorbells in support of a candidate or a cause that you believe in. Interest and advocacy groups, everything from the local NAACP or LGBT group to environmental or world peace organizations, welcome all newcomers willing to aid the cause.

7. **Join a religious group.** Whatever your religion, the local church, synagogue, mosque, or ashram is an obvious place to get involved. If you're an atheist, agnostic, or ethical humanist, don't feel excluded; look for a local or nearby chapter of the Ethical Culture Society or other secular groups.

8. **Join a book club.** Book clubs are everywhere. To find a club that appeals to you, check the local library and bookstores.

9. **Join an on-line community bulletin board or chat room.** More and more communities have organized on-line chat groups, often hosted by major Web services such as Yahoo, where people come together to voice opinions, ask for recommendations, and promote local events. Do a Google search using your town or city's name to find them.

10. **Throw a party (see page 86).** The best time to invite all the neighbors over for a party is when you first move in, preferably before you've even unpacked the cartons. It's the only time you won't have to ask your guests to pardon the mess, because, after all, you've just moved in and you're swamped just remembering what floor you're living on or where the bathroom is. You won't be expected to cook anything fancy, and you're bound to garner plenty of return invitations. If you've been in

your place long enough to be expected to have straightened it up, you can organize a block party. You'll meet all the neighbors, but you won't have to worry about vacuuming the day before. Just make sure you do the groundwork: Find out the local regulations, get the permits you need, and inform the police department.

11. **Start a public access TV show.** Especially if you're a professional or business owner, consider producing a local TV show, either as a special or on a regular basis. It's much simpler than you imagine. Virtually every community has a local public-access station that's staffed by people who will take care of all the technical details. You come up with the content, the rest will be taken care of. It's absolutely free, and you might be pleasantly surprised by the amount of attention and feedback you get.

Find Volunteer Opportunities

Some are motivated by altruism, others by boredom, and some by a desire to spiff up their résumé. Others want to change the political system or do their part in the social compact. They're all volunteers, working without pay in jobs they find interesting, fun, and/or rewarding. It's never been easier to find a perfect volunteer opportunity, one that fits your personality, the things you find important, and the time you have available.

1. **Decide how much time you have.** Be practical. If you have a full-time job and a family, your schedule is probably already pretty full. That doesn't mean you can't find a couple of hours a week, but if that seems tough, you needn't commit yourself indefinitely. There are many opportunities available that run for a limited number of months, weeks, or even days. It's called "episodic volunteering" and works a bit like temping; it's perfect for people who want to volunteer but whose schedules vary, as well as for those who want to give volunteering a try without making a firm commitment. On the other hand, if you're retired, you might consider taking on something that's virtually full-time. Just be aware that a commitment is a commitment; the word *volunteer* doesn't absolve you from the usual rules that apply when you give your word about something.

2. **Give thought to what you want to do.** The first step in getting started as a volunteer is identifying what it is you want to do. This deserves some thought, because it can go way beyond helping with the local Girl Scout cookie sale or raising money for the school building fund. Walk dogs for the local humane society, play guitar at a weekly sing-along at a nursing home, help reunite Holocaust victims through the local Red Cross; there really is no limit to what you can do. Or where. A recent check of on-line volunteer-matching sites (see more on this below) turned up an opportunity to help with a two-week AIDS education program in Belize and the chance to teach English in China. In fact, the choices are so varied, deciding where to donate your time and skills may be the most demanding part of volunteering. With that in mind, consider these:

- *Continue what you've always done.* This is an obvious one: Teachers may enjoy tutoring, doctors can help out at a community center, accountants can do pro bono work for a nonprofit organization, business people might help start-ups in the community or advise a nonprofit about writing a business plan or developing a marketing strategy.

- *Do something you've always dreamed of.* OK, there are limits here. You're not going to get a gig singing backup for Madonna at her next charity performance. But if you're an engineer and you always dreamed of helping villagers in India set up an irrigation system, you might very well find an opportunity to do it. If you have a skill, there are volunteer opportunities where you can put it to use.

- *Practice a hobby.* Again, if you're good at it—whether "it" is photography, cooking, or playing tennis—you can do it (or teach it) as a volunteer.

- *Learn something new.* You can use a volunteer opportunity to learn a whole new field. If you've always been interested in anthropology but never had the time to get real experience, volunteer in a society or social setting you'd like to learn about. If you've always been curious about astronomy, volunteer to be a docent at the local planetarium.

3. **Find opportunities the old-fashioned way.** Look around your community for ways to help. Religious institutions, schools, local Ys, the United Way, and Red Cross all need help; just ask. The advantage is you stay in your own backyard; the disadvantage is that you limit your experience to your own backyard.

WEBSITES LISTING VOLUNTEER OPPORTUNITIES

VolunteerMatch (*www.volunteermatch.org*).
Started in 1998, the San Francisco-based nonprofit hooks up individuals with more than 30,000 organizations across the country. It also works with companies to encourage employee volunteerism through corporate programs.

Action Without Borders (*www.idealist.org*).
First called the Contact Center Network, Action Without Borders was founded in 1995 to build a network of neighborhood contact centers that would provide a one-stop shop for volunteer opportunities and nonprofit services in communities around the world. It maintains a database of more than 46,000 nonprofit and community groups in 165 countries.

One Brick (*www.onebrick.org*).
With chapters in New York City, Chicago, and San Francisco, One Brick has worked with about 150 volunteer outfits since its founding in 2001. It is known for its focus on "commitment-free volunteering"; events typically last three to four hours and are followed by food, drink, and socializing at a local cafe.

Youth Service America (*www.servenet.org*).
Servenet is a great resource for children and young people interested in volunteering. It partners with thousands of organizations committed to increasing the quality and quantity of volunteer opportunities for young people in America, ages 5 to 25, to serve locally, nationally, and globally.

On Your Feet Project (*www.onyourfeetproject.org*).
This group targets individuals ages 18 to 35 and tries to integrate popular culture with volunteerism. Activities vary from interviewing-skills workshops for the homeless to letter-writing campaigns for (possibly) wrongfully convicted prison inmates.

4. **Find opportunities via the Internet.** If you're looking for something beyond what's available locally or if you're not yet well connected to your community, the Internet is the way to go. Sites that match volunteers with groups looking for them have radically transformed volunteerism. Using the Internet to find volunteer positions vastly increases the range and scope of what you can do. You can limit your search to your zip code or to a given distance from it, but you don't have to. You can pick a place and search there, even if it's overseas. You can search for opportunities at specific organizations, or you can list your skills and interests and search that way. For instance *www.volunteermatch.org* has almost 30 master categories to choose from, everything from arts and culture to crisis support, religion, and sports and recreation. Within categories, you can add keywords to narrow the search further.

5. **Be a virtual volunteer.** Perhaps the most interesting way the Internet has expanded volunteer opportunities is by allowing "virtual" volunteering. Once again, Volunteermatch.org is among the pioneers. A virtual volunteer doesn't have to show up at a specific location at a certain time. So long as you have access to a computer, the Internet, and a phone, you can join the legion of people who make a difference. A recent search for virtual volunteers turned up opportunities for illustrators, typists, board members, CPAs, editors, someone to do video captioning, and a translator fluent in Vietnamese. The only thing not found was a virtual dogwalker.

Organize a Grass-roots Campaign

◆◆◆

Organizing a grass-roots campaign for a good cause can be highly rewarding and allow you to connect in a meaningful way with your neighbors. The process is time-consuming, but there are tools and techniques you can use to get your campaign off the ground without giving up your day job.

1. **Don't try to go it alone.** Whether it's a political campaign you want to help or a policy in your town or city you want to change, there are almost certainly people in your community who already agree with you. Start by

canvassing likely groups. For instance, if you want to lower the speed limit in your town, attend meetings of the Parent-Teachers Association, where parents will probably be more than willing to get behind your campaign. If your cause is an addition to the local library, reach out to independent bookstores, book clubs, and educational organizations. If your issue is of national significance, such as environmentalism, national health care or civil rights, contact local chapters of organizations that promote your cause; in all likelihood, they can offer practical assistance in organizing a local campaign. And don't forget your friends; if you can recruit just one friend to help with the recruiting, the task will be far less daunting and might even be fun.

2. **Use the Internet.** The Internet can be just as influential in building networks of activists to work on local issues as it was during the 2004 presidential campaign. One of the most useful and easy-to-use Web tools is Meetup (*www.meetup.com*). Meetup is a Web-based collection of literally thousands of interest groups, covering everything from animal rights to Zionism. People who want to join a group simply sign up, for free, and browse, either by topic or location, for groups that meet their interests. When you find a group you want to join, you simply click on the group's welcome screen, and soon you will receive notices of face-to-face meetings, often in coffee shops, schools, or churches. If you choose to start a new group, you can post it on the site for a $12 monthly fee, which your eventual members will share. Anyone who signs in looking for a group in your area that matches your description will automatically be directed to the site Meetup provides for you. It's extremely effective and easy. A group of Yale students used it to help set up a grass-roots campaign to support Wesley Clark's 2004 presidential bid.

3. **Tap into the expertise of national grass-roots organizing groups.** A number of interest groups offer formal training for people trying to start local grass-roots campaigns. The Wellstone Action Network, for instance, founded by the children of the late Senator Paul Wellstone and his wife, Sheila, offers practical training for grass-roots organizers. The Orion Grassroots Networks is a coalition of more than 800 groups that offers support to grass-roots organizers for a yearly fee of $45.

Search for People On-line

It's theoretically possible to find just about anyone on the Internet, but if you don't want to spend an inordinate amount of time doing it, you should begin by figuring out the best places to look. Is the person an expert in a field? An alumnus of a certain school? An enthusiast who might belong to a Web interest group? Narrowing the field is the best first step whenever you're looking for something or someone. From there, try one or more of the following tips:

1. **Search on-line White Pages.** Couldn't be more obvious, right? But if it works, it couldn't be easier. If you know where the person lives, you're halfway there. Use one of the major search engines, such as Lycos's *www.whowhere.com*, Yahoo's *people.yahoo.com*, or Switchboard's *www.switchboard.com*. Another powerful search site is *www.pandia.com/people*. These sites don't include unlisted numbers, of course, and they may not be absolutely up-to-date, but most often your search will start and end here.

2. **Search by subject.** If the person you're looking for is an expert in a particular subject, you might try searching a database of experts, such as *www.allexperts.com* or the Yearbook of Experts at *www.expertclick.com*. To find similar databases, go to *www.refdesk.com/expert.html*.

3. **Do a Web search.** Just type the person's name into a search engine; if he has a Website or if she's been mentioned on one, you're likely to be directed to that site. Next, you can either call directly or call the site's organization and go from there.

4. **Search on-line chat groups.** Check the chat groups of subjects the person is interested in. Yahoo Groups is a good place to start. You might have to join the group in order to search posts, but membership in Yahoo Groups is free.

5. **Check public records.** The public records for many locations are available on-line. These include property records, immigration records, marriage and divorce records, even criminal records.

6. **Check by school.** If you know where the person went to school, you can check Alumni.Net (*www.alumni.net*). You'll have to join, but membership

is free. Not every school is represented, and not everyone from a registered school is necessarily included, but this is definitely worth a shot.

7. **Use a pay-for service.** One of the biggest and best commercial services is Knowx, *www.knowx.com*. It provides access to a large number of databases that cover everything from lawsuits and liens to owners of aircraft or boats. Fees typically range from $1.50 to about $10 per single search for individuals.

[Correspondence]

Pick the Right Stationery

◆◆◆

Is stationery necessary? No. Is it a gracious, civilizing addition to a busy life? Definitely. In your e-mail-, cell-phone-, blackberry-dominated life, however, you may be unsure how to choose the right stationery for a particular occasion. Start with the first two entries on this list, and expand from there as the fancy strikes.

1. **Fold-over notes.** These are perhaps the most versatile of all stationery pieces. They typically measure 4¼" × 6½" and can be printed on the front with your name, your name and address, or just your initials. They're perfect for thank-you notes, replying to or offering invitations, and simple catchups with distant friends. You can even use them for condolence notes. Fold-over notes can be purchased readymade, albeit blank, in almost any stationery store, but if you're going to purchase any type of printed stationery, this is the one to get. Choose white or cream paper, a simple type font, and an all-purpose ink color, such as black, blue, or green.

2. **Monarch stationery.** This is another option if you're choosing only one kind of stationery. Measuring 7¼" × 10½", monarch sheets are slightly smaller than regular business letterhead, which makes them a little more personal. They're appropriate for almost any correspondence, including personal letters and personal business letters. Each sheet is printed with your name, name and address, or your initials. They can also be printed with only your address, which makes them useful for any member of the household or even for guests.

3. **Informals.** Paradoxically, informals are the most formal of stationery. These are small, folded cards that may have a panel embossed on the front; they are appropriate for formal invitations. Traditionally, these cards were printed with a person's proper social name and title: Mrs. John Smithers Witherspoon, Doctor Phineas Alexander Spock, for example. Now, you can go with plain old Jane Witherspoon or James (not Jim) Spock. In the old days, informals were used mainly for formal invitations, but now they might serve the same function as fold-over notes, which makes them slightly redundant.

If you're bothering with custom-printed stationery, you probably should pay at least a little attention to the etiquette of correspondence. The essence of etiquette of any kind rests on three *C*s: common sense, custom, and courtesy.

Common sense. If you're sending an invitation, make sure you include all of the vital information: who's doing the inviting (you, you and your spouse/partner/boyfriend/girlfriend), where the party is, and when to show up. Be specific about whom you're inviting: If it's a couple, use both names; if it's an entire household, say so; if you're including someone's boyfriend or girlfriend of two weeks, include that person's name.

Custom. Custom evolves. What was unacceptable decades ago might be perfectly appropriate now, but certain rules never seem to change. If you are sending a formal invitation, such as to a wedding, spell out the invitee's full name and title: Doctor John Harvey Doolittle, not Dr. J. Doolittle. Don't use abbreviations when you address the envelope, and send children over 18 their own invitations. If it's the sort of event that generally means a gift, and you don't want one, say so. "No gifts, please"; "May your good wishes be your only gift to us"; or words to that effect are all appropriate. Never make suggestions for a gift, even if you've registered with a bridal registry at specific stores. Also, writing "money appreciated" is never in good taste.

Courtesy. Courtesy trumps custom. If anything that is customary might offend someone, bend the rules.

4. **Store-bought cards.** Keep a stock of birthday, get–well, and congratulations cards on hand. When you see a clever one or a particularly pretty card, buy it; someone's birthday is always coming up, and if you have the card in your desk drawer, you're much more likely to send it than if you have to rush out and find one. Also, stock up on enclosure cards; that way, you won't have to pick up a special card each time you give a gift.

5. **Do-it-yourself alternatives.** Anyone with a computer and an ink-jet printer can design and print stationery of all sorts, from fold-over notes and calling cards to monarch-size stationery. These work very well for informal invitations and for birthday or holiday cards; they allow you to personalize your message with photos and special designs. They don't, however, take the place of beautifully printed formal stationery.

6. **The externals.** Printed stationery is ordered with printed envelopes. Although envelopes for formal cards and wedding invitations generally are printed with the return address on the back flap, for most other envelopes the return address should be in the upper left-hand corner on the front. Keep a supply of stamps on hand, particularly attractive, special-issue stamps, but don't use oversize stamps on formal stationery. Be careful when it comes to holiday stamps; people may be offended by religious themes and others could take umbrage at the overly cute or sentimental. Play it safe, and skip the "love" stamps.

Write the Perfect Thank-You Note

In the age of e-mail and instant messaging, there's still no substitute for a handwritten thank-you note, but for many of us, writing one is a daunting task. It shouldn't be—not if you remember a simple formula: PBS (prompt, brief, and specific).

1. **Be prompt.** Time, the physicists tell us, is relative, and so is promptness. The best time to write a thank-you note is the day after you've received something to be thankful for, such as a weekend stay. But that isn't always practical. Some experts say wedding gifts should be acknowledged within a month of returning from a honeymoon, but etiquette maven Amy Vanderbilt says the bride and groom have 6 to 8 weeks from the time of the event. To be certain, the best way of avoiding thank-you-note anxiety is to write as soon as possible, rather than as soon as it's comfortable. Postponing the inevitable only makes the anxiety worse.

2. **Keep it brief.** If you think of your note as an essay, sitting down to write it will feel like taking the SATs. It's just a note, after all; it's not meant to express your deepest feelings.

3. **Be specific.** "Thank you for the lovely gift" doesn't cut it. At the minimum, you should say what the gift was and something about it: "The purple vase is the perfect color for my orange bathroom" or "I've been dying to read about the history of Estonian agriculture." If you're thanking a friend for a weekend stay, mention one of the highlights of the visit, such as a great meal or even how you enjoyed talking about your college days together.

4. **Don't rely on preprinted notes.** If you don't have personal stationery, use plain stationery or a blank card. If you have printed thank-you notes, they don't absolve you of the duty to write a genuine note, complete with mention of the gift. Never use professional letterhead for a social note.

5. **Include a photo.** If you've taken pictures during an overnight stay, include one or two with your thank-you note to make it that much more memorable. If you're thanking someone for a gift, a picture of you with the gift is a nice touch.

6. **Be diplomatic.** Maybe the chocolate-covered bacon strips aren't your idea of a fun dessert; perhaps the painting on black velvet of the Chihuahua in a pink tutu doesn't go with the Rothko in your living room. Still, assuming the intention of these gifts was benevolent, they deserve sincere thank-you notes. If you're having trouble thinking what to say, remember it's the thought that counts. About the Chihuahua painting, you might thank the giver for recognizing your love of dogs; for the chocolate-covered bacon strips, say how kind it was for the giver to indulge your passion for dessert. You haven't been untruthful, and you've acknowledged the giver's good intentions.

7. **Write it by hand.** Even if your handwriting defies the expertise of cryptologists, a handwritten thank you, with all its idiosyncrasies and personal touches, is always preferable to a totally legible computer-generated note.

Write an Appropriate Condolence Letter

◆ ◆ ◆

Writing a condolence letter is always hard, and there are no easy, formulaic rules that make it any easier. But when someone suffers the death of a loved one, a condolence letter can go a long way toward filling with love and friendship the gaping hole that's left by this loss.

1. **Don't be formal.** Just the fact that you took the time to sit down and write a personal note is itself a comfort to the bereaved. This is an intimate gesture, and the best condolence letters approach the tone of a conversation.

2. **Be personal.** Don't reach for words of universal wisdom; they'll only fall on ears deafened by the cataclysm of loss. Say what you really feel. If you were shocked to hear of the death, say so. If you are deeply saddened by it, talk about your own grief. If there's something that will be gone from your life now, write about that. Just don't make the mistake of saying you know how the recipient feels, because it's presumptuous, and you don't.

3. **Write about the deceased.** If you knew the deceased, mention something you remember with particular fondness about her. It might be something trivial but emblematic of her strengths: "I'll never forget when I tried, hopelessly, to coordinate that dinner for the family, and she rescued me by bringing over the fancy canapés at the last minute." By recalling something specific, big or little, something you remember with love, you'll be offering a great gift to the bereaved.

4. **Write about the relationship between the mourner and the deceased.** Another way to honor the deceased is to write about the positive relationship he had with those he left behind. If you didn't know the deceased well, you can be general, but, as always, the more specific you are, the better. "The way your father helped your littlest ones put the train set together and his delight in playing the role of chief engineer is a legacy of kindness and patience that will pay rich dividends for the rest of your children's lives."

5. **Be honest.** Don't stretch. Say what you can, but don't say more than you mean. False sentiment is worse than none at all. If you really didn't

know or like the deceased, keep your focus on the survivor and express your sympathy for his loss.

6. **Don't be morbid.** Don't dwell on the details of death. If the circumstances were truly horrendous, you needn't avoid them—absolute silence can be deafening—but don't drag them out and express your own shock at them.

7. **Be sensitive.** Even if death comes at the end of a terrible illness, survivors don't want to hear it's a blessing. Whether a stillbirth or the death of a nonagenarian, death is always difficult.

8. **Be brief.** Just knowing that you really care and that you, too, cherish the memory of the loved one is what's important. This need not be the final word. If you were really close to the person who died, you can write a longer memoir about him later. After the immediate rush of grief is past, a longer remembrance will be appreciated, but now may not be the time.

9. **Offer concrete help.** Simply saying, "Please call if there's anything I can do," only puts the burden on the bereaved. If you want to help, offer something concrete, like doing the shopping, cooking meals, babysitting, or helping with the responses.

10. **Do it yourself.** This is one of those occasions when a store-bought card just isn't enough. You may choose to send a sympathy card, especially if you hardly know the bereaved, but don't just sign your name; write at least a line or two of your own.

Write an Effective Complaint Letter

A good complaint letter isn't about getting the rage out; rather, it's written to get attention and, when appropriate, restitution. Here's a basic guide to writing a complaint letter that gets results.

1. **Exhaust the obvious routes first.** If there's a problem with a product or service, the first thing is to simply bring it to the attention of the person with whom you've dealt. If the widget doesn't work, ask the salesperson

to take it back or give you a replacement. If the spaghetti's cold, ask the waiter to heat it up. Only if you're refused satisfaction should you move on to a written complaint.

2. **Address the person in charge.** Don't write "To whom it may concern"; the problem is probably that it hasn't concerned anyone in the first place. You need to determine where the problem really lies. Was it with the local branch of a large corporation or with a basic policy of the corporation as a whole? Is it with the repair department or with billing? Once you've determined the area that should deal with the issue, find out who's in charge of that area. This may mean calling the local or national headquarters of a company. Be sure to get the correct spelling of the person's name, his title, and address. Don't address your complaint to the CEO. This does nothing but alienate the people below her to whom the letter will no doubt be referred.

3. **Be polite.** No matter how annoyed or righteous you may feel, you won't get results by being sarcastic or rude. Don't threaten, at least not with the first letter; a friendly, even complimentary, tone encourages the recipient to respond in kind. Asking for help to resolve an issue is more often effective than threatening nuclear disaster if you are refused.

4. **Be concise.** The longer your letter, the better chance that it will be skimmed, or skipped entirely, rather than read. Keep it short, factual, and to the point.

5. **But be precise.** Focus on the five guiding rules of journalism: who, what, where, when, and why. Say what went wrong, when it happened, whom you dealt with, and what steps you've taken thus far. Don't forget to include your own name, address, and phone number, and perhaps your e-mail address.

6. **Say what you want.** If you want a refund for a defective product, say so. If you want a replacement sent via express mail, spell it out. You might want to be compensated for your inconvenience: If, for example, a repair was done incorrectly on your leased car, and you have to take another half-day off work to go back to the dealer, perhaps you can ask the dealer to compensate you with an additional mileage allowance. If you've incurred dry-cleaning bills, state the amount and ask to be reimbursed. Or perhaps you just want an apology. Whatever it is, don't keep them guessing.

7. **Include documentation.** Send copies, not originals, of receipts and/or pictures of the damage.

8. **Make sure your letter is received.** Pay the post office to send your letter with a "confirmation of delivery," or if you want proof that it was received by the person to whom it was addressed, send it via certified mail.

9. **Follow up.** If you haven't received a reply in a reasonable period of time, follow up your original letter with another one, this time with a copy to the next level in authority, and state what you intend to do if you get no satisfaction. Be reasonable—you're not going to bring the company to its knees—but be real: Small claims court or the state department of consumer affairs may be appropriate, and for serious issues you might say you will turn to legal counsel.

[Social Life]

Work Any Room

(or How to Talk to Just About Anybody)

◆ ◆ ◆

Whether you're at a party or a business networking event, you may be intimidated by the idea of walking up to a stranger and starting a conversation. Many, perhaps most, people feel this way to one degree or another. The secret to working any room is to wade right in and do it. Here are some suggestions to get you started.

1. **Arrive early.** This may be the last thing you want to do, but consider how much less intimidating it is to be in the room as it's filling up than to walk into a crowd in full swing. When you arrive early, you can meet people one at a time, and even be the one to introduce newcomers to one another!

2. **Focus on the other person.** Remember that everyone is feeling a bit awkward and focus on putting the other person at ease. This will relax both of you and help you feel more in control of your environment.

3. **Fake confidence.** This is one of the best ways to relax and work a room: Pretend you are a confident person. If it helps, imagine you're someone whose social skill you admire. Think "How would Oprah act if she were here?" "What would Matt Lauer do?"

4. **Ask good questions.** Just about any question is a good one, because it puts the focus on the other person. But try to ask open-ended, rather than yes-no questions. A few possibilities:
   - "Why are you here?"
   - "How do you know the host?"
   - "How about those shrimp puffs?"
   - "What an interesting ring; is it a family heirloom?"
   - "Where are you going on vacation this year?"

The question doesn't have to be broadcast-quality interviewing, just something to get some back-and-forth conversation going with the other person.

5. **Bring up movies.** Whether the gathering is for business or pleasure, talking about the latest movie can be a great gambit. Movies are a fairly broad common denominator and are much safer than religion or politics. Even if you don't go to the movies a lot yourself, you can always lead with,

"Everyone has been talking about the new [fill in name of blockbuster here]. Have you seen it? What did you think?"

6. **Wear your name tag.** Some people disdain name tags as corny, but name tags can be an enormous social aid, saving you and others from the embarrassment of not remembering a name. Wear yours high up on your lapel, where it will be easy to spot when you're shaking hands.

7. **Read the other person's tag.** Greeting a stranger by name can be disarming and downright charming when you accompany it with a smile and a warm handshake. If you're not sure how to pronounce the other person's name, all the better: You've got your first question all ready for you!

8. **Ease away gracefully.** Ending a conversation is sometimes more difficult than starting one. But if you want to work the room, or just remove yourself from a conversation that has died a natural death, you need to master this technique as well. Try one of these phrases:

   • "It's been great talking to you." (This can work just fine when accompanied by a warm handshake and sincere smile.)

   • "Really nice catching up with you. I'm going over to get more ice."

   • "If you'll excuse me, I want to grab some more of that sushi."

   • "Thanks for chatting. I'll look forward to seeing you again."

If all else fails, you can always say you need to powder your nose or wash your sticky hands.

Tips on Tipping

Tipping is so much a part of American society that it's taken for granted as part of the cost of eating out or staying at a hotel. But who to tip, when to tip, and how much to leave is sometimes confusing enough to provoke anxiety. Although the amount considered standard will vary a bit, depending on the city or region of the country you're in, you can use these general guidelines to ease the uncertainty.

1. **Tip waiters on the pretax total.** Calculate the tip for your meal service based on food and drink, not the sales tax. The standard amount for

good service is 15 percent to 20 percent. If your service has been satisfactory, leave a 15 percent tip. If it has been superlative, consider leaving 20 percent. If your child threw spaghetti all over the walls and floor, you asked for several substitutions on your meal, and your waiter remained courteous and helpful, by all means push your token of appreciation past the standard 20 percent. But don't be intimidated into tipping. Tips are, after all, an expression of appreciation for good service. Aside from those occasions when a specific gratuity is stipulated for restaurant parties over a certain size, tipping for meal—or any service—isn't mandatory. That said, waiters work hard for a living and are often paid minimum wage or less, with the expectation that tips will make up the difference. Also keep in mind that your waiter generally shares his tip with the other servers who assisted at your meal, such as the bartender and busboy.

2. **Wine steward.** If you're at an elegant restaurant and are served by a wine steward, tip that person 15 percent to 20 percent of the cost of the wine.

3. **Don't forget buffet staff.** Even though you brought your own food to the table, those who filled your beverage order and cleared the plates deserve a tip. Ten percent is standard for buffet service.

4. **Tip cloakroom attendants when the service is free.** If your coat spends the evening in the cloakroom and there was no charge for the service, a $1 per coat tip is fine. If you've left extra baggage, or if you've received extraordinary service, a $2 tip is appropriate.

5. **Ladies room attendant.** If she hands you a towel, leave about 50 cents. If she provides extra service, helping you with a drooping hem or other minor catastrophe, leave a dollar. Feel free to leave the room without tipping if the attendant simply presides in a chair.

6. **Parking attendants.** When your car is delivered and the tires aren't smoking, a $1 tip is standard, even if you've paid a parking charge. If the attendants are particularly courteous, prompt, and careful with your wheels, go for the $2 tip.

7. **Taxicab and limo drivers.** For a short hop in a cab, a $1 tip is more than decent. If you've traveled from your home in the hinterlands to the airport, shoot for 15 percent to 20 percent. Depending on the amount of help you've received with your luggage, you may choose to add a one-dollar per bag tip to the total.

8. **Hotel maid.** If you've spent more than one night in a hotel room and had good housekeeping service, leave at least one dollar per night per guest. Put the money inside an envelope from the hotel's stationery stash and mark it clearly for the housekeeper.

9. **Hotel concierge.** If you'll be asking for a fair amount of help from the concierge during your hotel stay, an up-front tip of $10 to $20 is a smart idea. Otherwise, you may tip this person after each special service (making dinner or theater reservations, arranging a sightseeing tour) or leave a lump sum at the end of your visit. Tips should be based on the complexity or difficulty of the service performed, usually from $2 to $10.

10. **Hotel bellman.** Unless your bags are unusually heavy, one dollar per bag is fine. If your luggage is awkward or heavy, or if you're at a swanky hotel in a large metropolitan area, the standard would be $2 per bag.

11. **Doorman.** You don't have to hand the doorman a dollar every time he opens the door for you, but a dollar for hailing a cab or shielding you with an umbrella would be appreciated.

12. **Home deliveries.** The pizza delivery guy gets from $2 to $5, depending on the distance traveled and perhaps the weather he has braved to present your large pepperoni. Other types of deliveries, such as furniture or appliances, generally warrant anywhere from $5 to $10 per person. Let the level of courtesy and service be your guide here. Surly unhelpful delivery people don't necessarily merit a tip.

13. **Personal services.** Your hairdresser, unless she owns the salon, gets the standard 15 percent; give the shampoo person a couple of dollars, a bit more if you received extra special care such as a scalp massage or beverage service. The same 15 percent applies to manicurists, eyebrow waxers, and so forth. A massage therapist will appreciate a 15 percent tip, unless he's the owner of the business, in which case you don't need to tip for each service.

HOLIDAY TIPPING

Tipping during the holidays is a way to say "thank you" to those service providers you may not tip on a regular basis. On a less altruistic note, holiday tipping is a way to ensure, or at least increase the chances for, good service the rest of the year. With all of these, include a personal note expressing your appreciation.

The people in this category include:

Postal carrier. Postal workers are not supposed to accept cash; gifts are limited by USPS regulations to a maximum $20 value.

Newspaper carriers. From $10 to $30 is typical.

Trash and recycling collectors. From $10 to $30.

Pet sitters. A gift certificate or cash in an amount at your discretion

House cleaners. Typically the cost of one week's cleaning

Building superintendent. Depending on where you live, a standard tip can be anywhere from $20 to $200. Check with your neighbors. This goes for doormen, too, if you live in an apartment.

Any regular delivery people. From $10 to $30, depending on the quality and frequency of the service and the length of your relationship.

Salon owners. If the person who cuts your hair owns the salon, you don't need to tip her after each service. But a gift, gift certificate, or cash at holiday time is a nice gesture. A typical holiday offering would be something in the range of your usual charge for a haircut or coloring.

Personal trainer. You may give this person a gift, gift certificate, or cash. Use the cost of one session as your guide.

Landscaper. The cost of one week's service or a gift certificate.

SOUTH BURLINGTON COMMUNITY LIBRARY
550 Dorset Street
S. Burlington, VT 05403

Post the Perfect On-line Dating Profile

You don't have to be perfect to write the perfect dating profile. What you can do perfectly, or nearly so, is describe who *you* are and the kind of person you'd like to meet. Here are some tips to get you launched into the land of virtual romance.

1. **Check out the competition.** Before you write anything about yourself, study the women or men you'll be competing with for attention. Doing this will help you steer away from clichés. There are plenty of folks who say they love walking in the rain and looking at the sunset. Even if you like to do these things, featuring them in your dating profile won't make you stand out from the crowd.

2. **Stalk your quarry.** Next, cruise the lists of potential dates in the age and geographical range you've selected. If you find any that are particularly interesting, don't hesitate to take words or phrases from their profiles and use them in yours. This will make it more likely that you will pop up on the screens of people you'd like to meet. For example, if "fly-fishing fan," "bookworm," "wacky sense of humor," or "film noir buff" describe who you are or characteristics you're looking for, by all means, work these phrases into your profile.

3. **Create a memorable screen name.** This is your basic identity in the virtual dating world, so make it count. After you've surfed the competition, you'll have a better idea of which names work and which fall flat. Screen names like "QTPIE3" or "JOE12" won't say much about you (or your originality), but "TreeHugger" or "ShutterBug" might—that is, if you're an environmentalist or a photographer. Stay away from the "LUV2MEETU" sort of handle, because the only thing it suggests is that you're desperate to meet anyone who sees your profile. Reach a little further to convey who you are or what you enjoy; you could choose "CHATSOVERCOFFEE," if that's your idea of a good get-acquainted date.

4. **Craft a grabber headline.** After your screen name, your headline makes the next greatest impression. Ideally, it should say something about who you are and who you're hoping to meet. Go for something to pique cu-

riosity or even get a smile or laugh. "Well grounded guy seeks sparks" or "Frequent flier looking for seatmate" will give the right person more to go on than "Sincere guy looking for nice gal." You get the idea.

5. **Write vividly.** Just as your high school English teacher suggested, your writing will be more effective when you use colorful detail and give specific examples. Don't just say you enjoy outdoor sports. Describe how much you love to play softball and mention the year your team played several innings during a hurricane. If you are funny, don't just say "I'm funny," *be* funny. If movies are your thing, name a few favorites and say what you particularly like about them. Maybe even use a juicy quote from one or two.

6. **Be confident.** Mentioning that you feel awkward or can't believe you're actually posting a dating profile does not project confidence. You'll be more attractive if you come across as someone with healthy self-esteem. On the other hand, don't feel you have to be someone you're not. Have the courage to show who you are and even use a bit of charming self-deprecation: "Love to play the piano; whether my neighbors love listening is anyone's guess."

7. **Post a photo.** You dramatically increase your chances of being noticed when you post a photo, preferably more than one. Your primary photo should be a close-up; people want to see you. Your secondary photos can feature you in action on the ski slopes or at work in your office, but try to make all your photos interesting. Avoid using photos that include other people; those scanning the listings shouldn't be left wondering if that's your ex-husband or girlfriend standing next to you. Also, don't use any photos from which another person has obviously been cropped out. If you're a wild and crazy type, go ahead and use the shot from last Halloween, when you dressed up as a skunk.

8. **Protect your privacy.** Keep any mention of your last name or e-mail address out of the profile. When you arrange a date, make sure you set it up in a neutral, public place. Never invite strangers into your home, no matter how friendly or harmless they may seem.

Throw a Party

The secret to throwing a great party in your home is, well, not really a secret at all: planning and preparation. Planning early and preparing carefully will make your party as much fun for you as it is for your guests. Here's how to make sure a good time is had by all.

1. **Make lists.** No surprise here. In fact, make three different lists to help you keep everything straight. First, create a **guest list** to give you some idea of the number and nature of your guests. Preparing for a party of old college pals is very different from planning for your grandmother's 80th birthday celebration. Next, make a **shopping list** of everything you need to buy, from food and beverages to candles and cocktail napkins. Also make a **tasks list,** a list of all the tasks you need to do right up to the moments before the party starts. It's a good idea to create a separate list of everything you must do on the day of the party. Keeping this list separate may help you maximize focus and minimize frazzle as the appointed hour approaches.

2. **Send invitations.** Do this two weeks before the party. If your party is to take place on a popular evening, such as Oscar night or Halloween, or during a busy time of year, give guests even more lead time. Whether you mail the invitations or send them via e-mail, let your guests know whether a meal will be served. Ask your guests to RSVP or send "regrets only" by a particular date so you can keep a head count and minimize surprise guests.

3. **Plan your menu.** Whether you plan to cook all the food yourself or call a caterer, you should decide on the menu at least two weeks ahead. (Keep in mind that you may need to book your favorite caterer months in advance, and you can cook and freeze many homemade items several weeks in advance.) Making early decisions about the food minimizes the chance that you'll need to dash to the store at the last minute for items you forgot, toothpicks and cocktail sauce for that shrimp, for example.

4. **Stock the bar.** Wine, beer, hard liquor, and nonalcoholic beverages (aside from orange juice) all keep nicely, so stock up well ahead of time and spare yourself 11th-hour errands.

5. **Get help.** An extra pair of hands will go a long way toward easing your stress before and during the event. If your party will be large, consider hiring a professional bartender or even a college student over the age of 21 to mix and pour beverages. Your own child or a neighborhood teenager looking for some extra money might take coats, replenish the buffet table, and whisk away dirty plates and cups.

6. **Round up extras.** If you plan to borrow tables, chairs, linens, serving dishes, an ice chest, or any of the innumerable items you may need and don't own, do it as far ahead of time as possible. Stash these items in your garage or basement until the day of the party.

7. **Plan and set up music.** Will you be playing background music or are you hosting a dance party? Choose your CDs or program your MP3 player with an ear for the tone of your event. Plan and prepare your music at least a few days ahead of time. You don't want this critical part of the atmosphere to get lost in the frenzy of last-minute preparations.

8. **Find a place for everything that needs a place.** Where will you stash the coats (or gifts)? Where will you set out the food and the drinks? Where will people dance? Designate a location for all functions, keeping in mind how people must flow through the space. Be sure to find a discreet, but handy, area for the trash receptacle, especially if you are using disposable plates and cups.

9. **Decorate.** Never underestimate the power of an attractive setting to turn your party into something special. Even if your gathering doesn't call for balloons or streamers, you can create a festive atmosphere with flowers and candles (and maybe even a few paper lanterns). Put small bunches of flowers in several locations around the house or apartment and scatter or group votive lights so they will cast their magic spell without setting anyone's sleeve on fire.

10. **Clean house judiciously.** You want your home to look fresh and inviting, but there's no sense going crazy with the vacuum cleaner in every nook and cranny. Make sure the bathroom is clean and supplied with soap, guest towels, and toilet paper. Remove any pet hair from furniture and then just turn down the lights. There will be plenty of cleaning to do the day *after* the party.

11. **Be an attentive host.** As host, you are responsible for smoothing the entry of each guest. Introduce newcomers to at least one other person,

point them toward food and drink, and unburden them of coats, bags, and so forth. Above all, keep smiling. No matter what large or small catastrophes emerge, it's up to you to make everyone feel comfortable and glad they came.

TIP: Have a good friend on call the day of the party. If the last minute finds you short on shrimp or out of ice, you will have someone who can save your bacon by stopping at a store on the way to your home.

PARTY PORTIONS

Keep these rules of thumb in mind when planning food for entertaining, but always consider your knowledge of the guests and adjust portions accordingly.

Nibbles

Figure six bites per guest when snacks precede a meal.

When hors d'oeuvres *are* the meal, estimate that guests will eat about four or five hors d'oeuvres in an hour and a half. For a three-hour party with 30 people, figure 300 pieces.

The longer your party and the larger your guest list, the greater the number of selections you should offer.

The Main Meal

Poultry, meat, or fish—8 ounces when you have a single entrée, 6 ounces per dish when you offer two or more entrée courses.

Pasta—Use a serving spoon to estimate, but generally figure 2 ounces for a side dish, 3 ounces for a first course, 4 ounces for a main dish.

Rice, grains—1.5 ounces as a side dish, 2 ounces for a main dish such as risotto.

Potatoes—5 ounces.

Vegetables—4 ounces.

Beans—2 ounces as a side dish.

Green salad—Use a salad server to estimate a portion, but generally figure one ounce of greens per person.

Desserts

1 slice of cake or pie or one pastry per person

4 ounces of a creamy dessert such as pudding or mousse

5 ounces of ice cream

When serving two of the above, reduce each by a little less than half.

Tips for an attractive and tasty assortment of food

Don't repeat ingredients. For example, don't serve lasagna for dinner and cheesecake for dessert.

Consider the colors, textures, and temperatures of the food that will be served and make sure there is variety.

Create food stations for casual parties. People tend to congregate around food, so give them plenty of reason to circulate.

Organize a Family Reunion

For far-flung families, large and small, reunions can be a valuable way to stay connected. The key is to make it as easy as possible for everyone to attend.

1. **Give advance notice of date and time.** Depending on how far they are expected to travel, people need at least a couple of months to clear their calendars. A year in advance is not too long. Pick a date and time that works with almost everyone's schedule so the greatest number of family members can attend.

2. **Pick a suitable location.** Find a location that is reasonably easy to get to or one that everyone agrees would be worth the extra effort required to reach it. Consider whether the venue is large enough or intimate enough for the size of your family.

3. **Book a block of hotel rooms.** Family members may have more fun if everyone stays at the same hotel. If you book a block of rooms for the reunion, everyone should get a reduced room rate, and you can often get a complimentary suite or coupons offering a discounted breakfast for your party. Family members can reserve their rooms individually by calling the hotel and identifying themselves as members of your reunion party.

4. **Arrange transportation from the airport or train station.** If your family is staying at a hotel, find out whether the hotel offers complimentary shuttle service from the airport or train station. If not, try to coordinate flight or train arrival times and hire a van or town car to pick up arriving family members.

5. **Attend to children's needs.** If very young children will be invited, find a banquet hall or hotel that has a separate space where they can enjoy suitable activities. Consider hiring a baby-sitter to oversee the kids so the adults can be free to enjoy the party.

6. **Create special memories.** Your family is the theme of the party, so shower the room with touches that are meaningful to you.

   - *Photos.* Ask everyone to send you two or three old family pictures. If your family grew up near the beach, enhance your family theme by mounting the photos in frames decorated with seashells or nautical stripes. Honor lost loved ones by placing their photos on a mantle or special table decorated with flowers or candles.

- *Music.* Ask each family member to name a couple of songs that bring back special memories. Burn a CD mixing everyone's songs and play it as background music during the party. If you hire a DJ or band, supply a play list and ask that particular songs be dedicated to Cousin Jack or Aunt Sophie.

- *Games.* Games involving trivia from the past are lots of fun. Have someone ask questions about family history and award points and prizes for the highest number of correct answers. Pin the name of a family character on each person's back; that person has to guess who he is, based on how the other guests treat him or talk with him or the memories they discuss with him.

- *Food.* If your family had special family recipes, cook or have the caterer create those dishes for the party. Were lobster bakes a highlight of your childhood? Did Dad love eating peanuts at the ball game? Did everyone rave about Grandma Thora's cheesecake? Incorporate as many favorite foods as possible into the menu. Grandma Thora may be flattered if you ask her to make her famous cheesecake.

- *Décor.* Complete your family theme by decorating your party with images or themes that evoke your past. You might decorate the table with baseballs signed "Dad" and tied with raffia and small bags of peanuts. If you grew up on a farm, stack hay bales around the room or decorate the tables with loose bouquets of wildflowers. Bigger budget? Hire backdrops from a rental company depicting a farm, city skyline, or a blown-up photo of your childhood home.

Stock a Bar

The key decision when it comes to stocking a bar is whether or not to do it. Just because you're planning a party doesn't mean you have to offer everything from Cosmopolitans to Singapore Slings. A bottle each of red and white wine, plus club soda, ginger ale, and beer are probably de rigueur, but if neither you nor your friends are serious drinkers, you really needn't go further. If, however, you do a lot of entertaining and often include a cocktail hour, this list should provide the staples of a well-stocked bar. If you're starting from scratch and you intend to buy everything on the list, you might want to start by landing a second job. Instead, think of getting something from each category and filling in as you move up the corporate or professional ladder or closer to that big inheritance.

Hard Liquor

1. **Vodka.** This is the most popular hard liquor in the United States. It's the basis for lots of easy drinks, but premium vodkas, especially flavored ones, have become a stand-alone drink.

2. **Scotch.** Each connoisseur has her own favorite, but if you're buying just one, go for a good one, such as Dewars™ or Glenlivet™. Skip the very expensive premium scotch; it's meant to be sipped, like fine brandy.

3. **Gin.** Gin is the basis for many classic cocktails as well as the super-easy gin and tonic.

4. **Bourbon.** Real bourbon, made from corn, comes from Kentucky. Cheap is probably not a good idea since it can be harsh. A good bourbon, such as Booker's™, is much softer and can have surprising complexity.

5. **Rum.** Here the choice is between dark (more flavorful) and light (more suitable for summer drinks). Haitian rum is particularly flavorful.

6. **Vermouth.** Again, there are two basic kinds: dry (for martinis) and sweet (for sipping over rocks).

7. **Tequila.** This one is optional.

Wine

The key here is to steer a path between Thunderbird™ and Cheval Blanc™ '53. It is fine to stock one or two whites and reds and a couple of nonalcoholic choices. If you're uncertain about choosing, go to a good wine shop, give the salesperson your price range, and ask for some recommendations.

1. **White.** Choose at least one dry white and one that's on the sweet side. Perhaps the most popular white is the usually somewhat sweet Chardon-

nay (domestic Chardonnays are more likely to be sweet; French ones slightly drier). A popular dry white is pinot grigio.

2. **Red.** Merlot is a crowd pleaser (forget the movie *Sideways*). Inexpensive options include Beaujolais and Cabernet/Shiraz blends from Australia, but if you are looking for an inexpensive red wine and you aren't familiar with any, it is often recommended that you to stick to Cabernet Sauvignon.

3. **Nonalcoholic.** For nondrinkers and designated drivers.

4. **Champagne.** Maybe not for the big party, but good to have on hand for special occasions. Some domestic sparkling wines now rival their French counterparts.

Liqueurs

Perfect with coffee or in place of hard liquor, liqueurs are also essential for certain cocktails. Triple sec, an orange liqueur, is used in margaritas, along with tequila and lime. A good strategy is to stock a few liqueurs of distinctly different flavors. Since Grand Marnier™ and Cointreau™ are both basically orange flavored (they're both triple secs) choose one or the other. Include one coffee-flavored drink, such as Kahlúa™, and one Irish drink, such as Bailey's Irish Cream™. Brandy is an alcoholic beverage distilled from wine or fermented fruit juice. Cognac is brandy distilled from white wine, kirsch is cherry brandy, and slivovitz is plum brandy. Brandies are not sweet and contain as much alcohol, if not more, as hard liquors. Choose the flavor that appeals to you.

Nonalcoholic Beverages and Mixers

1. **Juices.** These are used as mixers or drunk on their own. Include tomato, orange, and cranberry.

2. **Club soda, tonic, and ginger ale.** These, too, can be drunk on their own or used as mixers.

3. **Soft drinks.** Cola, 7-Up™ or an equivalent, and flavored seltzer. Include regular and diet versions.

4. **Bottled water**

5. **Ice**

Garnishes and Spices

Garnishes include lemons, limes, orange slices, and maraschino cherries. You also need Tabasco sauce, olives, cocktail onions, and bitters.

Hire an Event Planner

◆◆◆

For really special occasions, you can save yourself time and trouble by hiring a professional event planner. New York City area event planner Carol Beaugard points out that experienced planners can anticipate problems and attend to fine points that might not occur to a layperson, and professional planners can usually save money for their clients by negotiating better terms with vendors. Beaugard suggests that for more spectacular affairs, you choose an event designer. Designers offer a more comprehensive service than planners; they usually create themes and supervise production elements, including lighting, special effects, unique entertainment, and activities. Here are some tips on hiring an event planner or designer.

1. **Make decisions before talking to the planner.** Think about your objective for the event before you get on the phone. In addition, be ready to talk about your style, taste, and personal vision. You should also know the following:

   The type of event (corporate function, social affair, special event)
   Approximate date and time of the event
   How many guests will attend
   Your budget

2. **Check on-line to find an event planner in your area.** First check the Web-sites of industry associations, such as the International Special Events Society (ISES) (*www.ises.com*) or the International Society of Meeting Planners (ISMP) (*www.iami.org*). You can also try *www.partypop.com*, *www.respond.com*, *www.specialeventsite.com*, *www.gatheringguide.com*, and *www.decidio.com*.

3. **Ask detailed questions.** Have a list of questions ready so that you don't forget anything.

- What experience do you have in the event-planning industry?
- How many events similar to mine have you planned?
- What duties are included in your fee? (See below for items that should be in the contract.)
- What are the costs for your services and how are you paid? Are you paid a flat fee, per project, or on a percentage basis of the entire event budget? Is there an additional charge for you to manage the day of the event?
- How many staff members will you need and what are the fees for their services?
- How will you be dressed for the event?
- What professional associations or organizations do you belong to?
- Can you provide referrals?

4. **Draw up a contract.** Make sure the planner's contract specifies that each of these duties will be performed:

- Site selection and assessment
- Vendor referrals
- Budget preparation
- Contract negotiations
- Planning event theme, design, and management
- Planning menus, programs, and special activities
- Development of time lines, calendars, itineraries, and registration procedures
- Arranging entertainment, decorations, signage, production (sound, lighting, technicians, etc.)
- Managing travel, hotel accommodations, parking, and transportation arrangements
- Arranging any necessary permits and certificates
- Providing publicity, sponsorships, and volunteer management
- On-site management on the day of the event
- Coordination of deposits and final payments for vendors

Create a Cozy Guest Room

Whether you have a spare room to dedicate exclusively for guests or must turn your child's bedroom or a den into guest quarters, think of the little things that will make your friends or family comfortable for the duration of their stay. Some of the amenities that will be appreciated include:

1. **A comfortable bed.** If the mattress is old, purchase a foam "egg crate" to put under the mattress pad. These do wonders to poof up an uncomfortable mattress. Fold an extra blanket at the foot of the bed for those who tend to get chilly at night. Offer two pillows even if you have a single guest, preferably one soft and one firm.

2. **Box of tissues.** There's nothing more awkward than waking up with a sneezing fit and having to stumble around looking for toilet paper to blow your nose.

3. **Bottle of water.** This is a nice touch. Place one next to the bed or somewhere in the room.

4. **Adequate closet space.** You may have to move some of your own items temporarily, but make sure there are a few empty hangers and enough room for your guests to hang their clothing.

5. **Clock or clock radio.** Don't make your guests ask for a wake-up call; give them at least a bedside clock. A clock radio is a nice touch if you have one to spare.

6. **Wastebasket.** Supply a place to put those crumpled tissues and any other debris a tidy guest may wish to dispose of inconspicuously.

7. **Fresh flowers.** Okay, so you're not running the Ritz, but a few fresh stems in a simple vase lets your guest know her visit was anticipated with pleasure.

8. **Reading material.** If you have any books about your town, or a local magazine featuring your area, by all means leave them in the guest room. A book of short stories can also be a welcome find by a guest who may have forgotten to pack bedtime reading.

> **TIP:** Equip the guest bath with clean towels and a reasonably fresh cake of soap. Toothpaste, shampoo, and a hair dryer will be welcome surprises.

Be a Great Guest

You're the guest. That could mean being waited on, taking it easy, taking advantage, and never being invited back. Or it could mean taking a part, being considerate, having a great time, and getting another invitation. Whether it's a cocktail party or a weekend in the country, being a great guest takes little more than common sense and a modicum of propriety.

1. **RSVP.** If you're invited, make sure you say whether or not you'll come. If your host bothered to send an invitation or even leave a voice mail, it's incumbent on you to respond, promptly. And then stick to what you've said, short of a real emergency (a subsequent, more attractive invitation, doesn't qualify).

2. **Arrive on time.** If your host says seven, don't show up at seven-thirty; it could mean a really dry roast. Cocktail parties allow more leeway, but don't push it. Arrive within a half-hour of starting time. On the other hand, never show up early. You might be stuck chatting with the five-year-old while your host tries to stuff the copy of *People* to the bottom of the magazine pile, leaving *The New York Review* on top.

3. **Don't come empty-handed.** But don't bring anything that needs immediate attention. If you bring flowers, bring them in a vase. Better yet, bring a plant or a bottle of wine. Depending on the occasion, you could bring special hand or bath soap, candles, or any number of thoughtful non-necessities.

4. **Be appropriately helpful.** If it's a formal affair, don't volunteer to help in the kitchen; that's what the "help" is for. If it's a casual dinner among friends, offer to pitch in.

5. **Don't monopolize the host.** You may not know anyone else, but the host does. Greet the host, but then move on. Even if you're shy, you can always ask the stranger next to you how she knows your mutual friend. Remember, as a guest at a gathering, you have a certain obligation to be social. If it doesn't come naturally, think of it as a role that you play for a time.

6. **Use your inside voice.** Don't be raucous, don't gesticulate wildly, and try to avoid tripping over furniture or feet.

7. **Be careful.** Don't rest a wineglass on a narrow shelf on the theory that it's probably wide enough. In other words, be extra careful of your hosts' home and furniture.

8. **Eat, drink, and be merry.** This is no time to announce that you've started your annual fast or that you've become a vegan. Don't force yourself to eat something you loathe or are allergic to, and don't drink alcohol if you ordinarily wouldn't, but don't announce what you intend to boycott. Just eat what you can, and don't comment on what you can't. Comparisons are always odious, unless the present meal truly is the best you've ever tasted. If you don't love everything, confine your comments to what you can honestly praise. If the food is truly awful, limit yourself to warm words about the company and the occasion.

9. **Don't tour the house unless your host invites you to.** Don't wander into rooms unless they're filled with other guests, don't open closed doors, and don't look inside the medicine cabinet.

10. **Don't outstay your welcome.** How do you know when it's time to leave? One way is to take your cue from others and not linger after others start to leave. Another is to be sensitive to your host. When she stops offering more coffee, when it's late and the conversation lags, it's probably time to say "good night." Don't make your host mention how early he has to get up or how tired she is before you take your leave.

11. **Say "thank you."** Even better, write it out. A call or e-mail will do, but a handwritten note is even better. And don't skip the "thank you" just because the individual is a good friend. Even a quick call after an evening together says that you value the friendship and don't take it for granted.

THE ART OF HOUSEGUESTING

A houseguest is something between a member of the family and a zoo animal. You want to be liked, you want to do your part, but you don't want to break anything or do something inappropriate. And you don't entirely understand the language. Each situation is unique, but there are some general rules that, if followed, assure a warm welcome and an invitation to return.

Arrive on time and under your own steam. If the invitation is for Friday evening around dinnertime, don't assume dinner's at eight. Ask when your host really expects you, and make sure you arrive on time. If possible, get there under your own power. If that means a cab from the airport, so be it, even if your host offers to pick you up.

Bring what you need. Think ahead and come prepared. Bring all your own stuff: sunscreen, bathing suit, rhino repellent. Sure, you can always borrow a sweater, but try not to.

Be self-sufficient. Entertain yourself when your host is busy or just wants some time alone. You can read, walk, snooze, watch TV (with the volume adjusted so only you can hear it). Don't expect your host to fill every minute of your stay with planned activities. You're not at summer camp.

Be helpful, but not intrusive. Definitely offer to do the dishes, but don't undertake spring cleaning. Guests who do the dishes and then proceed to scrub down the kitchen and wash out the refrigerator may be implying that the host isn't a good housekeeper.

Don't make yourself at home, whatever your host says. Take a soft drink from the refrigerator, but don't help yourself to the special delicacy your host brought back last summer from a trip to Paris. Don't rearrange the furniture in your room or adjust the central heating; don't use the phone to make long or long-distance calls; and don't presume to use the computer to check your e-mail unless you ask.

Don't parent. If your host has children, don't interfere. Maybe the kids eat ice cream for breakfast because they're allergic to cornflakes. Also, don't suggest the proper way to feed the cat. It won't be appreciated, no matter how well intentioned.

Expect to be fed, but not every meal. Offer to take your hosts to dinner once or twice, depending on the length of your stay. Offer to fix breakfast or even dinner, but if your host declines the offer, don't insist.

Fess up. The vase didn't fall, you dropped it; the potted plant didn't commit suicide, you snapped the stem. If you broke it, don't wait for your host to find out; confess up-front. If what you broke was valuable, offer to pay for it. If the offer is refused, send an equally valuable gift.

Leave no trace behind. When you leave, take all of you along. That means no stray hair in the bathtub. In fact, your host should have no physical evidence of your presence at all. That means leaving your room exactly as it was when you arrived, with the linens stripped and left in a laundry pile and the bedspread back on the bed.

Send a thank-you note. Definitely send a note and possibly a gift. If you've taken photos during your stay, you might include the best ones.

Choose a Great Gift for Your Husband

◆◆◆

"I don't care. . . . I don't want anything. Really." Does this sound familiar? The husband of the species can be a little difficult to read when it comes to gift buying. Maybe your man really doesn't want anything for his birthday or for the holidays. More likely, he just doesn't want to have to think about it at that moment. So your role, as the thoughtful spouse, is to figure it out anyway and come up with a gift that will wow him. Here are some tips to help you with this Herculean task.

1. **Listen when he talks to friends.** You don't have to bug his phone calls. Just pay attention to his small talk with the guys. That's when he's most likely to talk about "guy stuff," translation: things he'd like to own and to do if he could.

2. **Think about his passions.** No, no one is suggesting that you buy yourself a black lace teddy for his birthday (although it may be worth considering!). Think about other kinds of passions or interests he may have, anything from cooking to sports cars.

3. **Upgrade him.** If your husband is a techie, would he like the latest software to make his handheld organizer even more efficient? How about an MP3 player or other 21st century device? If he already has the latest gizmo, you might give him a gift card so that he can download more music without feeling guilty about the expense.

4. **Consider giving an experience.** Let's say your husband is really into fast cars. Of course, he drives a minivan or takes the train to work every day. But maybe he'd like nothing more than to spend a day learning how to drive a sports car around hairpin curves. This can be purchased as a package! Search the Web for high-performance or extreme driving schools to find one in your area. If cars are not for him, try rock climbing, sailing school, a gourmet cooking class, or a day at a spa.

5. **Present him with an opportunity.** Is he a movie buff or wannabe screenwriter? Chances are that your local college, university, or adult extension school has classes in screenwriting—or in pottery, watercolor painting, or do-it-yourself home repair. If you listen carefully, you'll know which of these courses might be an exciting chance for your husband to make his daydreams come true.

6. **Consider tools and jewels.** Depending on the kind of guy you're married to, a cordless screwdriver could really send him. Then again, cuff links from Tiffany's might put a sparkle in his eyes. Maybe he'd like both; only you can decide.

7. **Entertain or educate him.** A thoughtfully chosen movie or book might hit home. You might pair a novel or nonfiction book with a DVD on his favorite topic or historical event. If his idea of relaxing is to zone out in front of the History Channel, get him a DVD of the Civil War or WWII series. You can purchase these on-line from the History Channel or from your local public television Website.

8. **Think of his daily grind.** Does he stop at the local Starbuck's every morning on his way to the train? If he's a frilly coffee aficionado, maybe he'd be delighted with a milk steamer or a French press coffeemaker. Possibly he'd like to grind the beans himself on the weekends. Or, if he's a deeply serious coffee buff, consider a bean roaster. It doesn't get any fresher than that.

9. **Keep a gift receipt.** Okay, you're not a mind reader. Maybe you've struck out with the catcher's mitt you thought he'd love; or perhaps that cashmere turtleneck made his chin itch. There's no harm done as long as you let him know he's free to return your gift and come home from the store with the six pairs of tube socks he'd really rather have.

10. **Don't take it personally.** Whatever you chose, if you followed the steps above, you gave it your best shot. If you struck out with the catcher's mitt or the barbecue cookbook, remember that the gift you gave is not about *you* and accept his opinion gracefully.

Choose a Great Gift for Your Wife

Are you baffled—or paralyzed with indecision—when faced with the prospect of choosing a gift for your wife? If the item you settle on isn't received with the joy you hoped to inspire, both you and your wife could feel the disappointment. Here, then, is some help in unlocking the mystery of finding the perfect gift for that important woman.

1. **Think small and sentimental.** Choose something that speaks to your history, something perhaps to remind her of your first few dates. The soundtrack from the first movie you saw together or a framed photo from that romantic weekend in the Berkshires may mean more than a sapphire ring (not necessarily, but maybe).

2. **Package with flair.** Especially when you're giving a small and sentimental gift, splurge on beautiful wrapping and bows, and don't forget a carefully chosen card.

3. **Watch what she buys.** You can learn a lot by observing what she buys for others. Does she send gourmet food treats to your parents? Clothes to her sister? It's likely that she gives others gifts she would love to receive herself. Take note, and use her purchases as your cue.

4. **Enlist female help.** Women often love to help men with a gift-buying mission. Just make sure you take along someone whose taste you think your wife admires. A good friend or a sister can make all the difference in choosing a great gift.

5. **Buy brands she buys.** If your wife wears jewelry or clothing by particular designers, give her another article from that same line. Even if the item isn't an on-the-nose hit, you'll get big points for paying attention.

6. **Use a personal shopper.** Bring a favorite anything to an upscale department store and ask the personal shopper there to help you find something to go with it. You may come away with the perfect skirt or a just-right pair of earrings for that angora sweater she loves.

7. **Be stealthy.** Flip through catalogs or magazines she has read recently. When you see a folded page or, better yet, a marked item, order it!

8. **Be extravagant.** If all else fails, buy something so luxurious she'd never think of getting it for herself: a cashmere blanket, a year's worth of planted flowering bulbs, a gift certificate for the most upscale spa or salon in town.

9. **Beware of the practical.** Some women love to cook and would enjoy getting a high-end appliance that makes life in the kitchen easier. Others don't want anything that even smells like the kitchen. Even if your spouse is an avid cook, she may not consider a KitchenAide© mixer an appropriate birthday present. An anniversary gift that says "Cook up some spaghetti!" can stink, but Chanel© always smells like romance.

10. **Resist the temptation to give yourself a present.** When you discover that horse with a clock in its stomach at the flea market, ask yourself who it would really be for. You and your wife may have a lot of things in common, but a taste for white elephants may not be one of them.

Give Baby Gifts They'll Drool Over

◆◆◆

Sure, you can please any expecting mother with an adorable layette, a crib mobile, or the trendiest diaper bag. Heaven knows, she'll need a vast and bewildering array of clothing, accessories, equipment, and supplies, especially if this is her first child. But if you'd like to give a thoughtful present that will delight and surprise her—and one that is less likely to be a duplicate destined for return—consider the ideas below.

1. **Help her give thanks.** A box of pastel-colored thank-you notes and a roll of stamps would be a helpful present. She can reach for your box whenever she has a moment, and the energy, to dash off a note. Add a little notebook to record gifts, and she can check off each one when a note has been written. You've just made at least one part of her life a little bit easier.

2. **Give pampering, not Pampers™.** A gift certificate for a pedicure or massage might just make a new mother swoon with delight. To make sure she can take advantage of the gift, include an offer to baby-sit or to go along and cuddle the baby while mom is being indulged.

3. **Dress baby for later.** Many people give onesies and other tiny outfits the infant can wear right away. In nine to twelve months, however, the baby's wardrobe may be bare. Select an outfit or two for the baby to grow into. As you shop for the future, think of the season that should coincide with the size you are buying. This can be tricky, because some six-month-old babies fit into twelve-month-old clothing, but trying to coordinate size and season should ensure that you don't present a cute-as-a-button snowsuit that will fit perfectly on the Fourth of July. Consider buying clothing that spans more than one season, such as cotton sweaters, stretch pants, and T-shirts.

4. **Dress mama for nursing.** Now that the new mother is on her way to fitting back into her old jeans, she has a new wardrobe problem brought about by nursing. Special bras and blouses make nursing easy, but they can be expensive. Consider buying her some basic nursing T-shirts for everyday wear or a beautiful nursing blouse for special occasions.

5. **Entertain the bleary-eyed parent.** To a new mother, the multitude of nursing and soothing sessions can seem endless. A relaxing CD, an intriguing novel, or an upbeat DVD can help the hours pass more easily. Consider something frivolous, or at least unrelated to caring for the new

baby, to give her sleep-deprived brain a little vacation. If you think your friend would appreciate reading about other mothers who have made it through those first months and years and have some wisdom—and humor—to offer, see the list of books below.

6. **Help your bosom buddy.** Nursing can be initially more challenging than some new mothers expect. Consider giving *The Nursing Mother's Companion,* a classic book on the subject, along with a Brest Friend™ nursing pillow to help make the job more comfortable. You could also give her a breastfeeding support kit, which can be ordered from Earth Mama/Angel Baby *(http://www.earthmamaangelbaby.com/breastfeeding_support_kit.html)*. If your budget is larger, consider a glider chair and footrest.

7. **Be practical.** Avoid giving baby clothes that are too delicate to be machine-washed and -dried. Don't buy bottles or cups that are cute but hard to clean. In addition to making your friend's life a little more difficult, these hard-to-clean items invite bacterial growth.

8. **Start a library.** Books are always a good idea for children. Rather than buying the standard board books, which someone else might also give, you could purchase books for the future. Buy one or two hardbound classics of a particular series, and every birthday you can add to the collection. Include your favorite tales to make this gift more personal.

SOME FIRST-PERSON TALES FROM THE FIRST-BABY FRONTLINES

Operating Instructions. *A Journal of My Son's First Year,* by Anne Lamott

A Life's Work. *On Becoming a Mother,* by Rachel Cusk

Mother Shock. *Loving Every (Other) Minute of It,* by Andrea Buchanan

The Big Rumpus. *A Mother's Tale from the Trenches,* by Ayun Halliday

Guarding the Moon. *A Mother's First Year,* by Francesca Lia Block

Help a Friend with a New Baby

◆◆◆

Becoming a mother (or father) for the first time can be so overwhelming that there is almost no end to the help you can offer. The key is to know what kinds of assistance are most useful and welcomed by your friend. Here are some suggestions:

1. **Provide food.** You can do this in a couple of different ways. Prepare a meal that can be frozen and microwaved whenever it's needed. When you're planning a meal for a nursing mother, be conscious of foods she may be avoiding, such as cabbage, broccoli, onions, and spicy foods. You can also give a gift certificate to one of the restaurants in town that delivers. The busy new family might also appreciate receiving foods that can be served to friends and relatives who drop by to meet the baby. A gift basket of crackers, cheese, nuts, and other snacks would be appreciated. You might deliver a batch of homemade cookies to serve with coffee or tea. A pack of attractive cocktail napkins is a thoughtful touch!

2. **Become a chauffeur.** Offer to drive the new mother to the first pediatrician appointment. This might be the first time she is taking the baby out by herself, and having someone to help her get out the door with the baby and all the equipment should make it less stressful. Also, if you are a very close friend, offer to drive the new parents home from the hospital. This can be a wonderful gift, allowing the new parents to focus on the baby and savor the experience of bringing their first child home for the first time. Remember to disappear discreetly after you've helped them trundle everything into the house.

3. **Be spontaneous.** Instead of waiting for your friend to take you up on your sincere offer to "help with anything," call as you're going to the store and ask if there's anything you can pick up for her while you're there. If you're heading out to visit her, offer to stop on your way to pick up anything she needs at the pharmacy or grocery store.

4. **Do laundry and housework.** Use the same principal suggested above. Don't wait for your friend to ask; tell her you'll be over on Tuesday to do the laundry or the housecleaning. Your friend may not feel comfortable asking, or she may be so busy and overwhelmed that it doesn't even occur to her.

5. **Help her shower.** New mothers are often so busy attending to the infant that they can't find time in the day to take a shower. Offer to come by and sit with the baby for half an hour so your friend can get herself cleaned up and dressed for the day.

6. **Baby-sit while she's home.** Some new mothers don't feel comfortable leaving their new baby alone with anyone, however good a friend. If this is the case with your friend, offer to come to the house and sit with the baby while your friend naps, reads, catches up on e-mail, or does any of the numerous little tasks that are impossible with a brand-new baby at home. Of course, if your friend is willing, you can certainly offer to baby-sit while she goes out.

7. **Keep her company.** Being at home with an infant may keep a new mother busy, but it can also make her feel isolated and cut off from her friends. Offer to drop over in the daytime to chat, fix lunch for the two of you, or just listen.

8. **Provide historical photos.** If you are a relative of either parent, or otherwise have access to family photos, give her a few pictures of herself and/or the father as a baby. She will love comparing the photos to her baby and finding the little ways that the baby resembles mom or dad.

9. **Take digital photos.** When you visit at the hospital or in the first few days after the baby gets home, take digital photos and e-mail them to the parents so they can forward them to friends and relatives who live far away. Also offer to help your friend upload the photos to a Website.

10. **Offer interim clothing.** This is for mom, not the baby. If you happen to wear a larger size than the mom usually wears, offer her a few items to tide her over in those post-pregnancy baby weight months until she gets back into shape. This can really boost her morale, or even be a lifesaver, if she has an event to attend and nothing that fits her.

TIP: Whenever you call to chat or say congratulations, remember to begin the conversation by asking if it's a good time. Be prepared to keep the conversation brief.

Keep Holiday Shopping Hassle-Free

Nothing can tarnish the glitter of the holidays like schlepping through crowded stores and packed parking lots clutching a long shopping list. Imagine feeling joy instead of dread as December approaches, because you've already finished your holiday shopping. Sound too good to be true? It doesn't have to be. Here are some suggestions for turning your dream of a hassle-free holiday into reality.

1. **Cut your list.** You don't have to be a Scrooge, but your list may be longer than it absolutely needs to be. If you have been giving separate presents to everyone in your office, suggest drawing names. Do the same if you've been exchanging gifts with extended family—multiple cousins, nieces, in-laws, siblings, and stepchildren—or discuss confining gifts to the youngest family members. Chances are good that everyone will be as happy as you are to cut shopping time.

2. **Buy year-round.** Surely you've had the experience of seeing a great pair of earrings for your best friend during a spring sidewalk sale or a cunning little gerbil and hamster salt and pepper set for your rodent-loving cousin when you were browsing in July. By all means, buy the item when you see it, and stash it until December.

3. **Write a list and keep it with you.** Keep a slip of paper in the back of your wallet containing the names of those for whom you want to buy gifts. Check off the names as you purchase the gifts. This will keep you from buying more than you need and give you peace of mind as you see those names get checkmarked!

4. **Find a hiding place.** Designate a drawer, closet, or section of the basement or attic to stash those gifts you purchase during the year. Keeping them all in one place will eliminate that last-minute gift hunt when wrapping time rolls around.

5. **Shop at museum stores.** Some of the most original presents can be found at museum gift shops. If you're a museum buff, you'll have many opportunities to pick up truly inspired gifts on a regular basis.

6. **Purchase souvenirs when you travel.** Keep holiday gifts in the back of your mind when you're on vacation. This is another way to ensure that

the presents you buy are original and inspired, rather than grabbed in desperation at the last minute. Your friends will appreciate knowing they were on your mind while you were far from home.

7. **Don't be afraid of duplicates.** Sometimes the perfect gift for your friends in Iowa can also be the best choice for your pals in Pittsburgh. With some gifts, one size really may fit all. Here are some examples:

- *Gourmet items.* These can range from home-baked breads to cookies or upscale olive oil purchased on-line.

- *Easy-care greenery.* Amaryllis kits are reasonably priced and can be thrilling to receive. The smallest effort from even the brownest-thumbed gardener will be rewarded with a truly spectacular flowering plant.

- *Gift cards.* Many retailers have caught on to the fact that gift cards somehow seem hipper than gift certificates. The secret to making this gift seem thoughtful is to choose a card with each person's tastes and interests in mind.

8. **Let your keyboard do the shopping.** Some people never go to the mall anymore. Why spend the time and gas money when you can find pretty much anything you want on-line? And when you shop on-line for family and friends in other cities, you don't have to stand in line at the post office to ship the gift. One less holiday hassle!

Foreign Words and Phrases You Should Know

♦♦♦

Want to add some sparkle to your vocabulary? Or maybe you'd be happy just to keep up in a tête-à-tête with someone whose speech glitters with foreign expressions. Here are some frequently used terms from a variety of languages that you're likely to encounter in reading and conversation. Many have been adopted into English and are in *Random House Webster's College Dictionary.*

1. **Bête noire** [Fr. bet-NWARH]. Literally, "black beast." This phrase comes up when talking about something considered detestable, as in, "He used to enjoy golfing, but never mastered the game. Now it's his bête noire."

2. **Bon mot** [Fr. bon-MOE]. Literally, "good word." This refers to a witty remark. "She was popular at dinner parties because of her charm and frequent bon mots." (**Tip:** Don't pronounce the "s" at the end of French words.)

3. **Carpe diem** [Lat. kar-pay-DEE-um]. Literally, "seize the day." If you're trying to get a friend to forget about that early-morning meeting and go to a wild party, you might just say, "Carpe diem, pal!"

4. **Cognoscenti** [Lat. con-yuh-SHEN-tee]. This word comes from the Latin term meaning "to know." It refers to those who are educated or "in the know" on a certain subject, as in, "The chic gallery openings are always attended by the cognoscenti." The other thing to know about this word is that it's plural. If there is only one person who knows, she's a cognoscente.

5. **Deus ex machina** [Lat. DAY-uhs-eks-MAH-kuh-nuh]. Literally, "the god out of the machine." This term comes from Greek and Roman drama, when a god was abruptly lowered onto the stage by machinery to save a character from a difficult situation. In modern times, this phrase refers to a clunky plot device that comes out of nowhere to achieve a plot resolution. "The movie was really interesting until a deus ex machina ending spoiled the whole thing."

6. **Entre nous** [Fr. AHN-truh-noo]. Literally, "between us." You might share a tidbit with a close friend saying, "Entre nous, he's been dyeing his sideburns and mustache for years."

7. *Fait accompli* [Fr. FET-ah-kon-PLEE]. Literally, "accomplished fact." As in "There's no use applying for the job; Joe's appointment is a fait accompli."

8. **Hoi Polloi** [Gk. HOY- puh-LOY]. This often misused term refers to the common people, literally, "the many." Frequently hoi polloi associate it with *hoity-toity* and use it when they mean folks who are fancy-schmancy. Another tip: Strictly speaking, one doesn't say "the hoi polloi," because *hoi* means "the." So, if you want to be one of the cognoscenti, use it like this: "Do you want to get orchestra seats or would you rather sit up in the balcony with hoi polloi?"

9. *In medias res* [Lat. in-MEE-dee-uhs-RAYZ]. Literally, "in the middle of things." "The movie is hard to follow because it begins in medias res, and you have to figure out the plot from there."

10. **_Je ne sais quoi_** [Fr. zhun-SAY-kwah]. Literally, "I don't know what." This phrase is used to indicate that something is indescribable, usually indescribably good, as in, "My, this vegetable soup really has a certain _je ne sais quoi!_"

11. **Memento mori** [Lat. muh-MEN-toh-MOR-ee]. From Latin, "a reminder that you must die." Not a cheery term, but occasionally handy, as in, "Uncle Wilbur always slept in a casket. He considered it his memento mori."

12. **_Mi casa es su casa,_** also, more idiomatically, **_Mi casa, su casa_** [Sp. MEE-cas-uh-es-SOO-cas-uh]. It doesn't get any more literal than this expression of hospitality: "My house is your house."

13. **Pied-à-terre** [Fr. pee-ay-duh-TARE]. Literally, "a foot to the ground." Idiomatically, it is "a place to touch down." If you're lucky enough to have a pied-à -terre, you have an apartment in the city for part-time use, usually in a really great city where you'd like to spend the occasional weekend.

14. **Raison d'être** [Fr. ray-zohn-DE-truh]. Literally, "reason for being." If you love to garden, planting tulip bulbs might become your raison d'être each September.

15. **Schadenfreude** [Ger. SHAHD-un-froy-duh]. From _schaden,_ meaning "damage" and _freude,_ meaning "joy." This word refers to a malicious pleasure in the misfortune of others. _Schadenfreude_ was frequently used to describe the feeling some people had when domestic doyenne Martha Stewart was sent to prison.

16. **Sine qua non** [Lat. SIN-ay-kwah-NOHN]. Literally, "the essential element," as in, "peanut butter is the sine qua non of Aunt Frieda's sui generis stew."

17. **Sui generis** [Lat. SOO-ee-JEN-uh-ris]. Literally, "of its own kind." This word means "unique," as in, "Everyone at the potluck knew that Aunt Frieda's anchovy peanut butter stew was sui generis."

18. **_Weltanschauung_** [Ger. VELT-an-shau-oong]. Literally, "worldview." This term refers to a comprehensive worldview or philosophy of life. "His Weltanschauung doesn't allow for happy endings."

19. **_Weltschmerz_** [Ger. VELT-shmerts]. Literally, "world pain," sadness over the evils of the world or a weariness with the world brought on by that

feeling, as in, "Her gripping, yet depressing, novels were always tearjerkers, highly colored by her Weltschmerz."

20. **Zeitgeist** [Ger. TZITE-guyst]. Literally, "spirit of the time." This term is used in reference to the tastes, philosophy, and general feeling of an era, as in, "The zeitgeist of the roaring twenties was to have a good time because the war was over and you might as well live it up."

[Professional Life]

Network Effectively

A network is simply a circle of people knit together by trust and common interests. The object of professional networking is to widen the pool of people who know and trust you. The idea is that these people will feel good about connecting you with jobs, clients, or outlets for your work.

1. **Build trust.** The primary objective of networking is to build trust. Rather than trying to be impressive, you should strive to be honest and authentic. Instead of trying to reach some immediate goal, you should aim to connect with people and form relationships that will be enduring and productive. This means being consistent and being sincere. Listen at least as much as you talk. Remember, it's a relationship, not a one-time sale.

2. **Join, join, join.** Join professional organizations, but don't limit yourself to them. The relationships formed in social groups, community organizations, religious groups, even book clubs, can be invaluable sources of referrals and help. Of course, if it's a job you're after or professional help, professional organizations should be your first target. Join local and state chapters as well as national organizations.

3. **Do, do, do.** Joining isn't enough. You should become as active and visible in the organizations you join as possible. Volunteer for committee assignments, host meetings, and staff the phone banks; whatever the activity, be an active part of it. You needn't be the star; you just want to be visible to as many people as possible.

4. **Ask open-ended questions.** When you find yourself in conversation with someone, especially someone you've just met, avoid questions that can be answered with a simple "yes" or "no." Ask the who, what, and how kinds of questions that spark real conversation. In particular, ask about the other person. Two things will happen: You'll find out if he or she can be of help to you, and you'll go a long way toward impressing that person with your concern. People like to engage with and help those who are interested in them. Offer what you hope to receive. (See "Work Any Room (or How to Talk to Just About Anybody)," page 79, for more tips on starting a conversation).

5. **Develop your elevator speech.** It's amazing that we can spend years, decades even, doing something really well but still have trouble giving a

brief explanation of what we do or what's special about it. Spend some time pondering what makes you really proud about the work you do. What are your greatest accomplishments? Next, tackle the most difficult part: Boil it down to what you can say in 15 or 20 seconds. That's about as long as you're likely to be in an elevator with a hot networking prospect. Don't think of this as a sales pitch; think of it as an intriguing way to introduce yourself.

6. **Follow through immediately.** If someone gives you a lead or referral, follow up on it immediately. The person who offered the referral might well have gone out of her way and put her own reputation on the line. If, however, someone offers to make a call on your behalf, ask specifically when you should make the follow-up contact.

7. **Expand your network via the Internet.** The Internet offers an invaluable extension of your networking prospects. Participate in professional discussion groups and on-line forums. To find groups in your field, check *groups.google.com*. As you would in any community, participate actively. Consider starting a blog or a regular column for a Website or e-newsletter. Remember that networking on the Internet is the same as networking in person: It's about developing trust and relationships. Be helpful, and you're much more likely to get help from others.

Prepare the Perfect Presentation

◆◆◆

If you'd rather die than speak in front of an audience, you're not alone. Asked whether they would rather speak with or without notes to a full house at Radio City Music Hall or drop dead, most people would choose the latter. But if you've carefully prepared a stunning presentation, there's nothing to fear. Follow these pointers and choose life—even life in front of an audience—over death.

1. **Get the facts.** Find out how much time you'll have to make the presentation and allot about 20 percent of it to questions and comments. Know what audiovisual equipment is available on-site—computer, overhead

projector, microphone, slide projector—and bring anything else you might need. Ask for information about the audience and adjust your presentation to match its level of sophistication or technical expertise.

2. **Keep it sharp and simple.** Prepare an outline of the key points you want to make, keeping in mind the classic injunction, KISS: Keep It Sharp and Simple. Don't try to stuff too much into a single presentation, regardless of how much time you have. People can retain only so much. Write a rough draft that includes the main points of your talk, then go over it to make sure you haven't gone off on any tangents. You needn't write every word and phrase you're going to use; stick to the main points.

3. **Make it personal.** Try to include some "I" phrases and connect yourself and your topic to the audience. If it's a small group, you might make a point of addressing individual members by name.

4. **Use visual aids appropriately.** It's tempting to make PowerPoint the center of your presentation. It's slick, and it shifts the attention away from you. That's the problem. If your audience spends the whole time looking at a computer or projection screen, it won't come away with a sense of who you are or why what you're talking about is important on a human level. Besides, staring too long at a screen is an invitation to drift off and zone out. Use computer-generated aids strategically, but don't let them become the entire focus of your presentation. Follow the IMPACT rule: Visual aids should be **I**ntegrated into your presentation, **M**ove the presentation along, look **P**rofessional, be **A**ppropriate to the section where they're used, **C**ommunicate with absolute clarity, and be **T**echnically sound. There's nothing more disruptive than a recalcitrant video projector.

5. **Treat humor deferentially.** If you're Robin Williams, you can probably include some humor in your presentation. If not, be careful. Humor can be misconstrued or, worse, fall completely flat. And if it's too successful, people won't remember anything else. It's best to leave the jokes for later and focus on the topic at hand.

6. **Avoid unnecessary jargon.** Even if you're talking to people in the same line of work as yourself, relying too much on jargon suggests a lack of originality. Sometimes jargon is necessary, especially in technical fields, but if it isn't, don't use it.

MANAGE STAGE FRIGHT

Even polished performers suffer stage fright. They go on anyway, because they've learned that, uncomfortable as they may feel, stage fright is not symptomatic of anything about to go awry. You can use the same techniques as they do to get through the discomfort.

Remember, you'll probably live. Very few people actually die in the process of giving a presentation, and in all likelihood, life will go on after your talk, pretty much as it did before.

Focus on your talk. Make communicating what you want to say your primary concern. By consciously focusing on it, you'll divert yourself from your own feelings.

Take deep breaths. Deep breathing is a meditative technique that can slow your heart rate and induce a sense of physical calm. Just don't overdo it: You could hyperventilate and pass out.

Avoid medication. Don't take that tranquilizer unless you know it won't dull your mind as well as your anxiety. Some performers resort to medications called beta blockers, which slow your heart rate, but if you're not used to them, the results can be disastrous; a dead faint is not out of the question.

Know that it feels worse than it looks. You may feel your hands trembling, but your audience probably won't notice. No one can see the butterflies in your stomach.

7. **Practice, practice, practice.** Nothing will boost your confidence higher than knowing your material cold. Practice the presentation using just a card with keywords on it. Making a recording of your presentation is unnecessary, but you should give the talk out loud enough times so that you can do it even if you're distracted. If you can give your practice presentation in front of a spouse or friend, all the better.

8. **Prepare responses.** Anticipate questions and objections that might come up during or after your talk and prepare responses. Although it is impossible to anticipate every question, you should be able to adapt many of your prepared responses to answer questions that actually arise.

9. **Arrive early.** Even if you know the room, you should arrive early to make sure chairs are set up properly and that the equipment you need is working.

10. **Check the mirror right before curtain time.** Is your fly zipped? Lipstick on straight? Any parts of lunch still visible? Trailing any debris on the soles of your shoes? You don't want to be wondering why half your audience seems barely able to contain their laughter when you haven't said anything funny.

Prepare for Business Trips

Your flight is booked, your hotel room reserved, but there are hordes of details you need to consider before you leave on a business trip. Plan ahead, and you won't be stranded away from home and office without something that you can't—or really would rather not—do without.

1. **Print out a copy of your itinerary.** Include everything: flight details, land travel arrangements, all meetings, lunches and dinners, power breakfasts, sightseeing, and other important information about your trip. Especially important are the names and titles of all the people in your meetings and the addresses and phone numbers for every place you need to go.

2. **Make sure others have a copy, too.** Key people in your office, such as your assistant or, perhaps, your boss, should have a copy of your itinerary. Give one to someone at home as well.

3. **Tie up loose ends.** This is especially important if you'll be away for more than a few days. Return phone calls, take care of office routines that you usually perform on the days you'll be gone, and inform colleagues of pending issues.

4. **Change voice message and e-mail responses.** Change your voice message to state the days you'll be away, when you'll return, and whom to contact in your absence, and program your e-mail to send a reply automatically that you'll be out of the office until the date of your return. (If you plan to check your e-mail on the road, send the message anyway.)

5. **Anticipate delays and plan for down time.** Don't schedule appointments back to back, and leave plenty of time to get to and from the airport. Just as you should anticipate unexpected delays, you should anticipate gaps in your schedule. People run late, traffic is unexpectedly light, and you might find yourself with time on your hands. Bring reading material—leisure as well as work-related—and scout out interesting places before you leave home in case there's time for some sightseeing.

6. **Pack light.** Try to pack so that you don't have to check any luggage. If you must check a bag, check your personal items rather than your work. You can always buy a new shirt or blouse, but you can't replace the carefully prepared presentation materials. If possible, leave room in your baggage for the stuff you'll collect, especially if you're attending a long conference or a trade show.

7. **Bring an envelope for business receipts.** If you stuff receipts into your wallet or pocket, they're likely to be tossed out with the soiled tissues. Instead, keep all receipts in a manila folder or an envelope, and put them there as soon as you get them. Those $5 parking receipts can add up.

8. **Prepare for your electronic needs.** Pack chargers and accessories for your laptop and cell phone. Make sure you have a copy of essential documents on universally accessible external media, such as a flash drive or CD. That way, even if your laptop crashes, you can still wow them with your PowerPoint presentation. The flash drive will also allow you to back up any work you do while you're away.

9. **Pack your medications and essential toiletries.** Include the usual first-aid items, such as Band-Aids, tweezers, and antiseptic, as well as cold and stomach remedies and over-the-counter painkillers, in case of indisposition or indiscretion. Include all the prescription medications you need, and enough extra to cover yourself if your trip is unexpectedly extended.

10. **If you travel often, keep a bag prepacked.** Keeping a set of personal items—clothes, medicines, toiletries—packed in a second carry-on bag gives the frequent traveler peace of mind.

Hold Efficient and Effective Meetings

Economist, ambassador, and wit, John Kenneth Galbraith spoke for many a bureaucrat when he observed, "Meetings are indispensable when you don't want to do anything." Instead of dwelling on the truth in such cynicism, you can follow a few basic guidelines to make any meeting more productive and help restore credibility to the word itself.

1. **Ask yourself if the meeting is really necessary.** If all you need to do is provide routine information, putting it in an e-mail or intra-office memorandum would be a better use of your time.

2. **Think through your objectives for the meeting.** Ask yourself what you hope to accomplish. Are you looking for a brainstorming session? What ideas or plans should emerge from the meeting? Would you like to come away with a list of action items assigned to each staff member?

3. **Draw up a list of participants.** Once you know what you'd like to get done at the meeting, decide who should—and shouldn't—attend.

4. **Create an agenda, including critical information.** An agenda is a road map telling each participant where the meeting is headed. A well-planned agenda will help everyone stay on course. Write the objective of the meeting at the top of the page. Make a list of items to be covered, numbering them from most important to least important. Make it easy for your staff to keep important details together by putting the date, time, and location of the meeting on the agenda, as well as a list of the attendees.

5. **Attach background information to the agenda.** If you're asking the attendees to do preparation for the meeting, staple the necessary documents to the agenda. This may sound like grade school handholding, but busy people are not always as organized as they might be. Giving them some assistance will pay off for you in the long run.

6. **Use your agenda as the timekeeper.** Put the starting and ending times of the meeting on the agenda, and indicate the approximate length of time to be spent on each item.

7. **Stick to the agenda.** An agenda is useful only when it is adhered to; ignore it at your peril. Without the discipline of an agenda, a meeting can

meander off course, leaving participants frustrated and objectives unfulfilled. Your own credibility as the person in charge may also suffer.

8. **Don't use meetings to mete out criticism.** Never single out anyone for criticism at a meeting. Praise and encouragement work well in public, but negativity rarely does.

9. **Always start and end on time.** When you delay a meeting awaiting late-comers, you punish the punctual and reward those who stroll in late. When you end meetings at the advertised hour, you let staff members know their time is valuable and respected.

Relocation Tips

◆◆◆

Moving is always a strain, even if you're only going across town. But if your employer is relocating you, you will need to deal with work issues on top of everything else. This list offers tips specifically related to relocation due to a job. For general information on changing your abode, see "Moving," pages 250-268.

1. **If this is your idea, make sure it's a good one.** If you're requesting a transfer, or simply leaving one job for another in a different place, consider all of the issues involved, not just those involving your career. Do some research on the town where you may go. Find out such things as the price of housing, the cost of living, and the quality of the schools (if you have school-age children or intend to). Try to get a sense of the cultural and social climate of the place. If you're relocating from a big city to a small town or the other way around, you could be in for culture shock. Search the Web for sites covering the town or city, and see if there's a community chat group that you can join to get a feeling for the people. If you own your home, ask a local realtor how much he thinks you can get for it, and find out how much houses cost in the town where you intend to relocate.

2. **Know what kind of help your company will provide.** Often, when a large company asks you to relocate, it will take care of all of the details surrounding the move. If it's a permanent relocation, it might offer to sell

your house for you and help find you a new one. Make sure you understand the price parameters on both the buying and selling sides. Will the company also pay for moving your furniture and, if so, is the cost of packing covered? Will anyone at the new location be able to help with details like finding new schools? Will there be help finding your spouse a new position? If it's a temporary relocation, most companies will provide housing, but you are responsible for maintaining your permanent home; make sure the compensation, monetary or professional, is worth any additional expenses you may incur.

3. **Make contact with new associates well before the move.** Call the new offices and set up a time outside of business hours when you can chat with one or more of your new colleagues. This gives you a chance to talk about office politics and get an idea of what the social and cultural scene is like.

4. **Know what to do that first week.** The first days after a move are stressful. Find out as much as possible from your new boss or colleagues about what you'll be doing the first week at the new location. Knowing this ahead of time can relieve anxiety and help you prepare, allowing you to work as efficiently as possible despite the distractions of moving.

5. **Get specific information on overseas locations.** Relocating overseas is usually much more complicated than relocating within the United States. Before you move, you must settle medical care and insurance issues and fill out the paperwork needed for a driver's license. If you're moving to an established office, ask to talk with anyone who has made a similar move and find out what it was like, what problems came up, and what solutions worked best. If you have school-age children, you must decide whether to enroll them in a local, possibly non–English-speaking, school, or in a private school where English is spoken. One of the most important steps you can take to integrate into a new country is to learn some crucial customs beforehand, both business and social. They don't call foreign countries *foreign* for no reason. Things you take for granted in the States, such as shaking hands, working on weekends, and expecting business associates to act as friends, may not be the way things are done in your new home.

Negotiate Like a Pro

◆◆◆

"In business, as in life, you don't get what you deserve,
you get what you negotiate." —Chester Karrass

For many people, the idea of negotiating conjures images of tough guys driving hard bargains in smoke-filled rooms. But negotiation is simply part of the give-and-take of basic human communication; it's about finding a way to get what you want. Granted, the experience of negotiating is more intense if you're talking to a car salesman or asking your boss for a raise. Keep these suggestions in mind the next time you sit down to negotiate.

1. **Do your homework.** Knowledge is power. The more information you have as you begin the negotiations, the stronger your hand is. If you're negotiating for a car, for example, knowing the dealer's cost gives you a foundation for your offer. In any negotiations it is essential to know whether you can go elsewhere for what you want. If you can, you are in a more powerful position whether you're bargaining for a cell phone, an automobile, or a new home.

2. **Ask for more than you expect to get.** Never put your best terms on the table at the outset. You will need to give up something to get what you want, so begin by reaching higher than you expect to go. You can assume that the person you're negotiating with has done the same thing. This gives you both some wiggle room in approaching the deal.

3. **Approach the negotiation as a win–win situation.** When you want to get something from another person, it helps to consider his point of view. You will be more persuasive if you look for a solution that gives him some of what he wants.

4. **Keep the negotiation balanced.** Never give a concession without getting a concession. Keeping trade-offs on the table lets the opposition know that you won't be bullied into a deal.

5. **Develop your relationship.** Successful negotiations are based on relationships. Although you are talking about either abstract concepts or dollars and cents, your final agreement will rise or fall, at least in part,

based on the connection you establish with the other person. Put in a more old-fashioned way, "You catch more flies with honey than with vinegar."

6. **Touch on basic human needs.** You are more apt to negotiate successfully if you keep in mind that the most basic human needs include security, economic well-being, recognition, and control over one's life. You must ensure that the person with whom you are negotiating feels her needs have been met; only then can she feel good enough about the deal to agree to it.

7. **Don't be afraid of silence.** When rooms go quiet, people tend to get nervous. Don't be the one who rushes in to fill the gaps. If you do, you're liable to appear nervous or too eager. Going quiet can make the other person fear that you're losing interest. Let the silence work for you.

8. **Base your arguments on what the other person needs.** If you're asking for a raise, don't tell your boss why your family needs extra income. Outline the ways in which you have been valuable to the company and continue to be. Persuade your boss that it is in her best interest to keep you satisfied.

9. **Attack the issue, not the person.** If you suspect your opponent is using dirty tricks or inaccurate information to bolster his position, address those points directly. You'll get nowhere attacking character or starting a personal argument. Instead, say something that shows your knowledge but gives the other person an out. "I may be mistaken, but those figures don't jibe with the numbers I've come up with. Can we take a look at your source for that information?"

10. **Don't be pressured.** Many of us have had the experience of being trapped at a car dealership for hours and hours as the salesman periodically disappears into his "manager's" office to present your latest offer. This tactic is designed to exhaust you, so you'll agree to any terms just to end the process. There's no reason to succumb to such pressure. You can always get up and say, "I'll come back later, after you've finished talking with your manager about the deal you're prepared to offer."

[Physical Health]

Find the Right Physician

People often choose a physician the same way they choose a mate: They trust in blind luck, they accept a prearranged marriage, they hope to fall madly in love, or they simply settle for whatever is available. Sometimes these strategies work, but when they don't the consequences can be dire. At least when it comes to choosing a doctor, there is a more rational approach. The choice may be immediately narrowed by needing to find a physician who participates in a particular health insurance plan, but that usually still leaves a pretty large field. Here are tips to help assure a good choice.

1. **Know what makes you comfortable.** You don't have to love your doctor, but you must feel comfortable with him or her. Does gender matter? How about age? Religion? Nationality? Put political correctness aside. If deep inside you believe no one under 50 knows enough about life to give advice to others, you won't be comfortable with a 35-year-old physician, no matter how well qualified.

2. **Choose a hospital.** The best hospitals tend to attract the best doctors. They also have stringent standards that doctors who want admitting privileges must meet. Physicians associated with major teaching hospitals meet those standards and have access to leading specialists to whom they can refer you should the need arise. So you may want to choose the best hospital in your area and work from there.

3. **Ask for recommendations.** Although friends may not be best equipped to judge a physician's professional accomplishments and expertise, they're very good at judging how the office is run, an important factor in your overall satisfaction with the physician you choose. Ask if appointments can be had quickly when you're sick and if the office generally runs on time. Chronic waiting is a serious health problem.

4. **Determine board membership.** Virtually all physicians are board certified, but you want your primary-care physician to be certified in internal medicine, family practice, or, if you're old enough to qualify, geriatrics. Of course, if you have a particular chronic or acute problem, you want a physician certified in the appropriate specialty. You can check board certification at the Website of the American Board of Medical Specialties (*www.abms.org*)

or by calling them at 866–ASK–ABMS, or you can go to the DoctorFinder section of the American Medical Association's Website (*www.ama-assn.org*).

5. **Schedule interviews before you get sick.** If you can afford to, schedule interviews with two or three physicians before choosing one. Depending on the part of the country you live in, you may find physicians willing to schedule an initial interview at no charge, but this is unlikely to be the case in larger cities. Be sure to ask ahead of time what each physician will charge. Initial interviews won't be covered by your insurance company, so if you can't afford to pay for one, schedule a first visit. Some doctors insist on a comprehensive physical as the first visit, in which case the wait for an open appointment may be considerable; others are willing to schedule a routine office visit first and follow it up with a full physical later.

QUESTIONS TO ASK A NEW DOCTOR

Whether you schedule an interview or an exam, you should come prepared with specific questions to help you determine if you want a long-term relationship with this physician.

Will you accommodate my preferences for a specific health-care approach? If you have a definite preference in your approach to health care, ask if the physician is comfortable with it. For instance, if you believe in practices considered "alternative," such as chiropractic or acupuncture, make sure the doctor is like-minded. Most people now want to participate in their health-care choices, but some prefer that the doctor simply make all decisions. Spell out which you prefer and ask if the physician can accommodate you.

What tests do you regularly order and what do you check for? A doctor should be able to answer this question in a way that's comprehensive and clear to you.

Will you accept my insurance as payment or must I pay your office? Some doctors' offices bill your insurance company first and ask you only for the copayment or any charges your company won't cover. Other doctors require payment up-front, leaving you to deal directly with your insurance company for reimbursement.

What incentives and disincentives drive your practice? It's usually considered rude to suggest that money may be behind health-care decisions, but let's face facts—it often is. The pressures of financial incentives can seriously affect the quality of your care. Specifically ask if the practice is owned by a large corporation and how that corporation exercises its power. Is the doctor part of a preferred-provider plan or health-management organization? Is the doctor penalized if his patients' care is more complex and costly? Are prescription options limited by a certain formulary, an approved list of drugs? Is the doctor limited in the specialists to whom he can refer you?

Whom do I call if I get sick while you're away? Whether the physician is on vacation or simply gone for the day, you should know whom to call when the physician is not on call.

Do you mind if my partner, spouse, or friend sits in? If you're willing, so should the doctor be.

When to Call a Doctor

When you fall victim to a debilitating illness or are in a serious accident, there's no question: Call your doctor. But it isn't always easy to know whether a less dramatic symptom is cause for alarm (unless you're a hypochondriac, in which case the answer is always yes). How do you determine whether a symptom is just part of being alive or if it requires medical attention? Here are some broad guidelines for when to call your doctor.

1. **Call if you feel dramatically ill.** Any severe symptom that lasts for more than a few minutes warrants an immediate call to your doctor. Of course,

Although your primary concern when choosing a physician is the physician herself, her staff can have a real impact on your health care. How did the person react when you first called? Was he friendly or curt? Were you placed on hold and forgotten? When you showed up for your first appointment, were you treated with respect? Did you wait an inordinate amount of time? Find out who handles calls during lunch hours and on weekends and whether it's possible to get a message to the doctor when he's ordinarily not available. Is the office convenient to get to? Is there adequate parking or is it near the public transportation you usually use? These may seem like trivial issues, but if they become impediments to seeing a physician when you need to, they become serious health issues.

if you slam the window on your finger and it hurts like hell, you probably don't need expert advice unless you think it's broken. But if you develop a sudden sharp pain that isn't the consequence of lifting more than you should, if you feel dizzy or very light-headed and you haven't suddenly changed position, if you find it difficult to catch your breath and you haven't been exerting yourself, you may have a serious problem that needs quick intervention.

2. **Call if you've been running a fever for more than a couple of days.** If you have a cold and your fever is slight, give it at least three or four days, but if you don't see any reason for a fever, don't ignore it for more than two days. If a fever, even a slight one, comes and goes over a period of several days, make the call.

3. **Call if you have a high fever.** Don't play doctor and diagnose the flu. Any fever of more than 103°F is cause for concern.

4. **Call if you have symptoms of heart attack or stroke.** Obviously, a sharp pain in your chest that lasts for more than a minute or so, loss of sensation in your face or limbs, slurred speech, sudden visual changes, or shortness of breath all warrant an immediate call to your doctor, if not to

911. But heart attacks and stroke don't always present themselves in these obvious ways. You may not feel chest pain with a heart attack. Rather, you may simply feel a persistent bloated sensation, perhaps with nausea, or suffer sudden extreme fatigue, or notice a new, irregular or fast heartbeat. If you do experience pain or shortness of breath that gets worse with exercise, call right away. Symptoms of stroke can also be very subtle: A slight blurring of vision or confusion could be the only signs. If it passes, fine. If not, or if the symptoms come and go, it's time to call.

5. **Call about any unusual bleeding.** A bloody nose, unless it won't stop, doesn't warrant a call. Blood from any other orifice probably does.

6. **Call if you notice any significant mental changes.** This one is tricky, because some mental changes induce paranoia, but if you experience a noticeable change in your mental functions you should call a doctor right away. It could be a symptom of stroke, an allergic response, or a toxic reaction to a drug. Kidney or liver failure can also produce severe mental changes.

7. **Call if you suffer any loss of function.** If something has been working normally and suddenly doesn't, you should call your doctor. If you don't have the strength to do something you ordinarily do, if the directions for buying stamps at the post office vending machine suddenly make no sense, or if your left leg won't go where it's supposed to, call.

Prepare Questions about Your Health

The time to think of what to ask your physician is not when you're sitting in a paper gown on the exam table. Prepare for your annual physical—or any doctor visit—as you would for a business or professional meeting, with an agenda and a list of questions, as well as a summary of information your doctor is likely to need.

1. **List physical concerns and changes.** Patient, know thyself. A day or two before a scheduled doctor visit, take some time to think about how you feel. While you may feel fine at the moment, think about your physical state since your last visit. Have you been ill (even with colds or

stomach upset that you may consider routine)? Any aches or pains you attribute to normal aging? Weight gain or loss? Sleep problems? List all of your symptoms and include everything that's changed since your last visit; what seems unimportant to you may provide a clue to your physician and help in a diagnosis or evaluation. Your doctor will want to know when the symptoms started, how often they occur, and how long they last.

2. **List all your medications.** Your doctor needs to know about all medications you take and others you've been told to take, but don't. Make sure you have the names of the medications, dosages, and instructions for how to take them, and don't forget to include all over-the-counter medications and supplements.

3. **Write down your concerns and your fears.** If it concerns your health, it's never trivial. If you've given up an activity you used to enjoy, such as gardening or skiing, mention it. Writing a list makes it easier to bring up topics you might otherwise skip because they seem trivial or embarrassing, such as issues related to sex or incontinence. With the list in front of you, you're much more likely to talk about what really concerns you.

4. **Write down the answers.** Don't depend on your memory. Write down answers your doctor gives you, especially if they involve detailed or technical information. Better yet, bring a relative or friend to your appointment to serve as your note taker and support.

5. **Ask about alternative diagnoses.** If the doctor diagnoses a disease or condition, ask if there are alternative diagnoses. Ask how the doctor can rule them out.

6. **Ask what to expect from prescribed tests.** If the doctor suggests additional tests, ask what she expects to learn from them and what you should expect in the way of preparation, costs, and side effects.

7. **Talk about family members recently diagnosed with a disease or condition.** This isn't the time to pump your doctor for information about your uncle's hernia repair, but family history is crucially important. Your doctor needs to know if a blood relative has a relevant health problem. Also, knowing about the health of those close to you can help your doctor better evaluate your own emotional and mental health.

8. **Discuss any travel plans.** Your doctor may suggest immunizations or tell you to bring particular medications. If you take prescription drugs or

wear a medical device, you might need a note from your doctor to get through airport security, here and abroad, expeditiously.

9. **Ask about any new prescriptions.** Make sure you know exactly how to take any new medications you are given, when to take them, how long to take them, any special instructions, and whether the drugs may interact with any of the other medications you're taking or with over-the-counter medications. Are there any side effects? How long might they last? At what point should you become concerned about them and check back with the doctor?

10. **Ask what the numbers mean.** You may get some test results right away. Ask about the significance of these. Make sure you know what your blood pressure is and what it means.

11. **Know what to expect.** If you're ill, ask how long symptoms will last, when you can resume your usual activity, and if there are any dietary restrictions or suggestions.

12. **Ask if there are alternatives.** If your doctor recommends a specific treatment, ask what the alternatives are and the advantages and disadvantages of each. This is especially important if surgery is recommended.

13. **Know what to do next.** Do you need a follow-up exam or test? Should you ask for a second opinion? (Don't be shy about this.) If you need to see a specialist, ask what you should do to prepare for that visit. Should you call for test results, or will the doctor call you? When?

Over-Twenty, Over-Forty Checkups

◆◆◆

The annual physical remains the cornerstone of health care for most of us, despite the fact that the American Medical Association suggests an annual checkup is unnecessary for healthy adults with no symptoms of disease. Still, seeing your primary care physician once a year has a few benefits: It nurtures your relationship with this person whom you must trust to care for you when you *are* sick. It gives you the opportunity to get your annual flu shot. It serves as a time to be reminded to lose a pound or two and to exercise just a little more. A regular visit to your doctor is also the best way to catch early diabetes and other conditions before they become serious problems. When it comes to what is done at an annual checkup, your age plays a role. The older you are, the more checking is needed.

For All Adults Over Twenty

1. **Height and weight.** People in their twenties need to establish baseline values. Weight gain can be caused by everything from overindulgence to heart or kidney problems that cause fluid retention. Weight loss may indicate infection or cancer. Changes in height as you age could be a sign of osteoporosis.

2. **Blood pressure.** This should be checked at every office visit and certainly during annual physicals.

3. **Blood analysis.** The standard tests form a baseline when you're young and can also be an early warning of conditions and diseases that need to be dealt with before they escalate to serious problems. Tests include complete blood counts; thyroid, kidney, and liver function; cholesterol; and markers for inflammatory diseases and processes.

4. **Chest x-ray.** Not strictly a part of annual physicals, a chest x-ray should be performed at least once during young adulthood to rule out undetected chest infections and, again, establish a baseline.

5. **Electrocardiogram.** Once again, this test should be done at least once to establish a baseline and to rule out past, undetected heart damage or abnormalities.

6. **Screen for hernias and (for men) testicular abnormalities.**

7. **Dental exam.** A complete dental exam should be performed yearly. In addition to checking the health of your teeth, the dentist should carefully examine your mouth for any signs of cancer or other abnormalities. Routine cleaning should be performed twice a year, unless your dentist recommends more frequent cleanings.

For Those Over Forty

1. **Height and weight**

2. **Blood pressure**

3. **Yearly blood work.** The standard screens (including fasting blood glucose), plus, for men, a check of the prostate-specific antigen, or PSA, as a screen for prostate cancer.

4. **Mammogram.** Women should have a mammogram every other year between 40 and 50, and every year thereafter. For women with particularly dense or fibrous breasts, many breast specialists recommend digital mammograms. With a digital mammogram, the picture is made and stored electronically which allows it to be read instantly and altered, if needed, to improve clarity and help the radiologist interpret the image. Digital mammograms are recommended for women who are pre or peri-menopausal, under age 50, or who have particularly dense or fibrous breasts. Check with your insurance company to see if it covers digital exams.

5. **Pap smear.** This can be done once every three years, although women with human papillomavirus or a family history of cervical cancer should have this annually.

6. **Digital rectal exam (for men only).** This is a screen for benign prostate enlargement as well as for prostate cancer.

7. **Bone density.** This should be done for all women at onset of menopause. If the results are normal, it needn't be repeated for another four years. If there's evidence of bone loss, it can be repeated more often to see if medicine or dietary changes are working. Men need this test only if there's evidence of bone loss, such as significant loss of height.

8. **Eyes.** Eye exams can reveal more than poor eyesight. A careful eye exam can uncover a great deal about your general health. This is the one place, for instance, where a doctor can actually look at your vasculature without cutting you open. Don't confuse optometrists, who can measure your eyes for glasses, with ophthalmologists, who are physicians. Your primary-care physician should monitor your eyes at every annual visit, but it pays to visit an ophthalmologist at least once every two years as well, and make sure you're tested for glaucoma every two years. If you have a family history of macular degeneration, tell your ophthalmologist so you can also be checked for early indications of that condition.

9. **Colonoscopy.** This should be performed at age 50, and once every six to ten years thereafter. For those at higher risk—people with a family history of colon cancer and those with Crohn's disease, for instance—the first colonoscopy should be at age 40.

10. **Skin exam.** Yearly, to check for skin cancer.

11. **Urinalysis.** This can help assess kidney function and detect infections as well as early bladder cancer, which generally has no symptoms.

Practice Safe Sex

◆◆◆

It may be reassuring to read that 83 percent of heterosexual adults in the United States have never had a sexually transmitted disease (STD). Odds are in your favor, right? But if you examine that number from a slightly different angle, you get this fact: 20 percent—that's one in five—of all adolescents and adults in the United States has some type of STD. And consider this: One of those five has genital herpes, and *90 percent of those with genital herpes don't even know they have it.* So much for relaxing your vigilance because you think you know your partner pretty well. Here are the basics for practicing safe sex.

1. **Act like a professional.** This doesn't have anything to do with standing on street corners. Do as doctors, dentists, nurses, and other professionals do: practice "universal precautions." Taking universal precautions means these people assume that any patient may be infectious for all blood-borne diseases, such as AIDS and hepatitis B, and they take precautions accordingly. Unless you have been in a monogamous relationship for at least 10 years, assume nothing. Use a condom every time you have intercourse.

2. **Talk about it.** If you're embarrassed to bring up the subject of condoms or other protective barriers, maybe you don't know the other person well enough to be swapping bodily fluids. You definitely don't know him well enough to risk your life or health for him.

3. **Don't take "no" for an answer.** It truly is a matter of life or death whether or not you use a condom. If your potential partner isn't interested in taking precautions, put on your shoes and go home.

4. **Make sure it's latex.** Lambskin and polyurethane condoms are not quite as reliable as latex, so stick with that, and make sure it's fresh. Packages of condoms are marked with expiration dates; don't use a condom past its prime. If the condom hasn't expired but it has been in your wallet, back

pocket, or purse for a while, it may be dried out and cracked; don't trust it. Keep a fresh supply of latex condoms handy.

5. **Use only water-based lubricants.** Petroleum-based lubricants, such as Vaseline, baby oil, and most hand lotions, break down the fiber in latex condoms. Fluids pass easily through these tiny rips, making pregnancy and a variety of STDs possible. Use one of the many products created just for the occasion: KY™ jelly, Astroglide™, or any of a wide variety of other brand names. In a pinch, you're safe, and plenty slippery, with vegetable oil.

6. **Don't leave home without one.** If you cherish even the flimsiest of hopes that you'll wind up in bed at some point in the evening, be prepared. This goes for women as well as men. Females who count on the guy to be the condom custodian run the risk of having dangerous sex during a weak moment.

7. **Fall back on Plan B.** If you do find yourself in an amorous situation with nary a condom in sight, there are still plenty of possibilities for intimacy. Those details are best left to your imagination, but the bottom line is that as long as no bodily fluids are swapped you're home free.

Choose a Health Club You'll Use

The country's debt could be retired, perhaps, on the amount of money spent on health club memberships that never get used. If you've been considering joining a club, or if you've been one of those ghost members who've rarely shown up after joining, use the following tips to find a facility that you'll actually use.

1. **Make sure it's convenient to home or work.** Or both. Resist the temptation to join a club that looks like fun but isn't easy to get to. Decide on a workout schedule and select a club location that is convenient, depending on whether you'll be coming from home or from work. Also check out parking: Is there enough of it? And is it close to the club?

2. **Make a list of requirements.** Do you need child care? Do you want aerobics classes in the middle of the day? Are you hoping to practice yoga or kick boxing? Do you want to do lap swimming after work on weeknights? Study the club's schedules, and see whether its schedule fits yours.

3. **Tour the club.** Before signing up at a health club, make an appointment to tour the facilities. Or, better yet, get a visitor or day pass. It's important to visit the club during the hours you plan to use it. Take some time to hang around and decide if you like the feel of the place and if you're comfortable with the staff and members.

4. **Talk to members.** While you're on the tour, don't be shy. Ask your guide to give you some time to talk to members. They're the ones who can tell you how helpful the staff is, whether the equipment is well maintained and the locker rooms are kept clean, and anything else you'd appreciate knowing ahead of time.

5. **Study the contract.** At some point you should read all the fine print, but look especially for the following important items: Are you agreeing to a multiyear membership? A lifetime membership (they are illegal in most states)? What are the cancellation provisions? Are finance charges built into the monthly payments?

6. **Don't be pressured by the sales pitch.** Health clubs often pressure people to sign up immediately to take advantage of "special offers." Don't fall for that. Also know that, after you sign a large contract, there is a standard three-day cooling-off period during which you can cancel.

7. **Ask who will own the contract.** Sometimes health clubs sell contracts to third parties. When this happens, the club you joined may have less incentive to provide good service and keep you motivated to stay with your program.

8. **Ask about reciprocity agreements.** If you travel frequently, can you use the club's facilities in other states? Can you transfer your membership if you move?

Choose a Personal Trainer

◆◆◆

There are many reasons to hire a personal trainer. Getting buff or just getting into your swimsuit are two possibilities. If you are not naturally inclined to working up a good sweat, paying real money to a personal trainer can be just the motivation you need to show up at the gym on a regular basis. No matter why you choose a trainer, consider these tips to help you pick the right one.

1. **Ask about price.** Some gyms allow you one session with a trainer just to get you started and show you the ropes (and pulleys, and rowing machines, and all). This is included in your gym membership. But for ongoing help, you are likely to pay an hourly rate that ranges from $40 to $100, depending on where you live and the popularity of the trainer. Often you can save money by purchasing sessions in bulk. For example, a trainer who charges $50 an hour may shave the cost of one session if you pay for 10 sessions at a time. This has the advantage of keeping you motivated, but can become pricey if you skip sessions.

2. **Know the trainer's training.** Ideally, you want someone who has been certified by the American College of Sports Medicine (ACSM) or the American College of Exercise (ACE). He or she should also be certified in CPR. You should look for someone who has been practicing for at least a year and who is skilled at putting people through their paces. Ask how much training the person has had in diet and nutrition counseling. A trainer can't take the place of a nutritionist, but you'll get a twofer if the trainer can give you tips on an eating routine that will enhance your physical workout. Also ask if the trainer keeps current on research by reading and attending seminars.

3. **Make sure the chemistry is good.** Whether you work with a man or a woman, you should enjoy being with the person and feel confident in following that person's suggestions. To some extent, this is a matter of chemistry. Working out with a trainer can be fun, but in choosing this person you need to balance the fun quotient with a professional manner that inspires you to get through the exercise routine.

4. **Coordinate schedules.** If you do your best when working out first thing in the morning, look for a trainer who has that time available. Same thing if you can only dash in during your lunch hour. Your chances of sticking

with an exercise routine are much better if the schedule fits easily into your daily life.

5. **Check on approach to fitness.** A good fitness program should incorporate five aspects of physical health: strength training, weight management, cardiovascular exercise, nutrition, and flexibility training. Make sure the trainer you choose takes all these into consideration.

6. **Keep business policies in mind.** Find out how far ahead of time you can cancel a session without being penalized. It is usually 24 hours, but don't assume anything. Ask if the trainer carries liability insurance, and only choose one that does.

7. **Check references.** As always, before you shell out real money to hire a professional, ask for and check references. When you talk to the trainer's clients, ask the following:

- How reliable is he at keeping appointments?

- Does she inspire you to push yourself harder?

- Is he good at communicating? Do you easily understand what he's telling you to do?

- What would you say are her strongest and weakest points?

Get Exercise without Really Trying

There are those who like to run, lift weights, do aerobics, and generally work up a good sweat on a regular basis. Then there are the "others"—most folks—for whom the very idea of strenuous activity brings on a strong urge to sink into a soft chair with a good book. This list is for them.

1. **Buy and wear a pedometer.** This nifty little device—the best invention since sliced bread—clips to your belt and keeps track of the number of steps you take in a day. It can also tell you how many calories you've burned. When you can see how much you've accomplished at the end of every day, it's easy and inspiring to do even better the following day.

2. **Take the stairs.** You'll accumulate many more steps on your pedometer by avoiding the elevator, and you'll get your heart rate up at the same time. If you work on the 15th floor of a building, don't attempt the stairs all at once. Ride up to within a couple of flights of your destination and slowly work up to the number of flights you can master.

3. **Park in a faraway spot.** Think of the time and aggravation you can save by not even trying to get the best parking spot at the grocery store, the mall, or at work. All those steps you take count as exercise, and carrying your packages back to the car counts extra!

4. **Get a walking buddy.** This is a good way to spend more time with a friend you enjoy but hardly ever see. Set your alarms for the crack of dawn and meet for a walk before work, or before the kids get up. Alternately, schedule a lunchtime walk with a colleague or an after-dinner stroll with a mate.

5. **Buy a bike.** Think of the joy you got from riding a bike as a kid. It could be yours again—if you have a bike. Most any bike will do, but take the time to at least visit a bike shop. Modern bikes come in many forms: road bike, mountain bike, hybrid, or cruiser. A good salesperson can help you pick the one that best fits your needs. You may or may not want to bike to work, but you can certainly bike for fun on the weekends and after work when the weather's good. You could even turn that early-morning walk into a bike ride.

6. **Sneak in moves here and there.** You can stretch at your desk and do leg or arm lifts while you're on the telephone (unless you work in the middle of a crowded office!). When you're at home, pace while you talk on the phone, do leg and toe lifts while washing the dishes, and remember to pull in your stomach and breathe deeply from the diaphragm.

7. **Rock out while you dust.** Housecleaning can be fun and a decent aerobic workout if you play some rowdy dance music while you vacuum, scrub, and dust.

8. **Take the long way around.** If you work in a large office building, use the restroom on a different floor (taking the stairs, of course). Avoid using the elevator when you run errands or go to meetings. Walk to your usual restaurant for lunch instead of taking the car.

9. **Pick up the pace.** While you're doing that extra walking, swing your arms, walk faster than usual, and breathe!

10. **Try something different.** If you hate the idea of lifting weights, jumping around, or running, try Pilates, which emphasizes flexibility, core strength, and breathing; it may be just the thing for you. You could also try yoga, tai chi, or other eastern practices, which have converted many a couch potato into a regular exerciser.

Diet Successfully

Food for thought: *The average American woman is 5'4" tall and weighs 140 pounds. The average American model is 5'11" and weighs 117 pounds.*

If traditional dieting were an effective weight-loss method, this wouldn't be such a chubby nation. Americans spend more than $40 billion a year—roughly the equivalent of the federal budget for education—on their dieting obsession. The real secret to weight loss is to change your eating and exercise habits permanently. That's not as grim as it sounds. The Washington, D.C. area nutritionist and food writer Katherine Tallmadge suggests the following tips:

1. **Eat breakfast.** When you skip or skimp on breakfast, you increase the chance that you'll overeat later in the day. If you're not hungry for breakfast, eat something small, like a piece of fruit, and have a mid-morning snack.

2. **Eat a big breakfast, small dinner.** Try to eat a third of your total calories at breakfast. People who eat proportionately more in the morning eat fewer overall calories, an average of 300 fewer calories a day!

3. **Eat more whole grains.** People who substitute whole grains for refined flour products have lower overall body weight and a lower incidence of diabetes. Try to eat one serving of whole grains at every meal.

4. **Weigh yourself daily.** New studies show that people who weigh themselves daily learn more about what works for them and what doesn't. As long as you don't overreact if the scale shows a slight gain, you can profit from watching the weight fluctuations your body goes through. This is

not recommended, though, for people with eating disorders or who tend to obsess about their weight.

5. **Irritate the waiter.** First order salad, soup, or appetizer, *then* decide if you still want to order a main course.

6. **Eat more vegetables.** No surprise here. Research has shown that when you add veggies to a meal, either as salad, vegetable soup, or part of the entrée, you will naturally eat about one-fourth fewer calories.

7. **Do the numbers.** For every 3,500 calories you cut from your regular diet, you will lose one pound. If you eat 500 fewer calories each day you will lose one pound per week.

8. **Don't be a vending machine victim.** Bring fruit to work or school so you won't be tempted to eat a candy bar when you need a snack. Cutting out vending machine snacks can save 200 calories a day, a sizable chunk of that 500–calorie-a-day deficit you're aiming for.

9. **Use the 25-percent solution.** If you are planning to eat at a restaurant four times in the coming week, choose one occasion to splurge and eat light at the others. This way you can enjoy your favorite restaurant dessert, but you won't pay for it in weight gain. This technique works for parties during the holidays, too.

10. **Forgive yourself.** Everybody slips. In fact, the people who enjoy long-term successful weight loss have just as many incidents of overindulgence as those who ultimately fail. The difference is the fact that the people who succeed forgive themselves and move on rather than despairing and continuing to overeat.

Choose a Cosmetic Surgeon

There was a time when changing your appearance through surgery was considered to be the height of vanity and extravagance. No more. Now certain kinds of cosmetic treatments are so common they're considered fairly routine. In 2003 the number of cosmetic surgical treatments jumped 20 percent to a total of nearly 8.3 million procedures, according to the American Society for Aesthetic Plastic Surgeons. If you're thinking of joining the cosmetic cutting edge, here are some things to consider and questions to ask when choosing a cosmetic surgeon.

1. **Start with word of mouth.** But definitely don't stop there. If a friend has had a positive experience with a doctor, you should consider him, but don't assume he's the doctor you should select.

2. **Look closely at specific credentials.** In many states a variety of doctors, from dentists to gynecologists, can legally do cosmetic surgery, but they don't necessarily have the experience or qualifications you want. Make sure the doctor you choose specializes in the field of plastic surgery and is a member of the American Board of Plastic Surgery (ABPS).

3. **Study the boards.** Don't take the phrase "board-certified surgeon" at face value. There are many boards, some of them with impressive but essentially made-up names. The American Board of Plastic Surgery is the only board recognized by the medical community for plastic surgery. To find out if an M.D. you're considering is board certified, call the American Board of Medical Specialties (ABMS) at 866–275–2267 (866-ASK ABMS) or the American Society of Plastic Surgeons (ASPS) at 888–475–2784 (888–4-PLASTIC).

4. **Definitely shop around.** Many cosmetic surgeons charge for a consultation, but that fee is often folded into the cost of the procedure if you go with that doctor. If you decide against a particular doctor and don't recoup your consultation fee, consider it money well spent. You can save yourself time as well as money by calling the ABMS to check on a doctor before scheduling a consultation.

5. **Get the numbers.** Ask how many times the doctor has done this procedure. There's no precise number that qualifies a doctor as an expert, but you don't want to be among the first handful of people she's done this procedure on.

6. **Ask about limitations.** What is the best outcome you can expect? What is the least benefit you might wind up with? This is also the time to ask about possible failure rates or undesirable outcomes. No procedure is without its risks. Make sure you are aware of and comfortable with the potential downside to the procedure you're choosing.

7. **Examine before and after photographs.** Look at photographs of pa-

tients of each doctor you are considering. Make sure the photos have not been retouched, and find out how long after the surgery they were taken.

8. **Get names and numbers of patients.** Many doctors have a roster of patients willing to share their experiences. You can learn a lot from talking to a few former patients who have had the procedure you are contemplating.

9. **Find out about recovery time.** Some doctors downplay the aftereffects of a procedure, quoting optimistic statistics about the number of patients who have gone back to work the following Monday. Ask about a realistic recovery period, and ask how much help you may need immediately following the procedure. Talking to a former patient, as suggested above, can be very helpful.

10. **Ask about general anesthesia.** For certain procedures, doctors use general anesthesia, rather than light sedation (or "twilight sleep"). General anesthesia requires careful oversight and constant monitoring. Make sure a certified registered nurse anesthetist (CRNA) or board-certified anesthesiologist is present at all times, monitoring your heart rate, blood pressure, and oxygen saturation.

11. **Check up on location.** If the procedure will be done in an outpatient facility or in the doctor's office, is the facility Medicare certified and state licensed? You may feel foolish asking if the doctor's staff is ready with a crash cart when you're "only" having liposuction, but complications can and do occur.

12. **Go with your gut.** Once you've asked all the questions above and are satisfied with the answers, you should base your final choice on your instincts. If you're comfortable with the doctor and feel that the office runs in a smooth, friendly, and caring manner, go for it.

Stock a Medicine Cabinet

You undoubtedly know where your medicine cabinet is—probably in the bathroom—but do you have any idea what's in it? And why is this stuff there? Who brought it in, and when? If there's more than one person in your house, those questions become even more difficult to answer. Here's a rational plan for stocking a medicine cabinet and keeping it safe.

1. **Pain and fever remedies.** Acetaminophen (either Tylenol™ or a generic brand) is a good pain reliever that also reduces fever. (Never exceed the recommended dose, because an overdose can cause serious, life-threatening liver failure.) Ibuprofen (in the form of Motrin™ or a generic) is an alternative pain and fever reducer. Naproxen (Aleve™ or a generic) alleviates pain but doesn't reduce fever.

2. **Aspirin.** Adult-strength aspirin should be on hand in case someone in the house suffers a heart attack. Chewing one or two tablets while waiting for an ambulance can be a lifesaver (chewing reduces absorption time by half when compared with swallowing them whole). Don't, however, give aspirin to children or teenagers; it is associated with Reye's syndrome, which can be fatal.

3. **First-aid supplies.** These belong in your first-aid kit (see "Stock a First-Aid Kit," page 168).

4. **Hydrocortisone cream.** For minor skin irritations, such as insect bites and rashes, it's handy to keep this cream in both the medicine cabinet and your first-aid kit.

5. **Medication for diarrhea and stomach upsets.** Over-the-counter medicines, such as Imodium™ and Pepto-Bismol™, are handy for occasional use, but they should not be used for more than a day or so without consulting a doctor. Antacids, such as Tums™, are good for stomach upsets, but again, if the upset continues, you should check with your physician.

6. **Decongestant and cough medicine.** It's a good idea to check the label of your cold medicines. Many contain acetaminophen, and if you take one of these along with Tylenol™, you could unwittingly exceed the maximum recommended dose.

7. **Antihistamine.** Antihistamines, such as Benadryl™, are helpful with allergic reactions, but be aware that they may cause drowsiness.

8. **Thermometer.** Invest in a digital thermometer rather than an old-fashioned glass one.

9. **Cotton balls and cotton swabs**

10. **Important phone numbers.** Keep a list of key phone numbers on the inside door of your medicine cabinet. Include your family physician, pediatrician, and any specialist involved in your family's ongoing care, such as a cardiologist or even a dentist. Also, post the Poison Control Center (usually 800–222–1222) and the emergency services phone numbers, especially if they aren't 911.

WHERE SHOULD IT BE?

As with real estate, location is critical when it comes to medicine. The bathroom is the perfect place for toiletries, but it may be the worst place for pharmaceuticals. Most medicine—prescription and over-the-counter—should be stored in a cool, dry place. If that describes your bathroom, fine. If not, think of another room. A kitchen cabinet away from the stove might do, so long as the kitchen itself doesn't get overly hot.

If possible, keep drugs and supplements in a handy location. Vitamins and other supplements, as well as medicines that need to be taken with meals, should be in or near the room where you eat. Barrier contraceptives should be near the bed. There are exceptions, of course. If a medication needs to be kept refrigerated, keep it in the refrigerator. And don't keep sleeping pills or other sedatives next to the bed. It's too easy to roll over and take one or more when you're in no condition to make a rational decision.

WHAT'S SPECIAL ABOUT CHILDREN?

Households with children need special supplies. These include acetaminophen, decongestants, antihistamines, and cough medicine formulated for children. Note that the "children's" medication is a different concentration from the "infants'" medication; do not use them interchangeably. You also should have a medicine dropper or oral syringe, child-safe suntan lotion and insect repellent, a digital ear thermometer, and a rehydration fluid, such as Pedialyte™. In case of accidental poisoning, keep a bottle of syrup of ipecac on hand to induce vomiting, but use it only if your doctor or the poison control center instructs you to do so.

TIP: Check expiration dates regularly. That antinausea prescription you got when you were pregnant with your teenager is of no use to you now, and it could even be dangerous. Even common remedies, such as aspirin, have expiration dates, which are not money-making schemes on the part of manufacturers. Medicines can deteriorate, lose their efficacy, or even transform into other substances over time. Make a habit of going through your medicine cabinet at least once a year to clear out items that have expired.

Master the Art of Sleep

◆◆◆

"Sleep," wrote Nietzsche in *Thus Spoke Zarathustra,* "is no mean art: for its sake one must stay awake all day." While great artists may be born, not made, and there's good evidence that some people are naturally talented when it comes to sleeping, it's entirely possible for the rest of us to master at least the rudiments of the art of sleep.

1. **Get up the same time each day.** Sleep is to a large extent a function of our body's internal clock, specifically its circadian, or 24-hour rhythm. The best way to keep this rhythm in sync with the daily cycle is to get up at the same time each day, whether it's a workday or a weekend day, whether you're tired or not.

2. **Go to bed at the same time each night.** This is actually less important than getting up at the same time each morning, but keeping to a regular schedule on both ends is a good idea.

3. **Reserve your bed for sleep and sex.** You don't want to do anything in bed but sleep and have sex. The bed is not the place to lie awake and think about today's problems or tomorrow's challenges. If you watch TV, chat on the phone, or do paperwork, you create cues for wakefulness, not sleep. If you're not sleepy, sit in a chair and read something light and unimportant, and don't watch the clock. Watching the clock can make you more anxious that you're not asleep and keep you awake longer. Just read until you're sleepy, and get into bed. If it's 2 A.M. and you usually get up at 7 A.M., you should still get up at that time.

4. **Limit naps to 20 minutes.** If you have only five hours of sleep, you are tired the next day. Naps are fine, as long as they don't involve deep sleep. Naps should last only from 10 to 20 minutes.

5. **Establish a before-bed ritual.** Make a conscious effort to wind down before going to bed by doing something relaxing. Walk the dog, read something light, listen to music (no Wagner or anything too strenuous), or watch some mindless TV. The point is to make it a ritual that signals bedtime. There's something comforting about these rituals, as parents know. The bath, the story, the tucking in, and the good-night kiss are simply rituals that ease the transition from the happenings of the day to the peace of night.

6. **Take a bath.** A warm bath relaxes the muscles and also raises the body temperature slightly. When you leave the bath, your body temperature falls, which mimics the natural cooling that occurs during sleep. Showers, however, can be too stimulating, and insomniacs, especially, should avoid them at night.

7. **Eat a snack.** It's true: Warm milk, which contains tryptophan, an amino acid that stimulates serotonin production, has a calming effect, and a little carbohydrate at the same time can enhance the effect. Also, eating a light snack—the key word here is *light*—will silence the growling stomach that can waken you and your partner in the middle of the night.

8. **Avoid caffeine.** Coffee and other foods containing caffeine will interfere with sleep, and it's not enough to limit caffeine intake in the hours right before bedtime. Caffeine can stay active in the body for six hours, so most people should avoid it after mid-afternoon.

9. **Avoid alcohol and tobacco.** Although alcohol is a depressant and can help you fall asleep, it has a rebound effect that can interfere with normal sleep patterns. Nicotine is a stimulant and can interfere with sleep for hours after the last puff.

10. **Avoid over-the-counter sleep aids.** These often contain an antihistamine, which can actually interfere with normal sleep patterns and affect alertness the next day. Melatonin can be helpful, but using it properly requires advice from your doctor; tryptophan supplements are controversial, and should be used only under a doctor's supervision.

11. **Exercise regularly, but not before bed.** Regular exercise is essential for proper sleep. Vigorous exercise late in the afternoon is particularly effective, but don't exercise strenuously within two hours of bedtime.

12. **Create a good sleep environment.** Obviously, your bedroom should be quiet and it should be dark, because darkness helps trigger the part of the circadian rhythm that induces sleep. The room should be cool—although not to the point of discomfort—because the body naturally cools during sleep and a cool room helps signal the body that sleep is imminent. Cold feet can turn up your internal thermostat, so if your feet are cold, wear socks to bed or use an old-fashioned hot water bottle to make those toes warm and cozy.

13. **Forget the sheep.** Studies have shown that counting sheep just isn't all that fascinating and leaves plenty of mental room for worry. It's better to get out of bed, write down your concerns, and try to remember that most problems seem less daunting in the morning. Or do what Napoleon is said to have done: Imagine a chest with lots of drawers, and stuff each problem into one of those drawers until they're all safely tucked away and there's nothing left but to go to sleep.

14. **Fantasize.** Nothing too stimulating, unless your partner is willing. Do for yourself what your parents did when you were little. Tell yourself a pleasant story; if you're lucky, you'll fall asleep *in medias res.*

15. **If all else fails, seek medical help.** Sometimes, insomnia requires professional intervention. If you try all these suggestions but still can't sleep, know that help is available. Check with your physician first; she may recommend short-term sleeping pills, melatonin supplementation, or tests at a hospital-based sleep center.

Pack for the Hospital

Think of a hospital visit as a minivacation, a time away from home. It's a casual vacation that won't require formal dress—or your scuba outfit. OK, that's stretching it a little. A hospital stay may pale in comparison to a few weeks on Martha's Vineyard or a stay with friends in the south of France, but you still need to think of what to bring to make your stay as comfortable as possible. A little forethought can help make your visit far less stressful. Here's a list of what to bring:

1. **Noise-canceling device.** This could be as simple as earplugs or as elaborate as special earphones that block ambient noise. If you don't want to hear your roommate's television or inane conversation, bring something to screen it out.

2. **Noise-making devices.** No, this doesn't mean party favors, firecrackers, or accordions. Think MP3 player, personal CD player, or portable radio with headphones.

3. **Insurance card and photo ID.** You might not get past the front door without these.

4. **Copies of advanced medical directives and medical power of attorney.** Make sure you go over these with your doctors beforehand, but also give copies to the hospital administration.

5. **A list of your medications.** Don't forget to include the dosage and time of day you usually take each medicine.

6. **Clothing.** You might as well be naked in those hospital gowns. Bring something for day and something for night. Don't assume the temperature inside will even remotely resemble the temperature outdoors. In winter, you might need a light short-sleeved T-shirt or pajama to sleep in, since hospitals tend to be warmer than ideal for sleeping. Bring a robe and nonslip slippers to ensure you don't break anything that wasn't broken when you came in.

7. **Don't bring valuables.** Remember that you can't take jewelry into surgery or radiology, so leave it at home. Also leave behind your credit cards and your money, except for some change for vending machines.

WHEN IT'S A BABY

Definitely the most pleasant reason to be in a hospital is the birth of a child. You should pack items for both the time when you are in labor and the time after the baby has arrived. During labor, you will need to relax, so bring music. An MP3 player or personal CD may work for the early part of labor, but later you may not want to be wearing headphones. Also, your partner or birthing coach might want to hear the music, too, so a portable CD player or radio may be a better choice. Soothing, perfumed lotions or massage oils are a good idea, and you might want a tennis ball or rolling pin for back massages (also useful for striking annoying doctors and nurses when they tell you one too many times to relax). Bring a still or video camera, a list of phone numbers to announce the news, and, if you're considerate, a snack for your coach, especially if you don't want him or her in the cafeteria at the crucial moment. Many hospitals permit a bottle of champagne for celebratory purposes after the birth (not before!), or you might prefer nonalcoholic sparkling cider.

After the baby has arrived, you will want a favorite nightgown (two if you need to stay in the hospital longer than a day). If you plan to nurse, these should open in the front. You should also have a pretty robe to wear when greeting guests. You might want some high-waist underwear, especially if you have a cesarean. Some new mothers stay in the hospital just one night; others need to hang around a bit longer. Bring things to pass the time just in case you end up in the latter group: Books and magazines are always good, but also consider bringing a stack of birth announcements to fill out and send, or a baby-name book if you've left that particular task for the last minute. Don't forget your going-home outfit (remember, the baby may be out, but you still won't fit into those designer jeans) and the car seat you now can't drive anywhere without.

[Mind and Spirit]

Choose a Psychotherapist

Put simply, psychotherapy is the process of gaining insight into your unique way of responding to the world and discovering the ways in which those patterns may work against you or make you unhappy. The goal of psychotherapy is to relieve symptoms, whether mild, moderate, or severe, and to improve the way you function by modifying thoughts, emotions, and behaviors. According to the National Institute of Mental Health, the single most important factor in successful psychotherapy is the relationship between the therapist and the patient. Finding the right "fit" between you and a potential therapist is even more important than the type of degree or professional training the person has. Mental health practitioners vary in skillfulness and style; finding the right one for you is a fairly subjective process. Here are some guidelines:

1. **Rely on word of mouth.** The best way to start a search for any professional, from a roofer to a psychotherapist, is to talk with friends who have had a good experience with someone. Your family doctor may also be able to provide some referrals.

2. **Request local referrals from organizations.** Contact the American Psychological Association (800–374–2721); American Counseling Association (703–823–9800); American Association for Marriage and Family Therapy (202–4520109); or the American Psychiatric Association (888–357–7924).

3. **Check the phone book.** Look in the Yellow Pages under psychologists, psychiatrists, social workers, marriage and family counselors, and licensed professional counselors.

4. **Check with your health-insurance provider.** Your insurance company may cover some counseling services, although sometimes you must choose from one of the providers with whom it has a contract. In any case, the company may supply a list of licensed providers in your area. Be aware that there is usually a limit on the number of visits an insurance company will cover. Also, keep in mind that the term *preferred* refers only to the contractual arrangement between the therapist and the insurance company; it is not necessarily an indication of quality or competence. That is a judgment only you can make.

5. **Give some thought to your reason for seeking psychotherapy.** If you can articulate this briefly, it will help you and the potential therapist recognize whether you two would be a good match.

6. **Contact the therapist before your first visit.** When you've identified at least three potential therapists, call each and ask a few questions.

   - *What is your education and training?* Psychiatrists have medical degrees and can prescribe medication but are not necessarily skilled in the psychotherapeutic process. Psychiatric social workers and counselors have master's degrees, and psychologists have doctoral degrees in psychology or psychotherapy. If a psychotherapist claims to be an "analyst," he or she should have certification from a psychoanalytic institute or school.

   - *Are you licensed?* Licensing doesn't guarantee skill or effectiveness, but it does mean the person has a certain level of training and has passed written and oral exams required by the state in which he or she practices. Many state governments offer free Internet licensee searches.

   - *Do you carry malpractice insurance?* Are there any outstanding charges against you?

   - *How much experience do you have?* This is important. Experience is one of the best indicators of effectiveness. Be specific. If you're looking for help with a particular problem such as addiction, obsessive-compulsive disorder, depression, or mood disorders, ask about the therapist's experience in that area.

   - *What types of cases do you work with most often?*

   - *What is your therapeutic approach or philosophy?* You don't need to hear an extensive treatise on this over the telephone, but you should get some idea of how this person works with clients. There are three major branches of psychotherapy: behavioral, cognitive, and psychodynamic. Behavioral, as the name suggests, focuses on changing unwanted behaviors through rewards, reinforcements, and desensitization. The goal of cognitive therapy is to replace negative or destructive thinking patterns with more balanced views that lead to more satisfying and productive behavior. Psychodynamic therapy may be longer-term than cognitive or behavioral, which tend to be more sharply goal oriented. Psychodynamic therapists work from the premise that personal history, genetic factors, and current situations determine behavior. Sessions will deal with the emotions and unconscious motivations that influence your actions.

- *How will I know when I'm finished with therapy?* What is the average length of time to reduce or eliminate the kind of symptoms I have?

- *What are your fees and what kind of contractual arrangement do you make with your clients?* Do you require that I pay up-front or will you accept assignment, that is, wait for reimbursement from the insurance company? Sometimes therapists require a commitment from you as to the frequency of visits, and they usually charge for missed appointments.

7. **Schedule appointments.** After talking with potential therapists on the phone, set up appointments with those you would like to meet. Be sure to ask about the charge for a first-time consultation. Most therapists do charge for this visit whether or not you decide to pursue therapy with them.

8. **Assess each initial meeting.** During and after your meetings with therapists think about your comfort level with each person. How was the chemistry? Did you feel you could talk candidly about yourself? You aren't looking for a new best friend, but you are looking for someone to collaborate with over a period of weeks, months, or even years. Your intuitive response to his or her personality is an important indication of how well you will work together. You will most likely do better with someone you consider warm and empathic. Ideally, you should come away with an idea of how the therapist views your issues and how this person will approach your work together. If you don't feel good about the first meeting, don't agree to more sessions.

TIP: Almost all HMOs and many other health plans require that you be preapproved for therapy sessions. You must call the insurance company *before* making an appointment with the therapist. Many plans will not pay for you to shop around. Nevertheless, these "shopping" visits are deducted from the annual maximum number of visits, which is usually from 12 to 25.

Recognize Depression, Addiction, and Eating Disorders

Depression

Nearly 10 percent of adults will experience serious depression at some point in their lives, according to the National Institute for Mental Health (NIMH). Depression is not the same as feeling a little blue, or down, for a few days. It is a potentially serious and debilitating condition that all too often goes untreated. In fact, the NIMH estimates that only about 20 percent of adults with depression get adequate treatment. The other 80 percent either don't realize they are depressed or believe they should be able to snap out of it on their own. Such suffering is unnecessary because most depressed people respond well to treatment: talk therapy, medication, or both. Below are the classic signs of depression as outlined by the NIMH. If you or someone close to you has experienced five or more of these symptoms for more than two weeks, see a doctor as soon as possible.

1. Sad, anxious, or empty mood
2. Feelings of hopelessness, pessimism
3. Feelings of guilt, worthlessness, helplessness
4. Loss of pleasure or interest in activities you once enjoyed, including sex
5. Decreased energy, fatigue, being "slowed down"
6. Difficulty concentrating, remembering, making decisions
7. Insomnia, early-morning awakening, or oversleeping
8. Appetite and/or weight loss or overeating and weight gain
9. Thoughts of death or suicide; suicide attempts
10. Restlessness, irritability
11. Physical symptoms that do not respond to treatment, such as headaches, digestive disorders, and chronic pain

Addiction

The word *addiction* is sometimes tossed around casually as in, "I'm addicted to chocolate chip cookies" or "My friend Sue is addicted to her wireless

Blackberry." It certainly is possible to become addicted to activities and substances as varied as sex, gambling, tobacco, and food, but the following two lists deal only with addiction to alcohol and drugs. It's not easy to know when someone's use of alcohol has crossed the line into the disease of alcoholism, or, for that matter, when recreational, if illegal, use of drugs turns into drug addiction. Only an expert—and the person in question—can truly make that diagnosis.

Alcohol

Many experts in the field of alcoholism rely on Alcoholics Anonymous (AA) as the best treatment for this disease. Here are the classic 20 questions printed in AA literature* for determining whether or not a person is an alcoholic.

1. Do you lose time from work due to your drinking?
2. Is drinking making your home life unhappy?
3. Do you drink because you are shy with other people?
4. Is drinking affecting your reputation?
5. Have you ever felt remorse after drinking?
6. Have you gotten into financial difficulties as a result of your drinking?
7. Do you turn to lower companions and an inferior environment when drinking?
8. Does your drinking make you careless of your family's welfare?
9. Has your ambition decreased since drinking?
10. Do you crave a drink at a definite time daily?
11. Do you want a drink the next morning?
12. Does drinking cause you to have difficulty in sleeping?
13. Has your efficiency decreased since drinking?
14. Is drinking jeopardizing your job or business?
15. Do you drink to escape from worries or troubles?
16. Do you drink alone?
17. Have you ever had a complete loss of memory as a result of your drinking?

*Excerpted from material appearing in the pamphlet, "Memo to an Inmate Who May Be an Alcoholic," and reprinted with the permission of Alcoholics Anonymous World Services, Inc. (AAWS). Permission to reprint this material does not mean that AAWS has reviewed and/or endorses this publication. AA is a program of recovery from alcoholism *only*; use of AA material in any non-AA context does not imply otherwise.

18. Has your physician ever treated you for drinking?
19. Do you drink to build up your self-confidence?
20. Have you ever been in a hospital or institution on account of drinking?

Drugs

Drug use can be more insidious than alcoholism simply because it's pretty obvious when someone has been drinking, but not so easy to spot when someone is under the influence of drugs. Here are some indications, but the list is, by no means, comprehensive:

1. **Change in mood or personality.** Drug users have unusual personality changes, including mood swings or inexplicable irritability, as well as sudden outbursts of laughter and giddiness. It's common to lose interest in or motivation for school, work, sports, or other activities that used to be important.

2. **Physical changes.** Opiates, and this includes most prescription painkillers, often cause pinpoint pupils. Those who inhale cocaine or other drugs may develop nosebleeds or itchy, runny, irritated noses that make them sniff frequently. Weight loss is common with cocaine and amphetamine abuse.

3. **Paranoia.** Some drugs, particularly cocaine, can induce paranoia. This may take the form of fear of police, but the user may become distrustful of family and friends, too. Paranoia can also be part of an overall personality shift, causing the user to avoid people and sometimes resort to extreme measures to remain isolated.

4. **Violent outbursts.** Amphetamine users are particularly prone to flashes of rage, but any regular drug user may have such outbursts, especially as the effects of the drug are wearing off. Nervousness and a tendency toward argumentativeness are also common.

5. **Lethargy.** In general, most drug addicts exhibit signs of sedation, confusion, impaired decision making, clouded judgment, and memory lapses.

Eating Disorders

In our society, which often equates thinness with glamour and in which dieting is a major preoccupation, the struggle to achieve a perceived ideal body can turn into a life-threatening illness. Although teenage girls and young women make up 90 percent of those with eating disorders, older women, men, and boys can also develop one of the three major types: anorexia nervosa (starving syndrome), bulimia nervosa (binging and purging), and binge eating. Recognizing eating disorders isn't easy, partly because it's hard to tell when weight loss crosses a line and becomes pathological, and also because shame and secretiveness are part of the diseases. Here are the major symptoms to watch for according to the National Eating Disorders Association (no one is likely to manifest all of them):

1. Skipping meals, taking tiny portions, or refusing to eat in front of other people
2. Mixing strange food combinations
3. Spitting out food before swallowing or rushing from the table to vomit when normal portions are eaten
4. Shopping and cooking for the household but refusing to eat the carefully cooked meal
5. Regularly giving reasons for not eating: not hungry, just ate with a friend, feeling ill, upset, and so forth
6. Becoming repelled by former favorite foods such as red meat and desserts
7. Eating a narrow range of "safe" foods
8. Reading food labels religiously and boasting about the healthful quality of what is eaten

Bulimia and Binge Eating

1. Gorging in secret, sometimes with specially purchased high-calorie binge food
2. Purging with laxatives or vomiting to get rid of the calories
3. Leaving clues that invite discovery: empty boxes, cans, and food packages; foul-smelling bathrooms; excessive use of mouthwash and breath mints; and, in some cases, containers of vomit poorly hidden.
4. Abusing alcohol or street drugs, sometimes to kill appetite, sometimes to deaden emotional pain.
5. Exercising compulsively

Heal a Rift, Apologize with Grace

Nothing can be more antithetical to the dominant culture of winning, success, and perfection than an apology, an admission that you've done wrong. But a sincere apology can also be one of the most powerful tools for strengthening a bond and bringing people closer together. Here are the basics of a graceful apology.

1. **Be specific.** Generalities, like "I'm sorry I hurt your feelings," won't do and actually give the impression that you don't understand what you've done wrong. If you're apologizing for something you've just said or done, articulate exactly what it was.

2. **Take responsibility.** One of the worst ways to apologize is to imply that the injury is the other person's problem, as in, "I'm sorry if that's such a sore subject with you." If your intention is to apologize, say you're sorry without making editorial comments about your friend's hypersensitivity.

3. **Don't try to justify what you've done.** Sure there may be a good reason why you did what you did. That's not the point. If you've decided to apologize, apologize. If you've done something hurtful that was completely inadvertent, try to make that clear. Attempts to justify contribute very little to the substance of an apology, and they make it appear that you're less sorry for the hurt and more interested in your own reputation.

4. **Give it time.** Don't rush through an apology and quickly move on to something more pleasant. The person you've offended may feel an immediate hurt, but how that injury resonates, what else it connotes, and what other issues it raises may take some time to become apparent to either of you. An apology is an opportunity to make a relationship stronger than it was before the offense. By being willing to endure your own pain for as long as it takes to soothe the other person, you're demonstrating the seriousness of your own commitment to the relationship.

5. **Don't expect absolution.** Just because you have unburdened yourself, that doesn't mean your injured friend must forgive you. Of course, that would be nice, but it shouldn't be your only goal in apologizing. If you aren't showered with expressions like "Oh, please, forget about it," you're not entitled to sulk.

6. **Do better next time.** If you injure someone's feelings or diminish his sense of self, or humiliate him, resolve not to make the same blunder again. That means paying careful attention to the way your words or action affected the other person. If you made the person feel stupid, find a way to make him feel smart; if you made her feel insensitive, you help her know you think she's particularly sensitive.

7. **Go one step further.** An apology is itself an act of generosity, because it's made at a real emotional cost to oneself. If you've just expressed your deep regret for knocking over a lamp, offer to pay for it. If that offer is refused, give your friend a gift commensurate with the broken lamp's value. If the mistake you're apologizing for was of a less concrete nature, you might want to surprise your friend with some flowers or another spontaneous act of generosity.

Choose a Feng Shui Practitioner

Feng shui (pronounced *fung shway*) isn't magic, despite the impression you might get from looking at various feng shui books (there are more than 300 currently in print), articles, and Websites. The Chinese words *feng shui* mean "wind and water," and the practice of feng shui is based on the perfectly reasonable belief that environment affects a person's well-being. In its classical form, feng shui analyzes a building and its physical setting to determine whether they support the people who live or work there.

As feng shui has become popular in the United States over the past decade, nearly as many variations have evolved as there are people practicing it, but there are still two major schools: Black Hat and Classical Compass. The Black Hat method was developed in this country about 60 years ago and considers the entryway of a room or building to be the starting place for feng shui analysis. The Classical Compass school is based on the original Chinese practice, which is nearly 6,000 years old. To put it very simply, the Classical Compass school, as its name suggests, uses the cardinal directions (east, west, north, south) to determine auspicious arrangements. If you're interested in hiring a feng shui practitioner to guide you in making your home or office a more pleasant environment, heed these tips lest you spend time and money in an unlucky way.

1. **Browse the array of feng shui books.** Begin your quest at your local bookstore or library, where you can become familiar with all things feng shui. This way you will be ready to talk to the various experts you encounter.

2. **Decide which school appeals to you.** Having studied the literature, you should have a sense of whether you are interested in Black Hat or Classical Compass feng shui. Since feng shui is an art, not a science, your own intuition about following one versus the other is as good a way as any to make your choice.

3. **Take care of first things first.** Living in an orderly, aesthetically pleasing environment can, indeed, make a difference in your daily existence, and you don't need to pay anyone to tell you that a dilapidated house is depressing. A home that's dirty, messy, or in need of repair generally creates problems for the people who live there. Don't spend money on a feng shui expert until you've fixed broken items, cleaned up clutter, repainted dingy walls, and so forth. If you feel overwhelmed by the mess and clutter around you, it's conceivable that you'd be better off spending money on a personal organizer than a feng shui consultant (see "Hire a Pro: Choose a Professional Organizer," page 22).

4. **Ask yourself if your goals are reasonable.** If you want to create a feeling of harmony, that's one thing. If you're hoping to solve serious financial or relationship problems, you may need to talk to experts in those areas first. Feng shui isn't magic, and it won't change your life in a dramatic way all by itself.

5. **Check for healers and designers in the Yellow Pages.** Despite the wide popularity of feng shui, you're not likely to find a listing for it in the Yellow Pages. Try looking under holistic healers or interior designers to see if there is a mention of feng shui. You can also try calling a few interior designers to see if any of them are trained in feng shui.

6. **Do a Web search.** A search on the Internet will yield many feng shui Websites, perhaps one for a practitioner in your area.

7. **Find a teacher.** Many local adult education centers offer classes in feng shui. Get a catalog and talk with the person who teaches the class. Don't be shy about asking the instructor for other practitioners you could interview.

WHAT TO ASK A POTENTIAL FENG SHUI PRACTITIONER

Some people refer to feng shui as psychology for the home. It's important to choose a home psychologist, or feng shui expert, whose personality and approach you relate well to. Ask each person you interview how long he has been practicing, what kind of training he has had, and how long he studied. Various certification programs exist, but their value to you is impossible to determine. Some feng shui experts also have a background in interior design, which is useful since this person will be asking you to spend time and money on rearranging furniture and accessories in your home. After the interviews, you should be certain the practitioner you choose is not making it up as she goes along.

Also be sure to ask about fees. Many feng shui practitioners charge by the hour, and this rate can vary from $40 to more than $100. Others charge a flat fee based on the square footage of your home or office. Insist that the person give you an upper limit for the total cost.

Practice Lifelong Learning

Research shows that besides adding enjoyment and enrichment to your life, continuing to learn as you age helps your mind stay nimble and sharp. Now it is easier than ever to find opportunities for learning outside of formal education, and the selection of these offerings is large and diverse. Try one of these routes.

1. **Extension and adult-education courses.** Almost every college and university offers courses for adults that don't require matriculation, courses you can take without enrolling in a degree program and worrying about your grade. Usually cheaper than for-credit courses, these range from in-

troductory to advanced courses in virtually every discipline. Similarly, high schools in many communities host adult-education courses in which you can learn to do anything from speaking a new language to refinishing your own furniture. These adult-ed courses can also provide a terrific opportunity to get your feet wet in teaching. All you need is the time, expertise in something others might be interested in, and the desire to share what you know.

2. **Elderhostel.** Adults 55 and over can take advantage of the literally thousands of programs offered by Elderhostel (*www.elderhostel.org*). This organization offers a no-hassle way to combine travel and education. Its trips include travel, food, and lodging, as well as lectures or workshops. The variety of trips is extensive, everything from a tour of the Louvre accompanied by an art-history professor to a five-day exploration of Yiddish songs and Jewish humor in the Borscht Belt.

3. **Internships.** Not just for second-year law students, internships, paid or unpaid, can be a perfect introduction to a second career or a chance to explore a lifelong interest. One way to find an internship is to take a course at a local college. Community colleges, in particular, which are often more geared toward adults, usually have an office that specializes in placing interns. At some community colleges you don't even need to take a class; you can pay a fee and gain access to internship programs. You can also take advantage of your own professional contacts. If you've been working in finance but want to try your hand at public relations (PR), talk to all the PR people you've met. Remember, you're not competing with them for a job; you're simply trying to see what the field is like by getting some hands-on experience. Peterson, the college-guide publisher, puts out *Internships*, an annual listing of opportunities. You can also log on to *www.careerbuilder.com* and *www.monster.com*, both of which have extensive listings.

4. **Adult camps.** Similar to Elderhostel, adult camps are minivacations focused on various subjects, from astronomy lessons, with the use of sophisticated telescopes and expert guidance from senior astronomers (*www.astronomycamp.org*), to guitar-making (*www.furpeaceranch.com*). A comprehensive source for information about adult camps is *www.grownupcamps.com*, where you can search by special interest.

5. **International exchange programs.** Whether you want to teach or study, you can find an overseas program that meets your needs. International ex-

change programs range from the well-known, high-profile Fulbright Scholar Program to Human Rights Watch (*www.hrw.org*), which places people in volunteer positions where they work toward advancing human rights worldwide. The Center for Interim Programs (*www.interimprograms.com*), which was founded to provide new experiences for students between high school and college, has expanded to meet the needs of adults looking for new careers, empty-nesters, and retirees seeking alternative experiences.

[Personal Safety]

Stock a First-Aid Kit

Accidents happen and medical emergencies arise. A well-stocked first-aid kit can help you deal with emergencies until professional medical help arrives and, if the crisis doesn't require a trip to the emergency room, a good first-aid kit may help you avoid a trip to the doctor.

Every household should have two first-aid kits, one in the home, handy to adults but out of the reach of small children, and one in the car. Not all items need be in your first-aid kit, but they should be within easy reach. These include items you should have in the medicine cabinet (see "Stock a Medicine Cabinet," page 145) such as a thermometer, painkillers, antacids, and diarrhea remedies. Be sure to keep the kit stocked by replenishing items as soon as possible after you've used them; check the items in the kit every six months and replace any medications that have expired.

1. **First-aid manual.** Every kit needs a small manual, preferably one with large and simple illustrations. Although this should be kept with the kit for reference purposes, you shouldn't wait until the heat of the moment to read it. Every responsible member of your household should read the manual ahead of time and understand how and when to use all items in the kit.

2. **Phone numbers.** The kit should contain a list of essential phone numbers, including the numbers of your physicians (family, pediatric, and specialists), the Poison Control Center (usually 800–222–1222), and the local police and fire departments, especially if you're not covered by 911. If you are covered by 911, make sure that number is listed, just in case a young child needs to make the call.

3. **List of medications.** Include the names and the dosages of the prescription medications each member of the household takes.

4. **List of allergies and other medical information.** Information on each member of the household should be included.

5. **Assorted Band-Aids**

6. **Nonstick gauze pads.** It is important to have nonstick dressing so that it can be more easily changed. Stock a variety of sizes, with at least three each of 2" x 2" and 4" x 4".

7. **Butterfly bandages**

8. **Elastic bandages**

9. **Tape**

10. **Antiseptic.** Wipes are okay, but a small bottle of liquid antiseptic, such as Betadine™, can be easier to use for larger wounds.

11. **Antiseptic ointment**

12. **Triple antibiotic cream**

13. **Hydrogen peroxide.** This is needed for deep puncture wounds.

14. **Scissors**

15. **Safety pins**

16. **Tweezers**

17. **Small flashlight**

18. **Thermometer**

19. **Disposable instant cold packs**

20. **Analgesics.** Pain and fever reducers include acetaminophen (Tylenol™), ibuprofen (Motrin™), and naproxen (Alleve™).

21. **Aspirin.** This can be chewed if a heart attack is suspected, but it should not be given to children.

22. **Antihistamine.** This can help with minor allergic reactions. Fast-acting over-the-counter brands are fine (don't choose drugs like Claritin(tm) that need to be taken for days before they're effective).

23. **Epinephrine.** Keep this in a preloaded syringe (a prescription item) if someone in your household has a life-threatening allergy.

24. **Cough suppressant**

25. **Activated charcoal and syrup of ipecac.** Use these only on the advice of a poison control center, physician, or emergency department.

26. **Dental analgesic**

27. **Antacid**

28. **Diarrhea remedy**

29. **Hydrocortisone cream**

30. **Cotton balls and cotton swabs**

31. **Sunburn treatment**

> **TIP:** You can purchase premade first-aid kits from most drugstores, and the Red Cross sells fully stocked kits for about $20. A complete first-aid kit makes a great gift for an elder or for someone getting a first car (or apartment) and for a family with children.

Keep Important Numbers by Your Phone

◆◆◆

A crisis is no time to look up a critical phone number. Keep the following phone numbers by your phone—upstairs and downstairs—and you won't waste time when you can least afford to.

1. **911.** Teach every member of the family how to dial this number in an emergency. Also teach them, and remind yourself, that this number should *only* be used in emergencies. A call to 911 to complain about the neighbor's barking dog could hinder emergency services to someone in a life-or-death situation.

2. **Emergency services other than 911.** Most cities and towns are served by 911, but if yours is not one of them, keep the phone numbers of the local police, fire department, and ambulance service next to the phone.

3. **Nonemergency police and fire department numbers.** If you have a question or need to contact the fire or police department for any nonurgent reason, say you smell smoke but can't confirm a fire, or you want to report vandalism, use each agency's nonemergency number.

4. **Poison control center.** (800) 222–1222.

5. **Primary-care doctors and pediatrician.** If you have a chronic disease, such as diabetes, your specialist's number should be on the list as well.

6. **Veterinarian.** Also include an emergency vet number for nights and weekends when your vet isn't around.

7. **Dentist**

NICE TO HAVE HANDY

The following numbers can be useful, but they aren't usually needed in a hurry. You could keep them on a separate list attached to the emergency numbers, in a conveniently located drawer, or even on the refrigerator door.

Pharmacy

Children's school numbers

Barber or hair salon

Newspaper circulation department. To report a missed delivery or soggy paper.

Home maintenance. Gardeners, lawn service, pool cleaner, and any other service you regularly use.

Takeout restaurants

Movie theaters

Baby-sitter

Pet sitter, dog walker

Train and bus information

Airlines. List your frequent-traveler membership numbers, as well.

8. **Home-alarm company.** To report false alarms quickly.

9. **Office and cell-phone numbers.** Even if you know them, your children or your baby- or pet sitter may not.

10. **Key family members.** List more than one and more than one household, in case your first choice is away.

11. **Key friends**

12. **Neighbors.** Again, don't rely on just one.

13. **Plumber**

14. **Electric company.** In case of a power outage, it may be difficult to find the phone book in the dark.

Burglarproof Your Home

◆◆◆

A determined and professional burglar may be hard to thwart, but your average crook is looking for easy pickings. You can definitely foil those bad guys by following these guidelines.

1. **Don't leave open invitations.** Keep your doors and windows closed and locked securely when you're asleep or away from home.

2. **Buy good locks.** Thieves keep a sharp eye out for flimsy locks that can easily be forced. Outfit your doors with deadbolt locks with a one-inch throw and a reinforced strike plate with three-inch screws. Your windows should have sturdy window locks.

3. **Secure sliding glass doors.** Put a dowel or broom handle in the track of the sliding door so it can't be opened, even if the lock is broken.

4. **Lock garage doors.** If you have an attached garage, always lock the interior door that connects to the house. Don't count on your automatic garage door for security.

5. **Plant unfriendly shrubs.** Prickly or very thick shrubs planted close to the house under your windows will discourage burglars, but beware of overgrown shrubbery around windows, entrances, and walkways. Keep hedges trimmed so they don't provide cozy hiding places for burglars as they do their dirty work.

6. **Keep exterior well lighted.** Low-voltage outdoor lighting is an inexpensive way to make your home look more attractive while it discourages intruders. It also helps visitors spot your address in the dark.

7. **Install motion detector lights.** These are particularly effective foils for would-be intruders. There's nothing like suddenly finding yourself in the spotlight as you're tiptoeing up the walk in your bandit mask.

8. **Always be home.** Well, you can't really do that, but you can create that impression, whether you are out for the evening or away on a two-week vacation. Employ these tactics:

- Use timers on lights, radios, and televisions.

- Keep some shades and curtains open to create an everyday, lived-in look.

- Never leave a message on your home phone saying you're out of town, or out of the house, for that matter; "Away from the phone" is a good all-purpose phrase to use instead.

- Stop your newspaper and mail delivery, or ask a trusted neighbor to collect them for you while you are gone.

- Leave a car parked in the driveway or invite a neighbor to park there every day or so. If you'll be away during a snowstorm, have a neighbor or a service come and shovel your walk and driveway.

9. **Invite the police.** Organize a neighborhood watch group, and invite a representative from your local police department to give an informative talk about keeping your individual homes and your neighborhood safe.

Hide Valuables Cleverly

The Chicago Crime Commission estimates that the average burglar spends about eight minutes inside a home. He moves quickly, of course, and checks all the obvious places first. Here are some recommendations for where and where not to stash your really valuable stuff.

1. **Avoid obvious places.** Dresser drawers, jewelry boxes, nightstands, desk drawers, and cookie jars are usually the first places a burglar will look.

2. **Skip the medicine cabinet.** Burglars are sometimes looking for prescription drugs, so don't hide anything valuable in bathroom cabinets, and don't stuff cash or jewelry into any kind of pill bottle.

3. **Head for the basement.** Basements are harder to get to, messier to look through, and generally less obvious places for hiding valuable items.

4. **Keep cold cash.** Some burglars may be hip to this idea, but most will be fooled if you wrap cash up in foil, label it as, say, fish, and put it in the freezer. This is a good spot for that extra cash you keep on hand in case ATMs go down in a blackout or other emergency.

5. **Hold the veggies.** Don't eat those frozen vegetables; instead, open a bag, hide jewelry or money inside, and close it up as you normally would.

6. **Foil pantry moths and burglars.** Those canisters you use to keep pantry moths out of your flour and cereal can double as cash and jewelry hideaways. Wrap small valuables in plastic wrap and sink them into the grains.

7. **Tennis anyone?** Make a slit in a tennis ball, squeeze it to open, and put your valuables inside; the ball will return to its original shape. Toss it in the box with the other sports equipment. Just be sure you don't mistakenly bring it to the courts.

8. **Use clever decoys.** You can purchase a number of items that are designed to look like regular home objects—cleaning products, books, and electric outlets—but actually conceal your grandmother's Tiffany silver.

Avoid Common Home Accidents

◆ ◆ ◆

Most people are so comfortable in their home that it's difficult to think of it as a potential minefield. The National Safety Council's statistics reveal two surprising facts: First, more people are injured in home accidents than in car crashes and workplace injuries combined; second, all home accidents are preventable. Here are tips to make your home safer.

1. **Let there be light.** Make sure all interior areas, not just hallways and stairs, are at least dimly lit at all times. Use automatic night-lights, even in the living room and dining room, so that you can navigate them in the dark if you need to.

2. **Remove clutter.** Objects get bigger and heavier in the dark. Avoid nasty bruises by keeping items where they belong. If you move a table, put it back; familiarity breeds safety when it comes to large objects. Also make

sure you pick up small objects, such as the dog's ball and the children's Legos(tm).

3. **Keep bathrooms slip-free.** Bathrooms are usually second to kitchens in the number of accidents occurring in them. This is probably because the bathroom is rarely carpeted, the floor gets wet, and you're likely to walk around in it with bare feet. If your bathtub or shower doesn't have a slip-proof surface, install adhesive strips or a nonslip mat designed to prevent falls. Use only nonskid rugs in the bathroom, and make sure anything you might grab to steady yourself, such as a soap dish in the tub, is sturdy enough to handle your weight. If anyone in the house is frail or unsteady, install special grip bars in the tub or shower and next to the toilet.

4. **Install smoke alarms and carbon-monoxide detectors.** Make sure these are located on every floor and in the basement. Test them and change the batteries when you change your clocks, in the fall and spring.

5. **Don't stand on chairs.** When changing light bulbs or dusting ceiling moldings, use a proper stepladder; never use chairs, cartons, or other improvised boosters.

6. **Install child-proof cabinet locks.** If you have children, grandchildren, or frequent young visitors, you should have child-proof locks on all cabinets used for dangerous items: cleaning products, medicines, even breakable glassware. Medicine cabinets can be reached by young children, who may climb on the toilet or sink, so drugs are best kept in child-proof containers in a less accessible, and locked, cabinet. This is also necessary if anyone in the house is in any way mentally impaired.

7. **Secure the garage.** Most people store many poisonous items, including antifreeze, paints, and motor oil, in the garage. Make sure young children don't have access to it.

8. **Set water heater no higher than 120° F.** This is a money saver as well as a safety precaution.

9. **Don't wear loose-fitting clothing when you cook.** Loose sleeves, scarves, and anything else that dangles and could brush into an open flame should not be worn in the kitchen.

10. **Clean up spills immediately.** Postpone cleaning spills, even for a minute while you're rushing around to get dinner on the table, and you

SAFETY TIPS FOR THE DRIVEWAY

Accidents at home happen, but when cars are involved the injuries are often worse. Avoid disaster on your driveway by taking these common-sense precautions.

Account for all adults, children, and pets before backing up. Remember that your rear-view mirror is blind to objects directly behind your car, so turn your head completely to scan behind you before you put the car in reverse.

Never leave your car running when you're not in it. A car can be a lethal weapon; keep control of it at all times.

Don't leave your car without taking the keys. Children are curious; teenagers, adventurous and naive. Leaving the keys can be as disastrous as leaving the car running.

Use cones or ropes to make the driveway a playground. When children are at play in your driveway, set up cones or ropes to keep cars away from them and to keep them from running into the street.

may slip and wind up eating your next meal in the waiting area of the emergency room.

11. **Repair loose banisters.** Make sure all banisters are secure before you need to rely on them.

12. **Train small animals to stay away from the top of the stairs.** It's hard to trip over a boxer or a standard poodle inadvertently, but cats and Chihuahuas can easily fall under your radar and send you flying from the top to the bottom of the stairs much faster than you're meant to go.

13. **Banish throw rugs from top and bottom of stairs.**

14. **Lock up guns.** Guns and ammunition should always be stored in separate locked cabinets.

15. **Update wiring and outlets.** Modern building codes usually require ground-fault circuit interrupters on electrical outlets in kitchens, bath-

rooms, and other places with access to water. These outlets provide quick-tripping circuit breakers that instantly shut off power if an appliance plugged into them experiences a short. If your home is older and doesn't have these life-saving outlets, hire an electrician to install them.

Keep a Healthy Home

In your attempt to care for your body, you visit your doctor regularly, gulp down supplements, and avoid saturated fats. You also steer clear of rabid raccoons and friends with the flu. But when was the last time you thought about the health of your home and how it affects your own health? Indoor air pollution—including the presence of dust, mold, and germs—can seriously compromise your well-being. Use this checklist to assure a healthy home.

1. **Keep it dry.** Moisture is probably the number one threat to a healthy home, because it encourages mold growth and provides a welcoming environment for bacteria. The humidity in your house should not rise above 50 percent. Buy a hygrometer at the local hardware store and monitor the humidity, which changes from season to season and day to day. If the humidity indoors rises above 70 percent, you should take action to remedy the situation. Use dehumidifiers in the basement and any rooms that tend to be damp, or install a central dehumidifier unit in a forced-air heating system. Use exhaust fans in the kitchen and bathrooms. If you live in a particularly humid environment, such as Florida, avoid vinyl wallpaper. It doesn't "breathe" and allows moisture to condense inside walls.

2. **Ventilate.** As homes have become more energy efficient, they've become tighter, meaning less air passes from outside the house to inside and vice versa. Although this is good for your fuel bill, it can result in unhealthy conditions, because moisture is allowed to build up inside. Keep a few windows open, if only a crack, and if necessary, use an air-exchange system that completely flushes stale air from the house and replaces it with fresh outdoor air several times a day. In cold climates use

an air-to-air heat-exchange system in which incoming cold air is warmed by air being moved out of the house.

3. **Seal any leaks.** This holds true from your roof to your basement, both of which should be monitored for leaks and regularly maintained. Even if you don't see water coming in, it may be seeping unnoticed from the roof to the space between the walls, where it will promote mold growth. If the basement shows any signs of leaks—cracks in the floor or walls or discoloration on walls—call a waterproofing specialist. The water you don't see, water that's been forced up from the ground into the spaces within the cinder blocks of basement walls, can be more dangerous than the puddle in the middle of the floor. If there is a puddle, however, it may be time to install a sump pump. Also check around windows for leaks, especially if your windows are old and made of wood.

4. **Change filters regularly.** Filters for a forced-air heating/cooling system, as well as those for your window air conditioners and dehumidifiers, should be changed before the start of the heating and cooling seasons. Filters for a central system should be checked once a month whenever the system is running. If you use a humidifier, flush it out regularly and follow the manufacturer's instructions about cleaning it to keep it mold- and fungus-free.

5. **Choose environmentally friendly household products.** These are less likely to give off noxious fumes.

6. **Use paints, varnishes, pesticides, and other harsh chemicals only in well ventilated rooms.**

7. **Don't accept dry cleaning that smells like the dry cleaners.**

8. **Don't allow smoking inside your house.**

9. **Clean conscientiously.** Clean all kitchen and bathroom surfaces after every use. It needn't be the kind of cleaning that will pass muster with your mother-in-law, but it needs to be sufficient to discourage bacterial and viral growth. This means using a disinfectant or bleach solution. Avoid cleaning products with antibacterials, which seem to promote resistant strains of bacteria.

10. **Dust dutifully.** Dust isn't just unsightly; it harbors mites and allergens.

11. **Air out new furniture, carpeting, and building materials.** These items often give off toxic fumes when first unwrapped, so give them time outdoors before bringing them inside your home. Ask that your new carpet be aired out before it's delivered, and try to arrange delivery of new furniture during seasons when you can keep the windows open.

12. **Check for radon.** Kits that are labeled "meets EPA requirements" are available at most hardware stores. If the house wasn't tested when you moved in, do it now.

13. **Avoid gas-fueled space heaters.** If gas-powered heaters are operated in a poorly ventilated room, they pose a serious threat of carbon-monoxide poisoning.

14. **Never run a car or gas-powered tool in a closed garage.** A gas-powered engine, running in an enclosed space, can create deadly levels of carbon monoxide.

Avoid Being a Crime Victim

◆◆◆

The most basic way to protect yourself from becoming a crime victim is to use caution and common sense at all times. Here are some tips from the National Crime Prevention Council to make you more street savvy.

At Home

1. **Don't hide house keys in obvious places.** Under a planter, under a doormat, in a mailbox, even on top of the doorsill are all routine spots where burglars look.

2. **Never put your name or address on your keys.** Better to lose your house keys than to give them to a criminal along with a note on where to use them.

3. **Don't trust strangers at the door.** Don't open the door to anyone you don't know, no matter how silly you feel yelling through a closed door.

Tell door-to-door solicitors that's your policy. Offer to call 911 for anyone who claims to need help (water, phone, bathroom); don't let him in. If a serviceperson comes to the door, make a phone call to verify the information he gives before letting him in.

4. **Never give personal information to any caller.** This seems obvious, but telephone scammers are getting more clever all the time. Your policy should be never to give out information (even if the caller says she has it and asks you to confirm) if you didn't initiate the call.

5. **Hang up on harassers.** The less you say the better. Any reply you give will only encourage a harasser.

In Public

1. **Be alert to your surroundings.** Pay attention to who is walking behind and ahead of you.

2. **Walk confidently.** Crime prevention experts say that muggers and rapists are more likely to target victims who appear vulnerable. Always act as if you know exactly where you're going. Stand up straight and make brief, self-confident eye contact with anyone around you.

3. **Carry a loud whistle.** Don't be embarrassed to use it if you even suspect you're in danger.

4. **Secure your valuables.** Women should hold their purses close to the body; a bag slung crosswise over the chest is a good choice. Men should carry wallets inside a coat (not pants) pocket.

5. **Give it up.** If a mugger does manage to grab your purse or wallet, don't fight it. Let it go and run.

6. **Lighten your load.** Avoid walking with a large load of packages or grocery bags. They'll slow your reactions and impair your view of your surroundings.

7. **Get away.** If you suspect you're being followed, cross the street, go into an open store, or quicken your pace to get to a well-lit area with people.

8. **Handle money discreetly.** Don't flash your cash, and keep careful track of your credit card; make sure you get it back after a transaction.

9. **Don't be distracted by your cell phone.** Cell-phone users have become popular targets for criminals, because they are so preoccupied by their conversation.

10. **Use care on public transportation.** Don't sit close to doors and exits, where you are more vulnerable to being attacked or robbed by a passing criminal. Be aware of who gets off a bus or train with you, and stay alert to make sure you're not being followed.

11. **Practice caution in elevators.** Take a quick look inside an elevator before you enter, and don't get on if you see someone suspicious. If someone you're uneasy about gets on with you, back out and wait for another car. When you're in the elevator, try to stand next to the controls. If you are attacked, hit the alarm and as many floor buttons as possible.

IF YOU ARE ATTACKED

Stay calm. Take a deep breath, if possible. You'll be better able to judge the situation and make good choices about what to do next if you remain calm.

Make noise. Scream or blow your whistle. The more noise you can make, the better. You may startle the attacker into fleeing, and you may attract the attention of someone in the vicinity who can come to your aid.

Avoid injury. If the attacker has a weapon, don't take the risk of resisting. If the attacker is unarmed, and you sense you could get away, fight back while screaming.

Attack critical body parts. If your life is in immediate jeopardy, do anything you can to hurt your attacker and get away. Concentrate your attacks at the eyes and groin. Jam your keys right into the eyes, if you can, and don't wait even a second to check the effect; just run and scream.

Protect your body. If you aren't able to get away, drop, curl tightly into a ball, and lace your fingers together at the back of your neck to protect your body as much as possible.

In the Car

1. **Keep car doors locked.** This is as important when you are in the car as when you park and leave it.

2. **Look around.** Check the inside of your car, front and back, before getting in. Once inside the car, lock it *immediately* and head to your destination.

3. **Keep your purse on the floor.** Driving with a purse on the seat next to you could tempt a thief to break in and grab it.

4. **Call police for breakdowns.** In the case of car trouble, put up your hood, sit in your car, and lock your doors and windows. Use your cell phone to call for assistance. If a stranger stops to offer help, ask through the window for him to call police or a tow truck or thank him and say that help is on the way. There is no need to roll your window down to communicate.

5. **Don't stop for strangers.** If a passing motorist indicates something is wrong with your vehicle, drive to a well-lit, populated area before getting out to check. Never stop in an isolated area to help someone in a disabled vehicle; use your cell phone to call for help instead. Don't stop for flashing lights on the highway unless you see a clearly marked police car. If you aren't sure that it is a police officer pulling you over, call 911 and ask for verification, or wait to pull over in a populated rest stop.

6. **Never pick up hitchhikers.** Haven't you seen enough slasher movies?

Take Reasonable Precautions

◆◆◆

The key word here is *reasonable*. There's no end to the precautions a person might take against unknown, unspecified dangers and disasters; people who try to take them all are called insane. That said, in our post-9/11, post-Katrina society, it makes sense to have a predetermined plan to deal with the unexpected.

1. **Take inventory . . . of everything.** Do you know what's in your wallet? After it's lost is no time to try to figure this out. Take the time to make

photocopies of your credit cards, driver's license, and anything else you carry in it. Do you know what's in your living room? Take a detailed inventory of your entire house, preferably including digital photos of every room. Include pictures of the outside areas, and don't forget cars, boats, RVs, and, if you're so fortunate, airplanes and blimps.

HAVE AN EMERGENCY KIT ON HAND

In addition to a supply of food and water, you should have an emergency kit and know where it is. Be careful not to make the kit so big that you won't be able to grab it quickly. Include:

Flashlight

Battery-powered radio

Extra batteries

Paper and pens

Cash and/or traveler's checks

Basic tools: screwdriver, pliers, small hammer

Knife

Scissors

Change of underwear for each person

Plastic sheeting

Duct tape

Trash bags

Whistle

2. **Keep a copy of the inventory at another site.** An inventory won't do you much good if your only copy is in your desk in the den and the house burns down. Choose a secondary site for an additional copy of your inventory. This could be at a friend's or relative's house or in your safe-deposit box. Just remember that in the case of a death, the safe-deposit box may be sealed. If you've had such valuable items as artwork and jewelry appraised, keep copies of the appraisals at home and at your secondary site.

3. **Know where your important papers are.** In addition to the inventory, you should know where copies of important papers are. These include insurance policies; birth, marriage, divorce, and death certificates; deeds; passports; professional licenses; vehicle registrations and titles; trusts and wills; and any other documents that are vital to your daily life or that you might need in case of an emergency. As with the inventory, copies of all of these should be in at least two places, at home and at a secure second location.

4. **Have an emergency plan.** After 9/11, a lot of attention was given to making an emergency plan, but how many people actually sat down and made one? If this is one of those things you've been meaning to do but put off in favor of more immediate needs, like your daily latte, stop procrastinating. If, however, you actually made a plan a couple of years ago, it's time to make sure that plan is still relevant (see "Have an Emergency Kit On Hand," page 183).

5. **Choose emergency contact people.** Pick a reliable friend or relative close at hand and another outside your area to serve as emergency contacts. These should be people who won't hang up and won't be hung over if you call at 4 A.M. Take a minute now to call each of them and ask if you can call on them for a drive to the hospital or a place to stay, in case of a local emergency. Keep their numbers—home, work, and cell—handy, and make sure everyone in your household has them.

6. **Keep a well-stocked first-aid kit.** Check your first-aid kit periodically to make sure it has all the supplies you need and that none of them is dried out or expired (see also "Stock a First-Aid Kit," page 168).

7. **Watch your gas tank.** Never let your car's tank reach empty; it should always be at least half full. Don't leave the job of filling the tank for the morning; what if you have to take Bisco to the emergency vet at 2 A.M. and the tank reads empty? It can be hard to explain, once labor begins, that you have to find an open gas station before you can get to the hospital.

THE EMERGENCY PLAN

Make sure every member of your household knows and understands the household emergency plan, which should cover the following items.

Know emergency contacts. You should have at least two emergency contact numbers, one local and one outside your immediate area, in case local phones are out. Every household member should either know these numbers by heart or have a copy with them at all times.

Locate shelters. Find out where the local shelters are and where you are supposed to go in case of a natural or man-made disaster. Call your local Red Cross office or governmental emergency organization for help figuring this out.

Know the best evacuation routes.

Find a sealed space. In case you need to stay put, know what to do. Get everyone, including animals, into an interior room, and, if the air is contaminated, seal the room as best you can with plastic sheeting and duct tape. Don't forget to take your food, water, and emergency and first-aid kits into the sealed space.

Know how to turn off utilities. Make sure you know how to turn off your gas, electricity, and water, in case authorities tell you to. Keep necessary tools near gas and water shutoff valves.

Understand the perils of high-rises. If you're in a high-rise, know where the nearest exit is and where another one is, in case the first is blocked. Stay clear of bookshelves, file cabinets, and other things that might fall. Move away from exterior walls and face away from windows and glass. Don't take the elevator, and stay to the right when going down stairs so you won't block or crash into emergency workers coming up.

8. **Keep a three-day supply of food and water.** And don't forget the paper plates and plastic utensils. The food, of course, should be nonperishable, and you'll need a can-opener (nonelectric) unless you have extraordinary teeth. Count on keeping about a gallon of water per person per day. This is not a get-it-and-forget proposition. Rotate your rations every six months or so. Even canned goods can become unappetizing, if not downright peculiar, after a while. Don't forget to pack pet food or plan on sharing some of your rations with your feathered or furry wards.

[House and Home]

Stock Kitchen Equipment

◆◆◆

If you would like to prepare simple meals but don't expect to master the art of French cooking, here is a list of basic kitchen equipment you should have on hand.

1. **Can opener.** More and more cans have pull tops, which someday may make can openers obsolete; until then, you need a handheld opener with a comfortable grip.

2. **Coffeemaker.** Even if you don't drink coffee, one of your guests may want a cup.

3. **Colander.** Choose either a plastic or metal colander for draining pasta.

4. **Cookie sheet.** Even if you're not a cookie maker, get a cookie sheet to put under those frozen pies and pizzas you heat up.

5. **Cutting boards.** Buy plastic cutting boards so that you can toss them in the dishwasher. You need a small one for cutting fruit and chopping garlic and one larger one for bigger jobs.

6. **Frying pans.** Buy an eight-inch skillet for scrambling eggs and a 12- or 14-inch pan for stir-frying and sautéing.

7. **Grater or planer.** Although they serve the same purpose as old-fashioned box graters, modern planers are much easier to use. The only catch is that each planer has only one size of shredding/grating surface, so you need two, a micro and a shredder. One size allows you to grate Parmesan cheese, the other, carrots.

8. **Knives.** You don't need many knives, but it's worthwhile to invest in quality. Sharp knives are not only less frustrating to use, they are also safer. You should have a small paring knife (4- to 6-inch) and one larger chef's knife (8- to 10-inch). A long serrated (saw-toothed) knife is handy for slicing bread.

9. **Measuring cups.** You can do fine with a Pyrex two-cup measure for liquids and a set of graduated plastic or metal cups for measuring flour, sugar, and other dry ingredients.

10. **Microwave oven.** If you've never had one, you'll wonder how you did without one for so long. A microwave is handy for heating everything

from a single cup of tea to a plate of leftovers, a baked potato, and individual microwave dinners.

11. **Mixing bowls.** Buy a set of nesting bowls, and you're covered for whatever you decide to stir up. The largest bowl can double for serving salads.

12. **Plastic containers.** Pick up a set of plastic containers with tight-fitting lids for storing leftovers in the fridge.

13. **Potholders.** Buy two flat ones and an oven mitt or two. Don't try to use dishtowels to lift hot pans; they aren't thick enough to provide adequate insulation.

14. **Roasting pan.** Roasting a chicken is easy and gives you great leftovers for sandwiches and salads during the week.

15. **Saucepans.** A one-quart pan is needed for heating up a can of soup, and a two-quart pan, for making rice and steaming vegetables.

16. **Stockpot.** This is simply a pot large enough to boil pasta for four or make soup from scratch. Make sure the pot has a tight-fitting lid and is heavy enough to distribute heat well.

17. **Teakettle.** Choose one that whistles and won't rust inside.

18. **Toaster.** That is, if you like toast. You can make toast in the broiler, but it's an iffy proposition. You may want to consider buying a toaster oven. They take up counter space, but are very handy for top browning open faced sandwiches with cheese or for heating items you want to keep crisp, such as small pizzas or slices of pie.

19. **Utensils.** Pick up a few wooden spoons, a plastic or metal spatula (to turn pancakes), a rubber spatula (to get the last of the tomato paste out of the can), a soup ladle, a large serving spoon, and maybe a set of tongs for picking up spaghetti or serving asparagus or green beans to company.

NICE BUT NOT ESSENTIAL

Pepper mill	Large slotted spoon
Baking pans	Sharpening steel
Vegetable peeler	Electric mixer
Oven thermometer	Garlic press
Meat thermometer	Blender
Salad bowl	Wooden toaster tongs
Potato masher	

Stock a Linen Closet

◆◆◆

The number of sheets and towels you should own depends to a large extent on how often you're willing to do laundry. The quality of the sheets and towels you own depends on your budget and your sensitivity to scratchy sheets. If you enjoy the feeling of soft sheets, purchase a minimum of 200-thread count. They cost a bit more, but the higher the thread count, the longer the sheet will last. With higher-quality sheets you can convince yourself you're being thrifty while indulging yourself with softness.

1. **Sheets and pillowcases.** For the sake of convenience, you should have two sets of sheets per bed. That way you don't have to scramble to do the laundry on the same day you change your sheets. You should have the same number of pillowcases per pillow as you have sheets for the bed.

2. **Mattress pad.** These provide both comfort for the sleeper and protection for the mattress. One per bed is fine, but it is handy to have an extra one in case you need to remake the bed from the mattress up in an emergency.

3. **Blankets.** Keep at least one warm winter blanket per bed and one lighter blanket or coverlet for summer use. Don't forget extra blankets for the guest bed.

4. **Comforter.** This is strictly a matter of preference, but a down- or synthetic-filled comforter (sometimes referred to as a duvet) is mighty cozy on a cold winter's night. Comforters are sold in various weights. Choose light, medium, or winter weight depending on your climate and whether you prefer to use it year-round or only in the deepest cold of winter. If you purchase a comforter, be sure to buy a duvet cover to protect it.

5. **Bath and face towels.** Figure on a minimum of two per person in the household.

6. **Washcloths.** It's not a bad idea to buy a set of matching bath and face towels that includes a washcloth. Even if you don't usually use a washcloth, it is nice to have a tidy set when you're setting up for a house guest.

7. **Bathmats.** Keep two on hand for each bathroom in the house so they can be changed weekly.

8. **Bathroom rug.** This is optional. If you do choose to have an area rug in the bathroom, make sure it can be laundered and has a nonslip backing.

TIP: Watch for white sales in July and January and stock up on sheets and towels then.

Fall Maintenance Checklist

◆◆◆

Take a cue from the squirrels and make preparations for the winter months before the weather turns so cold that working outside becomes difficult, if not impossible. Even if you live in a place where the climate is mild, temperature and moisture changes dictate certain chores in the fall. Follow this schedule for fall home maintenance, and you'll have that much less to do in spring.

1. **Clean gutters and downspouts.** Neglect your gutters or let them become clogged with fallen leaves and you risk wood rot, wet basements, pest infestations, and foundation damage. Check to make sure gutters are securely fastened, rain isn't leaking behind them, and water is draining properly and not pooling near the house.

2. **Check windows and doors.** Repair or replace damaged weatherstripping, and caulk cracks or gaps around edges of windows and doors before the weather gets so cold that the caulk won't set.

3. **Install storm windows.** If you have older windows with removable screens, replace the screens with storm windows, wash the screens and store them covered. Close the storms on windows with pull-down storms. If you have thermal paned windows and don't need to remove storms, do yourself a favor and remove, wash, and store the screens. Screenless windows allow more light into the house during those dark and dreary winter days.

4. **Check the roof.** Get up on the roof and look for loose shingles or obvious damage to flashing (the material, usually metal or plastic, that's used around angles to prevent leaks). If you see a few loose shingles and you feel comfortable up there, tack them down, making sure you use proper roofing nails and don't damage the roof. If you don't feel completely safe and you see more than a few loose tiles, call a professional roofer. Repairing a slate or clay-tile roof is trickier, so you may need professional attention from the start.

5. **Check chimneys.** If you have a fireplace or wood-burning stove, make sure the chimney and/or stovepipe is clean. Unless you're partial to soot, this is best left to a professional chimney sweep. Also check the flues that vent your heat and hot water systems, and inspect all chimneys for cracks.

6. **Pack up the patio.** Clean and store lawn furniture.

7. **Check the heating system and change filters.** Have a professional check your heating system early in the fall and repair any little problems that could turn into major ones at 3:00 in the morning on the coldest day of the year. Most oil-delivery companies offer an annual checkup as part of your contract; if you have a gas-powered system, your local utility should offer something similar. Clean and vacuum dust from vents, baseboard heaters, and cold-air returns. If ducts haven't been cleaned for

a while, this is a good time to call in a professional. Also, be sure to change the filters on forced-air heating systems. If you have central air-conditioning, the end of the cooling season is a good time to clean the outdoor compressor.

8. **Drain outdoor faucets.** If you don't drain outdoor faucets, you risk a burst pipe. Find the cut-off valves to all outdoor faucets and close them. Then, open the faucet on the outside to drain it. For long outdoor lines, you may need to use a compressor to blow out standing water. Disconnect hoses, drain them, and store them in the garage or tool shed.

9. **Trim trees and remove dead branches.** Do the easy stuff yourself, but if there are any signs a tree is sick—cavities or rotten wood along trunks or major branches, cracks or splits in trunks, a poor leaf season, or premature or unusual coloring and loss of leaves—call in a tree expert. A heavy snow, high winds, or a particularly wet fall can be the final straw that pushes a weak tree onto your roof, your car, or a passerby.

10. **Drain sprinkler system.** You might think about having the system blown out.

11. **Lay in winter supplies.** Make sure you have a back-friendly snow shovel stored in a handy location. If you're considering a snow blower, buy it now, when the greatest selection is available. Stock up on rock salt or chemical ice-melting crystals (if you have dogs, use a pet-friendly formula), and put out the winter mats, indoor and out, to handle mud and slush.

12. **Change the batteries.** When you set your clocks back at the end of October, don't forget to change the batteries in your smoke and carbon-monoxide detectors.

> **TIP:** Washing all your windows in the fall yields a double payoff. Clean windows allow more light into your home during the months when light is scarce, and your windows will stay clean longer because there's no pollen or insects to muck them up.

Spring Maintenance Checklist

◆◆◆

If the delightful spring air isn't enough to get you up and out, think of the money to be saved in home repair costs if you do these routine spring maintenance chores before it's time to fire up the barbecue or head off to the beach.

1. **Start with the roof.** The roof provides a great place from which to check on returning birds and blooming bulbs, and while you're up there you can check for winter roof damage. Ice can lift and damage shingles and flashing. Repair the simple problems yourself, but if many shingles are missing or curling, or if you notice weak spots or significant damage to flashing, call in a professional before the rainy season hits.

2. **Check your sump pump.** Make sure your pump is operating correctly and that the discharge pipe is clear.

3. **Go over your gutters.** Make sure gutters are clear and firmly attached and that the downspouts are discharging water away from the foundation. If you can't easily see your gutters and you don't want to climb a ladder, tape a mirror to the end of a rake and inspect them from the comfort of the ground.

4. **Regulate air conditioning.** Make sure lamps, televisions, and other heat-releasing appliances are away from thermostats for a central air-conditioning system; these appliances can force the system to turn on before you really need it. Also, change air-conditioner filters and vacuum the vents.

5. **Swap storm windows for screens.** If you did your fall maintenance, the screens should be clean and ready to install.

6. **Check attic fan.** Make sure your attic fan is operating properly. Open vents if you closed them for the winter.

7. **Examine your siding.** Modern vinyl siding is pretty maintenance free, but it's still a good idea to check for cracks, rust, or any signs that a piece has come loose. Wood siding is subject to dry rot and damage from termites. Crumbling wood signals dry rot. Bore holes and wings are evidence that termites are at work.

8. **Check caulking.** Make sure caulking around doors and windows is intact. If there are any gaps, apply new caulking.

9. **Shut down the furnace dehumidifier.** If you have central air conditioning, now is a good time to clean the furnace dehumidifier and shut the damper.

10. **Check and clean room dehumidifiers.** Follow the instructions in the owner's manual for maintaining your unit.

11. **Follow foundation walls.** Check for cracks or leaks in your foundation, and repair any you may find. Concrete caulk should take care of small cracks. For larger cracks, use a concrete patch.

12. **Inspect your deck.** Look for cracks that ice may have opened. Inspect the connections between the main structure and all railings and supports; tighten them, if necessary. Pour a glass of water on the deck; if it soaks in instead of beading, you should reseal the deck. Also, check for any signs of wood rot. If you see damage, call a professional. It's important to address damage early before it threatens the structural integrity of the deck.

13. **Change the batteries.** When the clocks move ahead, it's time to change the batteries in your smoke and carbon-monoxide detectors.

Stock a Do-It-Yourself Tool Kit

◆◆◆

Whether you live in a house, apartment, or even a ritzy mansion, sooner or later something is going to break, fall off the wall, or develop a leak. If the job is simple and you own some basic tools, you won't need to pay for an expensive repair every time something goes awry. Tuck these basics into a tool kit, and you'll be equipped to handle most common household repairs.

1. **Adjustable wrenches.** These open and close to fit larger or smaller items; you probably should get several, in different sizes. Make sure the handle is comfortable and that the adjustment knob operates smoothly.

2. **Caulking gun.** Get one that fits the standard tubes.

3. **Cordless electric drill.** No longer a luxury item, this can be one of the most useful tools you get, not just for making holes, but for driving or removing screws as well as for light sanding and buffing, with the appropriate attachments. How powerful it is depends on the voltage of the battery, which may range from 7 to 24 volts. Choose one with at least a 9.6-volt battery. Buy a complete kit, with extra battery, charger, and a variety of bits.

4. **Duct tape.** When you don't have the time or expertise, duct tape saves the day in a multitude of repair crises.

5. **Fasteners.** Keep a supply of screws, nails, nuts and bolts, and picture hangers in a variety of sizes.

6. **Flashlight.** Choose one that's small and light and has an adjustable lens.

7. **Glue.** Keep all-purpose glue, such as Elmer's™, as well as so-called superglue.

8. **Hammer.** Choose a hammer that has a head that won't, literally, fly off the handle. A 16-ounce hammer with a curved claw (for extracting nails) is heavy enough to drive nails into tough materials, but not so heavy as to be tiring to use. If you find this uncomfortable, try a 12-ounce model.

9. **Level.** Choose a two-foot long wood or metal level, not a plastic one. Smaller levels are acceptable for straightening pictures, but you'll appreciate the extra length for most home-repair jobs.

10. **Lock for your toolbox.** Especially if you have children, you should keep your toolbox locked; tools, in the wrong hands, are dangerous.

11. **Pliers.** There are four basic kinds of pliers, and you should get one of each: standard pliers, sometimes called slip-joint pliers, which adjust to two sizes, depending on the diameter of the object you're working with; needle-nose pliers, used for electrical work and for working in small spaces; diagonal, or wire-stripper/cutting, pliers, useful for stripping wires and cutting thin metal; and groove-joint pliers, sometimes known as tongue-and-groove pliers. These are larger, adjust to many sizes, and have longer handles for greater leverage. Never use pliers instead of a wrench, and don't try to remove screws by turning them with pliers; you're liable to break off the head that way.

12. **Plungers.** Otherwise known as plumbers' helpers. Get a smaller one for sinks and a larger one for toilets.

13. **Safety glasses or goggles.** Buy a comfortable pair and wear them whenever you do anything that might result in small missiles aimed at your face.

14. **Saw.** Buy a good quality, crosscut handsaw with a wooden handle, which is much more comfortable than plastic. It should have about eight teeth to the inch.

15. **Screwdrivers.** Buy a set of screwdrivers that contains at least three sizes of both Phillips and standard tips. Look for screwdrivers with nonslip grips and hardened tips. A handy alternative is an all-in-one model, which has a handle with interchangeable heads.

16. **Tape measure.** Get a retractable steel tape measure with a locking mechanism. A 10-foot length is enough for most jobs, but you might consider a longer one, perhaps 16 or 25 feet.

17. **Utility knife.** Get a metal knife with retractable, replaceable blades, and buy a set of blades.

Avoid Calling a Repairperson: Tricks of the Trade

◆◆◆

Things fall apart, as the poet William Butler Yeats noted, and when they do most people reach for the phone and call a repairperson. But there are plenty of repairs you can do yourself, saving big bucks while bolstering your self-esteem. Don't undertake anything you don't feel comfortable with or that might run afoul of local regulations, such as certain electrical or structural repairs, and if in doubt, check with the authorities. Keeping that in mind, here are some easy repairs that just about anyone can do.

1. **Unclog a sink or tub.**

   • *Use a plunger.* You need a regular plunger, not a toilet plunger, which has two cups, one inside the other. If the sink or tub is empty, pour a couple of cups of boiling water into the drain. Next, or if there's already standing water, add enough tap water to cover the top of the plunger. Make sure the plunger is completely and tightly covering the drain, plunge it forcefully and pull up; repeat several times.

- **Remove the trap.** If the plunger doesn't work, try removing the trap at the bottom of the U-shaped tube under the sink. Put a bucket under it and, using a wrench, unscrew the metal slip nut. Poke a straightened wire hanger up toward the drain to loosen anything caught in the pipe.

- **Try a snake.** Push the end of the snake into the drain and turn the handle. You may have to push harder to get around the bend in the pipe. You should feel some resistance as the tip encounters and then breaks through the clog. If it doesn't break through, you may have encountered a solid object. If you're lucky, when you pull the snake out of the drain, it will carry the solid object with it. If you can't get the snake down the drain, open the trap, as described above, and push the snake in toward the drainpipe or up toward the drain, if that's where the blockage is.

- **Run water.** This will help flush any remaining pieces of the clog past the trap.

- **Avoid chemicals.** Older pipes can be damaged by chemicals, and even the fumes can be toxic. If you must use a chemical product, never mix it with anything that contains ammonia. Drain cleaners tend to contain bleach (sodium hypochlorite); ammonia plus sodium hypochlorite produces chlorine gas, which can be lethal.

2. **Fix a stopped-up toilet.**

- **Use a plunger.** Let the bowl drain and add enough hot or boiling water to cover the top of a toilet plunger. Make sure the head of the plunger completely covers the drain opening. Push down several times to force the clog down.

- **Flush the toilet.** Flush several times to force any remaining pieces of the clog into the drainpipe. Be prepared to shut off the water supply behind the toilet if the bowl begins to overfill.

- **Try dish soap.** If plunging doesn't work, try adding dishwashing soap into the bowl. Let it sit for five minutes and try using the plunger. The soap can help dissolve fatty material.

- **Try a snake.** If this still doesn't work, try using a snake. Be careful not to unduly scratch the inside of the bowl.

- **Avoid chemicals.** Use chemicals only as a last resort.

3. Fix a leaking pipe.

- *Use duct tape.* For a pinhole leak, wrap the pipe tightly with duct tape. This is a very temporary fix.

- *Use a hose clamp.* For a longer lasting fix, use an automotive hose clamp with a bit of rubber. Wrap the rubber around the pipe and place the clamp directly over the pinhole leak and tighten.

- *Use a pipe clamp and gasket.* This is a semipermanent fix. Assemble the clamp around the gasket and tighten all four nuts.

4. Fix a dripping faucet.

- *Washerless faucets (single handle).* If you have a newer faucet without a washer, the hardest part about fixing it is determining the brand and model, information you need to get replacement parts. Take a digital picture of the faucet and bring it to your local hardware or plumbing supply store to see if someone there can identify it. Turn off both the hot and cold water supplies under the sink and open the faucet to let the water drain. Pry off the decorative cap and remove the screw beneath it. Pull the handle off. You should see a nut that holds the faucet stem or cartridge in place. Unscrew it and take out the old cartridge. It might be tight, so pry it out carefully. Underneath the cartridge you'll find various parts, depending on the brand of the faucet. Note the way these parts are assembled so you can replace them in the same order. Replace the old cartridge with the new one and reassemble.

- *Stem-type faucets (with separate hot and cold handles).* Turn off the water supply and open the faucets, as above. Remove the faucet handles, which are usually attached with a screw; the screw might be under a decorative cap that has to be pried off. Loosen and remove the lock nut under the handle and pull out the stem. In some cases, the stem itself is threaded, in which case, loosen and remove it with a wrench. (If the nut is deep-seated, you might need to buy a special wrench for this purpose at the hardware store; it's still a lot cheaper than calling a plumber.) Remove the rubber washer at the bottom of the stem. The washer may be held in place by a screw. Replace the washer with a new one. If you don't have one on hand, bring the old one to a hardware store to get an exact match. Reassemble everything in reverse order.

5. **Correct weak or uneven flow at a faucet.** Unscrew any in-line device, such as an aerator or water filter. Rinse off or replace the screen or change the filter.

6. **Get the lights back on.** If the lights suddenly go off, look out the window. If everyone's lights are out, report the problem to the electric company, then just sit back and wait for the company to make the needed repairs. If your neighbors have lights, check your circuit-breaker box. If you've lost power to the entire house, the main circuit breaker has been tripped. If it's just a room or two, just one of the circuit breakers should be in the off position. In either case, make sure as many as possible of the affected appliances and lights are switched off. Now push the affected circuit breaker all the way to the off position and then to the on position. That should fix the problem. If the lights go off again, there could be a short someplace. To find the offending light or appliance, turn them off, one at a time, and reset the circuit breaker until it stays on. This should isolate the offending light or appliance.

7. **Repair or replace a doorbell.** Doorbells run on low-voltage systems, so you can repair them without taking your life into your hands.

   • *Test the button.* Remove the button and turn it over to make sure the wires are firmly attached. If they aren't, reattach them. That should do it. If they're in place, try shorting them with a screwdriver or small loop of wire. If the bell doesn't work, the button needs to be replaced.

   • *Check the transformer.* Find the transformer, which is probably in the basement. Make sure the wires from the button and those to the bell are attached. If they are, test the transformer with a voltmeter or multitester, which you can pick up at the hardware store. Or, short it with a screwdriver; if you see a spark, the transformer is working. If the transformer is defective, replace it, but before you do, make absolutely sure the circuit breaker that feeds it is turned off, because the other side of the transformer is getting house current at full voltage.

   • *Test the bell.* If the button and the transformer are working, the culprit may be the bell itself. Again, look for loose or broken connections. Most bells have terminals for front and rear buttons, even if you have only one. Using a multitester, check for current by applying one end to the terminal labeled "front" button and one to the terminal labeled "trans." Repeat for the "rear" terminal. If current is running to the bell, but it doesn't work, replace the bell. If there's no current reaching the bell, the problem could be in the wiring between the transformer and the bell.

8. **Fix a garbage-disposal unit.** Turn off the power. Don't even think about sticking your hand into the garbage disposal unit unless you know the power is off. To be safe, trip the circuit breaker that feeds the unit. Remove any loose items. Run cold water. Press the reset button. (This is located on the bottom of the unit under the sink.) Turn the power back on and flip the wall switch. You might have to press the reset button again. If something is stuck that you can't remove, insert a disposal wrench, available at the hardware store, into the hole at the bottom of the unit in the center and wrench back and forth to free the blades. (Most units come with a wrench, so before going to the hardware store, make sure there isn't one taped to the side of the unit under the sink or in a special pouch on the unit.) If the blades turn, and you've pressed the reset button at least twice, the motor may be burned out, in which case it's time to replace the entire unit.

Find a Reliable Handyperson

If you think a Phillips screwdriver is a hangover remedy, you're probably not up to performing so much as a minor household repair. And even if you have a more than passing familiarity with the back aisles of your local hardware store, you will sooner or later lack the time, the expertise, or the patience to make repairs yourself. That's when a handyperson is essential. Here are some tips on finding one who won't undermine the foundation of your house—or your bank account.

1. **Decide how large the job is.** There's a considerable difference between a small job and a major renovation in terms of required permits and licensure. Also, the skill sets of various contractors compared with those of handypersons may be higher, broader, or both. A licensed electrician can replace an outdated and inadequate main circuit box, but he usually

won't make a house call just to install a single light switch, unless, of course, you're willing to pay a very hefty hourly fee. If you're looking for a contractor, see "Hire a Contractor" page 204, but if it is a handyperson you need, read on.

2. **Define the job.** This may seem obvious, but it's worth a little thought. Do you want to clean the grout in the kitchen or do you want to replace it? Does the paint in the bathroom need a touch-up or a complete makeover? Do you want someone to install the shelves you bought at Ikea or do you want something custom-made? You can't even begin your search until you know the parameters of the job to be done. Are you most interested in quality, price, or speed? The saying that you can only get two out of those three is worth heeding.

3. **Make a list and check it twice.** Handypeople often front-load the first hour, meaning they charge a minimum that's higher than their hourly rate just to show up. Some jobs require a setup, and that time may be the same regardless of how complex the work is. It therefore often pays to get as much done as possible at any given time. If you're having shelves put up in the den, decide now whether you really want that spice rack in the kitchen. You can save money by having both jobs done at the same time.

4. **Ask a friend or neighbor.** Consulting friends and neighbors is the best way to find someone reliable. Be specific about what you need. The person who helped your neighbor install a new washing machine or clean out her gutters may have no carpentry skills, so if your job requires fixing the wood railing on the back porch, you may have to look further.

5. **Check the obvious.** Look through the home-repair classifieds of your local newspapers or "pennysavers," as well as ads in the Yellow Pages (skip the Internet yellow pages; they're usually just lists of names and phone numbers).

6. **Dig deep.** Because the best handypeople often don't advertise (they get all the business they can handle through referrals), you may have to dig deep to find one. Ask for recommendations at lumberyards and hardware stores, as well as at Home Depot, Lowe's, and Sears. In fact, if you need someone to install a stove or air conditioner, these large stores may be the first stop, since they generally maintain subcontractors for this sort of work. Don't forget to ask apartment building and condo managers; most of them employ their own handypeople, who may be able to moonlight or recommend a colleague.

7. **Ask the right questions.** Before you commit, ask for references, especially if your source is someone other than a trusted friend. Remember, you're letting someone into your home, so it's not just the person's skills you need to be concerned about. Ask if the person has experience in the specific job or jobs you have in mind. That may not be important if you're looking for someone to rake your leaves, but if it's anything more complicated, you want to be sure the person can handle such a job and has done so successfully in the past. Your job should not be a learning experience for the person you are hiring.

8. **Ask for credentials.** What kind of licenses, if any, does the person have? Requirements vary from state to state and even from one locale to another. If the job involves electricity or structural issues, don't take chances; call your local building inspector or town hall to find out the requirements for the job and make sure anyone you hire meets them.

9. **Verify insurance.** Generally speaking, hire only a handyperson who carries liability insurance, even if you have some coverage under your homeowner's policy. If you're hiring someone to haul away trash, you may not need to insist on this, but when you hire anyone to work in your home, you could be liable if they don't have their own insurance. If the job requires the handyperson to hire helpers, make sure those workers are provided with worker's compensation. Ask to see evidence of this insurance.

10. **Get an estimate.** Some handypeople charge by the hour, others by the job. Either way, get an estimate for what you want done and ask what factors might drive the price higher. Some states require a written estimate for jobs over a certain amount. Whether you get a written estimate or a verbal one, let the person know your upper limit for the job. You don't want any surprises.

TIP: Some jurisdictions require handypeople who perform work over a certain dollar amount (usually $1,000—$1,500) to be registered with the state. This is separate from licensing requirements. Call your local building inspector or town hall to determine the requirements for your state.

Hire a Contractor

Home improvement projects (remodeling, reroofing, electrical, and plumbing) are the top source of consumer complaints nationwide. Although there are many reliable and competent contractors out there, the risk of hiring someone who does harm to your home or wallet (not to mention your nervous system) does exist. Major structural improvements involve the largest cash outlays made on your home, so there is a lot riding on hiring the right person. No wonder most homeowners approach hiring a contractor with a good deal of trepidation. Heed these tips, and you increase the odds of finding a contractor who meets your expectations.

1. **Get referrals.** This is always the place to start. Ask family, friends, and especially neighbors who've had work done recently for names of people they were happy with.

2. **Follow the rule of three.** To do a thorough search for a contractor, you should get at least three competitive bids.

3. **Don't take anyone's word for it.** No matter how trustworthy the contractor appears to be, and no matter how happy your neighbor was with the work done, get at least three references and check them. You'd be surprised at the number of people who ask for references and never check them. Don't assume that just because a contractor gave you a handful of names and numbers the news from all of them will be positive. Even clients who were generally pleased with a contractor's work may have some useful information to share about the experience. Here are some questions to ask:

    *   Was the quality of the work and materials what you expected?
    *   Was the project completed on time and within budget?
    *   During work, did the contractor keep you informed?
    *   Did the crew and subcontractors treat your property and family respectfully?
    *   Would you hire him or her again?

4. **Inspect completed work.** Check out other projects finished by the contractor you're considering. If at all possible, visit a current job site so you can see how his crew works.

5. **Check with local officials.** Call your municipality's building-code inspection department to find out what licenses a contractor is required to carry. Determine who (you or the contractor) is required to provide workman's compensation. This varies by locality, so take nothing for granted. It is also important to ask what permits should be pulled for the job you are planning. For a variety of reasons, including the future sale of your home, it's foolish to have major work done without those permits. You don't want to work with a contractor who skips permits routinely.

6. **Check credentials.** Now that you know precisely what is required, ask your contracting candidates to show proof of license, insurance, bonding, and workman's compensation insurance. Make sure any contractor you consider will pull the permits required for your job. Don't let anyone talk you out of pulling permits and proceeding without the municipality's blessing.

7. **Don't forget the subcontractors.** If your contractor will bring in electricians, plumbers, and so forth, get it in writing that these outfits are also licensed, bonded, and insured.

8. **Ask for itemized bids.** A seasoned professional should expect to prepare an itemized bid. Look for a bid that's detailed down to the kind of nails to be used and one that lays out a step-by-step plan for performing the job. The bid should include an estimate of labor costs. Prices for labor vary somewhat, but expect the total labor cost to be about 15 percent more than the cost for materials. The cost of materials is generally about 40 percent of the total.

9. **Get it in writing.** There's a reason they call them contractors. Make sure you have a carefully and completely written contract. Never sign a blank contract or one that isn't filled out entirely. If the job is to put a new roof on your house, will the old roof be taken off? How many layers of old roofing material will be removed? Who is liable for protecting your home if it rains while the roof is off? How will that be done?

10. **Document the dates.** Have the contractor specify the date on which the job will begin and the date it will end. Don't settle for number of working days, because that leaves too much wiggle room for starting the project. It is standard to include a clause excepting rain or other circumstances beyond the contractor's control.

11. **Schedule the payments.** This detail should be included in the contract. Beware of a contractor who asks for a large percentage of the money up front. Ten percent is standard, usually followed by three payments of 25 percent evenly spaced over the duration of the project. The final 15 percent shouldn't be paid until every item on the punch list (final details you want taken care of) is complete.

12. **Read the warranties.** Be aware that a contractor's warranty covers his work only. Usually there is a separate manufacturer's warranty for the materials used. If the manufacturer's warranty stipulates a certain method of installation, talk this over with your contractor and get the details written into your contract.

Shop for a Major Home Appliance

◆◆◆

If you dread the prospect of spending big money to replace your refrigerator, washing machine, or other large appliance, take heart. There is a chrome-plated lining to this cloud. New appliances with the Energy Star rating can cut your utility bill dramatically, usually at least 30 percent. For the typical family that spends $1,500 a year on utility bills, that's a hefty $450 saving. So maybe you can afford that sleek new refrigerator with all the bells and whistles after all!

1. **Decide on must-haves.** You may not be able to make a definitive list of all the features you want until you've done some browsing, but before you leave home take the time to list product features that are essential to you. Do you insist on a gas cooktop? Does your family consider an indoor ice and water dispenser indispensable? Knowing which options interest you helps focus your shopping.

2. **Shop locally.** Don't assume you should start your shopping at the largest so-called discount store you can find. A recent survey by Consumer Reports found that smaller, independent appliance stores outperformed the big-box stores in price, service, selection, and overall customer satisfaction.

3. **Shop around.** Unless you are absolutely pressed for time because a week's worth of groceries is spoiling inside your old refrigerator, visit at least a couple of stores and compare prices, selection, and service. If nothing else, visiting a couple of stores staves off the buyer's remorse that comes from realizing you compromised when you could have purchased exactly what you wanted at the store up the road.

4. **Do the numbers.** Figure out how much you are willing to spend on your purchase. Then decide how you'd prefer to pay for it. If you're going to buy on credit, you may be able to factor in favorable financing terms as you negotiate the deal with your salesperson. This can be done at large stores as well as mom-and-pop enterprises.

5. **Make smart money choices.** If you fall in love with a fancier and higher-priced item than you were figuring on, look past the price as you weigh whether or not to purchase it. Does it come with free delivery? That's worth at least $50 at most stores. Will the store set it up and install it for free or for a minimal amount? That's worth something. How about the warranty? Do you get a better deal on parts and labor with this one than with the less pricey model? And don't forget the energy savings factor. Most appliances now come with an Energy Star rating. If the choice is between an energy-efficient appliance and one with no such claim, the efficient model will save you money over the life of the appliance.

6. **Wait for the sale.** If you have the luxury of purchasing your big-ticket item whenever you choose (that is, not racing to replace an overworked washing machine that broke that morning), you can often get a good deal by timing your purchase strategically. The new big-ticket items, such as ranges and washing machines, usually hit the sales floor in September and October. You may get a great deal on last year's model by seizing the moment when dealers are trying to clear their showrooms for the new arrivals.

Hire an Interior Decorator

Whether you are planning a major redecorating project or just want help selecting the right fabric for your old sofa, you may want to hire a professional. Although it might sound like a luxury line item, the services of an interior designer could actually save you money in the long run by heading off costly mistakes such as impractical fabric choices or extra gallons of paint. Here are some things to consider before hiring a decorator and some tips on finding the right one for your project.

1. **Consider the scope and purpose of your project.** Whether you're working on one room or the entire house, give some thought to how you will be using the space you're decorating. Design considerations should include more than your favorite color choices: a rambunctious family of nine requires a very different decorating approach from a couple that entertains formally and frequently.

2. **Give some thought to your budget.** Although you may not know yet how much to expect your project to cost, set an upper limit on what you're willing and able to spend. As you're doing this, take into consideration how long you expect to occupy this space. For example, if you move every few years, you may not want to spend a large chunk of your budget on custom window treatments that will stay behind.

3. **Invest some time and money on shelter magazines.** Even if you don't usually daydream over interior-decorating magazines, now is the time to do it. Get in the habit of ripping out pages whenever you spot an interior that appeals to you. Don't worry about the details at this point; your goal is to make discoveries about your own likes and dislikes. If you do this long enough, you'll begin to see a pattern in your choices and learn more than you thought possible about your own taste and preferences. This information will be extremely useful in your initial meetings with the designer.

4. **Locate some candidates.** The Website for the American Society of Interior Designers (ASID) has a "find a designer" link and can be a great place to start. You may also get some good direction from the Franklin Report (*www.franklinreport.com*), a regional guide to interior designers. If you are on a very tight budget (and are willing to be adventurous), call the

interior design department at your local university or vocational school. You may find a talented student able to take on your design project for credit toward a degree.

5. **Interview designers.** Ask about hands-on experience as well as education and training and ask to examine the designer's portfolio. Definitely request a list of relevant references and check them carefully. Find out what services the designer has access to—furnishings, upholstery, carpentry, picture framing, etc.—and what the markup will be. Discuss your deadlines, and do a reality check on your time line to make sure the designer can work within your timetable.

6. **Check the chemistry.** Pay attention to your comfort level with the designer as a person. Because you will be working closely on a fairly intimate project, it's vital that you can communicate comfortably and feel that your priorities and concerns are taken seriously.

7. **Base your selection on a variety of factors.** Don't just go with the lowest estimate. Take into account your aesthetic and functional goals and consider how well each proposal seems to meet them.

TIP: The terms *designer* and *decorator* are often used interchangeably. The technical difference is that interior designers are formally trained and must pass a national test. They're also licensed by the state, which is relevant if you have a bad experience and want to press for financial redress.

HOW INTERIOR DESIGNERS CHARGE FOR THEIR SERVICES

According to the American Society of Interior Designers, there is no such thing as a "typical" or "customary" fee. The cost of an interior designer varies based on everything from her experience and reputation to the client's unique requirements. Generally, a designer's fees are based on one, or a combination, of the following methods:

By the hour. The charge can range from $50 to $250 an hour, depending on the designer and the region of the country.

Fixed or flat fee. Some designers name a sum to cover all costs, excluding reimbursement for expenses. Others may charge an upfront, nonrefundable fee.

Cost plus. This fee structure is based on the designer's purchase of materials, furnishings, and services at cost and reselling them to the client at an agreed-upon markup. At one time, this was the customary method of compensation for designers, but hourly fees plus a designer's markup for material and whole-project flat fees are becoming increasingly common.

Stock a Reference Library

◆◆◆

Every home library should have certain basic reference books, including but not limited to a good English dictionary, an encyclopedia, an atlas, and an almanac or yearbook. In addition to these, you should consider a book on etiquette, a basic home-repair book, possibly a French or Spanish dictionary, and a medical encyclopedia, so long as you don't confuse it with a sound medical education followed by years of residency training. Your special interests will dictate the rest. Here are the basics.

1. **Dictionary.** Look for standard editions, but be aware that the word *Webster's* isn't protected, so any company can use it in a title for any dictionary, even an old, warmed-over one. Check the copyright to make sure the dictionary you choose is newly updated. It should include new terms and up-to-date usage. Compare definitions for a couple of new tech terms to see which dictionary is most up-to-date. You can also compare dictionaries by reading the definition of the same word in each of them and considering which style of definition you prefer. Some dictionaries list the most common usage first; others list definitions in historical order. Finally, make sure your choice of dictionary has these other important features: clear pronunciation guide, list of biographical names, list of geographical names, and a brief style or grammar guide.

2. **Encyclopedia.** There are two basic choices: a multivolume set, which is costly and takes up lots of room (although you could purchase a CD-ROM version), or a single-volume encyclopedia, which sacrifices detail for affordability and a handy size. As with dictionaries, check the copyright to get an up-to-date version.

3. **Atlas.** These range from the elaborate, beautiful, heavy, and pricey to the compact, soft-cover, and affordable. Copyright is key, since an atlas, like a dictionary, can become obsolete with each new war and revolution. Decide what features you want in addition to standard maps: some atlases include demographic and economic data, topographic maps, and information about agriculture and weather patterns, all of which may or may not be of interest to you.

4. **Almanac or yearbook.** These terms are pretty interchangeable, although almanacs are often more eclectic in the information they provide, while yearbooks focus on basic country data and highlights of the news of the year. These need to be renewed each year, so stick with paperback editions.

5. **Video/movie guide.** Make sure you get the current year's guide and that it's cross-referenced by title, actors, and directors.

6. **Basic cookbook.** Unless you entertain at McDonald's and limit home cooking to microwavable pouches, you need at least one basic cookbook. In addition to recipes, this book should contain such handy basics as a roasting chart, carving tips, explanations of different grains and pastas, and cooking times for various meats and vegetables. It might even cover the essentials of cake baking.

GREAT SPECIAL-INTEREST WEBSITES

The Web, of course, is an infinite source of information. You might want to add these sites to your favorites folder.

American history. An exhaustive source of information on American history is at *www.ku.edu/carrie/docs/amdocs_index.html*. The site is organized by date from before the European discovery of America to the present day. It includes original sources as well as historical interpretations and outlines.

Biography. "Biography," the A&E program, maintains a Website with more than 25,000 entries at *www.biography.com*.

Business and economics. A comprehensive source of information about people, companies, and virtually all things business-related is *www.business.com*, which has links to other key sites arranged by topic.

Census and demographic information. The government's Website, *www.factfinder.census.gov*, is an endless resource for genealogy and general historical research.

General. Two priceless sites are *www.wikipedia.org* and *www.howstuffworks.com*. Wikipedia, a new phenomenon, is a free, Web-based encyclopedia to which anyone can contribute. By early 2006 it had more than 3 million articles on just about everything under—and above—the sun. As with any source, you should not count on Wikipedia for 100 percent accuracy. On technical subjects it has a slightly higher error rate than Britannica, the other large and popular Web based information site. Howstuffworks.com is the place to go for explanations about the way things work. Check out a few examples: "How does lock picking work?" "How does the stock market work?" "How does soap work?"

Law and legal issues. Go to *www.findlaw.com* for legal information by category, such as car accidents, estate planning, consumer law, marriage law, business law, and immigration. This site includes definitions, tips, and downloadable forms.

Language and literature. Texts, references, and verse are found, free, at *www.bartleby.com*. Another good general book site is onlinebooks.library.upenn.edu/ (enter it just this way, without "www").

Maps, country information, etc. If you don't have an atlas, find maps and other geographical information at *www.atlapedia.com*.

Medicine and health. Healthopedia (*www.healthopedia.com*) is a gateway to a huge collection of information on everything from alcohol abuse to Zollinger-Ellison Syndrome.

Movies. Internet Movie Database (*www.imdb.com*) is the first site to check for information about movies. You'll find everything from a complete list of screen credits to fascinating trivia to movie reviews written by professional critics and other imdb.com users.

Sports and recreation. ESPN (espn.go.com) and Sports Illustrated (sportsillustrated.cnn.com) are both linked to their respective television programs and provide comprehensive news about all sports subjects, including scores and background information on teams and players.

Weather. Accu Weather (*www.accuweather.com*) provides detailed information about weather, including maps, local forecasts, radar views, and breaking weather news.

7. **Thesaurus.** If you do any writing, personal or professional, a thesaurus is extremely handy. A thesaurus may be organized alphabetically or by category; your choice is a matter of personal preference. It's best not to rely exclusively on the rather limited virtual thesaurus in your word-processing system.

8. **Book of quotations.** The bigger the better. As with a thesaurus, how a book of quotations is arranged determines how easy it is to use. The most useful, generally, is a book arranged by topic or category. Look for a keyword index in addition to an author or source index.

[Housework and Other]
Emergencies

Go from Pigsty to Presentable, Pronto!

◆◆◆

Company is coming in half an hour, and your living room appears to have been tossed by a gang of burglars. The bathroom isn't looking particularly fresh either, is it? Don't worry; there's no need for top-to-bottom cleaning. All you really need to do is spiff up the public areas—generally the living room and the guest bathroom—making them look as attractive and welcoming as possible. Here's how to achieve maximum results with a minimum of time and energy.

1. **Clear the decks.** It is amazing what a ruthless round of tidying can achieve. Move through the living room quickly, picking up every item that doesn't belong there. Carry a large bag or laundry basket to perform this task more efficiently.

2. **Dump and close.** Decide which room of your home can accommodate the detritus and deposit the miscellany from the living room in there. Shut the door.

3. **Fluff and straighten.** Smooth slipcovers, fluff throw pillows, stack magazines and books neatly, arrange lamps and knickknacks attractively. Take a moment to survey the room. With the clutter removed and the remaining furniture and decorative items placed artfully, you are almost finished.

4. **Clean sparingly.** If you see actual dust bunnies, dead plant leaves, large pieces of lint or the like lying around, scoop them up with a wet paper towel. If you own pets and the upholstery appears to have a pelt of its own, put on a latex glove, dampen it, and run your gloved hand over the fur. As it rolls right up, put the fur in a paper trash bag (the fur will cling to plastic bags and be hard to manage). Use a Dust Buster® to pick up any leftover clumps.

5. **Make the bathroom sparkle.** It takes only a couple of minutes to make the bathroom gleam impressively. If the toilet looks unsanitary, pour in a little bleach and let it sit while you clean the rest. Remove the soap or anything else sitting on the sink and cover all the surfaces with spray-on bathroom cleanser (or simply wipe with treated disposable cloth (see "Stock Cleaning Supplies," page 223). Scrub or wipe until the dirt lifts and the sink sparkles. Rinse. Polish the faucet and handles with a paper

towel. Twirl the toilet bowl brush around a few times and flush. If the bathroom mirror, the top of the toilet tank, or other surfaces look grungy, wipe them with a paper towel. Put out a clean hand towel for your guest.

6. **Pat yourself on the back.** You have finished your household drudgery in record time. Everything that will be seen looks presentable. Don't worry about the rest until tomorrow.

Make Dinner from Thin Air

Whether you work at home or commute to an office, coming up with an acceptable dinner each evening can become a dreary chore. Keeping a cleverly stocked pantry and refrigerator eliminates some of the fuss and drudgery of cooking when you're exhausted, hungry, and short on time. Before you dash off to the grocery store with the shopping list that follows, think about the tips below and get ready for creative and stress-free meal planning.

1. **Forget the brown thing, white thing, green thing "rule."** Back in the old days, this formula governed the evening meal: Meat loaf, mashed potatoes, and peas. Pork chops, rice, string beans. You get the idea. A hearty salad with or without bread on the side can be a satisfying—and easy—meal.

2. **Look to the Big Three.** Canned, frozen, and dried foods are helpful working basics. If you have a variety of items in each of these categories, you have the makings of a satisfying and presentable meal.

3. **Dare to serve what you feel like eating.** If it's summer, and you're in the mood for corn on the cob and sliced tomatoes with mozzarella, go for it. If it's winter, and you want something cozy like a hot casserole but don't feel like messing with vegetables or salad, the family won't get scurvy or rickets because you served an imbalanced meal one night.

4. **Serve other meals for dinner.** Omelets or pancakes sound like fun tonight? Soup and sandwich more appealing than standard dinner fare? Rest assured, the Food Police have better things to do than break down your door if you feed the family breakfast or lunch at dinnertime.

5. **Think of balancing the week, not the meal.** In other words, you can feel free to wing it every now and then as long as you're not alternating nights of canned soup and Fruit Loops(tm). If you do serve up pancakes one night and a salad the next, a dinner with protein and vegetables the following evening will settle the score.

SHOPPING LIST

Pantry Items

Pasta, rice, and couscous. Stock whatever kinds you like, of course, but consider keeping both short and long pastas on hand for variety. Orzo is a rice-sized pasta that can be a wonderful base for an easy meal. Rice comes in a variety of flavors: consider basmati and jasmine for a slightly exotic effect. Stay away from instant rice, unless you don't mind stuff that tastes like the box it came in. Couscous takes almost no time at all. Boil the water, add the grains, and steam for one minute. This Middle Eastern grain can be a side dish or yet another base for a one-dish dinner.

Beans. Add beans and vegetables to pasta, rice, or couscous and presto! You have a hearty dish with no meat. Garbanzo beans, also known as chickpeas, are great for this, but black, kidney, pinto, and cannelloni (Italian white) beans are all reliable and good. Refried beans can make a quick casserole: Grate cheese on top and heat in the microwave.

Canned tuna, salmon, sardines, clams. Toss any of these into commercially made pasta sauce, and you're almost there.

Bottled pasta sauce. Experiment until you find one your family likes.

Bottled salsa. Add to chili or on top of that refried beans casserole!

Canned tomatoes. Buy tomatoes chopped or crushed in their own juice. You can add these to pasta or rice for a no-cook sauce or use them as a base to create your own sauce. Add them to a can of soup to stretch and zip it up. Sauté an onion with garlic, chili powder, and cumin, stir in the tomatoes with your favorite beans, and the next thing you know, you have a pot of meatless chili.

Oils and vinegars. Olive oil and balsamic vinegar are excellent basics for salad dressing and seasonings for vegetables. Keep a lighter-flavored oil such as canola on hand for sautéing or making salad dressings with a more neutral flavor. Spray-on oil is very good for greasing skillets and roasting vegetables.

Soy sauce, Dijon mustard, fresh garlic. Nobody needs to know how much preparing dinner bores you. Add a dash of any of these to whatever you're preparing to disguise your state of mind.

Herbs and spices. The variety of spices at the grocery store can make the noncook nonplussed. There are dozens to choose from, but you can get by very nicely with just a few. Start with oregano, basil, thyme, rosemary, cinnamon, curry powder, chili powder, cumin, and cayenne pepper. Salt and black pepper, too, of course.

Raisins. Golden raisins are especially useful, if your family likes them. You can put them in salads for a sweet surprise or add them to couscous with garbanzo beans to conjure the taste of far-off lands.

Canned chicken or vegetable broth. Prepackaged broth (preferably low-salt) enables you to add a bit of extra flavor to rice or couscous (use it instead of water) or gives you the makings of homemade soup (see "Five No-Brainer Dinners," page 221).

Refrigerator and Freezer

Eggs. Never underestimate the simple elegance of an herb and cheese omelet for dinner.

Butter or margarine. You can freeze butter and pop it into the microwave to soften or melt it as needed.

Plain yogurt. For a quick sauce that will add protein as well as flavor to rice or potatoes, mix 1/4 cup of extra virgin olive oil to a cup of plain yogurt. Add pressed or minced garlic and maybe some thyme, basil, or oregano, depending on what else you're preparing. This sauce is as good on fish or chicken as it is on rice. For an extra-healthy variation, use non- or low-fat plain yogurt.

Cheese. A tightly wrapped wedge of Parmesan will keep for weeks in your refrigerator and do wonders for that bottled pasta sauce. Avoid the variety that comes already grated in round cardboard containers and tastes like something you swept from under the bed. Jack and cheddar cheeses don't keep as well as the drier Parmesan, but they are worth having on hand. Grilled cheese sandwiches and tomato soup are almost everybody's favorite comfort food. Diced cheese adds protein to salads. Cheese slices make good snacks, and grated soft cheeses taste good on anything from toast to soup.

Nuts. Pecans and pine nuts are favorite freezer secrets. Walnuts, of course, can also be a welcome addition to salads, pastas, and casseroles. Toast the nuts lightly in a dry frying pan for a few minutes, or heat them on a cookie sheet in a 350-degree oven. Taking the extra moments to toast nuts pays huge dividends in flavor.

Onions. Stock red for salads and white or yellow for sautéing, although the latter can also go in salads.

Potatoes. Baked sweet or russet potatoes can be the centerpiece of a light, yet satisfying, meal. Top with any or all of the above: yogurt, salsa, cheese, beans, and chopped onions. You can even make quick and healthy "French fries" by spraying cut-up sweet or russets with oil and baking them at a high temperature (400 degrees) for about twenty minutes.

Bagged, whole baby carrots. Steam these to serve as a side dish or chop and add to salads. They're also handy to fend off the starving multitudes waiting impatiently for the main event.

Bread and rolls. If you have a big family and go through bread like General Sherman through Georgia, you won't need to refrigerate bread, which dries it out but retards mold. If you use less than a loaf every five days, however, keep bread in the fridge or, perhaps, the freezer.

Frozen vegetables. If you like spinach, buy it in large bags to pour out what you need. You can microwave or sauté frozen spinach and later add a dash of olive oil and salt and pepper for flavor. Other frozen vegetables, including broccoli florets, peas, string beans, and corn, are great for emergencies, but don't forget that fresh vegetables are as easy as rinsing, trimming, and steaming. The trick is to have them on hand. When you don't have fresh, frozen can be an ace up your sleeve.

Chicken sausages. You can buy and freeze fully cooked chicken sausages in a variety of flavors. Apple and chicken, sun-dried tomato and pesto, garlic and cilantro . . . the list goes on. Check your grocer's meat counter above the poultry. The great thing about these sausages, besides their taste, is that they're fully cooked and need only pan sautéing or microwaving to heat.

Chicken breasts, hamburger patties. Freeze these individually so you don't have to thaw a block of meat or an iceberg of chicken when you need only a meal for one. Always thaw meat and poultry in the microwave or refrigerator. Thawing at room temperature is an engraved invitation for bacteria of the very scary kind.

TIP: Eight ounces of uncooked pasta yields four cups cooked. If you are feeding a family of four hearty eaters, boil a full pound of pasta. If pasta is a side dish, figure on half that amount.

FIVE NO-BRAINER DINNERS

Chicken Soup. It's not just for colds. Heat a large (48-ounce) can of chicken broth and add diced chicken (leftover or canned), frozen vegetables, herbs, a dash of cayenne pepper, and diced potatoes or cooked rice. Simmer until the vegetables are tender. This will make four to six hearty servings.

Moroccan Sausages. For four servings, boil two cups of water and add one teaspoon each of cumin and curry powder, plus one-fourth teaspoon cayenne pepper (or to your taste). Meanwhile, sauté one or two packages of chicken sausages until heated through. (The sausages generally come four to a package. If you slice them, you can get away with fewer whole sausages.) Drain an eleven-ounce can of garbanzo beans and sauté with the sausage to heat. When the water has boiled, remove it from the heat, stir in one and three-quarter cups of couscous and a handful of golden raisins. Cover and let it sit for one minute, until the water is absorbed, then fluff with a fork as you pour it into the pan with the sausages and garbanzos. Stir well to mix. You can serve this with a salad, or you can sauté frozen vegetables with the sausages for a complete one-dish meal.

Orzo with Roasted Vegetables. Okay, for this one you need fresh vegetables. Just use your favorites, but to get you started here are some ideas: Try eggplant, onions, carrots, squash (zucchini, yellow, or winter squash, such as acorn or butternut), parsnips, asparagus, or tomatoes. Know that denser vegetables like carrots, parsnips, and winter squash take longer to roast than the moister, lighter-weight variety, so cut the denser vegetables smaller. Spray vegetables with oil and crumble herbs like oregano and basil over the top. Peel a few garlic cloves and toss them into the pan. Roast at a high temperature—400 degrees—for about thirty minutes, or until vegetables are as tender and browned as you like them. Stir once or twice as they cook. Onions become sweet and delicious when they've been allowed to cook until brown around the edges. As you put the veggies in to roast, boil a large pot of water and add a teaspoon or so of salt. When the water boils, add the orzo (a pound for a family of four) and boil about ten to twelve minutes, until it's tender. Drain, toss it with the vegetables, and add grated Parmesan or any cheese you like. If this is the main course for a family of four, you might use this generous assortment of vegetables: one medium eggplant, one large onion, one large tomato, one bunch asparagus (ends snapped off), one package mushrooms. Note: Use a large roasting pan so that you can spread the veggies out in one layer.

Quick Chili. It's almost redundant to say quick chili, because chili is a dish you can prepare with little time and fuss. To serve four, chop an onion and a clove or two of garlic. Sauté one pound of ground beef with the onion until the beef is just browned and the onion is translucent. Toss in the garlic and sauté for about thirty seconds. Add one twelve-ounce can each of chopped tomatoes and drained pinto, black, or kidney beans, and stir in about one teaspoon each of cumin, chili powder, and cayenne pepper (to taste). Simmer for about ten minutes or until the beef is cooked through and the mixture is hot. Drain off any fat before serving. You can omit the beef and serve your vegetarian chili over rice for a filling, meatless meal. To cut the fat content, consider substituting ground turkey for the beef. Be sure to spray the pan with cooking oil first.

Pasta and sauce. Or, as the Soprano family calls it, macaroni and gravy. Boil water for pasta and add one teaspoon of salt. As the pasta is cooking (angel hair/capellini takes only a couple of minutes; spaghetti, penne, and the denser pastas take ten to twelve minutes), pour bottled pasta sauce into a bowl and heat in the microwave. Toast a handful of pine nuts in a dry skillet to garnish your dish with flair. Garbanzo beans will make this more filling and provide a complete protein with the pasta. Serve sautéed or microwaved spinach with garlic on the side.

Stock Cleaning Supplies

◆◆◆

If you are reading this list, it may be safe to assume you're not a domestic diva whose idea of a good time is ironing sheets and finding new ways to make appliances shine. Instead, you're more likely to be someone interested in learning the bare minimum of equipment and supplies you need to make cleaning easy and, therefore, more likely to get done. This list is for you.

1. **Cleaning gloves.** These are must-haves for cleaning enthusiasts and phobics alike. Disposable latex gloves protect your hands from harsh cleansers, and they give you courage to tackle jobs you'd normally shrink from, like cleaning up pet accidents and wiping muck out of trash cans.

2. **Vacuum cleaner.** There's no getting around it: You should own one of these. A good quality vacuum is the best device for keeping your floors and rugs clean while expending a minimum of your time and energy. If you have allergies, invest in a vacuum cleaner with a HEPA filter. Canister vacuums store easily and can be powerful enough for most jobs. Uprights tend to take up more storage room and require more changes of attachments for vacuuming anything other than the floor (such as the upholstery).

3. **Small handheld vacuum.** Although it isn't a must-have, a Dust Buster™ can come in handy for picking up small dry messes, such as spilled flour and cookie crumbs.

4. **Feather duster.** These are great for quickly dusting books, knickknacks, and other small or delicate items you'd rather not move.

5. **Toilet brush.** Left alone, the bowl will grow unpleasant rings at the water line. You can purchase an inexpensive toilet brush, complete with its own holder, in most grocery stores. Stash a brush behind each toilet in the house to make the occasional cleaning more convenient—and therefore more likely.

6. **Disposable cleaning wipes.** These pretreated wipes are a dream come true for the minimalist cleaner: no mess, no fuss. Everything you need is soaked right into these handy individual wipes. There's a special wipe for cleaning virtually any room or surface in your home, from the bathroom and kitchen to wood floors and table tops. Keep a package of

bathroom wipes under the sink. Pull a couple out and have a go at the tub, toilet exterior, the sink, and faucet. Kitchen wipes multitask in a similar way: They will clean and shine everything from countertops to appliances.

7. **Sponge mop.** For those occasions when the entire kitchen or bathroom floor is dirty and the minimalist method just won't do, you should have a sponge mop. You can find inexpensive sponge mops with aluminum squeezers attached at most grocery and household specialty stores.

8. **Liquid all-purpose floor soap.** The brand is up to you, but odor and nontoxicity may be important considerations. Some disinfectant detergents leave behind a sharp pine smell that some people consider unpleasant. You might consider choosing one of the citrus-based "green" cleansers, which are nontoxic, biodegradable, and pleasantly scented, provided you like the odor of orange and lemon.

9. **Bleach.** This good old-fashioned standby is an excellent cleaner for numerous jobs, but if you have a septic system you should never put it down your drains. For those connected to town or city sewer lines, bleach disinfects and cleans toilet bowls, keeps drains running free (pour half a cup of bleach into each drain every few weeks and follow with a cup of boiling water), removes mildew from shower curtains and tub caulking (dilute one part bleach to three parts water in a spray bottle), and lifts most rust stains from porcelain sinks and tubs (use full strength). To clean the toilet bowl, pour in half a cup of bleach, let it sit while you clean the rest of the room, then swish away rings and soil with the toilet brush and flush. Wear an apron and gloves when using bleach, and be careful, fabrics can easily acquire ghostly spots wherever bleach has splashed.

10. **Sponges or paper towels.** The true minimalist will prefer to wipe spills with a damp paper towel, which can be thrown away. The more conservation-minded might prefer a sponge, which can be rinsed and reused many times before becoming landfill. If you do use sponges, rinse them thoroughly and allow them to dry after each use to prevent bacteria buildup and mildew. Replace sponges frequently.

Do the Laundry So You Can Recognize It Afterward

◆◆◆

Have you ever wondered where the crease from your permanent-crease slacks went after you took the laundry out of the machine? How the pink tint got on your white underwear? Why the sweater you wore last week looks like it might fit a Chihuahua this week? Solve those mysteries and more by following this simple checklist. You'll be delighted to find that the laundry coming out of the machine looks just like the laundry that went in, minus the dirt and grime.

1. **Read the label.** If you're in luck, it will say "dry-clean only," in which case, you're done (see "Interpreting Fabric Care Symbols," page 228). The label might say, "Wash in cold water" or the dreaded "Hand wash." Following the label instructions can preserve your clothes a little longer and make ironing less likely. You can often get away with washing "hand-wash" items on the delicate cycle in your machine, but if you try that shortcut, be sure to follow the instructions in number 7, below: "Pick load level, water temperature, fabric cycle."

2. **Sort the obvious.** Decisions, decisions. It seems simple: separate dark colors from light. But even here you may be stumped. Is sky-blue light or dark? What about pale orange? When in doubt, assume colors will bleed and keep them far away from whites.

3. **Sort some more.** There's more to sorting then separating light from dark. Delicate items can be segregated into a mesh bag to keep them from snagging, tangling, and unraveling altogether. Think about separating synthetics from natural fibers; mixing them can lead to pilling. Also, try not to mix very heavy items, like bath towels and jeans, with light ones, like blouses. Mighty wrinkles can result. If you have items that are really filthy, wash them separately; everything will come out cleaner in the end. And anything covered in something that migrates, like pet hair or grass clippings, or that naturally sheds, like fluffy bathroom rugs, deserves a machine all to itself.

4. **Check pockets.** A pocketful of used or virgin tissues can be a prelude to a long afternoon of picking tiny pieces of lint off a mountain of laun-

dry; a fountain pen clipped to a shirt pocket can seriously compromise an entire load; and the smallest crayon hidden deep in a child's pocket can render everything bright orange (or virtually any color known to Crayola™). A bank check can cause heartbreak if it goes through the entire cycle and comes out illegible, which it surely will if it was written for a substantial sum.

5. **Consider zippers and buttons.** Zippers should be zipped to prevent their catching on other items, but experts disagree about whether buttons should be buttoned or not. Shirts and blouses, unless still on your back, are probably unbuttoned; just leave them like that, unless fiddling with buttons seems like a good way to spend spare time. You might check collars and cuffs and unbutton them if they aren't already undone. Some laundry experts say this assures better cleaning and fewer wrinkles; another school considers it a waste of time. If the shirt or blouse needs ironing, having the buttons undone will make that job go faster.

6. **Treat stains.** Left to themselves, stains become immortal. Fortunately, you can kill them if you act quickly and decisively. Use either a pretreatment stick or a spray-on enzyme product, which act particularly well on biodegradable stains. Another option is to saturate the stain with liquid detergent. Whatever method you use, do it as soon as possible after the stain shows up. Let your chosen product remain on the clothing a few minutes before the wash and don't rinse it off.

7. **Pick load level, water temperature, fabric cycle.** Most machines give you choices for all three. Here are some ideas on what to pick.

   - *Use cold water for bright colors and delicates.*
   - *Use warm water for most other loads.* Warm water cleans better and faster than cold, and it helps remove wrinkles. Warm water is best for permanent-press items, colorfast darks, synthetics, and washable wools (unless the label says to use cold). Bleach works better with warm water than with cold.
   - *Avoid hot water.* It can yellow whites and has little advantage over warm water.
   - *Use a cold-water rinse cycle.* Cold water helps reduce the soapy residue.
   - *Don't choose an overly long cycle.* Eight minutes is usually the optimum wash cycle; longer cycles can actually redeposit soil on clothes.

8. **Measure your detergent.** Generally speaking, follow the directions on the detergent. Using too much can leave a soapy residue, while skimping can leave clothes less than brilliantly clean. Most manufacturers of top-loading machines recommend that you add the detergent first, then the clothes. If you have the patience, start the water and wait until the soap has mixed a bit before tossing in your wash items.

9. **Add the clothes.** Stuffing the machine full leads to spotty cleaning, wrinkles, and, if you're really unlucky, mechanical failure and massive repair bills. You won't save much money or time in the long run if your clothes get less than optimally clean, or, worst case, if you damage the machine by taxing its capacity.

10. **Be careful with additives.** If you add bleach, make sure your clothes can take it. Memorize the international symbol warning against the use of bleach (it looks like a black tepee with crossed sticks in front). Use liquid bleach only on whites, and even then, use it with caution; too much bleach can break down fibers and damage fabrics. Never use bleach on woolens, silk, or treated cotton. All-color bleach, as its name implies, is good for colorfast clothing and can actually make colors more vivid while brightening whites, but not always. If the label says no chlorine bleach, or if you know the colors run, don't use even the nonchlorine all-color bleach. If your machine has a liquid bleach dispenser, pour the measured bleach slowly into the dispenser only after the machine has filled and is agitating. If you don't have a separate bleach dispenser, just pour the bleach into the filled and agitating machine. In either case, the bleach should be added before you add the clothes. The same goes for fabric softeners: Either put it in the fabric softener dispenser or add the softener to the water before you add the clothes.

11. **Dry the clothes.** Don't let the load sit for hours in the washer unless ironing is your hobby. Remove the clothes and transfer them to the dryer as soon as the wash is done. Take the time to shake out shirts, blouses, and slacks; it shortens drying time and helps prevent wrinkles. Don't overload. Since dryers usually have larger capacities than washers, you probably won't have that problem if you dry just one load at a time. Keep these tips in mind:

- *Clean the lint screen before each cycle to prevent fire.*
- *Check care labels again.* Some clothes should be dried flat or on a line.

- *Don't just stuff everything in.* Separate items and give shirts, blouses, and slacks a few snaps of the wrist.

- *Use the cool-down setting, if your dryer has one, to minimize wrinkles.*

- *Throw in a fabric softening sheet to further discourage wrinkles and prevent static cling.*

- *Don't let clothes sit in the dryer.* Remove and fold them as soon as possible after the cycle.

INTERPRETING FABRIC CARE SYMBOLS

Fabric care symbols on clothing labels can be baffling. If you didn't know better, you might think they were some kind of hieroglyphics. Actually, they are the U.S. Federal Trade Commission's earnest attempt to communicate the best way to launder garments. Some of the most common are listed below with explanations. A diagonal slash through any of these means don't use that method on the garment in question.

Wash. You'll see variations on what looks like a crown. It's actually a tiny washing tub with wavy water at the top.

Bleach. This is a triangle, reminiscent of the radiation symbol for fallout shelters. To be safe, consider bleach the equivalent of a dose of radiation for your clothes. Use it sparingly and with caution.

Dry. A simple square, modeled perhaps on a dryer.

Iron. This symbol actually resembles an iron, especially your grandmother's, or great-grandmother's, flat iron.

Dry-clean. Circle.

[Flowers and Plants]

Collect Basic Gardening Tools

◆◆◆

If you love to garden, or think you might, treat yourself to a collection of the best-quality basic gardening tools you can afford. Don't bother with expensive power tools that get used only once a year, such as aerators and thatchers; these can be rented. Spend what you can on quality tools so that you can use them year after year and spend more time enjoying your garden and less time slaving over it. Pay particular attention to how well tools are made. Well-made tools are safer and more comfortable to use than poorly made ones, and they are likely to last much longer. Look for tools on which the blade or metal head are welded to a socket that fits up around the handle, not stuck directly into the handle, where it will soon come loose. If the metal part wriggles even slightly, don't buy it. Also, don't buy any tool you haven't held in your hand, imitating the motions you'd use in the garden. If the weight, shape, and overall feel of the tool isn't right, you probably won't use it.

1. **Standard shovel.** The shovel is the mainstay of garden tools. Use it for digging and for lifting and moving loose material. Choose a shovel with a round point; a square-point shovel is handy for moving larger amounts of material, but not for digging. If you plan on doing a lot of digging, look for a round shovel with a wider rim at the top; this will make it easier to use your feet for extra leverage. Taller people might consider a shovel with a long handle.

2. **Spade.** Essentially a small shovel, spades come in a variety of shapes. A garden spade is good for such basic chores as cutting and digging. Because it's smaller than a standard shovel, a spade is lighter and can handle more delicate jobs in tighter spaces. If you can afford a second spade, get a drain, or trench spade, which is even narrower and can be used in even tighter spaces.

3. **Spade fork.** Also known as a pitchfork, this is the tool you use to turn over soil and prepare beds for planting.

4. **Trowel.** A miniature spade, a trowel is essential for planting both annuals and perennials and for digging out weeds. You might want to have two of these: a narrow one for weeding and planting bulbs, and a broad one for flowers and seedlings.

5. **Hand cultivator.** This tool has either three or five prongs and is great for loosening soil around plants and for weeding. Choose one that's twelve to eighteen inches long; shorter ones are hard to use.

6. **Rake.** A bamboo rake is inexpensive and gentle on grass and plants. If you will be smoothing new or existing beds, get a ground rake as well. Ground rakes have a metal head and can be used to help aerate.

7. **Pruner.** A bypass pruner is essential for keeping plants under control. It works like a scissors, cutting stems cleanly without crushing them. To prune small branches, you need an anvil pruner, which has two blades, one sharp and one dull; the sharp blade comes down on a branch, while the anvil blade holds it in place.

8. **Watering can.** Use a watering can for small areas or on delicate plants that the stream from a hose might harm. Choose one with a two-gallon capacity to save steps and with a brass spout for durability.

9. **Large plastic trash can.** Make sure it's light, so you can easily drag it around with you. Plastic bags without the can blow around, turn inside out, and do everything they can to be infuriating.

10. **Gloves.** Unless you would like to display your dirty, scratched, and bleeding hands as testimony to your diligent work in the garden, buy at least one pair of good garden gloves. You won't be able to wear them all the time, but when doing cleanup work or dealing with thorny bushes or woody plants, you'll be glad you have them.

11. **Knee pads.** These save wear and tear on clothes and kneecaps.

12. **Wheelbarrow.** Either a plastic or metal wheelbarrow is fine, but make sure the one you choose has rubber wheels that won't go flat.

Grow Hardy Houseplants

There is hope for the horticulturally challenged. Although it may take a certain talent to coax temperamental orchids to flower year after year, some plants virtually grow themselves. Unless you actually plot against them, the following plants will survive just about anything short of fire or flood.

1. **Jade plant** *(Crassula argenea)*. With fleshy leaves and a trunklike stem, the jade plant can be thought of as a bonsai without the bother. It can grow as tall as three feet and just as wide. A jade wants at least a little natural light, and if it gets full sun the leaves often acquire an attractive red border. It likes to be watered sparingly, when the top soil is dry.

2. **African violet** *(Saintoaulia ionatha)*. One of the easiest-to-grow flowering plants, the African violet likes moist soil and light, either natural or artificial. The key to keeping this plant healthy is to fertilize it lightly each time you water, using a liquid fertilizer specially made for African violets, and to water only when the top of the soil is dry to your touch. Avoid wetting the leaves as you water and never water the center of the plant.

3. **Spider plant** *(Chlorophytum comosum)*. Really hard to kill, the spider plant is good for hanging baskets. It sprouts wiry stems with white flowers and little plantlets, which, if they touch soil, become new spider plants. Just make sure your spider plant doesn't invade your entire house, displacing other plants, children, animals, and humans. The spider plant does well in bright light, but full sunlight will burn the leaves. Water it at least once a week, but make sure the soil isn't getting soaked. The plant only needs to be fed every three to four months. If you use fertilizer every time you water your plants, dilute to half strength when you get to Spidey. Sturdy as they are, these plants can be sensitive to chemicals in tap water. If the tips of the leaves turn brown, switch to distilled or rainwater.

4. **Pothos** *(Epipremnum aureum)*. This is a lovely vine with green or variegated leaves that needs very little light, so it can creep across a bookcase or hang from a basket. Just water when the top soil is dry, and a pothos will live contentedly for years.

5. **Snake plant** *(Sansevieria trifasciata)*. This plant is also known by the frightening name Mother-in-law's Tongue, but that's a misnomer because it is actually a tolerant, easy-going plant that makes few demands on its hosts. It likes to dry out between waterings and even prefers to be root-bound, so it doesn't need to be repotted as it matures.

6. **Cast iron plant** *(Aspidistra elatior)*. As its name implies, this is one tough plant, renowned for its ability to withstand abuse and neglect. It has long pointed leaves, and one variety is striped. Give it tough love: Let it dry out between soakings and don't fertilize.

7. **Azalea** *(Rhododendron)*. This plant, with its abundant flowers, thrives in cool conditions with plenty of indirect light, although it can summer outdoors so long as it doesn't get too hot. Keep it evenly moist, but don't let it get waterlogged.

8. **Wandering Jew** *(Zebrine pendula)*. Equally at home with all denominations—as well as secular humanists and wiccans—the wandering Jew is a great hanging plant, with green or variegated leaves, and, from time to time, small lavender, three-petaled flowers. It likes some morning and evening sun but does quite well in just about any light conditions short of extremes of sun or shade. Fertilize with balanced liquid fertilizer once a month, and trim strands that turn brown to encourage new growth.

9. **Parlor palm** *(Chamaedorea elegans)*. If palms make you think of Miami, think again. This one, with its tropical-looking fronds, tolerates low light. Water sparingly and don't water until the soil is quite dry at least two inches down.

10. **Philodendron.** There are many species of philodendron, each with its own leaf shape and color. Some climb, others just sit there as a shrub. A native of South American jungles, this plant likes the filtered light it would find at home, but it tolerates anything short of darkness or strong, direct sunlight. Keep it evenly moist and mist the leaves when you think of it. Feed with liquid fertilizer in the spring and in midsummer.

TIPS ON CARING FOR POTTED PLANTS

These houseplants don't ask much of their owners. Most will cheerfully flourish for years if provided with the big three: water, light, and growing room. Here's how to give them the right amount of each.

Water judiciously. One way or another, plants tell you when something is not right with them. When leaves yellow and wilt, the plant is either calling for more water or, more likely, asking you to stop drowning it. Overwatering is probably the most frequent cause of failure with plants. To avoid doing it, test the soil before you water. Stick your finger into the soil. If soil clings to your finger, the plant does not need to be watered. If your finger comes up clean, go ahead and give the plant a drink. If you see yellowed or wilted leaves, consider how frequently you have been watering. If you've been watering daily, water less often; if you haven't watered within memory, be more conscientious. Also keep in mind that most plants appreciate a misting now and then; plants native to humid climates should be misted every day.

Provide the right amount of light. Here's a quick guide:

Bright, indirect light is found within two to four feet of east- and west-facing windows, and within three to six feet of south-facing windows. It is also reproduced under special grow lights.

Moderate light is three to six feet from east- and west-facing windows and eight to ten feet from south-facing windows. It is also found directly on a north-facing windowsill.

Low light doesn't mean darkness; it generally means the ambient light in the middle of a fairly well-lit room, or anywhere in a room near fairly bright artificial light.

Repot occasionally. Unless the plant prefers to be root-bound (snake plants, for instance), repot plants when the roots begin to compact into a tight ball or when they start to clog the drainage holes in the bottom of the planter. Use a planter two or three inches larger than the current one. Don't move the plant to a pot much larger than the original one or the roots will have a difficult time reestablishing themselves.

Fertilize appropriately. Most plants should be fertilized on a monthly basis, or at least every season. Use balanced, liquid fertilizer, but this is definitely not a situation where a little more of a good thing is better. Too much fertilizer can burn roots and kill plants.

Give First Aid to Dying Plants

◆◆◆

There is no 911 for dying plants, but if there were, it would connect directly to the plant police. Sure, some plants die a natural death, but most are done in by their well-meaning caretakers. To assure long, healthy lives for your plants, take action at the first signs of distress and avoid the most common causes of premature plant death.

1. **Overwatering.** The number one cause of plant death is overwatering. There are primarily two reasons for this. First, people mistakenly think that plants can't get too much of a good thing. Second, people water all plants on a single, rigid schedule. Different plants have different needs. Some evolved in wet environments, others in near-drought conditions. To assure plant health, respect those differences and water accordingly.

   • *Symptoms.* Yellow or brown spots, caused by fungus and overwatering, may appear on older leaves, or leaves may yellow from the outside toward the inner part of the plant. In more advanced cases, leaves may also appear limp and mushy, which indicates root rot.

   • *First Aid.* Don't water. If there's water in the bottom of a saucer, discard it and let the plant dry out a bit before watering again. If the plant is waterlogged (it will be particularly heavy), try gently lifting it out of its pot and setting it on absorbent paper towels or newspaper to help it dry out faster. If the roots are rotted, however, even emergency measures will probably be fruitless.

   • *Long-term care.* Find out from a local nursery which of your plants like a moist environment and which don't, and water each according to its needs. In general, don't water unless the plant needs it, and never let the plant wilt. All plants go through cycles when they need more or less water. Flowering plants, especially when they are in bloom, tend to like more water than those that don't flower, but all plants go through dormant periods, during which you should cut back on watering. Conversely, when they're in an active growth cycle, plants use water in greater quantities, so you may have to water more often. Let the condition of the soil be your guide; when the top soil is dry to the touch, water. Be careful to empty any water that runs into the container beneath the plant. Finally, be aware that although tap water is usually safe for plants, in places where the water has too much chlorine or fluoride it's a good idea to use either filtered water or to let the water stand in an open pitcher for twenty-four hours before using it for your plants.

2. **Lack of light.** Again, check with your local nursery or plant store to find out what kind and how much light your plants need. Even plants that live in the shade of large trees in their natural habitat may not have enough light in a suburban den or city living room.

   - *Symptoms.* Plants that are getting less light than they need may have pale foliage, lanky growth, and a general lack of luster. Flowering plants may have few flowers, and the color of those they have might be dull.

   - *First Aid.* Move plants to a window. Most flowering plants like south, east, or west windows, while some, such as African violets, prefer north light. If you can't put plants near a sunny window, fluorescent lights, placed fairly close to them, will do. However, when plants are in flower, keep them out of direct sunlight, lest the flowers become over-heated and collapse prematurely. Foliage plants can often tolerate less light. For them, a north window or a window with a light curtain to diffuse direct sunlight is usually fine. A plant suffering from too little light needs immediate help, but don't shock it by moving it from an interior space to a south-facing window in one step; a too-sudden shift to bright light could bleach or burn its foliage.

3. **Inappropriate fertilization.** Plants purchased fully grown were probably fertilized before you bought them and won't need to be fertilized right away. If you intend to discard a flowering plant after it drops its flowers, there's no sense worrying about fertilizing. But if your plant is a long-term companion, you should keep it on a regular diet, which, like your own, should be not too much, not too little, but just right.

   - *Symptoms.* The symptoms of too little fertilizer are often the same as those of too much or too little watering: yellow or pale leaves, leaf drop, and weak growth. Leaves with brown edges indicate that a plant has been overfertilized, as does a plant's stunted growth, which results from root burn.

   - *First Aid.* If your plant is showing signs of underfertilization, and you are certain that you're watering correctly and that the plant has the proper amount of light, you should fertilize. Use an all-purpose fertilizer formulated for houseplants and follow the directions carefully. More of a good thing, in this case, is usually too much and can result in burned roots. If the plant is wilted, don't fertilize until you've watered properly and given the soil a chance to dry slightly. Most plants appreciate a dose of fertilizer once a month, but during dormant periods in the winter don't fertilize. Remember that fertilizer will not cure plants suffering from the wrong kind of light or inappropriate watering; in fact, until you correct those problems, fertilizing can do more harm than good. The easiest way to correct for overfertilization is to flush the plant with a volume of water equal to three times the size of the pot. If you'd rather start fresh, take out the plant and wash the pot. Discard the old soil and gently tap off most of the soil clinging to the roots. Repot the plant with fresh soil.

4. **Root-bound.** A newly purchased plant is usually fine in the pot it comes in and, in any case, should be allowed to acclimate to its new environment before you repot it. As the plant matures it may outgrow its original pot and may eventually become root-bound.

   • *Symptoms.* When you see the roots emerging from the drainage holes of a potted plant, it's time to repot. Poor growth and the increased need for water are also signs that a plant is root-bound.

   • *First Aid.* Repot. Choose a pot one size larger than the pot the plant is now in. Using a pot that's too big can be just as bad as letting a plant languish in a pot that's too small. That's because the larger container can allow water to accumulate in the soil, displacing oxygen and causing root rot. Put some soil in the new pot, and gently lift the plant from its old pot, being careful not to tear the roots. Firm the soil around the root ball, but not so hard that it becomes compacted, which will make it difficult for the roots to take up water and nutrients. Allow room at the top of the pot to allow for watering, but don't water unless the new soil is particularly dry or the old soil was dried out. Keep the plant in its usual spot; repotting and changing location at the same time is a double stress.

5. **Insect infestations.** Your houseplants may be safe from marauding deer, fox, and the occasional brown bear, but that doesn't mean they have no natural predators. Insects and other pests can seriously damage and kill houseplants. The most common are aphids, spider mites, mealy bugs, and whitefly.

- **Symptoms.** Sticky spots on foliage suggest aphids; round or oval bumps or cottony masses are symptoms of mealy bugs; and tiny white spots on the leaves may be caused by spider mites, which can make the leaves look bronzed or washed out.

- **First Aid.** If you don't mind sharing your home with ladybugs, you'll have no problem with aphids, since ladybugs consider them especially delicious. Otherwise, treat aphids with the systemic insecticides malathion or diazinon. Spider mites need immediate attention, because they can quickly get out of control and become impossible to treat. Caught early, you can eradicate them by dipping the plant or spraying it with insecticidal soap. In some cases, a systemic insecticide also works. Mealy bugs are tough to treat because the cottony masses they create protect them from sprays. You can try touching each with a Q-tip dipped in alcohol. Diazinon is effective, but only if the bugs are thoroughly wetted. Since whitefly fly off at the mere hint of a spray, they can be treated only in the immature stages, before they can fly. At that stage, you can spray or dip the plant in insecticidal soap or treat it with diazinon or malathion.

6. **Fungus and mildew.** Incorrect watering and the wrong light conditions leave plants vulnerable to mildew and fungus, as well as mold.

- **Symptoms.** Mildew manifests itself as powdery deposits that may vary in color from white to brown. Leaf spot fungus shows up as yellow or brown spots on older leaves. Gray mold (botrytis) looks like a dense, gray mass on leaves and stems.

- **First Aid.** Mildew, which is often caused by low light conditions, is easily treated by wiping the leaves with a damp cloth. If it recurs, spray the plant with a fungicide, and place it in direct sunlight for a time. Leaf spot fungus is also caused by poor light and improper watering and can be treated the same way. Gray mold, unfortunately, is very hard to treat, and the best course is simply to discard the plant before the mold infects other plants.

Grow Vegetables and Flowers

◆◆◆

Growing vegetables and flowers can be a full-time occupation—the people who do this are known as farmers—but even if you have another job, you can enjoy fresh produce from your backyard and decorate your table with home-grown cut flowers. (Apartment dwellers should see "Try Container Gardening," page 244.) The trick is to choose plants that are suited to your climate zone and your particular property. Stick to easy, tried-and-true crops, especially if you're just starting out. The following are among the easiest and most rewarding vegetables and flowers that you might grow.

Vegetables

1. **Zucchini.** The only problem with growing zucchini is cultivating a group of friends with whom you can share the abundance. By midsummer you'll be stuffing them in neighbors' mailboxes. Plant seeds in rows, spaced a foot or so apart. Water the first day and, unless it rains, every two or three days thereafter until the seeds germinate. Once they begin to sprout, keep only the best seedlings, allowing about a five-foot circumference, more or less, depending on the variety. Prolific as they are, zucchini plants enjoy some fertilizer, unless your soil is particularly rich. Watch your crop for signs of the dreaded cucumber beetle and squash vine borer, both of which can be controlled with insecticide if caught early. Harvest your zucchini when it's four or five inches long; you can let it attain monstrous lengths, but it won't be as tender or tasty.

2. **Tomatoes.** Your first chore is to choose from the hundreds of varieties of tomatoes. If you plan to use them in salads, cherry and grape tomatoes are perfect; they tend to be very sweet, they ripen early, and they don't need to be sliced. For other purposes, choose one of the infinite varieties of full-size tomatoes. One popular choice is beefsteak, which matures later than some but is worth the wait for its full, flavorful taste and its one-slice-covers-the-sandwich size. It's easiest to plant seedlings in early spring, after the last frost. Plant twenty-four to thirty inches apart, and pour liberal amounts of water and liquid fertilizer on them the day you plant. Once they start to grow, stake the plants and keep them well watered. Try not to wet the leaves, because wet leaves make the plants susceptible to a

number of plant diseases. Avoid watering at night in hot and humid weather, and don't space the plants so close together that air circulation is compromised, a condition that promotes fungus. Use a fungicide if the plants do contract a fungus infection.

3. **Cucumbers.** Like zucchini—they're both members of the Cucurbita family—cucumbers are easy to grow, prolific, and can even be trained up a trellis or fence if your space is limited. Plant in rows or hills about one inch deep and two to three inches apart. Water as you would zucchini and, as with zucchini, pick the best seedlings and destroy the rest. Cucumbers grow quickly. They are tastier when small, so pick them regularly, which will encourage new cucumbers to develop.

4. **Lettuce.** The basic choices are head lettuce, such as romaine, Bibb, and iceberg, and leaf lettuce, such as red leaf, green leaf, oak leaf, and arugula. All are fairly hardy, but need to be grown in cool temperatures. Arugula is a good choice if you prefer a stronger-flavored green; it has a slightly nutty flavor with just a bit of bite to it. Leaf lettuce can be ready in as little as three weeks; head lettuce takes a little longer. No matter which you plant, you will have greens within six weeks. Since lettuce seeds are very fine, it can be difficult to space them properly; a good solution is to use seed tapes, available for most popular kinds of lettuce. Cover seeds with a fine layer of loose soil or starting mixture. You can practice succession planting, in which you start rows or sections every week or ten days to assure a continuous supply. Water well and fertilize; the faster they grow, the better they taste. Since lettuce prefers cool rather than hot weather, plant in the early spring and again in the fall.

5. **Green beans.** Green beans come in two basic types: pole beans, a vining variety that needs the support of a pole or trellis, and bush beans, which grow as small, bushy plants close to the ground. Pole beans have the advantage of producing for a longer period than bush beans, but pole beans take longer to mature. Both types yield great vegetables. Plant after the first frost, water well, and water again in two or three days if there has been no rain.

6. **Onions.** Easy to grow and with multiple culinary uses, onions belong in any home vegetable garden. The most popular are the slicing varieties—white, yellow (or Spanish), and the mild purple—and long-stemmed scallions, pearl onions, shallots, and leeks. It's easier to plant seedlings or "sets"—small bulbs—than seeds, which must be started indoors. Onions prefer rich soft soil or loam, but they're very tolerant of just about any soil, especially if you add fertilizer and keep it moist.

Flowers

1. **Marigolds.** Among the easiest of flowers to grow, marigolds have the added advantage of repelling insects. Some gardeners plant them around tomatoes to inhibit tomato worms and other bugs. Marigolds come in many colors besides the standard gold, including white, yellow, orange, and red. The plants also come in various sizes, from smaller than a foot to four feet tall. They like full to partial sun and can be grown from seed or from seedlings. They tolerate just about any soil, but you'll get bigger, hardier flowers if you fertilize once a month. Keep soil moist, but not wet, watering once or twice a week during dry spells. Marigolds flower around midsummer and continue to flower until the first frost. You don't even have to remove dead flowers, except for appearance's sake.

2. **Cosmos.** There's little that can go wrong with cosmos, which makes them a perfect choice for first-time gardeners. They grow quickly to a height of four or five feet and produce brightly colored flowers in all shades of white, pink, orange, yellow, and scarlet. They thrive in both full sun and partial shade. Cosmos can be sown from large seeds, which germinate quickly. They tolerate dry spells and need fertilizer just once or twice a season. Tall plants might need to be staked, especially if they're exposed to wind.

3. **Impatiens.** Impatiens love shade, and almost everyone loves impatiens. They're compact and come in a huge variety of colors, everything from white, blue, and pink to multicolored. They like acidic, moist soil, but you can compensate for poor soil with the right additives (see "Go Organic," page 242). Keep the plants moist, but not wet, and they'll bloom continually, without deadheading, until the first frost.

4. **Snapdragons.** Colorful and graceful, snapdragons are most easily grown from seedlings. They prefer full sun and grow well in even average soil, which you should fertilize once a month. Plant after the last frost and expect blooms in June. After the long-lasting flowers fade, cut back the stalk to about six inches and wait a little for new growth and a second bloom. Since they're hardy, they may bloom well into fall, even after a first frost. Snap them every once in a while just for the heck of it by squeezing their little mouths together.

5. **Zinnias.** An easy-to-grow, hardy flower, zinnias range in color from white to red to multicolored. There are miniature varieties as well as giant

ones that grow to over three feet tall. The hardest part about growing zinnias is choosing which ones you like best. They can be started early from seed indoors and transplanted outdoors once the seedlings appear and the first frost is over, or you can plant them directly outdoors from seedlings bought in a nursery. They tolerate just about any soil but grow best in rich soil or average soil enriched with fertilizer. Keep the soil moist but not wet. Blooms begin midsummer and continue until the first frost. Remove dead flowers to encourage new growth.

6. **Pansies.** These flowers are anything but the wimps the name suggests. Pansies are among the first flowers to bloom, right along early spring bulbs, and they keep on giving until late fall and can even survive a light frost. They come in virtually every color, even black (just don't tell them black is not a color). They can be started indoors from seeds, but they germinate slowly, so you might want to stick with seedlings from the nursery. Pansies like cool to warm climates, so if your summers are hot, plant them in shade or partial shade. Fertilize at planting and once a month thereafter. Remove dead flowers to promote new blooms.

GO ORGANIC

The long-time practice of using inorganic (chemical) fertilizers and pesticides on both home and commercially grown vegetation has yielded a bumper crop of toxic matter in our soil and water. Luckily, the trend is away from chemicals and toward a more natural approach to cultivation. There is nothing difficult or particularly complicated about organic gardening; you can adopt these environmentally friendly and healthy practices whether you're a novice gardener or veteran. You'll find that you can easily grow abundant flowers and vegetables without putting chemicals into your soil, water, or food. There is no shortage of information on organic gardening on the Web. Here are a few helpful sites to get you started: *http://journeytoforever.org/garden.html*; *www .goorganic.com.au/information*; *www.organicconsumers.org*; *www.gar den master.com/Pages/HowToGuides/HowToGuidesDisplay.asp.*

Organic Gardening Tips

Use compost rather than commercial fertilizer. Compost pays dividends to the organic gardener in many ways: It improves soil structure and texture, allows for better aeration, and increases the soil's capacity to hold water. Of course, compost also does an excellent job of promoting soil fertility while it stimulates healthy root development. There are dozens of commercial and noncommercial Websites with excellent background information as well as specific tips on how to get started composting. Begin by visiting these sites: *www.prohardware.com, www.compostguide.com, www.reducerubbish .govt.nz/compost/tips.html.*

Mulch with organic material. Spread flower beds and trees with three inches of wood chips or other organic material. This covering conserves water, adds nutrients, and discourages weeds. It also gives an attractive, finished appearance to your beds.

Add acid with pine needles. Mulch acid-loving plants such as azaleas, gardenias, hydrangeas, and impatiens with a thick layer of pine needles. Do this in the fall, and the needles will deposit their acid into the soil as they decompose.

Discourage pests with healthy soil. Your best defense against disease and insects is to maintain healthy soil and hardy plants. You can achieve both by sticking to species that thrive naturally in your climate region and soil type and by treating the soil kindly with the right nutrients and proper watering. These practices will ensure vigorous, healthy plants that can withstand the potential ravages of insects and fungus.

Wash away pests with soap. If hungry little aphids are chomping on delicate buds and ruining your outdoor flowers, spray the entire plant—stems, leaves (don't forget the undersides), and buds—with a very diluted solution of liquid detergent and water, then rinse with clear water. This method works on even the heaviest infestation.

Try Container Gardening

You don't need a large spread to enjoy gardening. If you live in an apartment or town house, you can still feed yourself, family, and friends with the fruits (and vegetables) of your labors. All you need are a few containers. And even if you do have a plot of well-drained rich soil, you might still consider container gardening, which offers certain advantages over garden beds. It's easier to control pests in containers, because soil contamination is hardly an issue, and individual containers can be treated without bothering other plants. Container gardens aren't necessarily slaves to the seasons, so long as you can control light and temperature. There are also psychological advantages to this type of gardening: Somehow less commitment is involved; if a plant doesn't work out, well, it's not as though its roots go deep into the earth.

1. **Choose a location.** If you put your containers outdoors, make sure they are within reach of a hose and that there is enough (but not too much) sunlight. If you choose to plant indoors, take care that your plants are safely away from radiators or heating vents, that they get enough light, either natural or artificial, and that they are not in the path of marauding children or pets.

2. **Decide what to plant.** Do you want fruits and vegetables, flowers, herbs, or a combination? Be practical. Virtually anything can be planted in containers, but growing oranges on your terrace overlooking Boston Commons just might not work. Also, don't choose poisonous plants if children or pets are a factor (see "Avoid Backyard Hazards," page 246). If you have full sun or plenty of artificial light, you can grow most flowers, fruits, and vegetables; if the location is shady, choose plants that thrive in shade, such as ferns, hostas, and impatiens. If you want height, try climbers, such as clematis, morning glory, or less vigorous climbing roses. Subtropical plants, such as bougainvillea, oleander, and hibiscus, work in areas that are really warm, but unless you live in a tropical climate, these plants will need protection in the winter.

3. **Choose appropriate containers.** No matter what they are made of, containers should have good drainage. Clay pots allow plants to breath, but they're not the most durable containers, especially if subjected to severe temperature changes. If your garden is on a solid, hard surface, you

might want to raise the containers on blocks an inch or two to provide better drainage. Avoid containers with narrow openings, and remember that cheap plastic pots can deteriorate in sunlight and don't allow plants to breathe. Wooden containers may rot, although redwood and cedar are fairly rot-resistant. Avoid wood that has been treated with toxic chemicals, such as creosote, because these chemicals can damage plants. Make sure the container is big enough to allow for root growth; deep-rooted vegetables, for instance, require deep pots.

4. **Arrange the containers.** Decide on how the containers will be arranged. Don't forget that although containers can be moved, they are heavy once filled with soil.

5. **Check up on them.** Container gardens can't be potted and forgotten. They fall prey to the same hazards that attack regular gardens: insects and plant diseases, extremes of temperature, wind, heavy rain, and rampaging children and animals. Check them frequently to see if they are parched, infested, or otherwise in need of attention.

6. **Use the right medium.** Don't just dig up dirt from the backyard. This may have pests, and it may be too acid, too base, too fine, or not fine enough. Compost is often a good medium. It's light, which allows roots to grow and water and air to circulate, and it's rich in nutrients. Add a bit of peat moss in the bottom to help with drainage. You can also buy potting soil from a garden supply center. Check the requirements for what you're planting to see if you need to add sand. You might want to forgo soil altogether and use a "soilless" medium, which is lightweight and sterile.

7. **Fertilize, but carefully.** For most plants, it is best to fertilize every two to three weeks with a water-soluble fertilizer. Read the instructions on seed packets and ask for advice at garden centers. Be aware that container gardens, which don't have the benefit of unlimited soil to absorb extra fertilizer, are more sensitive to overfertilization than regular gardens. Too much fertilizer can burn or even kill plants; even if it doesn't, an excess of fertilizer can cause plants to grow too tall with the leaves benefiting at the expense of fruit and flowers. An occasional application of fish emulsion and compost can add beneficial trace elements to your containers.

8. **Get the light right.** What you grow is determined in part by the amount of available light. This can be supplemented somewhat by using reflective material, such as aluminum foil, but if your patio is on the shady side of

the house you pretty much have to stick with shade-loving plants. Indoor gardens are more flexible. Although a sunny spot is best, you can supplement natural light with specially designed artificial lights or with a combination of warm white and cool white fluorescent tubes. As always, check with experts at garden centers about the light requirements for the crops you're considering.

9. **Water regularly.** Container gardens need water more frequently than regular gardens. Porous containers, such as clay, allow water to evaporate quickly; glazed or metal containers hold water longer. Just make sure you keep the delicate balance between allowing the soil to dry out completely and keeping it sopping wet. Fall in either direction, and your garden will fail.

Avoid Backyard Hazards

Ah, the garden: bucolic island in a sea of domestic responsibility; refuge from the cares of work and worry. True. But it is also a heartless, dangerous, and wild place where unsuspecting homeowners are prey to poisonous plants and rabid raccoons. By all means stretch out in the hammock, tend the tomatoes, and mow the grass, but beware. Wild things lurk in your own backyard. Here are a few to look out for.

1. **Discarded tools.** The rake thrown on the grass can disappear beneath the weeds, only to rise up and strike you on the forehead when you inadvertently step on it. Don't leave anything sharper than a paper bag lying around in the garden; trowels, pruners, shovels, shears, and the like are all accidents waiting to happen unless safely stashed in the garage or tool shed.

2. **Garden chemicals.** Fertilizers and pesticides—chemicals that make things grow and those that make them shrivel—are powerful and dangerous. The fact that it's illegal to pour unwanted pesticides down the drain or the toilet is your clue that these items shouldn't be handled casually. Although garden-store chemicals are allegedly safe when used according to directions, they're definitely not safe for kids and pets. Keep them bottled up and securely stored when not in use.

PERILOUS PLANTS

Here's a partial list of dangerous plants. *Partial* is the operative word. If you don't absolutely know a plant is safe, assume it isn't. You may still choose to include these plants in your garden, but if you do, you should understand the risks, especially to children and animals.

Really Dangerous

Daphne. A few berries can kill a child.

Dieffenbachia. The leaves can cause intense burning of the mouth and tongue, which can swell enough to block breathing.

Foxglove. The leaves can cause irregular heartbeat and, in large quantities, can be fatal.

Golden Chain. Can cause severe nervous-system symptoms: excitement, staggering, convulsions, and coma. Can lead to death.

Jasmine. Eating the berries can prove fatal.

Lantana camara. The green berries are extremely dangerous.

Larkspur. The young plant or seeds of larkspur can induce severe digestive upset and nervous system problems.

Laurels, rhododendrons, and azaleas. Eating any parts of these produces extreme digestive upset, depression, difficulty breathing, coma, and death.

Lily-of-the-Valley. The leaves can induce irregular heart rhythms and digestive upset.

Mistletoe. The berries have proven fatal to children and adults.

Nightshade. They don't call it deadly for nothing.

Oleander. The seeds of yellow oleander, which children may find attractive, are particularly poisonous, but the leaves and stems can also cause serious illness.

Poison hemlock. Another appropriately named plant.

Rhubarb. The stalks, cooked, are fine, but the leaf blades can cause convulsions, coma, and death.

Rosary pea, castor bean. Eating a single rosary pea or two castor beans can be fatal.

Yew. The berries and foliage can be deadly.

Treat With Caution

Buttercups. The irritant juices can severely damage the digestive tract.

Chilies. Delicious, but not to young mouths. While rarely truly dangerous, they can easily make kids very sick and impart a lifelong fear of spicy food.

Oak acorns and foliage. Takes a lot to be dangerous, but not that much to be sickening.

Wisteria. Many children get sick after eating a few leaves. Rarely dangerous, but definitely unpleasant.

3. **Devil plants.** Some plants have no place in the garden. Which ones do, depends a lot on who shares the garden with you. Most adults are fastidious about what they put in their mouths, but kids and animals are much less discriminating. Even a single flower of an autumn crocus (which resembles the spring variety, except for the blossoms, which are pink-violet, and leaves, which are elongated) can be literally deadly. See the list below for some common poisonous plants, but don't assume because a variety doesn't appear on this list that it's harmless. Check with the agri-

culture department at your local college or university before planting anything you're not sure is safe. Plants can be really nasty, going well beyond the annoying itch of poison ivy. Sweet pea, for instance, a showy, decorative climbing plant, can cause convulsions and permanent paralysis if the leaves, flowers, or seeds are eaten. Teach your young children not to eat anything in the wild unless they ask you first (raspberries are certainly okay), and make sure you watch them at all times.

4. **Wild animals.** Of course, you're not going to pet the bear in your backyard, but are you thinking of feeding the cute raccoon? Think again. He might be rabid or otherwise ill, especially if he shows up during the day looking hung over. There's no need to take arms against wild animals or attempt to rid your garden of them. Just be aware that they can pose certain dangers, especially to children and pets. Enjoy them or revile them; just don't feed them or try to touch them.

5. **Sticks and stones.** As the saying goes, these can break your bones, especially when you mow the lawn. If the grass is high or you're casual about inspecting the ground as you mow, make a habit of first going over the lawn to look for stray branches, rocks, and other debris. Any of these items, rendered airborne by your mower blade, could become a weapon.

[Moving]

Choose a Real Estate Agent

Buying or selling a home is one of the most significant financial transactions you can make. Choosing a real estate agent, therefore, warrants the same care and consideration you'd give to choosing an attorney or a financial adviser.

Whether you are a buyer or a seller, it is critical to understand the nature of the relationship you will have with your real estate agent. Because the rules regarding this relationship vary from state to state, you should begin your search for an agent by learning the rules that apply in your state. The Association of Real Estate License Law Officials maintains a Website with a link to each state. Go to arello.org and click on the "Regulatory Agencies" link to be directed to your state's site.

In some states an agent may represent both the buyer and the seller. This arrangement, known as dual agency, is permitted only with the written consent of both parties. Realistically, it may be difficult for a dual agent to advocate for both the buyer and the seller equally, but the National Association of Realtors code of ethics requires dual agents to treat buyers and sellers fairly and equally. Under this agreement, buyers and sellers have the option of forbidding the dual agent from divulging certain confidential information about them to the other party. Some firms also offer a form of dual agency called "designated agency" whereby one agent in the firm represents the seller and another agent represents the buyer. This option (when available) may allow each "designated agent" to more fully represent each party.

Whatever form of representation you choose, it is essential that you have a clear understanding of what your relationship is with your agent and what the agent is obligated to do for you in the transaction.

Yes, you can go it alone, but do you really want to? A good agent is well worth the commission when you factor in the time and energy you save, the likelihood that the transaction will go as smoothly as possible, and the real possibility that you'll get more or pay less than you otherwise would. Ask for recommendations from friends and colleagues, but don't stop there. Visit open houses and chat with agents. Take a card if you like the person and schedule a more in-depth interview. Talk to several agents to find someone you're comfortable with. As a buyer, you'll be spending a significant amount of time with this person, driving through neighborhoods and walking through houses, and your agent may learn details about your finances and other personal information that you might not share even with friends. If you're selling your home, you will depend on your agent to tell you what your house is realistically worth and how to make it more appealing to potential buyers.

Questions to Ask an Agent When Buying a Home

1. **Do you do this full-time or part-time?** Part-timers might be fine, but the odds are you'll get more attention and more flexibility from someone for whom real estate is a full-time job. Will a part-timer be able to make an appointment in the middle of a weekday? Will he have the detailed knowledge of neighborhoods that someone working full time can have?

2. **How long have you been doing this?** Again, newcomers may be highly motivated, but they won't have the experience evaluating homes and understanding neighborhoods that agents who have been in the business awhile might have.

3. **Can I speak with some of the clients you've helped in the past year?** If the answer is "no," end the relationship now. Make sure the agent can provide at least five references, and speak to as many of those people as you can.

4. **Do you represent any of the sellers whose homes you'll be showing me?** This is not unethical, but it must be disclosed during the first substantive conversation between the potential buyer and the agent. There are times when the perfect house for you may be represented by the agent you've engaged to help you buy one. This is a situation in which the dual disclosure becomes relevant. Be aware that any conversations along the lines of "I'd like to get it for $450,000, but I'm willing to go to $475,000" will be disclosed to the seller unless you have established a formal fiduciary relationship with the agent and have signed a dual agency agreement.

5. **How well do you know the neighborhoods I'm interested in?** The better an agent knows the neighborhood, the more savvy she'll be about home prices and about issues that may affect the value of a home in the future. Is a new school in the offing that would raise taxes? Is the backyard in the path of a proposed highway? Has a high-rise been approved that will obstruct your view of the mountains?

6. **Given what you know of my preferences, are there other neighborhoods you could suggest?** If the answer is "no," it should be because you've been explicit, and this is truly the only neighborhood that matches your criteria. Otherwise, a good agent should be able to suggest alternative areas that fit your requirements.

7. **Can you provide me with e-mail listings of houses I'd be interested in?** This can be a big time-saver. An agent can assemble ten or more houses that meet your general criteria and send you details about each, including pictures, via the Web. You can then narrow the list down to those you're most interested in.

Questions to Ask an Agent When Selling a Home

You should ask many of the same questions of an agent selling your home as you would of one who helps you buy one, especially questions about the agent's experience. Again, be sure to check references and find out how well the agent knows your area.

1. **How many homes like mine have you sold in the past year, and can I speak to some of your clients?** An agent who has sold just a few homes like yours in the past year is probably not the right one for you. Some agents specialize in certain price ranges; perhaps yours is out of that range. Others simply aren't very good salespeople. The fact that you see many of that agent's signs around town doesn't necessarily mean she is a good salesperson. Ask for specifics and check out references. Even if an agent lists several sales, all things being equal, choose the agent whose sales have been concentrated in your price range and your kind of home.

2. **What does your marketing plan include?** You'll want the agent to host an open house and print up attractive brochures showing your home's best features. Ask to see samples of what the agent has done for other clients. You want a media blitz, including ads—with pictures—in area papers and on every Website out there. Simply listing the house with the Multiple Listings Service is not a marketing plan.

3. **Can you help potential buyers find financing?** An agent who is financially savvy will be aware of the latest developments in mortgage financing. She will have contacts with lending institutions that may be able to help prospective buyers who might not meet traditional income or asset criteria. This can significantly broaden the pool of prospective bidders for your home.

4. **Can we talk about your commission?** Not long ago a commission of 6 percent was standard. Now, commissions are more often negotiable. That's not to say they can or should be cut to the bone. You want to keep your agent well-motivated and with enough potential revenue from the sale to finance an effective marketing campaign, but you needn't pay full price. Consider 6 percent a starting point for a serious discussion, especially if you are selling one house and buying another with the same agent.

Prepare Your Home for Sale

◆◆◆

Turning a "For Sale" sign into one that says "Sold" isn't a mysterious process. Because most prospective buyers can't see past an unattractive surface, you need to make sure your home looks fresh, inviting, and ready for move-in. You want to create the immediate impression that living in your house would be a very pleasant experience indeed. Here are some tips for preparing your home for the marketplace.

Prepare the Interior

1. **Fix anything that's broken.** Examine every room in the house to make sure nothing is in need of repair. If a burner on the stove doesn't light, fix it. If a window is cracked, replace it. People want to feel the home they're buying has been well cared for. A flaw you no longer notice can jump out at a prospective buyer.

2. **Clean and straighten everything.** That means everything in and out of sight; remember that every closet door will be opened. Make the beds, and leave no dishes in the sink or trash in the trash cans. If you smoke, don't smoke inside for at least a week and make sure the house no longer smells of smoke. That might mean a thorough cleaning, or possibly replacement of drapes, furniture, and rugs.

3. **Remove clutter.** You may not think of them as clutter, but in this instance, most of your family pictures and treasured souvenirs fall into this category. They don't mean anything to prospective buyers and actually interfere with

their ability to picture themselves living in your home. Also put away appliances and other extra items that may sit on the kitchen counter. Create as much clear, open surface as you can. Think roomy.

4. **Remove extra furniture.** Rooms with less furniture look bigger. If you have extra tables, chairs, or hassocks, see if you can store them at a friend's house.

5. **Touch up paint and wallpaper.** You might get away with simply washing dirty spots or carefully patching a small piece of wallpaper, but if the paint is really shabby or the wallpaper is in shambles, you must repaint. If you do repaint, choose a light, neutral color.

6. **Freshen up the bathroom.** Recaulk around the tub, if necessary. Also make sure bathroom tiles are clean and remove any stains from the sink and toilet.

Prepare the Exterior

1. **Touch up and clean the exterior.** Remove any stains or mildew and consider repainting details, such as trim, doors, and shutters.

2. **Fix and clean everything.** Make sure the porch light and the doorbell work, repair or replace old screens, and clean and polish handles and door knockers.

3. **Get the lawn and landscaping in great shape.** Mow, trim, edge, weed, cut back plants, and do what you always meant to do each spring to make your landscaping look inviting. At the very least, purchase pots of colorful flowers for the front porch area.

4. **Keep the garage door closed.** But don't think a messy garage is therefore acceptable.

5. **Clear the driveway of toys and cars.** Leave room for prospective buyers to park.

6. **Repair the driveway if it's cracked.**

"Stage" Your Home

1. **Seller, be gone.** Prospective buyers are much more comfortable looking over a house when the owner isn't looking over their shoulders.

2. **Relocate dogs, cats, and other four-footed creatures.** Take them with you, board them, just don't leave them to greet prospects.

3. **Lighten up.** A well-lit home is more appealing than a dark one. Open blinds and turn on lights in every room, no matter what the time of day.

4. **Refresh the air.** In addition to not smoking, refrain from cooking anything that will leave a strong odor in the house. If the weather is cold and you have a fireplace, consider lighting it for a cozy atmosphere. A slight wood-smoke scent is very warm and inviting. So is the aroma of freshly baked cookies, even if they started life in the frozen food section of the local supermarket. Fresh flowers are great; scented candles are a risk (some people find them offensive, and others might think you're trying to cover up a bad odor).

5. **Consider hiring a pro.** Your agent can probably recommend someone who specializes in "staging" homes for sale. These professionals really know how to make a home look its best. In addition to clearing the decks to make your home look more spacious than you believed possible, they can often provide just the right décor items or occasional furniture to highlight your home's best features.

Choose a Neighborhood

◆◆◆

If no man is an island, neither is a house. The location of your home is at least as important as the layout of the kitchen, and more so if you believe the old real estate saying that the three most important features of a home are: location, location, location. Before you even consider buying a house or renting an apartment, check out the neighborhood. No matter how great the backyard, no matter how spacious the closets, if it's in the wrong town or the wrong part of town, you won't be happy. Here a few items to consider in your evaluation of a neighborhood.

1. **Assess access.** If you work or go to school, how long and how expensive is the commute? Are the grocery stores, dry cleaners, library, and other stops on your errand circuit easily accessible? If you're religious, are

places to worship nearby? If you enjoy movies, museums, or concerts, are they easy to get to?

2. **Decide on environment.** Rural may be romantic, but it's also remote. Are you really willing to plow a long driveway in winter, drive miles to the nearest store, or live far from advanced health care? Urban can be exciting, but if you have children a city can present unique challenges for education, sports, and carefree play dates. Suburban can be stultifying for singles and demanding on parents, who have to ferry children everywhere. The key is to be realistic about your lifestyle requirements and to know which trade-offs you are willing to make if you can't have everything you want.

3. **Spend time on the streets.** Visit each neighborhood you're considering at different hours, during the week and on weekends. Is it too noisy? Too quiet? Does the air smell right? Are there people around or are the streets deserted? What's the traffic like during the middle of the day and at rush hour? Trust your instincts: If your gut says you won't feel at home, this won't be the place for you. If you feel comfortable, you might well have found a congenial home.

4. **Take the journey at night.** Come to the neighborhood at night using the mode of transportation you would use if you lived there. Do you feel comfortable and safe? Is it peaceful or too noisy? Are any stores open, or do they roll up the sidewalks after dusk? If you're in the habit of stopping for takeout after a long day of work and there's nothing open for miles around, this may not be the place for you.

5. **Talk to people who live there.** People are happy to talk to prospective neighbors, and if they're happy with their neighborhood, they'll try to share their enthusiasm. If they're dissatisfied, you can rest assured they'll let you know (unless it's their house that's for sale).

6. **Research the local schools.** If you're a parent or intend to be, learn the basic facts, including the percentage of high school graduates that goes on to higher education, the test scores, and how the schools rank versus others in the state. Ask about the average tenure of the teachers, the teacher-to-student ratio, and what the facilities are like. If you don't have children, it is still a good idea to find out if the schools are good, because this can be a big factor in the resale value of a house.

7. **Think about the future.** Consider what the neighborhood will be like in ten years. If the neighborhood is well-established, is near a major city, and

has a history of high demand, values are likely to continue to rise. But if the population is aging and new families aren't moving in, it might be heading for decline. Vacant, undeveloped lots could be signs of decay, or they might be opportunities for growth. The river view you prize from that sixth floor duplex might turn ugly if a new building sprouts between you and the river.

8. **Investigate tax stability.** Try to determine if taxes are fairly stable. You might be able to afford the mortgage and the taxes today, but what if the tax rate rises to meet the need for a new school? If the town relies on tax revenue from local businesses, are those businesses healthy or will they relocate in a few years, shifting a greater share of the tax burden to homeowners.

TIP: Many communities have their own Websites, which provide a wealth of information about the local economy, school system, and public amenities. Yahoo Groups hosts independent Websites that might give interesting, alternative views about neighborhood issues. Check out local newspapers and radio and television stations, and don't hesitate to call the police department to learn about crime rates and the department of education for information about the school system.

Choose a Mover

Choosing a competent, reliable moving company makes all the difference in getting you and your belongings to your new home in one piece. Here are steps to take that will help you choose a safe, reliable mover and save some money in the process.

ASSESSING A HOUSE OR APARTMENT

If you're purchasing a home or an apartment in a state that doesn't require a home inspection as a matter of course, hire a home inspection expert to look the place over carefully and provide a full, detailed report. If possible, choose an inspector who is a licensed professional engineer. These are engineers who have passed a national licensing exam and are entitled to use the initials PE after their names. If you're renting, you probably won't go through the expense of a formal inspection, but you should at least go over the following items before signing a lease.

Check utility costs. As the price of fuel continues to rise, this can be a significant part of your monthly budget. If you're purchasing, ask to see utility bills for the past twelve months. If you're renting, ask previous tenants or prospective neighbors what typical utility costs are, especially for summer and winter.

Make sure everything works. How well does the heating system work? Air conditioning? Is the electrical system up to code? If you're renting, are the appliances in decent shape or will you want them replaced?

Test the water pressure. Run the kitchen faucet or the shower while you flush a toilet and see if there's adequate pressure to maintain the flow.

Ask about the hot water supply. Can you take a shower and wash dishes at the same time?

Check for any water damage. Look for signs of mildew or water stains on the walls, ceilings, carpets, and floors. Cracks in the basement floor or walls are signs of water coming up from the ground or dripping inside the walls from a leaky roof.

Look for signs of pests. Check cupboards and drawers for signs of droppings. Baited traps are a dead giveaway. A professional home inspection should include a check for termites and carpenter ants.

1. **Step away from the keyboard.** Virtually all reputable moving companies maintain Websites, but if that's all they maintain, you're asking for trouble. Never rely on a company you've found on the Internet that you can't also find in a bricks and mortar headquarters. Also, avoid Internet moving brokers, who book moves and hand them off to companies you may never have heard of.

2. **Ask for recommendations.** Talk with friends, neighbors, and real estate agents. Real estate agents are good sources, because many of their clients have just moved and their recommendations are current. Also ask for names of companies to avoid so you don't waste time interviewing the wrong people.

3. **Begin with basic questions.** Ask these questions over the telephone of any company you're considering:

   - *How long have you been in business?* Stick to companies that have at least ten years experience.

   - *Are you licensed and bonded?* If you're moving within the state, the company should be licensed in your state; if you're moving interstate, it should be licensed with the Department of Transportation's Federal Motor Carrier Safety Administration. Ask to see copies of the registration certificate, but double-check at your state's Department of Transportation, Public Utilities Commission, or Bureau of Consumer Affairs. Check federal registration with the Department of Transportation at ai.volpe.dot/hhg/search.asp. You might also check the company at the Federal Motor Carrier Safety Administration's site, *www.safersys.org*, which also provides a "company snapshot" that gives vital information about the company, including its license numbers, physical address, and the kinds of cargo it's licensed to haul (it should be "household goods").

   - *Do you carry workman's compensation?*

   - *Are you a member of a trade association, such as the American Movers Conference?* Membership would make resolving any dispute easier. Don't accept vague or reluctant answers; if the company representative isn't forthcoming on the phone, hang up and keep dialing.

4. **Get in-person estimates.** Don't consider any mover who wants to give you a ballpark estimate over the telephone after asking about the number of rooms in your house and other general questions. Never accept an estimate

based on cubic feet or gross weight alone, and never sign an agreement with
any blank spaces. Reliable movers will meet you in your home to prepare
an estimate. As you get estimates, leave them out so movers know they're
not the only ones being considered. Insist on a binding estimate. It will
probably have a clause stipulating that the estimate can be exceeded by a
given percentage, with a stated cap as the maximum. You may pay less, but
you know up-front the maximum you can be charged. A nonbinding estimate is tantamount to no estimate at all. Get the specifics in writing from
at least three companies and beware of hidden costs. Always ask:

• Do you charge extra for bulky items, elevators, or stairs?

• Are moving supplies included in the estimate?

• Exactly how do you handle loss or damage, and what is your maximum
insurance coverage?

• Can you supply references? Make sure you call them.

5. **Double-check a company's insurance.** Once you narrow your choices, check the insurance coverage of each company you're seriously considering. Go to *www.safersys.org*, the Federal Motor Carrier Safety Administration's site. Click on "licensing and insurance"; this will bring you to a page that asks for the company's name or USDOT license number. Enter either and you'll be taken to a page that lets you download the insurance information about that particular company. The middle column lists "authority type." "Common" or "contract" should state "active." Toward the bottom is insurance. The company should have both BIPD (bodily injury and property damage) and cargo insurance. You should see the amount that's required and the amount on file for BIPD insurance and the word *yes* in both columns for cargo.

6. **Consider additional insurance.** Check with the company that handles your homeowner's or renter's policy. Your policy may cover goods during a move, but you may have to schedule certain expensive items, such as artwork or antiques. If you're not already covered, ask if you can buy coverage specifically for this move.

7. **Save money by packing yourself.** On local moves, packing can account for as much as half the fee. The advantage of packing yourself, in addition to saving money, is that you can label every item with as much detail as you like and in ways you'll understand: "grandma's holiday sauce dish," may be more meaningful to you than "misc. dishes." You can even use color-coded boxes, available from moving-supply companies. One caveat: If you pack things yourself, the moving company won't be liable for breakage.

Countdown to Moving Day

◆◆◆

Face it: Moving is hard. Short of strapping the furniture, pets, and kids to the walls and transporting your house to your new neighborhood, there's just no easy way around one of life's more demanding chores. The very thought makes you understand why some families stay put for centuries. Use this list to gain the security of knowing what you must do and when. As you tick off each item, you can enjoy a feeling of accomplishment.

Two Months before the Move

1. **Select a moving company.** See "Choose a Mover," page 258. Meet with the company representatives and go over all the details, including scheduling and packing, if they'll be doing that for you.

2. **Sort belongings.** Divide unwanted items according to what you will give away to friends, what you will donate to charity, what you will sell at a garage sale, and what you will throw away.

3. **Transfer school records.** If you have children, it is important to contact the new school to let them know your children are coming and to transfer their school records.

4. **Arrange for storage.** If you're planning to put some things in storage, make the arrangements now.

5. **Make an address list.** Start a list of people and businesses you need to notify of your new address.

6. **Make repairs.** Begin working on any home repairs you've agreed to make before moving.

Four Weeks before the Move

1. **Fill out change-of-address forms.** You can do this very easily on-line at USPS.gov or you can pick up a handy change-of-address kit at the post office. To receive important mail as quickly as possible, notify magazines, credit card companies, and friends and relatives directly.

2. **Contact utility companies.** Schedule service cutoff for the day after the move. Give each utility your forwarding address for any refunds. At the same time, arrange to have utilities connected in your new location. If you haven't sold the old house or apartment, keep the electricity on, and if it's winter make sure it remains heated when you leave.

3. **Order packing supplies.** If you're doing the packing, you can purchase packing supplies at the local Office Depot, Staples, or Office Max. You can also order from one of the many on-line sites that specialize in packing supplies.

4. **Plan a garage sale.** If you're planning a garage sale, pick a date and place an ad in the local paper to run a week before the sale.

5. **Get health records.** Call your local physician, dentist, and veterinarian to have your records sent either to your new home or to your new health-care providers.

6. **Think about your car.** If you're moving to a different state, call the Department of Motor Vehicles in your new location to find out about registration and licensing requirements.

Three Weeks before the Move

1. **Take inventory.** Make a list of all your possessions (see "Take a Home Inventory," page 312).

2. **Start serious packing.** Work on one room at a time, starting with the items you use least often. Consider packing a telephone book from your old town to make staying in touch easier.

3. **Make personal travel arrangements.** If necessary, secure plane tickets and rental cars or make sure your car is in shape for the trip.

4. **Make sleeping arrangements.** Depending on how far you're going and when the movers will arrive, you should arrange for a place to stay near your new home for as many nights as needed.

5. **Take care of the animals.** If you won't be driving to your new place with your pets, arrange to get them there. Ask your veterinarian if your animals are up-to-date on required shots, and ask if he knows a vet in the area where you're moving. When you pack your pet's food, make sure you keep a one- or two-day supply handy. Dogs, cats, and other furry and feathered creatures can't understand that their food will turn up sooner or later.

Two Weeks before the Move

1. **Return library books and videos.** Also return anything you've borrowed from neighbors.

2. **Take care of your old house.** If you haven't already sold the old place, make arrangements to maintain it. That includes the yard and periodic checks inside to make sure all is well. Also, notify the police that the house will be empty.

3. **Cancel deliveries.** Stop any regular deliveries you may get, such as the newspaper, and set up new deliveries at the new place.

4. **Call the mechanic.** Have your car serviced by your mechanic.

5. **Clean out wall safes and secret hiding places.**

The Week of the Move

1. **Dispose of flammable material.** Also, drain the gas and oil from any gas-powered tools, such as lawn mowers and snow blowers.

2. **Arrange for a baby-sitter.** If you have young children, you should have someone to watch them at both ends of the move.

3. **Pay outstanding bills.**

4. **Eat the perishables.** Give away any good stuff you can't eat and can't easily move.

5. **Pay the moving company.** Make sure you know exactly what method of payment the company wants. You may need a certified check for the basic amount and a regular check for any additional amount, up to the cap, or a credit card may be acceptable.

6. **Label items staying behind.** If you've agreed to sell or give items to the new tenants or owners, clearly label them with tags provided by the moving company or with your own tags.

7. **Make sure the movers have your new address, phone number, and your cell-phone number.**

8. **Take care of helpers.** Buy drinks, snacks, and disposable dishes and utensils for any friends and family who will help out on moving day.

9. **Empty your safe-deposit box and arrange for a new one in your new town.**

10. **Pack a survival kit.** See "Stock a Moving Survival Kit," page 268. Label this box "Last on/First off" so the movers know what to do with it.

Moving Day

1. **Be ready to direct the movers when they arrive.**

2. **Do a final walk-through of your old house.**

3. **Put out the trash.** Do another walk-through after the movers leave to make sure they've taken everything; pick up any stray trash and bring it to the curb.

4. **Lock the doors and windows.**

MOVE YOUR COMPUTER SAFELY

Of course you've backed up your computer data onto removable media, such as DVDs or an external hard drive. Now it's time to dismantle everything. Pack the computer, monitor, keyboard, and any peripherals carefully in boxes with plenty of cushioning. The computer and the monitor should get separate boxes. Label the cords and secure them with ties or Velcro straps. A copy of your most important files stored on an external hard drive or media should travel with you while your computer goes with the movers.

Stock a Packing Kit

If you plan to pack your own belongings, put together a kit of packing supplies and keep it in one place. You can buy preassembled kits from packing-supply companies—each designed for a specific room, with special boxes and wrapping supplies suited for items found in that room—but these tend to be expensive. It's easy to put together your own kit from supplies available at any home supply, hardware, or major stationery store, as well as from on-line suppliers. Here are the basics.

1. **Boxes.** You can get boxes from liquor and office-supply stores, but avoid boxes from grocery stores, because they can harbor insects. It's best to buy boxes from the moving company or from a large office supply store. New boxes are stronger, cleaner, and more convenient because their uniform size allows you to stack them more easily. Specialized boxes, such as wardrobe boxes, make packing and unpacking much easier.

2. **Bubble wrap**

3. **Rolls of two-inch packing tape with dispensers**

4. **Gaffer's or duct tape.** This is strong and can be used to secure rolled-up rugs and other bulky items.

5. **String.** Use it to secure furniture drawers or other items you don't want to risk putting tape on.

6. **Small plastic bags with twist ties.** Use these for those small items, such as screws, brackets, and fasteners, that tend to wander off by themselves.

7. **Felt-tip markers.** Get thick ones that really leave a mark, and get several different colors.

8. **Scissors and box cutters**

9. **Basic tools, including screwdrivers and a hammer**

HOW TO MOVE PLANTS

Movers generally won't move your plants, because plants usually can't survive the move. If you plan to take your plants, you must transport them in the car. If that's not practical, at least two weeks before you move, begin giving your plants to family, friends, or neighbors who would enjoy them. If you can't live without your plants, here's what to do:

Line sturdy boxes with plastic and put the plants inside, cushioned with bubble wrap. Put the boxes in the back seat of the car, making sure they won't tip over by holding them in place with suitcases or other bulky items.

Put taller plants on the floor.

Take cuttings from the garden and place them in floral tubes, add water, and cap them.

Unpack plants as soon as you arrive and water them if necessary.

Stock a Moving Survival Kit

These are the things you and your family need to get through the first few days in a new place, until you find the energy or the inspiration to begin to unpack.

1. **Kitchen items.** Disposable dishes and utensils; also aluminum foil, paper towels, a sponge, and dish soap. A can opener can come in handy, and perhaps a small sauce pan.

2. **Survival food.** You may exist on takeout the first several days, but you will no doubt want either tea or coffee in the morning. Pack coffee, filters, loose tea or tea bags, a coffee pot, tea pot, and kettle. Consider bringing a supply of high-quality chocolate, always soothing during stressful times. Don't forget to pack pet food, if you have pets.

3. **Bedroom items.** Sheets, blankets, pillows, and pillowcases.

4. **Bathroom items.** Towels, toilet paper, soap, and toiletries.

5. **Household items.** Flashlights, basic tools (screwdrivers, hammer, scissors), light bulbs, and trash bags.

6. **Automatic night lights.** Make sure every room and hallway has one. This is new territory, and you don't want to discover it on your back at the bottom of the stairs in the middle of the night.

7. **Personal items.** It may be useful to pack a suitcase with clothing, an alarm clock, and anything else you'd need for a day or two.

8. **Prescription medications for everyone in the household.**

9. **First-aid kit.** See "Stock a First-Aid Kit," page 168.

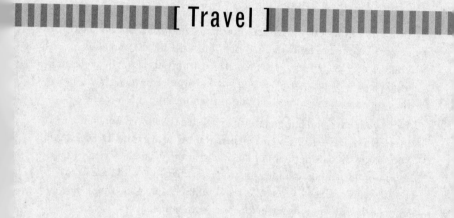

[Travel]

Get through Airport Security

Most people know the drill by now: Allow plenty of extra time in case of long lines at the security checkpoint; keep your boarding pass and photo identification handy; be prepared to have your carry-on bags searched; and wear as little metal as possible, because you will almost certainly have to remove it all to pass through the metal detector. Whether you are a veteran or a novice flier, keep all these tips in mind when you travel and you should breeze through security with as little fuss as is humanly possible.

1. **Don't be a comedian.** Even the most innocent joke about the teensy little explosive device tends to bomb at airports. Resist all temptation toward humor; security personnel are trained to react briskly at the mere mention of explosives or firearms. Remind any kids you're traveling with to take the process seriously as well. Penalties, even for humor, can be severe.

2. **Limit your carry-on baggage.** Each passenger is allowed only one carry-on bag and one personal item, such as a purse or briefcase. Don't overfill your carry-on bag; most airlines dictate that carry-on bags weigh a maximum of 45 pounds and measure no larger than 10" x 16" x 24". Additional items such as baby strollers and umbrellas are sometimes allowed, but check with your airline before you leave home.

3. **Leave prohibited items home.** Well, of course. But that means more than the obvious items like grandpa's antique saber or your favorite hunting rifle. Several seemingly innocuous items have been deemed "dual use" and banned for carrying on by the Transportation Safety Administration (TSA). Don't carry straight razors, Swiss army knives, or pointed metal scissors; many an otherwise innocent manicure set has been forfeited at the security checkpoint. Most blunt-tipped metal will be permitted, but it's often a judgment call of the screener on duty. No lighters of any kind and only up to four books of matches per person are permitted. Cigar cutters, corkscrews, and walking canes, however, are fine. If you just can't leave home without your firearms and ammo, you'll be pleased to know you can check them, so long as they're properly packaged and the airline doesn't object. For a complete list of items you can and cannot carry on or check in, go to the Transportation Safety Administrations Website, *www.tsa.gov*, click on "travelers and consumers," then "air travel," then "prohibited items."

There was a time when confiscated items were forever lost to their owners. Now about a dozen U.S. airports have mail-back kiosks just outside security checkpoints where fliers can purchase envelopes, labels, and postage to send their surrendered items back home. About a half dozen more airports have such kiosks in the works, and several airport gift shops located near security checkpoints have also begun stocking similar kits.

4. **Wear sensible shoes.** If you've previously worn a particular pair of shoes through security, they're probably okay, but even tennis shoes may have metal in them, so assume nothing. Whether or not your shoes set off the metal detector, they may require screening. Boots, platform shoes, and thick-soled footwear are likely to be screened, thanks to the fellow who tried to ignite one of his shoes shortly after September 11. Simple slip-ons are the best bet; even if you have to take them off, you won't cause others to wait while you put them back on.

5. **Dress for quick costume changes.** All coats and jackets must be removed and put through the x-ray machine, so wear items that are easy to take off and put on again.

6. **Charge your batteries.** PDAs, laptops, cell phones, and other personal electronics must go through x-ray, but even then you may have to turn them on to prove they're legitimate. If the batteries are charged, you'll be able to show the devices function as intended.

7. **Expect a thorough check.** It's not that you look suspicious; many inspections are random, and it can happen to anyone sooner or later. If you are asked to submit to personal or baggage inspection, you can request privacy. If your carry-on is full of dirty underwear and socks with holes, you can ask that it be opened out of sight of other passengers. Be cooperative, and remember that you're in a sarcasm-free zone.

8. **Leave gifts unwrapped.** If the security point's x-ray can't determine the nature of an object, you will be asked to display it. Just in case, save the tape and bows until you reach your destination.

TIP: If you have a complaint about your treatment at screening or about other security issues, call the TSA's Consumer Response Center at 866–289–9673.

MEDICAL ISSUES

The Transportation Safety Administration (TSA) has specific guidelines for people with disabilities or special medical needs. These are detailed on the Website *www.tsa.gov*. Click on "travelers and consumers," then on "persons with disabilities and medical conditions." If you have an implant that's likely to set off the metal detector, carry a note from your doctor to verify your condition. You will probably be screened with a hand wand or patted down. Make sure medicines are in their original containers, complete with prescription information. Diabetic supplies, including unused syringes, are fine, although used needles should be in an approved container. If you're wearing an insulin pump, you needn't remove it, but it will be subject to visual inspection. If you require a service animal, the animal can accompany you throughout security clearance, but you are responsible for controlling your animal. And if you're taking nitroglycerine, be aware that even small traces—did you use your laptop or cell phone after taking a pill?—can set off bomb-detecting equipment.

Upgrade, Fly Free, and Get on a Fully Booked Flight

◆◆◆

The days of showing up at the gate at the last minute and paying a pittance for an empty seat are long gone. Still, there are ways to get upgrades, a cheap seat, and in an emergency, a seat on a plane that is fully booked. There are no guarantees, but if you try these methods, you might wind up saving some money and getting extra legroom in the bargain.

1. **Volunteer to be bumped.** Airlines always overbook flights, counting on a certain number of cancellations. That usually works out well for the airlines, but occasionally everyone who bought a ticket actually shows up, and that's when there are opportunities for free tickets. If you don't ab-

solutely have to be on that overbooked flight, volunteer to be bumped. In return, you'll usually be guaranteed a seat on the next plane to your destination, you are sometimes given a meal voucher and a hotel room if the next plane is the next day, and, best of all, most airlines issue you an additional free ticket. These free tickets are usually good for a year and for any destination in the United States or Canada; on some airlines, they can even be used overseas. Occasionally an airline will offer cash compensation in place of an additional ticket.

2. **Stick with one airline.** Many airlines automatically upgrade elite members of their frequent-flier programs if a business-class seat is available. To maximize miles and earn elite status, try to fly the same airline whenever possible. The more miles you have the better, even within the stratospheric elite level, because the more miles, the higher your status, and the more likely it is you'll get the upgrade.

3. **Trade frequent-flier miles for an upgrade.** If you're already using 20,000 miles to pay for a ticket, another 20,000 might put you in the front of the plane. You'll spend more miles for overseas flights, but that's where an upgrade can be most valuable. Anyone can deal with coach from New York to Boston; New York to Tokyo is a different matter.

4. **Buy an upgrade.** You can simply pay the difference between coach and business class, assuming the seat's available, but some airlines (Airtran and America West, as of this writing) let you buy the upgrade for a nominal price if you're a member of their frequent-flier program.

5. **Upgrade via an e-ticket.** Some airlines (American and Continental, as of this writing) allow customers who use their e-terminals to purchase tickets to buy an upgrade at very little cost. The upgrade can be used on that flight if a seat is available, or on another flight. Generally, you buy the upgrade when you buy the ticket, but airlines sometimes allow passengers holding electronic tickets to upgrade at the gate.

6. **Ask.** This sounds too easy to be true, but it's worth a shot, especially if you've been inconvenienced by an airline. Airlines really do care what you think about them. If you've been bumped from a flight, ask for an upgrade on the next one. If this is a connecting flight, and there were problems on the first leg, politely complain to the ticket agent, who might offer an upgrade by way of apology. Since gate agents often have the discretion to issue upgrades, you might simply ask for one. Be charming and reasonable, and it might just work.

7. **Fly midweek.** Traveling on a Wednesday increases the chance that the plane won't be full. This means there could be a seat open in first or business class.

8. **Arrive early.** You can ask at the ticket window if there are any available first–class seats. If there are, you might be able to purchase an upgrade for a small fee.

9. **Be a courier.** This is for the fancy-free, because you may not know before you depart when your return flight will be. Also, remember that you probably won't be able to take anything with you other than what you carry on-board and that will be limited by what you've agreed to transport as a courier. If you're interested, you can find information at the Air Courier Association (*www.aircourier.org*) and at the International Association of Air Couriers (*www.courier.org*).

10. **Let your hardship be known.** Most airlines will do everything they can to get you on a flight if not getting on would be a true hardship. There are no absolute rules about this, so the only thing to do is ask. A qualifying circumstance would be attendance at the funeral of a close relative or a true medical emergency, not your last chance to catch the big act at a Vegas hotel.

Shop for Hotels and Airfares On-line

You *can* find great travel deals by surfing the Web, but take as your motto both caveat emptor (let the buyer beware) and whatever is Latin for "do your homework." The integrated travel Websites—including Travelocity, Expedia, Orbitz, and Hotels.com—are *not* designed to make it easy for you to find the lowest airfares and hotel rates. Nor is there any federal regulation of these sites. Travel expert Bill McGee, a consultant to the nonprofit, independently funded Consumer WebWatch, puts it this way: "The good news is that there's more competition. The bad news is that you have to work harder to find the lowest rates." Here are some tips to help you do that hard work successfully.

1. **Shop around.** Never assume that you can rely on a site just because you had good luck finding airfares or hotel deals there in the past.

2. **Dig deep.** The best rates will often be buried, even on the "better" sites. You must look carefully on each site to discover its "lowest to highest" sorting tool.

3. **Compare results.** This is especially important for airfares, because bookings are done in "real time," which means they can change rapidly. Expedia and Travelocity allow you to create an itinerary and hold a reservation, but they don't promise a rate will be held for you.

4. **Check fees.** Each site has its own agreements with individual airlines regarding fees for booking. A site may charge you to book with one airline, but not another. Another site may have a completely different fee structure. Don't assume consistency; these arrangements are always in flux. Check fees at each site each time.

5. **Check local sites for specific hotels.** You will almost always find the best room rate when you visit the local site of a brand hotel. For example, if you're looking for a Marriott in Tampa, don't start at the general Marriott site; go directly to the Tampa Marriott site. Also, don't hesitate to call the hotel directly and simply ask for a better rate or an upgrade. You'd be surprised how often you can get what you want just by asking.

6. **Take advantage of natural price troughs.** Resort prices in the Caribbean tend to drop around mid-April and rise again in December, and prices for hotels and airlines in general fall between Thanksgiving and mid-December and again during the first half of January.

7. **Beware of vague terms.** This is especially important when you're shopping for hotel rates. The integrated sites often feature a deal as "best value" or "exclusive rate," which sounds like a great find, but those encouraging labels don't necessarily translate as "this is the lowest rate."

8. **Don't fall for the "top of the page" trick.** Often airlines and hotels strike deals with travel sites to ensure their placement high up on the list of results. This means that when your results page pops up, what you see first might not be the best deal.

9. **Watch for hidden concessions.** Some truly great airfares come with stiff restrictions. Keep reading until you discover what you might be giving up for the big savings. Will you earn frequent-flier miles? Can the ticket be refunded? Changed? Upgraded? Do you care?

10. **Book airfares early.** Remember that not all airline seats are created equal, even if they're in the same row. Buying your ticket several weeks in advance may snag you one of a limited number of cheap seats available for that flight.

11. **If you must book at the last minute, try these sites.** By purchasing unsold airline tickets and hotel rooms, the companies hosting *www.site59.com* and *www.lastminutetravel.com* can offer packaged trips at deep discounts for people looking for quick getaways.

12. **Check out alternative airports.** Flying into Midway instead of O'Hare, or Manchester, New Hampshire, rather than Boston's Logan, can mean smaller crowds, shorter distances from curb to check-in, and, quite possibly, lower fares. Just make sure you don't spend the savings in higher cab fares to your destination.

13. **Avoid booking tickets on weekends.** That's when airlines typically try out higher fares; if sales are slow and other airlines don't follow suit, the fare may fall back on Monday.

14. **Check consolidators.** If you have to book an overseas flight at the last minute, check consolidators, which buy blocks of tickets far in advance or purchase them at the last minute for flights with many unsold seats. They typically advertise in newspapers, but don't list the airline's name, because carriers don't want to let the word out that they're selling tickets on the cheap. You can also ask a travel agent to find you a consolidator ticket. Unfortunately, they're rarely available for domestic flights.

15. **Remember the law of diminishing returns.** Sure, you can find rock-bottom deals if you search the Internet long enough, but is a $50 savings on an airfare or hotel rate really worth five hours of your time?

Manage Frequent-Flier Miles

♦♦♦

With credit cards that award one mile for every dollar you spend, and hotel and car rental agencies joining in to help, it is easier than ever to accumulate frequent-flier miles. Unfortunately, it's also harder than ever to use them. As major U.S. carriers tighten their belts in an effort to stay afloat, they are allocating fewer seats for award travelers. The result is that those easy-come bonus miles are not so easy go. Here are some tips for making the most of these potentially valuable, but slippery, perks.

1. **Forget about weekends.** Friday through Monday is the toughest time to book a seat using frequent-flier miles. Monday through Wednesday is your best bet for domestic travel. Tuesday through Thursday are the best days for international free flying.

2. **Plan ahead and be flexible.** Some airlines will allow you to book up to a year ahead of time, thus advancing your chances for a frequent-flier seat. If you are more spontaneous, try booking a reward flight at the last minute; occasionally, late cancellations make award seats available. Nothing beats flexibility for snagging a free seat. If you're able to travel on a variety of dates, and are willing to consider various destinations, you have the greatest chance of using up your miles.

3. **Burn miles.** Don't hoard your frequent-flier miles. These miles don't expire automatically as they once did, but since airlines themselves expire from time to time, it's best to use your miles as rapidly as possible. One way to do this, and get yourself the seats you want when you want them, is to turn over approximately twice the usual number of miles for your coach seat. For example, the average economy seat costs 25,000 miles. If you're willing to spend 40,000 or 50,000 miles for that seat, the airline will give you the same priority as a paying customer, vastly increasing the chance for you to get exactly the flight you want. Another attractive option is to use your miles to find out how the other half lives. If you book far enough ahead, you may be able to redeem your miles for an upgrade to business or first class.

4. **Save miles for expensive flights.** If there's a special fare available, it usually doesn't pay to use free miles for it. On the other hand, if you believe your airline is on the verge of financial problems, it's better to use the miles, even for a cheap flight, than to risk losing them.

5. **Use miles for miles.** Don't purchase stuff with your frequent-flier miles. Your miles are usually worth much more when used to purchase airline tickets than they are when used for merchandise.

6. **Stick to one airline.** If you fly five different airlines, you probably won't fly one enough to accrue meaningful mileage.

7. **Use a credit card to get miles.** Use a credit card with a tie-in to your favorite airline for everything you can: groceries, gas, even doctor bills. The more you charge on the card, the more mileage you accrue. Just be careful to pay the balance in full at the end of the month, because these cards tend to have higher interest rates relative to other cards.

8. **Know and use the program's partners.** Most programs partner with rental-car companies and hotels, but many also partner with other kinds of businesses, such as telephone companies and even florists. Know who your program's partners are and try to use them to maximize miles. Check the program's newsletter—snail mail or online—for new partners and program specials, such as a bonus of double miles for certain purchases.

9. **Search receipts for lost miles.** Go through your receipts for car rentals and hotel stays to make sure the airline hasn't failed to credit you with a qualifying purchase.

10. **Watch out for bankruptcies.** In the past, when airlines have filed for bankruptcy or been taken over by other carriers, frequent-flier members and their miles have generally been transferred to the new carrier or honored while the original one operates under bankruptcy protection (Chapter 11 bankruptcy). If an airline files for Chapter 7 bankruptcy, which requires liquidation, unused miles may be forfeited. If you're prudent, and your airline looks like it's in imminent trouble, use your miles rather than hope for the best.

Pack Suitable Clothing

Packing for a trip, even a weekend getaway, can reduce even a reasonably decisive adult to a state of hopeless confusion. What if we go to a disco? Am I ready for the beach? A blizzard? Horseback riding? It doesn't matter that it's a three-day stay with a friend in Cleveland; the possibilities multiply until the clothes you've laid out will hardly fit into two large suitcases. It doesn't have to be that way. If you think of your suitcase as a "world in microcosm, reduced to its essence," as novelist and poet Katherine Mosby puts it, you can embark with nothing more than a carry-on and arrive ready for anything. Here's how.

1. **Color coordinate.** Pick a neutral color and build your wardrobe around it, making sure that any piece goes with any other. You can add variety with colorful accessories like scarfs and jewelry. Dark colors and prints tend to show less dirt than light-colored solids. Leave anything that needs to be dry-cleaned, and make sure what you take is wrinkle-free.

2. **Make pieces do double duty.** A jersey-knit skirt may be able to double as a strapless dress. A blazer can take you out in the evening when worn with good pants and serve as an extra layer when coupled with jeans and a sweater for a cool morning stroll. Depending on the customs at your destination, jeans can be versatile—topped with a dressy blouse in the evening and paired with a work shirt for casual daytime wear. To keep jeans looking fresh longer, have them dry-cleaned and pressed before you go.

3. **Limit sleepwear.** Consider bringing T-shirts and sweats, which can serve multiple functions.

4. **Pack for layering.** Take light clothes that you can wear in layers for warmth rather than packing bulky sweaters. A thin cashmere sweater over a silk turtleneck can keep you just as warm as a thick wool cardigan.

5. **Resist the just-in-case syndrome.** If the weather suddenly turns freakish, you might be able to borrow appropriate clothes from your host, or if you're on your own, you can buy what you need.

6. **Wear your bulkiest outfit.** By wearing your bulkiest outfit while traveling you can save room in your suitcase.

7. **Eschew shoes.** Shoes are heavy and occupy a significant amount of real estate in your suitcase. Wear the heaviest shoes en route. Women should limit themselves to a maximum of three pairs, including the traveling pair; men can usually do fine with two pairs, tops. Leave slippers at home and use socks instead.

8. **Pack clothes you can trash.** If you take only your holey socks and tattered underwear, you can lighten your suitcase for the trip home by throwing each item away after you wear it.

9. **Ask about appliances.** Most domestic hotels provide a hair dryer and iron, but if you're traveling overseas, you may not be able to count on it. Call your hotel to find out what appliances are available. If you have to bring your own, make it the travel kind and don't forget the appropriate electric adapters.

10. **Pack for pickup.** Your suitcase may have wheels, but sooner or later you're going to have to pick it up to put it in the trunk of a car or in the overhead compartment of the plane. If you have trouble picking it up, you've probably packed more than you need.

STRATEGIES FOR YOUR CARRY-ON

The first thing to consider when packing your carry-on luggage is what you absolutely could not do without if your luggage went on to Bombay when your flight ended in London. Beyond those indispensable items, the possibilities for filling your carry-on are endless, and that's the problem: The space in your carry-on bags is not. Each passenger is allowed only one carry-on bag and one personal item, such as a purse or briefcase. Don't overfill your carry-on bag; most airlines dictate that carry-on bags weigh a maximum of 45 pounds and measure no larger than 10" x 16" x 24". Additional items such as baby strollers and umbrellas are sometimes allowed, but check with your airline before you leave home. This list assumes that you also are checking luggage; if you are not, you must prioritize this list and add a limited amount of clothing using the guidelines in the list above.

Stash medicine and toiletries. Prescription medicines should always be in your carry-on. They should be in the original bottles, with the name of the medication on them. Take travel sizes of your favorite lotions and toothpaste. If you need more than that, you can either pack it in your checked luggage or buy it when you get there. Don't bother with over-the-counter remedies. Your host or your hotel can supply them.

Take important documents. Carry your passport, tickets, and any other important documents with you on-board. If you don't own a fancy leather case for these items, a zip-lock bag is ideal: You can view and access documents easily, and the bag opens smoothly and closes securely. Include your itinerary and contact numbers for your hosts or hotels, as well as the confirmation numbers for hotel reservations.

Carry valuables. Don't travel with valuables that you don't absolutely need, but carry on those you do take.

Bring a list of items in your checked luggage. If you need to fill out a claim form, you'll know what's in limbo.

Take your cell phone and personal organizer. These will come in handy if something happens to your luggage or if you want to make a call while you're waiting to pick up your bags.

Pack a phrase book. If you're traveling internationally, take a phrase book in your carry-on for the country you'll land in. You can pack other phrase books in checked luggage.

Bring a change of clothes. In case the airline loses your checked luggage, it is helpful to have one change of clothes, including underwear, and a T-shirt to sleep in.

Prepare to Go Abroad

◆◆◆

Traveling abroad poses a few challenges you must meet before you even leave home. There are the obvious details to consider, such as passports, visas, foreign currency, and foreign languages. Then there are more subtle matters, such as cultural conventions and personal safety in an age of increased political and social instability. This list will help you take care of the basics before you leave home and guide you to sources for specific information about each country you may visit.

1. **Get or renew a passport.** A U.S. citizen must have a current passport to travel abroad. If you don't already have one, or if yours is expired, give yourself six to eight weeks to obtain it. The total fee for a passport is $97, including processing and security charges; renewals are $67. Expedited

AVOID WRINKLES

Unfortunately, cotton and linen, among the most comfortable fabrics to wear, are more difficult to keep fresh than some of the newer, engineered fabrics, such as Tencel. Rayon packs well, as does fleece, but fleece is not a viable choice for summer travel. When all else fails, and your clothing emerges from the suitcase looking like the two-thousand-year-old man, you have two options: Hang wrinkled items in the bathroom while showering, or call housekeeping to send up an ironing board and iron. The latter is a more reliable wrinkle remover than the old shower standby. Here are some packing tips to reduce wrinkles in whatever fabrics you choose.

Pack in layers that are tight enough to keep garments from shifting around and loose enough so they aren't jammed together.

Zip zippers and button buttons.

Cushion garments inside and out with the plastic coverings from the dry-cleaners or use tissue paper to minimize wrinkling.

Interlock garments and fold them into each other so that each piece cushions the other.

Fold garments into rectangles and then roll them from the bottom up.

Roll small items like socks and underwear into tight balls and tuck them into shoes or stuff them around the sides of the suitcase or wherever you have empty space.

Put more delicate items on top.

Place shoes and other heavy items in bags and put them in separate compartments of the suitcase, if possible, so they don't shift around and mash your clothes together.

service, which assures receipt of your passport within two weeks, is available for an additional $60 plus the cost of two-way overnight delivery. First-time applicants must go in person to one of the 7,000 acceptance offices, which include many courts, post offices, municipal and state buildings, and some public libraries. You need proof of citizenship in the form of a certified birth certificate (that is one with a raised stamp or seal), certificate of naturalization, or certificate of citizenship, and proof of your identity, such as a current valid driver's license. You also need two identical closeup color pictures of yourself, 2" x 2", taken against a white or light background, in everyday attire. The State Department provides a complete guide to getting or renewing a passport, including where to apply, at its Website, travel.state.gov/passport.

2. **Copy your passport information page.** Leave one copy at home with a friend or relative and keep another copy with you in a place other than where you keep your passport. This will make it much easier to replace your passport should it be lost.

3. **Apply for a visa.** Some countries require that your passport be stamped with a visa before you are allowed to enter. The visa authorizes you to travel within the host country for a certain period of time and, sometimes, for a particular purpose. Most west European countries don't require visas if you carry a valid American passport, but if you plan to venture outside that limited circle, you should definitely check with the country's embassy before you leave. For a quick check, visit projectvisa .com, which lists visa requirements for virtually all countries.

4. **Take preventive health measures.** Visit your doctor for routine care before you leave on a trip, especially if you plan to be away for more than a week or two. Make sure you have enough prescription medication to last for the entire trip, plus a little extra in case plans change. Carry prescription items in original bottles, with the prescription labels. Also make sure your routine vaccinations and immunizations are up-to-date and that you receive any immunizations specifically needed for the countries you'll be visiting early enough for them to be effective by the time you arrive. To find out what immunizations are needed for every locale, check with the Centers for Disease Control at *www.cdc.gov/travel*.

5. **Consider travelers' health insurance.** Most health insurance policies won't cover you if you become ill abroad, and those that do might require that you use an in-network provider, who could be far from where

you actually become ill. Check with your regular health insurance provider or insurance agent, your travel agent, or with one of the many companies that provide long- or short-term health policies, such as TravelersMed.com (800–584–3513 or *www.travelersmed.com.*) and World WideMedical (*www.worldwidemedical.com*).

6. **Leave a copy of your itinerary behind.** A close friend or relative back home should have a copy of your itinerary. If you're going to an out-of-the-way place, you might also want to leave a copy with the local U.S. embassy or consulate. That way, in case of an emergency back home, someone will be able to contact you.

7. **Check your ATM card.** The cheapest way to get local currency is through an ATM, but not all PIN numbers work abroad, and some banks restrict how much you can withdraw and from which accounts you can make withdrawals. Check with your bank ahead of time to avoid unpleasant surprises.

8. **Notify your credit- and calling-card companies.** A purchase charged from Brunei may look suspicious unless you've notified your credit card company that you'll be using your card there. Also, notify your telephone calling-card company so they don't put a "theft and loss" hold on your card. While you're at it, ask for the access numbers for the countries you'll be visiting.

9. **Get alternative credit cards.** If you don't have more than one credit card, get another. It is best to carry more than one card from different issuers (a Visa as well as American Express, for instance), in case one or the other isn't accepted.

10. **Investigate driving requirements.** In most European countries, and many others, a valid U.S. driver's license is all you need to drive or rent a car, but you can check with the American Automobile Association to make sure. If you need an international license, the AAA can issue one for a small fee. Also, make sure you know the rules of the road and the driving customs where you're going. You'll get in trouble pretty quickly if you try to drive 45 miles per hour on one of Germany's fast-paced autobahns, and you won't last long driving on the right side of the road in Britain.

11. **Be careful.** Don't be paranoid, but be at least as vigilant against trouble abroad as you would be at home. Don't wear flashy jewelry unless you're

going to a ball; don't carry your computer in a case that screams "expensive, steal me." And remember your manners; charm and respect can go a long way toward diffusing even threatening situations. If you're traveling to countries experiencing social or political instability, check with the State Department at *www.state.gov/travelandbusiness* for any current warnings. Warnings are listed by country and updated continuously, as conditions change.

Stay Safe in Hotels

The ads would have you believe it's your home away from home, but a hotel room is just a public space you rent for a limited time. The key to staying safe is to remember that you're not in your own bedroom and to take some common-sense precautions.

1. **Insist on security the moment you check in.** Don't let the clerk announce your room number. If he inadvertently does, ask for another room and tell him to write it down, not say it aloud.

2. **Don't advertise the fact that you're a single woman.** If you're a woman traveling alone, make the reservation as Mr. and Mrs. If the hotel policy is to charge extra for a second person, call the front desk shortly after your arrival to say that "Mr." has to cancel.

3. **Avoid hotels with metal keys.** Rooms with electronic keys are much more secure, because the electronic code is automatically changed each time a guest leaves.

4. **Choose a safe room.** Try to avoid the first two floors, where most thefts occur. Conversely, avoid anything above the sixth floor, since many fire ladders don't reach any higher. The safest rooms, although not necessarily the most quiet, those that are clearly visible from the elevator or another center of activity.

5. **Inspect the room.** Prop open the door with your luggage and check out the room. If you've asked for a smoke-free or allergen-free room, make sure that's what you've got. Check that there are no rooms that connect

to other rooms; if there are, make sure that they are securely locked. If there are sliding doors leading to a balcony, make sure they can be securely locked and that all windows have working locks.

6. **Have an escape plan.** Study the fire exit plan on the back of the door and physically scout out the nearest exit and a secondary route.

7. **Check for bedbugs.** Partly because the use of DDT has been banned and no new insecticides have been developed to fight them, and partly because of the increase in foreign travel, bedbugs, once the scourge only of bowery dives, are showing up as uninvited guests at even five-star hotels. Throw back the bedspread and look for small brown creatures about the size of an apple seed. Check around the seams of the mattress and box spring, especially along the welting, where bedbugs like to hide. Any little brown stains you see could be blood stains, a dead giveaway of a past invasion. These bugs are hardy and tenacious. They hide in mattresses, carpets, furniture, and even behind picture frames, and they can hitch a ride in your luggage and take up residence in your home when you return. Don't take chances; if you see signs of bedbugs, check out.

8. **Keep your door shut and locked.** If someone knocks, use the peephole to verify the person's identity, even if you've ordered room service. If you are at all unsure about the individual at your door, call the front desk to make sure the person is legitimate before opening the door.

9. **Don't hang the "Make Up This Room" card.** Call the front desk if you want your room made up outside the usual housekeeper's cleaning hours.

10. **Take care of valuables.** Use the safe or carry valuables with you. This includes anything you absolutely don't want to lose, including your laptop, jewelry, and credit cards. Also, never leave your house or car keys behind in the room.

11. **Ask about neighborhood safety.** No matter how it looks, don't assume the neighborhood is safe at night. Ask the hotel staff whether it's safe to walk to nearby restaurants or movies. If they voice any reservations, don't hesitate to ask for shuttle or taxi service or an escort to your car.

12. **Always use the hotel's main entrance.** If you're driving, make sure the parking area is well lit and open. If it isn't, ask for an escort from your car.

13. **Leave a light on.** Also, leave the TV on and hang the "Do Not Disturb" card on the door to create the impression that the room is occupied.

14. **Bring a flashlight.** Power fails and fires happen. Be on the safe side, and always pack a small flashlight and keep it by your bedside.

Hail a Taxi in New York City

◆◆◆

This skill comes under the heading of "life in the big city." Any tourist can get lucky fluttering a hand from the curb, but it takes a savvy traveler to grab a cab during rush hour. The good news is that there are more cabs than ever, and the $1 peak-hour surcharge, in effect from 4 to 8 P.M., Monday through Friday, makes it more likely than ever that you'll find a cab in rush hour.

1. **Stand at a corner.** This doubles your chances of getting a cabbie to stop, because you can get the attention of cabbies coming from two directions.

2. **Make eye contact.** It's hard for a driver to ignore someone who's staring into his or her eyes. Also, cabs are stop-and-go affairs; if the driver actually looks at you and sees you getting into the cab, he won't take off while you're only half in.

3. **Don't ignore rule two even if the light is red.** Never assume a cab stopped at a red light won't take off as soon as the light turns green. Always make sure you have the driver's attention before opening the cab door. If the light's been red for more than a few seconds, the driver will signal you to meet him at a safe corner when the light changes. Once the driver acknowledges you, that's your cab, even if someone else is waiting on the other corner.

4. **Capture your turf.** Stand at the edge of the street. If you stand on the sidewalk someone could swoop in and take the cab right out from under you.

5. **Know where cabbies are headed.** Put yourself on streets where taxis head to pick up fares. For example, you're more likely to find empty cabs on streets headed toward the train station than away from it.

6. **Loiter near a hotel.** You don't want to become a suspicious character, but if you need a cab, try walking to a hotel or big restaurant where you're likely to find cabbies waiting for business.

7. **Hail off-duty taxis.** Don't ignore cabs with the "off-duty" lights on. Under the Taxi and Limousine Commission's "going my way rule," off-duty cabbies are allowed to take fares on their way back to the garage, so long as the driver turns on the "occupied" light and records the trip in his log when you get in.

8. **Make your luggage disappear.** When you're headed for the airport during rush hour, do what you can to make your luggage inconspicuous. Cabbies hate to get caught in long lines of rush-hour traffic leaving the city.

9. **Flaunt your luggage.** If you're going to the airport at an off hour, make your suitcase as visible as you can. There's nothing like a long trip against prevailing traffic, with an extra tip for schlepping luggage, to warm a driver's heart.

10. **Go where the action is late at night.** Cabbies know where the likely fares are at unlikely hours. For example, twenty-four-hour news organizations, such as the CBS studio on West 57th Street, are cab magnets in the hours after the 11 P.M. newscast. Hospitals and late-night clubs also draw cab drivers looking for large fares in the small hours.

11. **Get a receipt.** It probably won't happen, but what if you inadvertently leave your Stradivarius violin in the cab? You're in a much better position if you can tell the Taxi and Limousine Service the number of the cab you left it in, and that number is right on the receipt. Just call 311 and report the missing Strad. With any luck, you'll be playing it in Carnegie Hall that very night.

12. **Forget about shift changes.** The Taxi and Limousine Commission points out that only about 20 percent of New York City cabs are fleet-owned. That means there's no particular time when cabs are headed back to the garage.

HAILING CABS IN TOKYO, PARIS, LONDON, AND MOSCOW

Tokyo

The first things you'll notice are the white gloves. Cabs in Tokyo are clean, which may come as a shock to Americans. They're also courteous—not just the drivers, but the cabs themselves. The passenger door, on the left, swings open when you approach and opens by itself (with an assist from the driver) when you depart. The difficulty with taking a cab in Tokyo comes in telling the driver where you'd like to go. As with so many cabbies in New York, drivers in Tokyo may not speak English, at least not the kind of English you speak. Also, the street arrangement is perhaps the most Byzantine on Earth. To compound the possibility for confusion, buildings are frequently unnumbered. If you're headed anywhere other than a major hotel or other popular destination, circle it on a map and hand the map to the driver. For all the potential difficulty in taking a cab in Japan, there is this good news: You will find all the drivers exceptionally polite. They would consider a tip an insult.

Paris

When you want to hail a cab in Paris, go to a taxi stand. The stands can be found at large intersections and in popular locations, such as tourist destinations and shopping areas. If only for economy's sake, use the taxi stands rather than calling for a cab; Paris taxi drivers start the meter when they set out to collect you, instead of when you get in. Many residents and businesses maintain accounts with cab companies, so if you have a connection you might use it to make arrangements the night before. Just don't count on finding a cab late at night, as you might in New York. To call a cab, try Alpha Taxi (01–45–85–85–85), Artaxi (01–42–41–50–50), Taxis G7 (01–47–39–47–39), or Taxis Bleu (01–49–36–10–10). Technically, tipping is not required, but

10 percent is standard. Keep in mind that the Metro goes everywhere, and it's quieter and more reliable than just about any other subway in the world.

London

London cabbies are legendary for their uncanny ability to find just about any address in town. This knowledge is a requirement for a cab license here. The big black cabs are extremely comfortable, but after 10 P.M., when a 50 percent surcharge goes into effect, they can be quite expensive. The minicabs cost less, but the experience just isn't the same. Cabs are easily hailed on the street, but become scarce late at night. A 10 percent tip is expected. To call a cab, try Dial a Cab (020–7253–5000) or Parkward (020–8838–4242). To make calls within London, dial only the last eight digits.

Moscow

The usual way to hail a cab is just to stick your arm straight out and wait for the first pile of scrap metal, otherwise known as a gypsy cab, to pull up. Confirm the destination and agree upon a fare before your ride begins. Be prepared to bargain; sometimes drivers will negotiate a flat, rather than a metered, fare. The average taxi fare in Moscow is Rb10.

Two important tips: Never pay until you've retrieved your luggage from the cab. Never get into a cab that already has a fare inside. It can help to know which side of the street to hail from, since if you're on the wrong side, the one-way system in Moscow can cost an additional fifteen minutes. Ask a native for advice. Having the exact fare is helpful, because drivers often don't have change, or won't admit to it if they do in the hope of acquiring a de facto tip. Otherwise, tipping is not expected. There is a central number for radio taxis (095–927–0000), or you can call Moscow Taxi (095–238–1001).

Instruct Your House Sitter

◆◆◆

You have been given a three-month assignment abroad, or maybe you just want to get away to the shore for a few weeks. You could cancel the newspaper, turn down the thermostat, set the automatic light timers, and hope for the best, or you could hire someone to live at your house while you're away. Here are some suggestions for finding and preparing a house sitter.

1. **Be specific about what you expect.** It's standard practice, and wise, to draw up a contract spelling out the house sitter's responsibilities. Typically, a house sitter is responsible for keeping up the house and its contents, caring for pets, watering the garden and houseplants, and attending to emergency situations. Standard contracts are available from most house-sitting agencies, or your attorney can provide one.

2. **Make sure the sitter is familiar with your alarm system.** Give your house sitter the combination for the alarm, and make sure she knows what to do in the event of a false alarm or a malfunction. Give her the number of the alarm company and the nonemergency number of the local police. Explain how to set the alarm, how to disarm it, and when to do both. Make sure the sitter knows which windows and doors are included in the system and which windows can be left open and how wide.

3. **Introduce the neighbors.** Neighbors can provide important information in unforeseen circumstances, and they can be an invaluable source of help in case your house sitter needs an extra hand. Face-to-face meetings are best, but at the least make sure your house sitter has the neighbors' phone numbers. Also make sure you tell your neighbors about your house sitter, so they will know the person going in and out of your house isn't a burglar.

4. **Provide essential phone numbers.** Leave a list of numbers that includes a plumber, an electrician, the pool maintenance company, your insurance company, and any other service you usually use (garbage collection, tree person, lawn-sprinkler company, etc.). Include numbers where you can be reached, as well as those of key relatives.

5. **Explain your pets' habits and needs.** If you have animals, you've chosen a house sitter who's comfortable with them, but don't take anything

HOW TO FIND A HOUSE SITTER

The virtual community is a great place to start a search, but don't forget your real community. As usual, start your search by asking friends and neighbors for recommendations. You might also try asking at local colleges and universities, especially for vacation periods and summer getaways. Local real estate agents may be a good source: People hoping to move into the community who haven't been able to find a residence, or those whose real estate closing is weeks or months away, may be delighted to get early entrée to the community through house-sitting. Next, go to the Internet. The house-sitter Websites include:

www.housecarers.com. This is one of the largest sites in the field. Through the site's confidential message system, homeowners and house sitters match needs and availability. The site also includes a comprehensive guide for both homeowners and prospective house sitters.

www.housesitworld.com. This is another search site, but not as comprehensive as housecarers.com.

www.sabbaticalhomes.com. As its name implies, this is a site that focuses on academics, although it's open to anyone. Most of these are for long-term assignments, and many offer to trade homes for the period.

www.mindmyhouse.com. This site matches homeowners with house sitters by state or city.

www.craigslist.com. The site every college student or graduate searches for just about anything.

for granted. Spell out your pets' habits, hiding places, and needs, and make certain your house sitter is comfortable meeting them. Leave your vet's name and number.

6. **Spell out what's off-limits.** If you don't want your house sitter using your computer, drinking from your wine cellar, or eating your truffles, say so. Perhaps you don't mind if the house sitter invites friends over for dinner, but you might not be thrilled if he or she (or they) hosts a class reunion in your backyard. Inviting someone you don't know well to live in your home is, by definition, a matter of trust, but it shouldn't be a blind leap of faith. It's a good idea to entrust very precious, uninsured, or irreplaceable items to a friend or family member while you're away.

7. **Leave clear instructions about bills.** Sometimes the sitter is responsible for paying utility bills, sometimes not. You may want to arrange to pay recurring bills, such as the mortgage or property taxes, through automatic deductions before you leave. Other bills might need to be handled on an ad hoc basis, possibly by having the sitter forward them to you. The important thing is that you and your sitter know who is responsible for paying which bills.

8. **Go over your house's idiosyncrasies.** If the furnace makes a strange noise when it comes on, tell the sitter, so she doesn't panic. Be especially conscious of your everyday routines around the house a week before your final meeting with the sitter, and note anything that someone else might not expect. You may know the back burner is on the blink and shoots flames three feet high, but your sitter won't unless you mention it.

Plan an Exotic Vacation

◆◆◆

A vacation is a chance to get away, to expand the daily circumference of your life into new territory. Some vacations, however, can take you into a wholly different sphere. There are plenty of opportunities to travel to more exotic locations than London, Paris, or Rome, but there are precautions to take and decisions to make before you leave. Here are the basics.

1. **Decide what you mean by exotic.** Are you willing to go into largely un-charted territory, where you'll find few of the comforts and amenities you're used to, such as paved roads and potable water? Do you want to explore a single aspect of a more developed place, such as the catacombs of Rome or the folk culture of the Balkans? Are you looking for outdoor adventure, such as mountain climbing, or extreme sports, such as heli-skiing? Options that were available to only the very rich just twenty years ago now are often no more expensive than a routine trip to Disneyland.

2. **Consider your health and physical condition.** Certain exotic vaca-tions, such as exploring the remote mountain regions of Tibet, demand top physical conditioning and very specific skills. In other des-tinations you could be exposed to extreme climates. Don't underesti-mate the physical demands of a vacation off the beaten path; in all probability you'll need more energy than you would for a week tour-ing Rome.

3. **Review the CDC's travel section.** If you're going anyplace even a bit unusual, check the excellent travel section of the Centers for Disease Control and Prevention's Website (*www.cdc.gov/travel*). It will tell you what immunizations and precautions you need to take for virtually any destination, as well as diseases and other health risks found there. You'll also learn what to bring with you, how to stay healthy during your trip, and what, if anything, you need to continue to do after you return (for instance, if you've been to a place where malaria is endemic, you should continue to take your antimalarial drugs even after you return).

4. **Check the State Department's Travel Warnings list.** You should do this whenever you travel abroad, but it's especially important when you travel to less-developed countries. The site, at *www.travel.state.gov*, is up-dated to reflect current conditions, and you should check it when mak-ing plans and just before departure.

5. **Bone up on your destination.** Do the usual preparation any traveler should do before going to new places, but go one step further. Ask for in-formation from your destination's embassy or consulate, search the Web for sites and blogs about the area, and spend some time in the library reading and looking at pictures to get an idea of the physical terrain.

GIVE WHILE YOU GET: VOLUNTEER VACATIONS

A volunteer vacation can be particularly rewarding. You immerse yourself in a foreign culture, meet local people, share their lives, use your expertise, learn something new, and return knowing that you've made a difference in the lives of others. There can be tangible benefits as well. Sometimes your travel costs are tax deductible; often accommodations, meals, travel within the country, and attendance at cultural events are free. On top of all that, you'll have the opportunity to visit places and interact with people in a way that a traditional vacation could never provide. Here are some resources:

Action Without Borders (*www.idealist.org*) lists opportunities in 165 countries. One of the recent listings: Help protect the reefs off Fiji and create a World Heritage site there (advanced diver training and certification included).

Earthwatch (*www.earthwatch.org*) offers opportunities to participate in scientific and cultural research throughout the world. A recent project involved studying the likelihood that Russian folk music traditions will be maintained in modern Russian culture.

Global Volunteers (*www.globalvolunteers.org*) offers opportunities to volunteer for one to three weeks in any of twenty countries, helping with village construction, health care, and child-care training.

Habitat for Humanity (*www.habitat.org*) provides a chance to spend anywhere from one to three weeks helping to build permanent and temporary housing in countries all over the globe, including this one.

6. **Buy the right travel health coverage.** An accident or unexpected illness in a remote location could require medical evacuation, so if your destination is remote, be sure your travel insurance includes evacuation coverage. Even if there's a hospital nearby, it may not function at a level you are accustomed to. A hospital in a remote area of a less-developed country might not have an x-ray machine, blood bank, or sterile needles. The cost of evacuation to a first-rate hospital in a nearby country can run as high as $75,000. Protect yourself with insurance that can cost as little as $4 per day.

||||||||||||||||||||||||||||[The Law]||||||||||||||||||||||||||||||||||||

Know When to Call a Lawyer

◆ ◆ ◆

Reviled, distrusted, the butt of countless jokes, lawyers are best encountered on television; unless, of course, you need legal help. Then they're indispensable. Sooner or later, most people will need a lawyer. Here are some of the most common circumstances under which you should seek legal counsel.

1. **You're arrested or charged with a crime.** This one may seem obvious, but don't forget that a serious driving mistake may well be a crime, not an infraction.

2. **You are served with a search warrant.**

3. **You are served any legal papers.** Such papers may come in the form of a subpoena, summons, complaint, or demand for arbitration. It's important to call a lawyer immediately, because you may only have a few days in which to respond without incurring a default judgment or penalty.

4. **You are being sued.**

5. **You feel you are entitled to sue someone or some entity.** If you're instigating the suit, don't do it frivolously. Unless you've suffered a meaningful financial loss that can be objectively measured or damage to your reputation that will result in serious financial loss, it may not be worth the costs of suing.

6. **You're involved in an automobile accident that results in injury or any significant property damage.** Call your insurance company immediately, but if the accident is serious, call a lawyer as well. Your insurance agent might be able to advise you, but also listen to your instincts.

7. **You've been unable to resolve a disputed insurance claim.**

8. **You want to write a will, a living will, or an advanced medical directive, or you want to have a trust or estate plan drawn up.** You can download the forms from the Internet, but it may be worth the fee to have a lawyer review them, especially if there's a large amount of money involved or if you want to delegate responsibility for carrying out your wishes to someone other than a spouse or blood relative.

9. **You're contemplating a divorce, entering a permanent domestic partnership arrangement, adopting a child, or are having problems with child support or visitation.**

10. **Your divorce agreement is not being honored.**

11. **You think a family member isn't getting the help that a government agency should provide.**

12. **You think a dependent or infirm family member is being unduly influenced by someone else in the family or by an outside person.**

13. **You believe you've been discriminated against at your job.**

14. **You're being subjected to a hostile working environment for any reason.**

15. **You're contemplating bankruptcy.**

16. **You are involved in any real estate transaction.** Many states require that you be represented by a lawyer if you buy or sell a home, but whether the state requires it or not, you should always have a lawyer review any real estate transaction before you close on it.

17. **You're buying or selling a business.**

18. **You're involved in a publishing venture, are offered a book deal, or are making a movie or creating anything for actual performance.**

19. **You want to patent or copyright something.**

20. **Another professional, such as an accountant, tax adviser, or financial adviser suggests it.**

BEFORE YOU MAKE THE CALL

Calling a lawyer may not be the first step toward resolving a dispute. If you have a problem with a product or service, first try to resolve it amicably (see "Write an Effective Complaint Letter," page 75). If you think you're not receiving something you are entitled to from the government, ask to speak with a representative of the agency involved. If that doesn't work, try your elected representative. Special interest groups, community organizations, professional associations, and volunteer agencies may also be able to help.

Choose a Lawyer

◆◆◆

The first step in choosing a lawyer is defining why you need one. Like physicians, lawyers tend to specialize in certain areas. Once you know what kind of lawyer you're looking for, ask for personal recommendations. Don't limit yourself to asking friends and relatives; ask other professionals, such as your doctor or accountant, and, if it isn't an extremely private matter, check with business associates and colleagues. Your local bar association will provide a list of lawyers, but it won't make recommendations or endorsements. Once you've assembled a list of names, talk to each of them on the telephone and, if you like their answers, schedule an in-person interview. As with many professional relationships, chemistry counts.

On the Phone

Start with a phone call to narrow the list of lawyers who might be worth the time (and possibly money) for a face-to-face interview. Before you make the calls, take some time to clearly summarize the issues of your case so you can present them succinctly and clearly. Ask these questions:

1. **Do you handle this kind of case?** Some lawyers limit their practices to particular areas of the law, such as discrimination issues, real estate, and intellectual property. If you want to sue Disney for stealing your idea about a foolish rabbit, don't even consider a real estate lawyer.

2. **How long have you been handling cases like mine?** If the lawyer just switched from entertainment to criminal law and you're accused of a crime, continue your search.

3. **Would you personally represent me, or would one of your associates handle my case?** You want to interview the attorney you'll actually be working with.

4. **Do you charge for an initial interview? If so, how much?** Many lawyers are willing to meet with you for a half hour without a fee to explore your case and see if the two of you are a good fit.

5. **How are your fees calculated?** Different types of cases are charged in different ways. Some of the most common are: a contingency basis, for which the attorney receives a percentage of the award if you prevail; a flat

fee, which is common in drawing up will or trust documents; and an hourly rate, more typical for divorces or criminal or civil litigation.

6. **Can you give me a rough estimate?** If your case will be charged on an hourly basis, ask for an estimate of how many billable hours it will take. A lawyer should at least be able to give you a meaningful range. He may say, for instance, that an uncontested divorce might run between $1,500 and $2,500; a simple will $500; a complex suit might be charged at an hourly rate of $400 and take anywhere from 100 to 300 hours of work.

In Person

Before you set up an appointment, contact the local bar association to make sure no actions are being taken against the lawyer and that he or she is, indeed, a member of the bar. Interview likely candidates in person to help you determine how well you get along, whether you're comfortable with the lawyer's approach to your case, and how the process will go. Come prepared with all the vital information, such as facts, dates, and the names, addresses, and phone numbers of anyone connected with the case, and with any relevant paperwork or documents.

1. **What are the strengths and weaknesses of my case?** Don't expect a detailed answer, but the lawyer should be able to tell you roughly what she thinks your chances of prevailing are.

2. **Will it go to trial or might we settle?** Again, it's early in the ball game, but you might ask if the lawyer has been able to successfully settle cases like yours without the expense and bother of going to trial. If so, what does he think you might roughly expect to win.

3. **Do you often take cases like mine?** If so, roughly how many have ended favorably for your client?

4. **What do you think the likely time line is?** How long should this take from start to finish if we can settle? If we go to trial, when might that be?

5. **What other fees might be involved?** Ask for an estimate of your total costs, including any court fees, research fees, copying fees, charges for expert witnesses, certified stenographers, private investigators, and the like.

6. **How will you bill me?** Do you require an up-front retainer? Will I be billed at the end of the case? Can I make a payment arrangement?

7. **Will you sign a fee agreement?** Many states require a written agreement if the estimated services will exceed a given amount. In any case, it's a good idea to have your agreement in writing, even if it's for a range, rather than a specific figure. Your fee agreement should specify what services the lawyer will perform, the type and amount of fees he'll charge for them, and how other costs will be billed.

8. **Will I be ultimately in charge?** This is an important issue. Some lawyers simply go ahead and take whatever actions they deem necessary; others will consult you before doing anything you haven't already approved. Make sure you understand exactly how this lawyer would proceed if you hired her.

9. **How often will I hear from you?** Don't expect to hear directly from the lawyer every few days, but make sure you're comfortable with how the communications between you will work. Should you feel free to call him directly? Will you be going through an assistant or a secretary?

Prepare for Small Claims Court

◆◆◆

Small claims courts exist for quickly settling disputes between two parties in which the amount of money at stake is relatively small. The definition of small may vary from state to state, but generally the maximum is somewhere between $3,000 (in New York) and $7,500 (in Minnesota). The atmosphere in small claims court is much more informal than in regular civil courts, and many small claims courts prohibit representation by lawyers. Resolutions are fast; it might be no longer than three weeks between filing a claim and getting a judgment, as opposed to waiting months or years in regular civil courts. In many states, both parties are required to submit to arbitration before proceeding to court, and this can be extremely effective. Since Maine instituted mandatory arbitration, the number of cases that have gone on to small claims court is down by 50 percent. If you do proceed to small claims court, you'll increase your chances of winning your case if you pay attention to the steps in this list.

1. **First, ask for what you want in writing.** Even if you've had a conversation about the matter and been turned down, ask the other party for what you want in a clear, straightforward letter. Mention that if you don't receive satisfaction, you intend to take the matter to small claims court. This shows you're serious, and it's also a required first step in many jurisdictions. Further, since both parties must personally appear in small claims court, just stating your intention is often enough to settle the issue.

2. **Decide whether the effort will be worthwhile.** Before instituting a suit, think about whether or not the person or company you're suing has the assets to pay a judgment against them. Does the person have a steady job? A bank account? Is the company likely to remain in business and is it profitable? Judgments are often good for many years, and circumstances change, but if the amount is small, the trouble and expense of collection may not be worthwhile.

3. **Call your county clerk to arrange for a court date.** If both parties live or do business in the same county, that's where your hearing will be held. If not, the clerk will tell you where to bring your action; often, if you're suing a business, the case will be heard in the jurisdiction where the company does business or is headquartered. Ask about filing fees, how and when they must be paid (often in cash), and what you need to bring to file the claim. You'll probably need to provide the clerk with the full name and address of the person you're suing or the principal of the company who will answer the suit. This is needed so that the defendant can be served the necessary papers.

4. **Verify the court date and arrive on time.** You should be notified of the trial date in writing. If you don't receive written notification within two weeks of filing your claim, call the clerk to see if there is a problem. In any case, always call to verify the date, and make sure you and any witnesses you plan to call arrive on time. If one party fails to appear as scheduled, that party loses by default.

5. **Collect supporting documentation.** Whether you're bringing the action or defending yourself against an action brought by someone else, what you bring to court is often more important than what you say when you get there. Make sure you have all the receipts, correspondence, letters from third parties, such as experts or witnesses, photographs, advertisements falsely hyping the product you bought, and anything else that might support your version of the truth.

6. **Prepare your statement.** Rehearse what you plan to say in court. Remember, your statement should be in plain English, not legalese. It should include a clear, concise statement of your complaint, the steps you've already taken to resolve it, and a concrete proposal for a settlement.

7. **Anticipate how the other side will respond.** You may have a good idea from previous conversations with the other party how he intends to defend himself. Think of each point he is likely to make and prepare a simple response to it. If your case has actually wound up in court, don't expect the other side to simply agree to all your points. That person is there because he intends to contest your version of the case.

8. **Be prepared to walk away without satisfaction.** You should understand before you even begin the process that collecting on a judgment may not be guaranteed. Even if the judge rules in your favor and awards you a cash settlement, the court may not have any provisions for actually collecting it. You may have to file a separate case to collect on your award.

Prepare for Traffic Court

◆◆◆

If you were going 50 miles per hour in a 25-mile-per-hour zone, you're clearly guilty of speeding, and you should pay the ticket and make a solemn vow to drive responsibly. But not every ticket is so clear-cut. Unsafe driving can be a subjective judgment call. Even if you have broken a traffic law, it could be worth going to court to fight the ticket or agree to plead guilty to a lesser charge. A moving violation will probably cost you insurance points, and insurance points mean higher premiums. If you show up in court and plead your case, you might be offered a deal that either reduces the points against your driving record or eliminates them altogether. If you do decide to fight your ticket, here are tips that will give you an edge.

1. **Be polite.** No matter how outraged you feel, don't let it show. Be polite and respectful. This is, after all, a court, and whether you personally like the judge or police officers involved, you need to show respect for the institutions they represent. Dress neatly, stand straight, without slouching, and address the judge as "your honor."

2. **If it's serious, hire an attorney.** If you're in danger of losing your license, or if the penalty could include a hefty fine or even jail time, hire an attorney. The stakes, in this case, are just too high to simply hope for the best. In fact, if the charge is serious, the judge might suggest you be represented by counsel. If you can't afford one, the judge will assign a public defender to help you.

3. **Request the police report.** You're entitled to know exactly what you're charged with and the statements of any witnesses involved. Get this information before going to court. Compare what you're being charged with against the definitions in the State Vehicle Code or any other code that applies, and see if you think your conduct did, in fact, violate the code. If not, prepare an argument that details why you think you're innocent.

4. **Bring all the documentation you can.** If you say you didn't realize you were speeding because your speedometer was broken, bring a letter to that effect from a mechanic. If the speed limit or other traffic sign was damaged or not clearly visible, bring photographs to prove your point. If it's an accident and you don't have photographs, draw a clear diagram that you can give to the judge.

5. **Find witnesses to testify on your behalf.** Perhaps the incident took place in front of a store and a clerk witnessed it. The testimony of a credible eyewitness could be persuasive to a judge.

6. **Emphasize your good record.** If you agree that you were wrong, be contrite and emphasize your outstanding driving record. Just remember, the judge will have your record in front of her. If this is your seventeenth bust, don't lie; just pay the ticket.

> **TIP:** In some states—New Jersey is one—you can plead guilty to a generic "unsafe driving" charge that carries no insurance points if this is your first offense in a certain period of time and you have a valid license and an otherwise clean driving record. However, you might incur a hefty surcharge for this privilege. Check with your insurance company to see how much your insurance would increase if you simply took the points and paid the ticket. If that amount is less than the fee you'd pay for the reduced charge, you might not want to contest the ticket.

FIGHTING A SPEEDING TICKET

Speeding tickets represent a special case, because they usually come down to your word against the officer's, and laws vary from state to state. If you want to contest a speeding ticket, follow the rules above, making sure to bring all the documentation you have to court. You should know if your state laws use absolute or presumed speed limits. In absolute-limit states, you're guilty if you go even one mile over the limit. In presumed-limit states, you're presumed guilty if you go above the posted limit unless you can justify your speed because of road or traffic conditions. Obviously, it's easier to defend yourself in a presumed-limit state, especially if you were traveling just a little over the limit. There are various defenses, depending on the circumstances.

General Defenses

There were extenuating circumstances. This could work so long as your circumstances were dire: You were rushing someone to the hospital, for instance. Being late for a date or rushing to deliver a PowerPoint presentation to your boss probably won't work in your favor.

You weren't going as fast as the officer claims. It's your word against his, and judges tend to side with the officer, but it can't hurt to try.

You had to drive above the posted limit to avoid a serious consequence. This could be because of sudden mechanical problems or the onset of a serious medical problem.

The road, traffic conditions, and your car's safety equipment made the speed reasonable. This argument works only if you're in a state where the presumed-speed limit rule applies.

Radar Defenses

Radar systems can't really pick one car out of a pack; whether the speeding car was yours remains the officer's discretionary call. Here are some possible arguments.

The officer was tracking another vehicle. This can be your word against his, but if there were a large number of cars at the time, the officer may not be able to swear it was your car he tagged.

The officer's radar was compromised. A photograph showing that the officer had to shoot his radar through an object between your car and his presents a pretty good defense. If the officer was trailing you, his reading could have been compromised by highly reflective signs, power lines, power stations, or other vehicles moving around you in dense traffic.

The equipment wasn't maintained or the officer wasn't properly trained. These are difficult defenses that require an attorney's help, because you must subpoena records. If the possible costs of a guilty verdict are great enough, these defenses might be worth at least considering.

Know and Protect Your Rights

◆◆◆

The basis of the U.S. government is that all people have certain rights. Those rights are guaranteed and protected by law, and they cannot be abridged without due process. The preamble to the Bill of Rights makes it clear that the rights that follow are actually restrictions on the original Constitution, which itself restricts government powers. In other words, the entire Constitution and the Bill of Rights, in particular, are meant to clearly restrict the power that government has over the governed. Here are your most basic rights and some information on how to protect them.

1. **You have the right not to talk to the authorities.** The Fifth Amendment provides an absolute right to remain silent when questioned by the police, Federal Bureau of Investigation, Immigration and Naturalization Service (INS), and any other law enforcement agency or representative. Even if you are arrested, you are not obligated to talk to anyone. Only a judge can compel testimony, and even then you have the right not to testify against yourself. If you are arrested you can request an attorney and refuse to answer any questions or divulge any information except on the advice of an attorney. If you're driving a motor vehicle, however, you are required to show your license and registration if asked for them.

2. **You can voluntarily surrender your right to remain silent.** Although you're guaranteed the right to remain silent, if you agree to talk to authorities, anything you say can be used against you. This extends, of course, to any written statements you make. You may still refuse to answer specific questions, unless ordered to do so by a judge.

3. **Minors also have the right to remain silent.** Even people under eighteen have the right to remain silent when questioned by authorities, including school authorities. Minors detained at a juvenile facility, unless accused of a serious crime, usually have the right to be released to the custody of their parents or guardians. Students caught cheating, blowing bubblegum, or making disrespectful faces at their teachers can refuse to talk when hauled off to the principal's office, although it's unlikely to endear them to anyone. Students should be instructed, at home if not at school, about their basic Constitutional rights and the fact that they enjoy the same protections as adults.

4. **Noncitizens have the right to remain silent.** People who are not U.S. citizens can also refuse to talk to authorities. If a noncitizen is stopped by an INS official or any law-enforcement agent, he might well consider asking for an attorney before voluntarily answering any questions, even questions regarding his immigration status.

5. **You have the right to be free from "unreasonable searches and seizures."** The Fourth Amendment guarantees that you cannot be stopped and searched nor can your house be entered without a court

warrant or a reasonable suspicion that a crime is taking place. If a policeman knocks on your door and asks to enter, you have the right to refuse.

6. **If an officer or other agent has a warrant, you must allow a search.** You have the right to see the warrant, and the search is to be limited to what is specified in the document. If the officer asks you to hand over material that is not specified in the warrant, you can refuse. You may choose to comply with any request, but if it isn't specified in the warrant you can't be compelled to do so.

7. **If you're stopped while driving, your car may not be searched unless there is reason to believe you've committed a crime.** The same restrictions against unreasonable search and seizure that apply to your home or office also apply to your car.

8. **If you are stopped by an authority on the street, ask the reason and ask if you're free to go.** If you're free to go, simply leave. You have no obligation to remain or talk to anyone unless you are told that you are suspected of a crime. If you are not free to go, you are being detained, although you are not necessarily arrested. If you are being detained, the officer has the right to frisk you, which means a pat-down on the outside of your clothing. Women have the right to request that they be frisked by a female officer. You do not have to submit to any other search. If you feel that the officer is violating your rights, you should speak up, but you should not physically resist. Insist on a lawyer and refuse to answer any questions, even if you are arrested.

9. **You have the right to advocate for change.** The First Amendment guarantees the right of individuals and groups to advocate for change of laws, policies, and even the form of government. The government can limit these rights only to assure the general safety, as when it legislates against maliciously yelling "fire" in a crowded theater when in fact there is no fire. These rights extend to students, who have the right to organize groups, even if the groups support unpopular causes. Again, there are reasonable limits, but they tend to apply only to hate groups or those advocating the immediate, violent disruption of normal school activities.

10. **You have the right to a fair and speedy trial.** The Sixth Amendment guarantees these rights. Local laws may define just what "speedy" is, but if you are arrested, you have the right to be told of the charge against

you. You are also entitled to know your rights to bail as well as what rules govern how long you can be held. Of course, if you are arrested, don't rely on the authorities to advise you of all your rights. Ask to see a lawyer immediately, and remember that if you don't know a lawyer or can't afford one, you are entitled to free, prompt, and competent representation.

[Money]

Take a Home Inventory

Taking a home inventory has got to be a close second to making a will when it comes to the list of tasks we'd all like to postpone indefinitely. But if you suffer a major loss from fire, natural disaster, or crime, without a current home inventory, your chances of being properly compensated by your insurance company are slim. You needn't do the whole inventory at once. Breaking the task down into manageable bits—even just one room a week—makes it much more likely that you'll actually do it. Taking a home inventory really isn't as daunting as it may seem if you follow these suggestions.

1. **Photograph everything.** With digital cameras, photographing every room of your house, as well as the outside of it, is relatively easy.

   - Take wide-angle shots of entire rooms; should your house be destroyed, this will help establish the scope of the loss.

   - Open closets and take pictures of their contents.

   - Take close-up shots of all important items, and include details, such as the brand of an appliance, or the titles and dates of your first-edition books, that might help establish value.

   - Remember to record the contents of the attic, basement, garage, and outbuildings.

2. **Make a descriptive list.** A picture may be worth a thousand words, but you're going to need words to describe exactly what's in the pictures. Be as specific as possible, and include the date an item was purchased as well as the serial numbers of major appliances.

3. **Save receipts.** Save receipts for all major purchases, as well as for any repairs or improvements you have made to your home.

4. **Have major items appraised.** If you have valuable artwork or antiques, have each piece professionally appraised, and make sure you keep the appraisals up-to-date. Markets can swing wildly, especially for collectibles, and what was worth a few hundred dollars five years ago could be worth thousands today.

5. **Don't overlook the small things.** Small items can add up quickly. Just because you don't eat off Royal Copenhagen china doesn't mean your

dishes are worthless. Don't bother with detailed descriptions, but include the number of dishes, silverware, dog beds, books, and other small items in your inventory.

6. **Include the big picture.** Go outside and photograph and describe the house as a whole, as well as the landscaping and any improvements you've made, such as decks or patios. Remember that trees and plants can be expensive, as can fences and swimming pools.

7. **Don't rely on computer software to do the trick.** Many computer programs include a home-inventory template. These may provide a handy fill-in-the-blank format, but they are unlikely to be complete or reflect your actual belongings. Nor will they provide the documentation you may need, like receipts and pictures, to support an insurance claim.

8. **Keep it current.** Whenever you purchase a major item or undertake a home-improvement project, update your inventory to reflect it. Even if you don't make any major purchases or changes, review the inventory once a year to update all those little things you've acquired.

9. **Keep it safe.** Keep one copy at home, but keep another, with a duplicate set of pictures and all original receipts, appraisals, and other documentation, in a safe-deposit box. You might even consider keeping a copy with a friend or relative in another city, just in case your entire neighborhood, including your bank, becomes inaccessible. Your insurance agent might also keep a copy for you.

Calculate Your Net Worth

◆◆◆

If you don't know where you are, you can't figure out how to get somewhere else. That, in a nutshell, is one good reason for calculating your net worth. If you don't know what you're worth today, you can't make rational decisions about work, vacations, retirement, or charity. Calculating your net worth is fairly simple; it's just a matter of sitting down and adding up all your assets and subtracting your liabilities. Assets are either liquid or illiquid. Liquid assets are things you can turn into cash quickly, including the balance in your checking account, savings bonds, stocks of large companies, and mutual funds. Illiquid assets take longer to convert into cash and include your house, artwork, most things you'd have to sell, money that's owed to you, and equity you may have in a private company. Liabilities include mortgages, credit-card debt, car and college loans, and any financial obligations you've undertaken.

1. **Gather all the relevant documents.** Get all your current bank statements, investment statements, credit-card bills, mortgage statements, and life-insurance policies. If you've lent money to others, gather the loan agreements. Once you've put your hands on all the current documents, separate them into two piles, one for what you own, and one for what you owe.

2. **Have valuables appraised.** You need to know the current value of your house and any other real estate you own, as well as the blue-book value of your cars. If you have jewelry beyond your watch or a pair of gold earrings, have it appraised. Get appraisals for artwork and antiques. It doesn't make sense to include things like ordinary household furniture, unless you plan to sell your bed and sleep on a park bench, but do include your wine collection, unless it's mainly Thunderbird™. Be very conservative in calculating the value of any electronic equipment, because it tends to depreciate very rapidly. The purpose of adding up all your assets is to see what you're worth this year, not this minute.

3. **Add up all your assets.** Include all your liquid assets, such as cash in the bank, as well as your less liquid assets, such as the things you've had appraised. Include money that's owed to you unless you think it unlikely you'll ever be paid back. If you're definitely due deferred compensation or a bonus, include it. The key word is *due*; don't include what you merely hope for, even if you're absolutely sure you deserve it. If you're due stock options, assign them their current market value.

4. **Add up your loans.** This includes the principal on all your mortgages, the outstanding balances on your credit cards, car and education loans, and any personal debts.

5. **Calculate other financial obligations.** These include current and back taxes, current and back alimony, current medical bills, and similar unpleasantness.

6. **Subtract all your liabilities from all your assets.** The result is your net worth.

Calculating your net worth is fairly straightforward, but what does the number really mean? If you have ongoing financial obligations, such as alimony or child support, if you have elderly parents or young children who might need your help down the road, you need to take these circumstances into account when assessing how much you really have. Furthermore, the value of your assets can change over time. Neighborhoods become more or less desirable, collectibles go up and down in value, and even cash has no fixed value, but changes with inflation. Net worth is just a snapshot of what you're worth at a given moment, not what you'll be worth in ten years, even if you stop working and stop buying new toys. If you're going to give your grandmother's engagement ring to your daughter, it's not really part of your net worth, even though technically you own it now.

Be careful not to overestimate what you can actually walk away with were you to sell everything. Remember that if you have a $25,000 gain in a stock, when you sell it, you'll pay taxes on that gain, and if you're fifty-one years old and liquidate your Individual Retirement Accounts (IRAs), you'll probably pay a penalty and taxes on any gains. Similarly, you won't realize the full equity in your home after you subtract real estate agent fees, the other costs of selling, and any taxes you may owe on your capital gain.

Manage Monthly Bills

Paying monthly bills promptly is a thrifty habit. Late fees are creeping into the stratosphere, and the damage late payments do to your credit rating can cost literally thousands when it comes to financing such big-ticket items as a car or house. Here are suggestions for making this monthly chore as easy as possible.

1. **Make a special place for all your bills.** It could be a folder on your desk, a specific drawer, or a bill box; just don't allow bills to slip underneath piles of other mail where they can languish unattended. Some people find a "tickler" file handy. These files are divided into separate compartments for each day of the month. File bills in a compartment for a day that is at least a week before they're due. In other words, if a bill is due on the tenth, put it in the compartment labeled the third. Check the file each day and pay that day's bills.

2. **Write the due date on the outside of the envelope.**

3. **Consolidate due dates.** Many companies allow you to change your billing cycle; arrange to have your bills due on two days each month to simplify the process for you.

4. **Choose a place for outgoing mail.** It doesn't help to write the check, put a stamp on it, and leave it on your desk for days. Choose a place for bills to be mailed near the door or where you keep your car keys; that way, you'll mail them the next time you leave the house.

5. **Consider automatic payments.** Many companies, including utility companies, mortgage lenders, and some credit-card issuers, offer an automatic payment service and debit your bank account on a certain day each month, either for the minimum amount due or for an amount above the minimum that you specify. You always have the option to change the amount or cancel the arrangement, but this system assures you don't miss a payment. Just be sure you have the available funds in your account at least a day before each debit is scheduled.

6. **Take advantage of on-line banking.** Most banks provide a service that allows you to pay bills on-line. This is extremely convenient and has the advantage of saving on postage. For many payees, such as utility companies and major vendors, the funds are transferred electronically, so payment happens overnight. You can pay virtually any bill on-line. For individual bills, such as your landscaper or your physician, a physical check is mailed by your bank. Since payment doesn't happen overnight, be sure you order these payments with enough lead time to allow for the check to be processed and mailed by your bank. This isn't complicated, however, because most banks' systems will tell you approximately how long it will take for your payment to be delivered.

7. **Use an on-line bill-paying service.** If you sign up for an on-line service, such as Paytrust's (*www.paytrust.com*), you can have bills sent directly to the service, which will pay them for you by debiting your bank account. You'll pay for the service, of course, usually about $13 a month for twenty-five bills, but if you consistently pay late charges because you just can't organize your bill paying, this could actually save you money over time. You'll receive an e-mail from the service each time a bill is due along with a digital picture of the bill, so you can still check it. If it's correct, you simply authorize payment, and it's done. If you travel frequently, this can be particularly convenient, since you can take care of your bills anywhere you can get Internet access.

Get the Most from Your Money

One person's luxury is another's bare necessity. There are as many ways to save money as there are to spend it. Here are some relatively painless economizing ideas that can help you get the most out of what you spend.

Food

1. **Plan meals a week at a time.** Plan meals to take advantage of specials, and do your shopping once a week for basic items. Fewer trips to the grocery store mean fewer chances to buy something you don't need.

2. **Make a list.** Shopping with a list reduces the number of impulse purchases you're likely to make. When you consistently shop with a list and buy only items on the list, you save money.

3. **Eat before you shop.** When you're hungry, it's nearly impossible to resist picking up snacks and other treats you had no intention of buying when you left home. Shopping when you're full helps curb impulse purchases.

4. **Use coupons.** It's amazing how much you can save by simply clipping and using coupons, but don't fall into the coupon spending trap: Use coupons only for items you would buy anyway.

5. **Buy generic.** Bulk couscous, for instance, costs just 25 percent of what prepackaged brands cost, and it's indistinguishable. You can buy bulk oatmeal, rice, and many other staples this way. Similarly, store brands of everything from canned beans to laundry detergent usually cost less and are comparable in quality to products with better-known labels.

6. **Brown-bag when possible.** When eating at a restaurant isn't required for social or business reasons, take your lunch to work.

7. **Join a food co-op.** This is especially rewarding if you have a large family. You generally volunteer to bag food once a month or do other chores. In exchange, you share in bulk purchases that can save real money. You might also have access to produce from local farmers or other suppliers that might not be available otherwise.

8. **Buy fruit and vegetables in season.** Produce that is in season is generally better quality as well as less expensive than fruits and vegetables imported from out-of-state or out of the country. In the winter, skip the tomatoes and put diced apples in your salads.

Household

1. **Share power equipment.** Share the purchase of snow blowers, tillers, power washers, perhaps riding lawn mowers, and other expensive power equipment with several neighbors.

2. **Choose Energy Star appliances.** Refrigerators, washing machines, air conditioners, and such that qualify for the EPA's Energy Star rating save energy and, thus, money. These appliances may also qualify for special rebates or credit from state or local governments or from your utility company.

3. **Maintain your home.** Do minor repairs immediately; don't allow small problems to become serious structural issues.

4. **Turn down the thermostat.** Turn down the thermostat five to ten degrees at night, then turn it up again in the morning. This eight-hour drop in energy use can save 5 to 10 percent of your heating bill.

5. **Manage your hot water heater.** Water heating typically accounts for 16 percent of your utility bill, the third largest energy expense in your home. For every ten degrees you turn down your water heater, you'll save 4 percent on your energy bill. Setting the temperature to 120 degrees also

helps prevent scalding accidents. Also, wrap your hot water heater with insulation to keep the water hot longer.

6. **Use energy efficiently.** Close doors to rooms that aren't being used, turn off lights, and use high-efficiency fluorescent bulbs where possible. Close the damper on your fireplace when it's not in use.

Clothing

1. **Resist impulse purchases, but take advantage of sales.**
2. **Coordinate.** Keep odd colors to a minimum and focus on neutrals or the basics, especially for work clothes.
3. **Accessorize.** Well-chosen accessories can turn a few basics into a number of different outfits.

Transportation

1. **Walk more.** It's cheaper than driving, and you'll probably get a bonus savings in the form of lower health-care costs.
2. **Car-pool.**
3. **Adjust automobile insurance.** Raise the deductible on all your automobile insurance policies and carry only the legally required coverage (public liability and damage) on older cars. Unless it's a classic car, the insurance premiums on theft and collision coverage usually aren't worth the costs.
4. **Plan vacations and avoid last-minute trips.** The earlier you plan a get-away, the more likely you'll find cheap fares or be able to take advantage of frequent-flier miles.

Make Extra Cash Quickly

◆◆◆

Tired of the old tried-and-true ways to make some extra cash: bottle returns, Ponzi schemes, and bank robbery? There are plenty of other ways to make extra money without risking life, limb, or liberty.

1. **Old standbys.** These are simple and require no long-term commitment. They include yard sales, baby-sitting, pet sitting, house sitting, lawn mowing, and the like. They work, especially if you're looking for a little extra once in a while. But if you're looking for something more, read on, because even these old standbys can be converted into more prosperous, long-term enterprises.

2. **Get a seasonal job.** Holiday time is perfect for picking up extra cash as a temporary salesperson. Most large chain stores list available jobs on their Websites; check out *www.macysjobs.com* for local listings of jobs at Macy's. Don't forget about local stores, which always need extra help around the holidays. If local stores have already hired all their holiday help, offer to be available on-call to fill in if someone calls in sick.

3. **Sign up with a temp agency.** If you have basic office skills, sign up with one or two temporary placement agencies. Even if you aren't proficient in Excel or more complex business programs, you may still be called upon to answer phones or file when a receptionist calls in sick.

4. **Sell stuff on eBay.** This can be a one-shot thing or a full-time business. Either way, you have to register as an e-Bay seller on the site. Registration is free, but there's a very small charge for listing items and a percentage charge if you actually sell. Take a digital photo of what you're selling, click on "Sell" at the top of any e-Bay page and complete the "Sell Your Item" form, which includes a place for the description, photo, shipping, and payment methods (definitely set up a PayPal account). The process is easy, and e-Bay will walk you through it.

5. **Sell stuff on LiveDeal.** If you've decided to unload granny's armoire or that rowing machine you haven't used in years, post it for free on LiveDeal.com. This service connects you to people within driving distance who are interested in what you've got to sell. The service also works for buying, of course, but you're not in a position to be spending your cash at the moment, remember?

6. **Offer personal shopping and errand services.** This is particularly easy during holiday seasons, although if you're interested in a longer-term project, it can become a part-time business. Advertise in local papers and on community Websites.

7. **Make pixels pay.** If you're proficient with a computer and have a scanner and a photo-editing program such as Photoshop, you can earn

money effortlessly by transferring photos to CDs or DVDs. If you're handy with a video-editing program, you can do the same with camcorder tapes. People will also pay to have their music CDs transferred to their iPod.

8. **Offer desktop publishing services.** Another computer skill that can be turned into quick cash is desktop publishing. If you've got a good design sense, you can offer personalized greeting cards, stationery, and invitations to individuals and local businesses.

9. **Be an extra.** If you live in New York or Los Angeles, there's a good chance you can get extra work for films and television. It's not easy—you might be asked to show up on a hot summer evening dressed in winter clothes because the TV show being shot in August will be shown next February—and the hours can be long and the pay low, but it's a chance to rub elbows with the stars, or at least stand within one hundred feet of them, and it gets you bragging rights, plus some extra dough. To get started, register with an agency that handles extras (there's at least one in most major cities). You must pay a small fee (less than $100) to the agency, which might take a simple photo of you and post some information about you on its Website. Watch out for side-scams: The agency might suggest you get a headshot taken by their super-expensive photographer, or have a résumé printed on "industry standard" paper (8" x 10", so that it fits on the back of a headshot). Neither is usually necessary for strictly extras work, but if you want them, you can probably get them cheaper elsewhere. If you can't find a local agency, you can register on-line with *www.moviex.com/extras* for a $10 fee. Finally, you can just try showing up at a shoot, but that's a long-shot, because it depends entirely on someone already scheduled failing to appear.

10. **Be an Avon person.** Yes, person. Avon reps don't have to be women, and cosmetics is a perennial moneymaker that's virtually recession-proof. Avon is the largest consumer direct sales company in the world, and it now offers wellness and fashion products in addition to the traditional cosmetics. The start-up costs are less than $50.

11. **Be a courier.** It may conjure images of secret agents, but you really can make money hand-delivering vital packages. The major shipping companies (such as DHL, UPS, and Fed Ex) offer these services, and you can expect to earn about $20 per hour plus travel and expenses.

12. **Shop for bucks.** Retail firms employ "secret" or "mystery" shoppers to provide feedback on their customer service. The hours are extremely flexible, and it's a perfect part-time or spare-time job. Get started by registering with one of the literally hundreds of shopping services agencies, which you can find by Googling "secret shopper."

> **TIP:** Beware of get-rich-quick and "easy cash for working at home" schemes. Envelope stuffing almost never pays enough to make it worth your while, and there's nearly always a catch. Also, never accept a "business opportunity" that requires you to pay a fee or purchase inventory up-front with the promise of riches to come.

Refinance Your Mortgage

When mortgage rates drop, people with higher, fixed-rate mortgages should think about refinancing their loan to lower their monthly payments or to reduce the term of the loan and save themselves money in the long run. People with adjustable mortgage rates might consider refinancing to lock in at lower rates and ensure that their payments won't increase. Here are the basics to consider if you're thinking of refinancing.

1. **Add up closing costs and calculate your break-even point.** Closing costs include the points the lender charges, attorney fees, appraisal costs, the title search, and any other one-time fees. If refinancing reduces your monthly payment by $125, and your closing costs are $6,000, you won't break even for four years; unless you plan on staying put for at least that time, you'll lose money by refinancing.

2. **Calculate the time value of the money saved.** The money you save from refinancing comes in the future, while the costs of refinancing are immediate. You lose investment opportunities on the money you pay

today, while the future savings will be in tomorrow's dollars, which will be worth less than today's. How much less depends on the rate of inflation, which changes annually and, thus, is difficult to calculate, but to ignore these issues is to distort the real costs of refinancing and the real savings you might realize.

3. **Consider tax implications.** The tax implications of holding a mortgage that's mostly paid off can be positive or negative, depending on your tax situation. During the early years of a mortgage, almost all of the payment goes toward interest, which translates into large tax deductions. If you're in a high bracket, these can be valuable. As you continue to pay, more and more of your payment goes toward the principal. That means your equity increases, but your tax deductions decline. If you're in a very high bracket and need as many deductions as you can find, it might pay to refinance, perhaps borrowing more than your remaining mortgage, even if your monthly payments don't decline. These are complicated calculations, best left to your accountant.

4. **Consider security.** If you have an adjustable rate mortgage, you might want to lock in a decent rate by converting it to a fixed-rate loan. Again, you have to consider closing costs and the possibility that your monthly payment might actually increase, but if you plan on staying in your home for more than a couple of years, a slightly higher monthly payment might be worth the security of knowing your mortgage payments will never increase.

5. **Beware the prepayment penalty.** If your current mortgage has a prepayment penalty, you have to consider that along with all of the other costs. It could wipe out any savings you might otherwise realize.

Choose and Use a Credit Card Wisely

Despite the bad reputation credit-card debt has given to plastic spending, there are some very good reasons to have a credit card. Certain transactions, such as renting an automobile or securing a hotel room, are possible only

REVERSE MORTGAGES

If you're sixty-two or older and you've built up a lot of equity in your home, you might consider a reverse mortgage, which can convert that equity into a lump sum, a monthly payment, or a line of credit. The amount is based on calculating the youngest borrower's age, the appraised value of the home minus whatever you owe on it, and the limit for your county, which is set by the Federal Housing Administration. You remain responsible for maintaining your home and for paying taxes on it, but you're protected against possible declines in the house's value, since the FHA insures the lender against any loss. The home must remain your primary residence, and when you die or move, the loan comes due. If your heirs want to keep the house, they must pay off the balance. Of course, if the home has appreciated, your heirs can choose to sell it, pay off the balance, and keep the difference.

when you have a credit card, and many other transactions—such as Internet shopping—are a whole lot more convenient when you've got that little square of plastic in your wallet. Aside from the access and convenience, there is another compelling reason for credit-card ownership: Using a credit card responsibly is an excellent way to build the good credit rating necessary for making life's largest purchases, such as a home or a car. On the other hand, overspending on that same credit card can have a ruinous effect on your credit rating. To make sure your card works for you, not against you, begin by choosing the right card for your needs.

1. **Be realistic.** The ideal way to use a credit card is to pay your balance in full once a month. If you know you will do that, you can focus less on obtaining a card with the lowest interest rate and more on what the credit card company can do for you. If you will carry a balance over from one month to the next, finding the lowest possible interest rate and fees should be your primary concern.

2. **Know the APR.** The APR, or annual percentage rate, is simply the interest rate charged on your unpaid balance, expressed as a yearly percent-

age. The periodic rate is the rate applied to your outstanding balance each billing period to figure out finance charges.

3. **Search for grace.** The grace period is the amount of time between your purchase and the date interest begins to accrue on that balance. Most cards offer a standard grace period, which means that you owe no interest if you pay your bill in full each month. A card with no grace period begins charging interest immediately on the day the charge is incurred. Don't choose a card with no grace period; make sure your card offers at least a twenty-five-day grace period.

4. **Ask what the card can do for you.** If you're sure you can pay off your balance every month, consider choosing a card that gives you something back for every purchase you make. Credit card awards come in a wide variety of forms. You can receive anything from frequent-flier miles to contributions to your favorite charity. The catch is that award cards generally charge a flat annual fee (usually under $100) for the privilege of accruing those awards, and these cards rarely have a low APR. If, however, you spend enough money every year to build up significant rewards, shop around for a card with the perks you want.

5. **Check other fees.** Most credit cards charge a hefty fee for cash advances (usually a percentage of the advance). Most cards also charge a fee for late payment and for charging above a set limit. Read all the fine print and look for any hidden fees.

6. **Translate the terms.** The dollar amount next to the words "amount due" on your monthly statement is *not* your total balance. Instead, it's the minimum payment required to keep your tab current with the card issuer. If you pay only the "amount due," you will *not* be paying off your entire balance, and you *will* begin accumulating debt as interest is tacked onto your remaining balance.

7. **Pass up store cards.** Cards issued by individual stores, such as department stores, usually carry interest rates that are higher than other credit cards. Although store cards may offer a discount on the day you open the account, they're rarely worth the higher fees involved.

8. **Report card loss immediately.** There is a $50-per-card limit on how much you're liable for if your card is lost or stolen, but you won't be responsible for any charges made after you report the loss. You'll avoid tremendous headaches if you report the loss immediately.

9. **Consider acceptability.** American Express is accepted at fewer places than Visa or MasterCard. Generally, Visa is accepted overseas more often than MasterCard.

10. **Don't accept more cards than you really need.** Your credit rating can be affected by the number of credit cards you have in your name, whether or not you actually use them. When you apply for a loan, the lending institution can consider the maximum credit you carry, not just what you actually owe, in determining whether to grant the loan. In qualifying you for a loan, the institution will assume that you can charge up to the limit on any card in your name. The best strategy is not to apply for or accept more cards than you really need.

> **TIP:** Try to pay your balance each month. Credit cards rarely offer interest rates competitive with other forms of credit, so it's a bad idea to accumulate appreciable debt on them. If you need to charge something you can't pay for at the end of the month, use an equity line of credit, if you have one, to pay off the card.

Prevent Identity Theft

◆◆◆

Once upon a time, if you kept your hand on your wallet and your eye on your purse, you could feel reasonably safe from pickpockets and thieves. But the world has changed radically in the past couple of decades. The growth of the Internet has given rise to the much more sophisticated—and harder to prevent—crime of identity theft. Identity thieves can rob you blind without going anywhere near your wallet, purse, or home. These thieves pilfer enough personal and financial information to make off with vast sums from your bank and credit-card accounts before you even know you've been robbed. Identity thieves often don't stop with simple stealing; they have been known to assume the identity of their victims and perpetrate other frauds in that person's name. The Federal Trade Commission estimates that between 7 million and 10 million people a year fall prey to this crime. While you can't hide your identity under the mattress, there are practical and effective steps you can take to keep it reasonably secure.

1. **Adopt a strict need-to-know policy.** Don't give out personal information unless it's absolutely necessary. The person at the checkout counter doesn't need your phone number and address to take your cash. Don't provide it. Don't give your social security number unless it's legally required. Doctor's offices, for instance, frequently use it to identify you; ask if you can use another number instead. And never carry your social security card with you.

2. **Plug computer leaks.** Guard your computer with a firewall, software or hardware that prevents hackers from accessing your computer data via the Internet or through a wireless network. Install good computer-security software that includes a firewall, antivirus, and antispyware software. Make sure the software for these protections is always active and up-to-date. Don't open e-mail attachments from unknown senders, never reply to unsolicited e-mail with personal information, use imaginative passwords, and when you do transmit sensitive information, as when ordering on-line, make sure the site is encrypted (look for the image of a closed lock somewhere on the page).

3. **Fight "phish."** If you get a phone call or e-mail message allegedly from your bank or credit-card company asking you to "verify," "update," or "confirm" your account information, don't do it without first checking to see if the call or e-mail is legitimate. It may well not be. Such phony communications are typical of a fraud known as *phishing*, in which the scammers attempt to elicit information that will allow them to steal your identity. Phishing e-mails and phone calls frequently have an urgent, ominous tone (we'll close your account if you don't provide this information immediately). If you receive such a phone call, ask for the phone number; look up the number yourself to verify its authenticity; and only then should you call back. If you receive an e-mail that seems suspicious, do not click on the link. Similarly, if you receive a call announcing that you've just won a great prize or qualify for a low-rate major credit card, and the caller asks for personal information on the pretext of establishing your identity, hang up. If you're the optimistic and trusting sort, you could ask to have the prize information sent to you in writing. Never

divulge any personal information, in person, on the phone, by e-mail, or by snail mail unless you're absolutely sure the address and the business are legitimate. Forward phishing spam to www.spam@uce.gov and to the company, bank, or organization impersonated in the phishing e-mail. Most organizations have information on their Websites about where to report problems.

4. **Don't trash your identity.** Don't throw away papers with your personal information without shredding them first. This includes bills, unused convenience checks from credit-card companies, explanation of benefits from insurance companies, and pay stubs. If the document includes your social security number or other personal information, shred it so that it can't be reconstructed.

5. **Be stingy with your financial information.** Banks and credit-card companies often share information about you with their affiliates, but they need your permission to do so. Unfortunately, they may have your passive consent if you don't "opt out" by checking a box instructing the institution not to share information with their affiliates (see "Opt Out," page 329). Make sure you communicate to all of your financial institutions that you don't want them sharing any information about you with anyone, affiliate or not.

6. **Keep checks lean.** Don't include your phone number or social security number on your checks. Actually, the only thing you need to have on your checks is your name. Anything else is superfluous and an invitation to identity theft.

7. **Check statements carefully.** Make sure you receive all your credit-card and bank statements every month. If you miss a statement, call the company immediately because your statement could have been stolen or diverted to another address. Tell the company that your bill is missing and you suspect fraud. Check all transactions, even for small amounts, and make sure you recognize them. Identity thieves may test out a stolen card number by making a small purchase; if it goes through, the next month they charge the plasma TV. Better yet, don't wait for statements; check accounts on-line weekly.

8. **Secure snail mail.** Don't put outgoing mail in an unsecured mailbox. Drop mail into a mailbox or at the post office. By the same token, don't leave incoming mail sitting in an unsecured mailbox. If you'll be away for

OPT OUT

Every time a "preapproved application" from a finance, mortgage, or credit-card company lands in your unlocked mailbox or in your trash without being shredded, you're at risk for identity theft. These offers are based on information companies purchase from the consumer credit-reporting companies, Equifax, Experian, TransUnion, and Innovis. You can opt out of receiving these potentially dangerous nuisances with a single phone call (888–567–8688) or on-line request (*www.optoutpresecreed.com*).

You also should consider opting out of all those catalogs that clog your mailbox and could become another source of information for potential identity thieves. By intercepting the catalogs, thieves know what companies you do business with and where you might have charge accounts. To opt out of these write Abacus (P.O. Box 1478, Broomfield, CO 80038) or e-mail Optout@abacus-direct.com. Include your address, your previous address, whether you've moved within the last year, and the full name of everyone at your address who wants to opt out of receiving unsolicited catalogs.

While you're at it, register all your phone numbers with the national Do Not Call list. You'll eliminate nuisance calls and avoid the occasion to reveal personal information over the phone. Call 888–382–1222 from the number you want to register, or go on-line to *www.donotcal.gov*. You will receive a confirmation e-mail containing a link to click. Be sure to click that internal link; it is the agency's way of verifying that the request actually came from you.

a while, ask your post office to hold your mail. If you move, don't file a permanent change-of-address form. The postal service actually shares this information with a National Change of Address database, which marketers who pay a licensing fee can access. Use a temporary change-of-address form instead; your mail will be forwarded for a year, plenty of time to contact the businesses and magazines you want to have your new address.

9. **Check credit reports.** One of the best ways to see if identity theft has already hit is to check your credit history. Recent federal legislation allows you to get one free credit report (technically called a credit file disclosure) per year from each of the three national credit bureaus: Experian, Equifax, and Trans Union. Since you can only get these reports once a year, it's a good idea to spread your requests over the whole year, ordering one every four months. You can order your reports by calling the toll-free number, 877–322–8228, or you can check your credit history on-line at *www.annualcreditreport.com/cra/index.jsp.*

> **TIP:** If you believe you've been scammed and have provided your Social Security number, call the Social Security Fraud Hotline at 800–269–0271.

Choose an Accountant

◆◆◆

An accountant can do much more than help with your tax preparation. In fact, if tax preparation is all you need, see "Consider an Enrolled Agent," page 332, and save yourself some money. But if your finances are complex enough to warrant the need for tax planning, budgeting, and strategic financial planning, follow the tips below to find yourself a good accountant.

1. **Ask for referrals.** As always, ask family, friends, and colleagues if they're happy with their accountants. Just understand that, like dentists, lawyers, and any other professional, the accountant who's appropriate for one person may not be appropriate for another. Discount the advice of someone who tells you his accountant lets him deduct everything; he's either exaggerating or working with an accountant who does.

2. **Check your state's Board of Accountancy.** Certified Public Accountants (CPA) are licensed by each state, but because states tend to use the Uniform CPA exam, accountants licensed in one state usually enjoy rec-

iprocity in other states. If you're looking for a CPA in your area, you might contact the local chapter, which won't offer recommendations but will give you a list of licensed accountants in your area.

3. **Check for specialization.** Accountants often specialize, and you should determine what, if any, specialization suits your needs. If you're an artist, writer, or filmmaker, for instance, you might want to narrow your search to accountants who specialize in entertainment or intellectual property. If you're a doctor, lawyer, or other professional, choose an accountant who works closely with members of your profession.

4. **Make an appointment for an interview.** Select a few of the most likely names and call to set up an interview. Ask ahead of time if you'll be charged. Accountants' rates can range from $150 to $400 per hour, so don't set up ten interviews just because the accountants are all located within a two-block radius.

5. **Check the aggression level.** Some accountants are willing to push the envelope when it comes to deductions and the way transactions are structured; others are more conservative. Choose an accountant who matches your own comfort level.

6. **Consider size.** Do you prefer a solo practitioner or someone who works in a firm, large or small? If you go with a large firm, much of the work on your account might be handled by assistants. That's not necessarily a bad thing, because the work of assistants, especially if they aren't CPAs, should be billed at a lower hourly rate.

7. **Check communication style.** Will you have access to the accountant throughout the year or just at tax time? Can you call, or must you make an appointment? Don't expect calls to be free, but if you have a quick question you might not want to schedule a full hour's appointment.

8. **Know how you'll be billed.** Ask for the accountant's rate, how you'll be billed, and what additional services, such as copying and filing fees, you can expect to pay.

9. **Ask about audits.** Not all accountants are willing to represent you before the Internal Revenue Service. If you should be audited and the accountant represents you, expect to be charged for the service unless the audit is the result of a mistake the accountant made.

CONSIDER AN ENROLLED AGENT

If you don't need the ongoing advice of an accountant but you feel your tax situation is too complex to handle by yourself, consider using an enrolled agent. These people are licensed by the Treasury Department to represent you before the Internal Revenue Service (IRS) in the event of an audit and are often retired IRS agents. They usually charge less than CPAs but are knowledgeable about tax matters and are actually the only professionals tested by the IRS. They are required to take continuing professional education courses and are governed in their practice by the same Treasury Circular 230 that governs attorneys and CPAs. You can find an enrolled agent by checking with the National Association of Enrolled Agents at *www.naea.org*.

Choose a Financial Planner

If you think financial planners are just for the very rich, think again. A financial planner can help you define financial goals and propose a savings and investment plan to help you reach them. A planner can also coordinate estate plans with your attorney and advise on the way specific investment and insurance choices might affect your overall financial health. As with the other professionals in your life, choosing the right financial planner is an essential first step and one that takes a bit of thought. The first step is to ask friends, relatives, and colleagues for referrals. Your attorney or accountant might also be excellent sources.

Once you've collected a few likely candidates, set up face-to-face interviews. The relationship with a financial planner is one of trust, and it could be a long and fairly intimate one, because your financial planner will know details of your income and lifestyle that even close friends may not. Ask these questions of planners you're considering.

1. **What are your credentials?** A number of organizations offer certification in financial planning (see "Where to Go for More Information," page 335), and you can check with these organizations to see whether a particular financial planner is entitled to use initials such as CFP (certified financial planner) and PFS (personal financial specialist) after her name. Only certified public accountants (CPAs) are eligible to become personal financial specialists. Financial planners must register with either the Securities Exchange Commission or a state security agency. Ask where he's registered and check with that agency to make sure he's never been the subject of any disciplinary action. If a planner isn't registered, strike him from your list.

2. **How are you compensated?** This is key. Financial planners earn money in one of three ways: from fees only, from commissions, or from a combination of the two. A commission-only arrangement means that if you don't buy products recommended by the planner, he makes nothing. Many financial experts (Jane Bryant Quinn and Suze Orman among them) advise hiring only a fee-based planner. The argument is that a commission-based compensation presents a conflict of interest because the planner has a financial stake in selling you particular investments.

3. **How long have you been a financial planner?** A lawyer who specialized in financial and business law for decades and who has just set up as a financial planner may be able to offer tremendously valuable advice, but as a rule of thumb look for someone who's been a financial planner for a minimum of ten years, long enough to have been through at least one complete economic cycle.

4. **What is your investment philosophy?** More specifically, what is your approach to my situation? An aggressive investment approach may be appropriate for a young family, but not for someone approaching retirement. Also, make sure you're comfortable with the person's philosophy. Some people are risk takers, others aren't; go with what makes you comfortable. If the adviser uses terms you don't understand, such as "market timing," "technical analysis," or "future value," ask for an explanation. If she can't provide one in a way you clearly understand, she's not the planner for you.

5. **What kind of clients do you most often work with?** Ask the planner to describe her typical client. If it sounds like you, it could be a good match; if it doesn't, you might want to keep looking.

6. **Will I be working directly with you or with your associates?** Also ask if the planner is comfortable working with your attorney and accountant. Some planners insist on working with their own professionals, and this may be a deal breaker for you.

7. **How do you choose investments?** Does the planner choose from a broad universe of possibilities or does she limit herself to products from certain companies? Does she subscribe to research services and, if so, which? What criteria must an investment meet for her to consider it?

8. **Will the plan be tailored to me and my circumstances?** The answer to this one has got to be "yes." It's easy enough to get a generic plan for free from most stock brokers. What you're looking for is someone who will spend the time with you to understand your particular circumstances, plans, and obligations and tailor a financial strategy specifically to meet them. A planner should consider not just your investments, but also your total assets and debts, your profession, and your lifestyle, to understand your complete financial picture.

9. **How and how often will we communicate?** There's no single right answer, but you should be in touch at least quarterly. Also, you should sit down at least once a year, face-to-face, to review any changes in your situation, how the plan is progressing, and what, if any, fine-tuning is needed.

Choose a Method for Stock Trading

◆◆◆

Once upon a time, if you wanted to buy or sell stocks or bonds, you went to one of the large brokerage companies, opened an account, paid high commissions, and hoped to ride the bull. That all changed in 1975, when full-service brokerage houses lost their monopoly and discount brokers entered the picture. With the explosion of e-trading, now you can even buy and sell from your laptop computer wherever and whenever you like. Still, you must decide how much help you want and where to open an account. Here are pointers to narrow the choices.

1. **Choose a full-service broker if you want a lot of service and advice.** These are the traditional houses, such as Merrill Lynch. They offer a full range of services, from stock and bond trading to financial planning and mortgage brokering. Theoretically, you can handle most of your financial transactions through a full-service broker, but you'll pay top dollar for the one-stop convenience. Full-service brokers maintain staffs of stock and bond analysts, economists, and statisticians whose expertise is available to the firm's brokers. However, there's usually a two-tier system, in which institutional clients, such as large pension funds and major corporations, have much more personal access to this research than the brokers who handle individuals. In any case, never be lulled into the notion that the broker is your friend. The broker is in business to make money for himself, first. Nor should you confuse a broker for a financial

adviser, although all full-service brokerage houses provide new clients with a financial plan. A broker is not a disinterested party; if you don't buy, he doesn't earn, and frequently, when there's a choice between an in-house product or an outside one, his commission is higher if he sells his own company's brand, whether it's a mutual fund or an insurance policy handled through the firm's subsidiary.

2. **Use a discount broker if you don't need frequent advice.** The line that used to separate discount from full-service brokers is blurring. Many discount brokers, such as Charles Schwab, offer services that look pretty much like those of full-service firms, but their prices are lower, often much lower. They usually don't provide the comprehensive planning that full-service brokers claim to offer, but for that, you're probably better off hiring an independent financial planner (see "Choose a Financial Planner," page 332). Discount brokers may not have their own dedicated research teams, but they have access to and subscribe to all the major on-line research services and often provide their clients with at least limited access to them. Like full-service firms, discount brokers offer margin accounts, several types of retirement accounts, and money-market sweep accounts that deposit cash directly into an interest-bearing account that can be accessed through checks or a debit card.

3. **If you're a seasoned trader, go with a deep-discount broker.** Deep-discount brokers are essentially order takers. You tell them what to buy or sell and they execute your order. They provide no advice or research, but the cost per trade is extremely low, and some will offer flat fees regardless of the number or price of the shares you trade. The deep-discount brokers do not maintain branch offices.

4. **Scrutinize service quality.** Unless you're going with a deep-discount broker, consider the level of service offered by the firm. You'll want easy access to the person who handles your account. If you trade actively, you'll want assurance that access to your broker is fast throughout the trading day. You'll also want some assurance that trades will be executed promptly. If you trade very actively, you'll probably want to be able to buy and sell through your computer. If so, make sure the platform the firm uses (the interface you see on your computer screen) is clear and that you find it easy to use; programs from various brokers can vary enormously. Finally, make sure the statements the firm provides are easy to understand. You or your accountant will appreciate that at tax time.

E-TRADING FUNDAMENTALS

Open an account with one of the many on-line brokerage houses, and you can start buying and selling stocks and bonds anywhere you have access to the Internet. On-line trading can save you a lot of money, but only if you're an active trader. If you aren't comfortable with the financial world, if you don't know how to read an annual report or interpret a stock chart, Internet trading is not for you. For people who buy or sell a few times a year, it's probably not worth the bother and could actually be more expensive than using a regular broker. If you decide e-trading is for you, choose an on-line broker that meets the same basic requirements for stability and service that you would want from any other broker. In addition, pay attention to the following points:

Make sure your Internet connection is fast and reliable. If your connection fails, so will your ability to buy or sell.

Be sure you're comfortable with the program you'll be using.

Be willing to put time into research. Some on-line brokers offer access to research, others don't. You'll have to spend quite a bit of time researching companies and staying on top of financial and economic news if you're to successfully trade on your own. If you're not willing to make that substantial investment of time and effort, stick with a full-service or discount broker that provides advice.

Make sure the broker provides real-time quotes. The standard fifteen-minute delay that characterizes stock quotes available through the regular on-line sources, such as Yahoo or MSN, is not good enough. Unless you're a very casual investor—in which case e-trading is not for you—you need to have real-time quotes in order to trade.

If you plan to trade on multiple exchanges, make sure the broker can execute trades on them.

Check fees very carefully. While per-trade fees may be low, there may be annual fees or execution fees that can actually make on-line trading more expensive than trading through a discount broker.

5. **Ask about minimum account balances.** Some brokers require a minimum investment to open an account. If the minimum is more than you want to invest, go elsewhere.

6. **Make sure the firm has SIPC coverage.** Don't open an account with a firm that isn't covered by the Securities Investor Protection Corporation, the government-sponsored entity that insures brokerage accounts.

7. **Ask for an information packet.** Do your homework before choosing a brokerage firm by studying the information packet from the firms you are considering. The packet should detail all the services offered and the fee for each. Because the brokerage field has become so competitive, it will be worth your while to familiarize yourself with each firm's fee structure and compare costs. Some firms that used to charge maintenance fees for IRAs may waive those fees if you ask. But until you study a variety of information packets, you won't know a bargain from a boondoggle.

Choose a Charity

◆◆◆

Giving to charity should be more than a well-intentioned impulse. It should be an informed choice and part of your overall financial plan. Here are some steps to make your giving both meaningful and effective.

1. **Decide what proportion of your income you want to give.** Since the appeals are endless, it's a good idea to incorporate charitable giving into your overall financial plan, so you neither give too much nor fall prey to impulse donations. Include charitable contributions in your yearly budget and keep track of donations.

2. **Resist pressure.** Don't give out of guilt or because someone's at the door pressuring you to save a child or an entire ethnic population. There's no dearth of disasters, and you can't solve all the world's problems. Make it a general rule never to donate in response to face-to-face appeals or unsolicited phone calls.

CHECKING ON CHARITIES

A number of organizations can provide information about particular charities. Among the most useful:

The Wise Giving Alliance (*www.give.org*). Associated with the Better Business Bureau (BBB), the Alliance tells you whether the charity meets the BBB standards. The site also provides tips on charitable giving.

Guidestar (*www.guidestar.org*). Guidestar offers financial details on more than 850,000 nonprofits. If you're considering a large donation, Guidestar can provide a detailed report for $59.

American Institute of Philanthropy (AIP, at *www.charitywatch.org*). The AIP grades charities, based on the percentage of money that goes to the stated cause, as opposed to administrative and fund-raising expenses. One caveat on this: Don't compare one kind of charity or cause to another, because different types may have very different profiles. Museums, for instance, necessarily have expenses that food banks don't.

Charity Navigator (*www.charitynavigator.org*). Charity Navigator uses financial data to analyze a charity's health. You can see charts for specific charities that detail financial information, such as revenue and expenses, and that compare the charity to others that address similar issues.

3. **Choose your causes.** Choose charities that address issues that are personally meaningful. Since you can't support everything, do what the big donors, like Bill and Melinda Gates do: Choose a cause that's close to your heart.

4. **Research the organization.** Just because the brochure shows a sad-eyed child or a bedraggled puppy doesn't mean your money will be going to

sick children or abandoned dogs. Check out the organization before you send the check (see "Checking on Charities," page 339).

5. **Beware of sound-alikes.** You've heard of the National Cancer Society, but is there such a thing as the Cancer Society of the United States? Make sure you're sending your check to the charity you really intend to support.

6. **Consider your estate plan.** Including charitable giving in your trust or estate can have tax benefits, while extending your charity beyond your lifetime.

End-of-Year Tax Strategies

Ideally, you should plan strategies for minimizing your tax liability starting in January, not December. But if you have postponed tax planning until the last minute, consider some of the strategies on this list. Just understand that nothing can substitute for the advice of a professional accountant (see "Choose an Accountant," page 330).

1. **Maximize retirement contributions.** Contribute as much as you can to your employer's retirement plan before the end of the year. If you're self-employed, set up a retirement plan or max out your contributions. If you're self-employed and miss the year-end deadline, you can establish a Simplified Employment Pension Plan—Individual Retirement Account (SEP IRA) up to the April 15 filing deadline. The rules for many of the plans have changed recently, so it's best to review your retirement savings strategy with your accountant to make sure you take advantage of new limits and special deductions available for small-business plans.

2. **Delay income and accelerate expenses.** If you can, delay receiving income until after December, unless you anticipate that you'll be in a higher tax bracket next year. Prepay as many expenses as you can. For example, make an extra mortgage payment, and if you make estimated tax payments, prepay your first-quarter estimated tax. If you own your own business or are self-employed, consider purchasing items such as office supplies or equipment that you'll need during the first quarter of next year. This allows you to claim the expenses on this year's return.

3. **Pay state tax early.** If you would be making a state income tax payment in the first quarter of the new year, write that check on December 31 and take the deduction on your federal taxes this year.

4. **Review your charitable contributions.** If you haven't made all the contributions you budgeted for the year, make them now (see "Choose a Charity," page 338).

5. **Donate stock.** If you have appreciated stock that you're considering selling, reap a larger benefit by donating the stock to charity. You can take the stock's fair-market value as a deduction, and your only out-of-pocket cost is what you initially paid for the stock.

6. **Take losses and postpone gains.** Although the capital gains rate is lower than it used to be, it's still standard practice to defer taking gains on appreciated stock and selling sagging stocks before year-end. But don't trade just to take advantage of losses for tax purposes. If a stock is down, but you feel it will bounce back, it might not be worth the transaction costs of selling now to take the loss and buying it back for possible future gains.

7. **Spend on your health now.** If you itemize deductions, medical expenses that exceed 7.5 percent of your adjusted gross income are deductible. Don't overlook weight-loss programs or even a gym membership if they're suggested as medically necessary by your doctor.

8. **Turn junk into deductions.** Choose year-end to clean out your closets, your children's toy chests, and to rid your basement of household goods that are no longer used. If the joy of closet cleaning doesn't move you to action, perhaps the promise of additional tax deductions will get you going.

Take Overlooked Tax Deductions

◆◆◆

No one is eager to pay more income tax than absolutely necessary, but many of us do just that because we overlook tax deductions to which we're entitled. Check this list to make sure you're not missing any.

1. **Mortgage costs.** A point is part of the fee sometimes charged for a new mortgage. One point equals 1 percent of the total mortgage amount. Points you pay when you acquire a mortgage for your primary home are fully deductible on your federal income taxes. This is also true for points that are part of a home equity loan used to make repairs on or to remodel a primary residence. Legal fees involved when you buy a home are also tax deductible.

2. **Publications related to tax and investment matters.** If you subscribe to an investment research service, for instance, you can deduct the expense of the service, as well as publications you use strictly for investment purposes.

3. **Professional publications and dues.** If you're a self-employed professional, you can deduct the cost of publications, services, and membership dues in professional organizations.

4. **Professional services and in-kind donations.** If you donate your professional services or make in-kind donations to charities, the costs of those services (billed at your usual rate) or merchandise are tax-deductible. If you're a writer and you write a brochure for a charity, you can deduct whatever you would charge a regular client for similar work. You can also deduct for mileage, gas, and parking if you use your car to perform services for a charity.

5. **Health Insurance.** This is deductible only if you are self-employed and itemize your deductions. In addition, deductions are available for the new Health Savings Accounts, but you should consult with a tax expert, because there are somewhat complex rules involved in setting these up.

6. **Expenses related to medical care.** If you itemize deductions and reach the threshold for medical deductions (7.5 percent of your adjusted gross income), don't forget to deduct expenses related to obtaining medical care, such as travel and parking costs.

7. **Deductions for the self-employed.** Self-employed people frequently fail to take advantage of all the deductions to which they're entitled, either because they don't know about them or because they're afraid taking them might trigger an audit. Although it is not a good idea to stretch the limits of what is a legitimate deduction, you shouldn't fail to take all that you're entitled to. Consider these:

- *Home office.* You can deduct the costs of space in your home that's dedicated to your work. Measure the space you use exclusively for work and calculate what percentage of your total home that is. You're entitled to take that percentage of most of the costs of your home, including routine maintenance and utilities, as a deduction. For details, as always check with your accountant.

- *Car.* If you have a car that you use only for your work, you can deduct the costs of maintenance, insurance, and gas. You can also amortize the purchase price. If you've bought a truck or SUV that weighs more than 6,000 pounds, you can deduct up to $25,000 the year you purchase it. The cost of passenger cars that weigh less than 6,000 pounds must be amortized, with a maximum deduction of about $3,000 the year the car goes into service.

- *Fixed assets.* You can deduct the cost of computers, file cabinets, and other equipment. The maximum amount allowed changes from year to year, although the cap in 2006 stands above $100,000. If you exceed that cap, you must amortize the value of purchases over a period of years. Your accountant has tables that show the expected life of various kinds of equipment. In addition, you might be able to deduct the costs of certain parts of commercial or rental property you're constructing or purchasing over a relatively short period.

- *Child care and other help.* Even if you run a home-based business, you can deduct expenses for child care. You might even be able to deduct expenses for other household help, including lawn care, if these costs are necessary for maintaining your home so that you can work with clients there.

- *Conferences, continuing education, trade meetings.* So long as it's associated with the continuing conduct of your business, these expenses and expenses related to them are deductible. Just remember that you cannot deduct the cost of education necessary to enter or qualify for a profession.

- *Phones, cell phones, and Internet services.* If you have dedicated lines for these, you can deduct the entire cost. If not, you can deduct that percentage that reflects business use, but you'll need to be able to substantiate that with copies of itemized bills.

KEEPING TAX RECORDS

Keep tax documents. Keep anything related to your taxes, such as receipts, bills, canceled checks, and various tax forms, including W-2s and 1099s for at least three years, the statute of limitations for the Internal Revenue Service (IRS) to conduct most audits. To be on the safe side, however, it's best to keep records for six years, because the IRS can audit returns that old if they suspect that income was underreported by 25 percent or more. If you're thinking of committing fraud, hold those records forever, because there's no statute of limitations on fraud.

Keep records of all home improvements. Although you can't deduct them from your income taxes, the costs of home improvements will offset the capital gains you realize when you sell the house.

Keep receipts for business and medical expenses. This is especially important if you're self-employed. If you use an account or a utility for both business and personal expenses, keep a diary of all business-related expenses.

Plan for Retirement

◆◆◆

If you think working is hard, wait until you get to retirement. Better yet, don't wait; think about it now. If you're still years from retirement, focus on financial planning; if you're almost there, start thinking seriously about how you want to spend your retirement years, because there could be many more of them than you suppose. There are three broad areas to consider: financial, mental, and physical. Here are tips for each.

1. **Save as much as you can.** Look at most retirement planning programs and you'll risk a serious fright. The suggested sums needed for retirement

are truly astonishing, but no one can accurately project what inflation will be or how the health-care system—the source of most retirement anxiety—will work twenty or thirty years down the road. You need to save as much as you can, but you shouldn't seriously compromise life in the here and now. The earlier you start a disciplined saving plan, the more money you'll have, thanks to the power of compound interest.

2. **Take full advantage of 401(k) plans.** These offer an immediate tax deduction, tax-deferred growth, and, frequently, a partial match of your contributions by your employer, which is essentially found money. If your employer doesn't offer a 401(k), open an IRA (individual retirement account); if you're self-employed, start a SEP (simplified employee pension) plan. There are different kinds of IRAs, so check with your accountant to see which is best for you.

3. **Pay attention to asset allocation.** Most retirement plans offer investment choices. Diversity is the rule, but there are other factors to consider. If you're young, you should probably be aggressive in the funds you choose. As you reach retirement age, shift more money into fixed-income and other conservative investments, but even then don't neglect stocks in favor of bonds. With longer retirements, the lower long-term returns on bonds can result in a loss of real income, as bonds fail to keep pace with inflation.

4. **Dip into retirement funds only for emergencies.** Don't be afraid to save as much as you can, because in certain circumstances, and depending on the kind of retirement fund you have, you can tap these funds without a penalty. Illness is one such circumstance, and a first-time home purchase may be another. Check with your accountant before you touch retirement funds. The laws governing use of these funds can be complicated. Most withdrawals will incur not only taxes but early-withdrawal penalties. Money becomes available without penalty at age 59½. You will pay tax on these funds, but chances are you will be in a lower tax bracket once you've retired.

5. **Structure your mortgage so your house is paid off when you retire.** If you have a traditional thirty-year fixed-rate mortgage, but you're less than thirty years from retirement, consider paying additional principal each month or see if you can restructure the mortgage to permit making payments twice a month, which has the effect of lowering your overall interest payments. If you're thinking of refinancing, consider a fifteen-year term (see "Refinance Your Mortgage," page 322).

NOW THAT YOU'RE FREE

Consider teaching. Local school systems, community and four-year colleges, and libraries and museums welcome people willing to offer courses in their fields of expertise. Retired professionals can teach part-time to earn extra income, or they can serve as volunteer mentors. Community centers and adult-learning centers also provide opportunities to teach what you know, either on a volunteer basis or as a part-time job.

Volunteer. There are almost unlimited options for volunteering, from helping people in your own community to lending your expertise to developing communities across the globe (see "Find Volunteer Opportunities," page 62).

Stay off the couch. One of the dangerous traps of retirement is slowing down physically to the point where you endanger your health. You may have to make a point of adding exercise to your life now that you don't have the daily walk to the station. Park a few blocks from stores, use the stairs rather than the escalator at malls, mow your own lawn, or join a gym. The point is, the more physically active you are, the more likely you'll enjoy good health in your retirement years. Remember that it's never too late to start. In fact, if you've been tied to a desk job for years, retirement can be an opportunity to finally get yourself into good shape. Don't begin an exercise program before visiting your doctor for a thorough checkup, and start slowly and persevere. Exercise needs to be a lifelong habit, not a quick fix.

Schedule regular physicals. If you move when you retire, you'll have to plan for your health care in a new community. Ask your current physician for referrals to doctors where you plan to move. Even if your physician doesn't personally know anyone, he or she can recommend good hospitals in the area that can refer you to local physicians. (See "Over-Twenty, Over-Forty Checkups," page 132, for details on what tests and physical exams you need.)

Stay mentally active. Learn a new language, take courses in subjects you always meant to study but never had time to pursue, read more and watch TV less. Most studies suggest that keeping mentally active is an essential ingredient for preserving your faculties into old age.

6. **Try a practice round.** There are many ways to spend time in retirement. Some people want to travel, others consider trying a second career; for some, endless rounds of golf seem attractive, others want to go back to school and get another degree. You won't really know what best suits you until you try it, so make no permanent commitments until you're certain what will really satisfy you. Try to take off for a prolonged period while you're still a few years away from retirement, to test the waters. If you're lucky enough to work at an educational institution and qualify for a sabbatical, take it as a dry-run for retirement. Some employers are willing to let employees take a prolonged leave without pay, which can serve the same purpose as a sabbatical. Just don't buy the house on the golf course until you rent it for a few months to see if that's where you want to be.

7. **Take a course or find a support group.** There are many programs across the country geared toward helping people make the transition to retirement. Civic Ventures, a San Francisco-based nonprofit, runs a program called The Next Chapter, which is designed to assist prere-tirees in establishing "connections and directions" to help them answer the question, "What's next?" Next Chapter groups are like student unions for the baby-boomer set, a place to hang out with peers and trade tips, experiences, and resources. To find a group near you, or to access Next Chapter resources, visit the Website at *www.civicventures.*to *org/nextchapter.*

8. **Check out community colleges.** Community colleges are shifting more of their resources toward addressing the needs of retirees. They often serve as lifelong learning centers and offer life-options seminars as well as courses on financial issues and other practical aspects of retirement. They frequently offer short courses on volunteer opportunities as well as training for possible second careers (see "Practice Lifelong Learning," page 164).

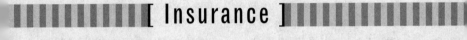

[Insurance]

Designate Beneficiaries

Designating beneficiaries on individual policies and accounts is the only way you can be assured that your assets will be distributed as you intend. Just naming people in a will isn't enough, because a beneficiary named in a particular account or policy trumps a beneficiary named in a will. For instance, if you name your children as the beneficiaries of your entire estate, but you still list an ex-spouse as the beneficiary of a life insurance policy and an old retirement account, your ex-spouse gets the life insurance and the retirement funds; your children wind up with the house and the collection of old LPs.

Designating beneficiaries is rarely a one-time task. You should review your beneficiaries periodically and certainly any time you experience a major life change, such as divorce or the birth or death of a loved one. Here is a list of things to consider when designating your beneficiaries.

1. **Know exactly what you have.** If you haven't already done so, make a list of all your assets. List every savings account, every investment account, every life insurance policy, and all your property, from real estate to heirloom jewelry.

2. **Know which assets require a beneficiary.** Certain assets must have a named beneficiary. If you fail to name one, the state will do it after your death, and its choice might not coincide with your wishes. A basic rule is that you must name beneficiaries for assets that will bypass probate and go directly to heirs. These include retirement accounts, annuities, and life insurance and disability policies.

3. **Decide who gets what.** This, of course is a personal decision, and sometimes a difficult one, but failing to decide can cause endless destructive squabbling among your heirs and legal and administrative fees that can substantially reduce the value of what you leave. When no beneficiary is clear, decisions will be made by the state.

4. **Keep the list up-to-date.** Deciding who gets what should be done periodically. As children grow up, they might need less protection; as spouses age, they might need more. New members of the family are born, and old ones die and relationships change. If you've designated an ex-spouse, that's who gets the asset, not the spouse who survives you.

5. **Don't name your estate as a beneficiary.** An estate must go through probate, which could delay distribution of assets, and an estate may be subject to taxes; assets distributed directly to a beneficiary are usually not.

6. **Don't name minors as beneficiaries.** Minors cannot control assets, so a court will appoint a guardian, either a person or a financial institution, which could incur costs that would diminish the value of the inheritance. Rather, name a guardian yourself or set up a trust to administer the assets for the child.

7. **Name contingent beneficiaries.** Many insurance policies and retirement accounts ask that you name contingent beneficiaries in the event the primary beneficiary predeceases you. It's a good idea to name contingent beneficiaries for all of your assets, even those that don't require one. If the primary beneficiary dies and you haven't named a contingent beneficiary, the heirs of the primary beneficiary might try to claim the assets even if you've named other people in your will. The claim may be denied, but not without a host of legal and court costs.

8. **Consider establishing a trust.** Trusts are not just for minor children. If you don't know whether a beneficiary can responsibly handle a large, lump-sum bequest, you might want to set up a trust and stipulate how and under what conditions proceeds should be distributed. This can be especially important if the beneficiary is incapacitated or mentally incompetent.

9. **Watch out for the tax man.** Assets passed directly to a spouse are not subject to taxation during the spouse's lifetime; however, when the spouse dies, assets may be taxed if they exceed the limits in place at the time of death (the limit is scheduled to reach $3.5 million in 2009). Anyone with substantial assets should discuss how best to structure estates and trusts so as to minimize taxation across a number of generations.

Choose Homeowners' Insurance

Homeowners' insurance is not an option; it's a must-have. Virtually all mortgages stipulate that you have it, but even if you own your home outright, you need homeowners' insurance to protect you against loss of your home and possessions and against liability should someone be injured on your property. Here's what you should consider when buying coverage.

1. **Determine what it would cost to rebuild your house.** If you have a mortgage, the minimum insurance you can carry is the amount of the mortgage, but that's rarely enough to cover the replacement of your home. The minimum insurance you should consider is the amount it would cost to completely rebuild your home from the foundation up. Just what that amount would be will depend on the kind of home you have, the architectural details, and the materials used. If you want to be able to duplicate an older, distinguished home, get an estimate from an architect or builder who specializes in building or rebuilding homes like yours.

2. **Get coverage for special risks.** Standard insurance won't cover you for loss due to floods. For this, you need to purchase separate flood insurance, available through the National Flood Insurance Program, administered by the Federal Emergency Management Agency. If you live in a state subject to extreme weather, your homeowners' policy may not cover damage due to winds and wind-driven rain and hail; in many of these states you can buy coverage against this kind of damage through a special pool established by the state. If you live in an area prone to earthquakes, you probably need a special rider or separate coverage against earthquake damage.

3. **Insure your possessions for what it would cost to replace them.** There are two basic kinds of coverage, *actual cash value*, which gives you the replacement cost, less any depreciation, and *replacement coverage*, which gives you the current amount of what it would cost to replace the item. Here's the difference: If you purchased a television five years ago for $500 and had actual cash value insurance, you might receive a payment of $100 were it damaged or stolen; if you had replacement coverage, you would receive the cost of an equivalent new set. Replacement coverage is more expensive, but you might offset the extra cost by increasing your deductible. In any case, in order to assure you receive proper payment for

any losses, it's essential to maintain a thorough inventory of your possessions (see "Take a Home Inventory," page 312).

4. **Make sure you have adequate liability coverage.** Standard policies usually include $100,000 of liability coverage, but most insurance experts consider this too little. Consider raising this to at least $500,000 or even $1 million. You can purchase an umbrella policy, which provides $1 million in liability insurance for as little as $150 per year.

5. **Add a personal floater to cover special items.** Standard insurance, even replacement coverage, may not cover particularly expensive items, such as art, antiques, and jewelry. To fully cover these items, buy a special personal floater for them. You will probably have to furnish a certified appraisal of each covered item, but for the added cost you'll get broader coverage, including theft or loss away from home and claims not subject to any deductible.

6. **Ask about extras.** You might want to include loss-of-use coverage, which covers temporary housing costs should you have to move out of a heavily damaged home. Inflation protection, which adjusts your coverage to account for inflation in rebuilding costs, is usually worth the small extra cost.

7. **Shop around.** Not all insurance policies are created equal, and the differences might go beyond cost. Use an agent you trust (ask for referrals from friends and family) and ask her to compare policies from more than one company. Be aware that some agents represent only one company; go with an independent agent who represents a number of different insurers. Ask how you can reduce premiums. Often, companies offer special deductions for certain safety measures, such as the installation of security systems, and many companies offer deductions if you have other policies, such as automobile or health, with them. You can significantly lower premiums by opting for a higher deductible. Make sure you ask about service. Some companies are known for providing fast and courteous service should you have a claim; others are notoriously difficult. Finally, make sure the company is financially sound; you can check this with A. M. Best, Co. (*www.ambest.com*), J. D. Power and Associates (*www.jdpower.com*), or your state department of insurance.

RENTERS NEED INSURANCE, TOO

If you rent, be aware that your landlord's insurance won't cover you should your possessions be damaged or stolen. Cover your property with a renters' insurance policy, and protect yourself with liability coverage. As with homeowners' insurance, you have a choice between covering your belongings for their cash value or, for a higher premium, for replacement value. The rules that apply to high-value items are the same, and you still need a home inventory.

Save Money on Automobile Insurance

◆◆◆

There may be no such thing as cheap car insurance, but there is no reason to pay more than you have to. Follow these tips to get the best rate.

1. **Shop around.** The Internet has made comparison shopping for car insurance, like comparison shopping for cars, much easier. Sites such as *www.insureme.com* and *www.insweb.com* walk you through the basic questions, such as your age, whether you or anyone you plan to include on the policy has had any accidents in recent years, and the make, model, and year of your car. They then return a number of quotes from a variety of firms. While you probably don't want to choose a company on price alone—service counts, especially if you have a claim—knowing the going rate will help you negotiate with your current or prospective insurer.

2. **Consider insurance costs when you choose a car.** Insurers consider a variety of factors when determining your insurance rate. Among them are the relative costs for repairs of the vehicle and how desirable the car and its parts are to thieves. These factors may vary from one part of the country to another. Call your agent and ask for an insurance estimate before you purchase a car.

3. **Ask for discounts.** Most companies offer discounts if you have other policies with them, such as homeowners' insurance, or if you insure more than one car. They also offer discounts for certain safety and antitheft features. Don't forget to ask for senior discounts if you qualify. At the other end of the age curve, companies offer discounts to students who complete a drivers' education course, and some even offer discounts to students who maintain good grades.

4. **Clean up your driving record.** Moving violations, which put points on your license, drive insurance rates higher. If you've accumulated points, see if your state allows you to eliminate them through a safe-driver course. Accidents also increase your premiums. The only thing you can do about higher premiums that result from a poor driving record is to make sure the premiums decrease when you again qualify as a safe driver, usually after a period of three years with no violations or accidents.

5. **Keep your credit score high.** Companies charge higher premiums to people with a poor credit history, and they sometimes increase premiums if you're late with a payment or two. Obtain a free copy of your credit report from each of the three major reporting agencies—Equifax, Experian, and TransUnion—and ask them to correct any errors and inform your insurance company of the corrected record. You can order your reports by calling the toll-free number, 877–322–8228, or on-line at *www.annualcreditreport.com/cra/index.jsp.*

6. **Don't pay for what you don't need.** If your car is paid off and is worth less than a couple of thousand dollars, it might not pay to have collision and comprehensive coverage on the vehicle. If you're a member of an auto club, you may already have certain coverage, such as rental car and towing, through the club. Don't pay for the same things twice.

7. **Increase your deductible.** Increasing the amount you pay before your insurance kicks in can reduce premiums significantly, but don't choose a deductible that is so high you'll have trouble meeting it.

8. **Choose a lower tort option.** The right to recover damages after an accident is known as a tort option. Some states offer a choice of a limited tort, in which you essentially waive the right to sue for pain and suffering. You may still collect for medical and other out-of-pocket costs. A full tort option means that you may sue for pain and suffering, damages over and above out-of-pocket expenses. Accepting the limited tort option can reduce your insurance premium by as much as 20 percent.

Buy Long-Term Care Insurance

No one questions the need for health insurance, and if you own a home you undoubtedly have homeowners' insurance. Chances are, however, you don't carry long-term care insurance. Should you? The answer is complicated. It depends on a variety of factors, including your financial position and your actuarial status. That is, how much money do you have and how long will you live? You can answer only one of these questions with any precision, of course, and there are several other factors to consider in the decision. Keep these suggestions in mind as you determine whether long-term care insurance is right for you.

1. **Beware of salespeople and sales literature.** Long-term care policies are complicated, with wide variations in charges, deductibles, rules that determine qualification for benefits, inflation protection, and renewability. Seldom are these spelled out in the sales literature, and agents selling these policies are not likely to focus on their more disturbing aspects. Courts have ruled that the contracts themselves, not the sales literature, determine which benefits can be claimed. Because these contracts are complicated, have yours reviewed by an elder-care lawyer before signing.

2. **Calculate the odds.** Your chance of spending at least some time in a nursing home is as high as 50 percent. That statistic certainly seems to suggest that everyone should have long-term care insurance, but it's not that simple. Consider this: Of the men and women who live to age sixty-five, one-third will spend at least three months in a nursing home, one-fourth of those over sixty-five will spend a year or more, but fewer than 10 percent will spend five years or more in a home. Of course, long-term care doesn't apply only to a stay in a nursing home; it could involve receiving help at home. Still, qualifying to receive benefits can be tricky, depending on the language in your policy.

3. **Pay attention to the fine print.** Every policy has a gatekeeper on the insurance company's payroll who determines when the policyholder becomes eligible for benefits. Generally the policyholder must be unable to perform a certain number of activities of daily living (ADLs) before qualifying. These ADLs include bathing, dressing, walking, moving from

a bed to a chair, using the toilet, maintaining continence, and eating. Some policies require that a person be sick or injured to collect benefits; other policies will pay upon receiving a doctor's certification that a nursing home is necessary. The fine print determines whether or not you'll be deemed eligible for benefits, so it's important to understand exactly what the fine print says.

4. **Make sure you can continue to pay the premiums.** If you don't maintain the policy, you can't collect on it when you need it. Most people are unable to pay the premiums as they get older. The U.S. General Accounting Office (GAO) confirms that of those who buy coverage at age sixty, 95 percent will have dropped it by age eighty, when they are most likely to need it, and the majority drop coverage after only ten years. Premiums can, and almost always do, rise from year to year, and payments that are affordable to begin with may well be unaffordable only a few years later.

5. **Listen to the smart money.** Many financial experts, including *Smart Money Magazine,* advise that people with assets of less than $200,000 should not purchase long-term care policies. At that income level people generally can't afford the premiums. Many in that group qualify for Medicaid, which provides medical services for people with low incomes and few resources. People with modest incomes are probably better off shoring up their savings by increasing their 401(k) contributions or saving in an IRA account. Long-term care policies are primarily for people with substantial assets—at least $1.5 million—that they want to preserve. Even individuals in this category should consult a financial adviser to help weigh benefits against the costs.

6. **Opt for compound inflation protection.** If it is to be worthwhile, a policy must include compound inflation protection. Assuming annual inflation at 6 percent, prices double every nine years, so a policy that initially pays $200 per day, would have to pay $400 per day after nine years to cover the same percentage of nursing home expenses. If the policy offers simple, rather than compound, inflation protection, it might offer an additional 6 percent per year, but over nine years that would come to just an additional $108 dollars, rather than the $200 that would keep you even. As time goes on, the disadvantage becomes even worse, so that in eighteen years the policy offering compound interest protection would pay $800 per day, while the one offering simple interest would provide just $416.

7. **Consider only the strongest companies.** Check a company's rating with A. M. Best (*www.ambest.com*) and choose only companies with the highest rating. Limit your choices to companies that have offered long-term care insurance for at least twenty years. Even large long-established insurance companies have exited the field after a few years, because they've made serious pricing errors or simply misjudged the complexities of geriatric care.

TIP: You can get free, unbiased assistance in understanding long-term care insurance policies, as well as a list of companies selling such insurance, by contacting your state Health Insurance Assistance Program. The number in each state is available from the toll-free Elder Care Locator at 800–677–1116.

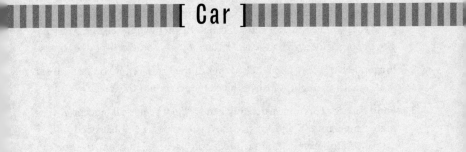

[Car]

Stock a Car

♦♦♦

Luck and cars break down at the most inopportune times. If the two break down simultaneously, you might find yourself in a situation ranging from the merely inconvenient to the life-threatening. Stock your car with the following items and you'll be prepared to handle any breakdown safely and with a minimum of discomfort.

1. **Cell phone.** A fully charged cell phone can be a literal life saver in an automotive emergency. Don't drive even a short distance without one. It's a good idea to keep one of those cigarette lighter battery chargers in your glove compartment so you're never caught with a dead cell-phone battery.

2. **Water.** Have at least a gallon of water in the car. Even if you don't need it, the radiator might. Change the water every month or so.

3. **Food.** Energy bars are particularly handy. They keep well (except in very high temperatures), and for the most part they pack a balanced mix of carbohydrate, protein, and fat in a small package. In a pinch, they can substitute for a meal.

4. **A map of the area you're traveling in.** A map will give you a good idea of where you are, which can be vital if you have to call an emergency roadside service.

5. **Fully inflated spare tire.** Check the pressure in your spare at least every three months, and pump it up if need be.

6. **Small flashlight.** Store a flashlight in the glove compartment, and check the batteries periodically.

7. **Small portable radio.** If your electrical system fails, this will help you stay in touch with the world outside.

8. **A first-aid kit and essential medication.** Keep a first-aid kit in your car (see "Stock a First-Aid Kit," page 168), and if you have a health condition that requires lifesaving medication, such as insulin for diabetes, make sure you have it with you at all times. Some medications have short expiration dates, so you may not want to keep those in the car; just make sure you have what you might need with you whenever you drive.

9. **Jumper cables.** Make sure these have fully insulated handles.

10. **Tire-changing kit.** Even if you are an AAA member or have access to another roadside service, it's a good idea to carry a portable tire inflator, plus a jack, lug wrench, and block of wood for emergency tire changes by the side of the road. You should also have an aerosol flat-tire fixer, which can work wonders for certain kinds of tire damage.

11. **Flares.** Stock flares or other warning devices, such as reflective triangles.

12. **An accident report form.** You can get these from your insurance company or from an auto club. The form guides you through the process of gathering all the information you need in case of an accident.

13. **Pen and paper.** These can come in handy for anything from recording a sudden brainstorm to writing the names of witnesses. You never know.

14. **Registration and proof of insurance.** Most states require that you carry both, but even if your state doesn't, it's a good idea to keep them in your glove compartment in case of an accident.

15. **Paper towels and window-cleaning fluid.** If the inside windows of your car are smeared or frosted, the windshield-wiper system won't help.

16. **Fire extinguisher.** A small, five-pound, A-B-C type fire extinguisher is all you need. Make sure you know how to use it; you don't want to be reading instructions by the light of leaping flames.

17. **Camera.** If your cell phone has one, that's all you need. Otherwise, keep a disposable camera in the glove compartment to record accidents, signs, and broken meters, should you get an undeserved parking ticket.

AND FOR WINTER ...

Stock the following extra items during the winter months (unless you live in a warm climate, of course!):

A blanket	Cat litter, sand, or traction mats
Ice scraper and snow brush	A small snow shovel
Gloves and extra socks	Extra antifreeze

Maintain a Car

◆◆◆

The key to minimum-expense car ownership is regular maintenance, and unless you're seeing flames shooting out from under the hood, it's not too late to adopt good maintenance habits. Consider your vehicle owner's manual the bible on just what those habits should be. Follow all the suggestions in the manual, and you will minimize costly repairs. Here are the basic guidelines for routine maintenance:

1. **Opt for the "severe driving" option.** Manuals frequently have two maintenance schedules, one for "normal driving" and one for "severe driving." Look at them carefully, and you'll realize that you probably fall into the severe category. This term simply translates to "average," as opposed to "ideal" driving habits. Severe driving includes making multiple short trips and driving in stop-and-go traffic. Normal driving is marked by long highway trips. If you do all highway driving and your trips last at least thirty minutes, go with the normal schedule. Otherwise, follow the maintenance schedule for severe driving.

2. **Change your oil and filter every 3,000 miles.** Also, check the oil level every other time you fill your gas tank and add oil if necessary.

3. **Check belts every time you have the oil changed.**

4. **Make sure all lights work and check tire pressure once a month.** Ask someone to make sure your brake lights work, and visually inspect all running lights monthly. Buy your own tire gauge, and check tire pressure when your tires are cold. Keep in mind that you'll need more air in your tires to maintain optimum pressure during winter months.

5. **Rotate tires and inspect brakes every 6,000 miles.** You can have this done every other oil change.

6. **Change the timing belt after 60,000 miles.** The belt may last longer, but if it fails, the best that can happen is you'll grind to a halt; the worst is you'll burn out your engine. It's better to be preemptive on this one.

7. **Replace belts and hoses when you change the timing belt.** Again, belts and hoses may last longer, but after about 60,000 miles they're on borrowed time.

8. **Maintain the battery terminals.** Keep battery terminals clean, and test the battery after four years. Many people routinely replace the battery after the warranty period expires.

9. **Flush the coolant system and replace fluid at least every 40,000 miles.** You might even want to observe the old rule of thumb, which is to do this every two years.

10. **Replace air and fuel filters every 15,000 miles or so.**

11. **Check fluids at least every six months.** These include brake, power-steering, coolant, and transmission fluids. It's not a bad idea to look under the hood every few times you visit a gas station; if the coolant level is often low, you might have a leak in the system.

12. **Check the air-conditioning system every spring.**

Choose a Good Mechanic

◆◆◆

The worst time to look for a mechanic is when you need one. Start your search for a mechanic as you would for a primary-care physician, when all is well. Once you find a mechanic you like, be a loyal customer. Although another shop may charge less for a particular repair, you'll probably wind up spending less in the long run if you stick to a mechanic you trust. You'll also avoid nagging suspicions that you've been taken for a ride. Here are tips for finding a mechanic you can count on.

1. **Take a new car to the dealership.** Dealerships can be the most expensive place to take your car for maintenance and repair, but if your car is less than three years old it's probably covered by a comprehensive warranty, which can make the dealership your best bet. Cost aside, the dealer will have the right parts, the best tools, and the mechanics with specific training to work on the make and model of your car. Also, if something goes wrong with your automobile during the first year, you definitely want the dealer to handle it. If a major defect shows up and it can't be fixed after three attempts, check your state's lemon law. You may have the right to a replacement vehicle from the dealer.

2. **Ask for recommendations.** Ask friends, relatives, and colleagues in the area if they have a mechanic they like. The longer they've been happy with a particular mechanic, the more valuable the recommendation.

3. **Look for accreditation.** The National Institute for Automotive Service Excellence (ASE) is the main accreditation body for auto mechanics. Service professionals are certified by the ASE after passing an exam and meeting certain experience requirements. Shops with a large percentage of certified ASE mechanics are awarded the institute's Blue Seal. Search for a Blue Seal shop in your area at the Institute's site, *www.ase.com*. Note that certification doesn't guarantee honesty, only competence.

4. **Check for awards and endorsements.** See if the shop has won an Automobile Association of America endorsement, which includes quality warranties and overall customer satisfaction among its criteria. Also, check for membership in the local Better Business Bureau and any other local civic organizations.

5. **Ask what kinds of cars the shop usually services.** If they specialize in American cars, your Ferrari may be better off someplace else.

6. **Look for certificates of continuing education.** Mechanics should be regularly updating their knowledge about the cars they work on. See if the shop displays certificates attesting to the courses its mechanics have completed.

7. **Look for easy-to-access pricing information.** Prices, including parts and per-hour labor rates, should be prominently displayed.

8. **Ask what the shop does if a car that isn't running right tests out okay.** If the mechanic says that has never happened, keep looking. It happens to every mechanic sooner or later, and the right answer is the shop does further research, consulting the manufacturer's bulletins and the latest manuals, all of which are available on-line or on CD-ROMs.

9. **Test the mechanic.** Take your car in for an oil change or a very minor problem and see how they handle it. The staff should be courteous and complete the repair when they say they will. If they can't handle a minor repair to your satisfaction, you won't want to trust them with a major problem.

10. **Read your bill.** This is always a good practice, but it's especially important when you don't know the mechanic. Don't be shy about asking questions if you don't recognize the itemized replacement parts or don't

understand the labor charges. Check to see that the warranty information is included on your receipt.

Deal with an Accident

◆◆◆

The National Highway Safety Transportation Administration (NHTSA) estimates that on average the typical driver is involved in some sort of automobile accident once every six years. That means if you haven't had the distress of even a fender bender, chances are you will at some point in your driving career. Whether you're in a serious or minor accident, you are required to take certain steps, and these may elude you in the stress of the moment. Keep this list in your glove compartment and use it to guide you in the event of any type of accident.

1. **Pull over.** If you're blocking traffic, pull off the road, but move your car the shortest distance possible to preserve details of the accident. If you can't pull over, put your emergency flashers on.

2. **Call 911.** Even if the accident seems minor, it's best to call for help. If anyone is injured, medical assistance will be needed. If the road is blocked, the police will be needed to redirect traffic and clear the accident scene. Finally, insurance companies require a police report.

3. **Take police officers' information.** When the police arrive, get the officer's name, badge number, and station phone number. Ask when you can receive a copy of the accident report.

4. **Exchange information.** Insurance companies and automobile clubs have blank forms that you can fill out at the scene of an accident. Keep one or two of these in the glove compartment (see "Stock a Car," page 360). Make sure you exchange all relevant information with any other drivers involved, including:

   • Name, address, and phone numbers, including work numbers

   • License plate number and driver's license number

   • Insurance company's name, address, and phone number (copy this information from the insurance card)

- Make, model, year, and color of the car
- Names, addresses, and phone numbers of passengers and any witnesses

5. **Write a description of the accident.** The blank form from the insurance company will have instructions on how to draw a picture of the accident, showing the direction both cars were traveling and how they collided.

6. **Take pictures.** If you have a camera with you, whether a disposable one you carry in the glove compartment for just this purpose or a cell-phone camera, use it to take pictures of the scene and of any damage to cars or other property.

7. **Make no agreement at the scene.** Don't let the other party talk you into settling up at the scene or "handling this among ourselves." Additional damage or health issues may arise later, and accepting an offer would compromise any future claim.

8. **Don't admit fault.** No matter what you think happened, don't admit fault and never sign anything at the scene.

9. **Go to the hospital.** Don't assume you are fine just because you don't feel pain immediately after the accident. It's not unusual for symptoms of injury to have a delayed onset. If you do need to file a claim for personal injury, having postponed medical treatment may work against you.

10. **Call your insurance company.** Call as soon as you can. Most companies have a twenty-four-hour number for reporting accidents. The company or your agent will tell you what steps to take next.

Buy a Car

◆◆◆

The great news about buying a new car today is that the age of sticker shock is over. Even car salesmen rarely point to the sticker and say that's the bottom line. The bad news is that if you want to save money and get the best deal you can, you must invest some time and effort in research. The savings you'll realize if you follow these suggestions can be substantial.

1. **Think about the car you want and need.** Your lifestyle will suggest the features you are likely to prize most highly. If you have a large family and possibly a dog or two, cargo space may top the list. For those same reasons, you may consider safety and economy most important. Passenger room, styling, and luxury options are all legitimate concerns, although they may not always be possible all in the same vehicle. As with any purchase, focus on the most important factors and see how you can squeeze in the secondary ones.

2. **Narrow your choices.** Read *Consumer Reports'* annual car issue, check the car magazines, and ask friends who own cars you're considering what their experience has been.

3. **Go for test drives.** Visit dealerships, browse around, and arrange test drives of at least your top three choices. Just make it clear that you're just looking and not buying. This is very important. Salespeople know that the impulse buy is their most profitable sale and that you're most likely to be vulnerable when you're really enthusiastic about a car you've just driven. It's also the worst time to make a decision. You need to go home, think about it, and prepare yourself to make the best deal.

4. **Jot down sticker information.** This includes the make, model, serial number, sticker price, and a list of all the options of the car you want.

5. **Check prices on the Internet.** At this point, you're ready to find out what the car really costs. Many Internet sites reveal information that goes beyond sticker and manufacturer's suggested retail price (MSRP). *Kelley Blue Book* (*www.kbb.com*) and Edmunds.com (*www.edmunds.com*) are among the most popular sites. At Edmunds.com you can choose a model and pick the options you want, and the site will show you three prices: the MSRP, the dealer's invoice price, and the price that customers in your geographic area are paying for a car equipped exactly as you've specified. You'll also see a list of any incentives that may be available. If you like, you can solicit bids from several dealerships in your area.

6. **Investigate financing costs.** Sites like Edmunds.com and Kelley Blue Book can provide quotes on financing from a variety of financial institutions. You should also check with your bank to see what rates it charges current customers for new-car financing. Prequalify for financing at the best rate you can find.

7. **Visit the dealer, but don't reveal your hand.** The salesman will probably ask if you want to finance the car and if you want to trade in your old car. Don't answer either question. Stick to the car you want to buy and the price you're willing to pay. Financing and any trade-in come after you've struck a firm deal.

8. **Make an offer.** Armed with the dealer's invoice price and the price paid by the average customer, make an offer between the two. Generally speaking, a fair price is $100 to $300 over invoice for a lower-priced car and $300 to $500 over invoice for a more expensive one. Say you'll buy the car today for that price, but emphasize that your offer is firm and specify that you will keep any applicable rebate.

9. **Be firm and skip the extras.** If the salesman hesitates, start to leave. If he tries to sell you undercoating or some such extra, refuse. Be firm. You know what the dealer paid, and you're offering to pay a bit more for a quick deal. Be polite and friendly. Mention that you could actually simply get the car on the Internet for this price, but you'd rather deal with a local business and establish a long-term relationship.

10. **Talk about financing and any trades.** Only when the salesman has agreed to your price should you talk about either of these issues. You already know what you can finance the car for. If the dealer can do better, fine; if not, go with the cheapest rate, for which you're already prequalified. For your trade-in, check the value of your old car as you would check the value of the car you're buying, on the Internet. The same sites that offer new-car pricing can tell you what you can expect in trade for your old car. Used-car pricing is highly subjective, however; it depends on the condition of the car, its age, and mileage. If you're trading it at the dealership, you'll be offered less than you might get from a private customer, but you'll avoid the hassles of a private sale.

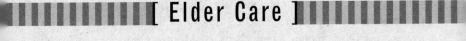

[Elder Care]

Choose a Nursing Home

◆ ◆ ◆

For a variety of reasons, placing a loved one in a nursing home is one of the most difficult tasks a family member can face, and determining the right time to make the change may be the most painful part of the undertaking. For that reason, it's important to solicit all the help that's available. If possible, share the task with other family members. When a loved-one is moving from a hospital to a nursing home, the hospital's discharge unit or social-services office can usually provide help. You might also receive help from your church, synagogue, or mosque. Although it may be difficult to do, try to approach this emotional task as you would any other major decision: rationally, systematically, and armed with as much information as possible. This list will help you cover the basics.

1. **Select several nursing homes to compare.** Try to get recommendations from families who have placed a loved one in a nursing home. Ask your primary-care physician if she can recommend a local geriatrician who might be helpful. Because the cost of nursing-home care can exceed $70,000 per year, it's best to find a facility that participates in Medicare. Consider homes that are within easy visiting distance for as many family members as possible.

2. **Schedule tours with people who work there.** If you tour a facility with a social worker or director of nursing, you will have a different experience than if you are escorted by a marketing representative, which is more likely to be the case if the home is a for-profit facility. Try to arrange to visit during mealtime so you can observe the treatment of residents who need assistance with eating. Before you leave the facility, make it a point to talk with a few residents and visiting family members.

3. **Use your senses as you take the tour.** How does the place smell? Basically, it shouldn't. A strong odor of air freshener or disinfectant may mask a lack of sanitation and patient care. A sweetish or rotting smell may indicate bed sores that aren't being properly treated. Watch the behavior and note the apparent mood of the residents, as well as the attitude of the staff. Are staff members pleasant, friendly, and helpful in their exchanges with patients? Also keep an eye on the following:

- *Patients' clothing and grooming.* Residents should be neat and clean, of course, but look for extra touches, such as nicely arranged hair, jewelry, or scarfs on the women. Such details suggest that staff members take special care to assure patient dignity.

- *Individual rooms.* Look for photographs and other personal items. Some facilities allow residents to bring a couple of pieces of furniture from home, which can make the transition easier.

- *Accessible hallways.* Hall passages should be brightly lit and wide enough for two wheelchairs to pass each other. Walls should have handrails on both sides.

- *Patient privacy.* If your guide takes you into an occupied room or opens closets without asking the resident's permission, privacy is not respected and neither is the patient.

- *Patient activity level.* Observe whether patients are lying in bed or are up and active, even if they are in wheelchairs.

- *Mealtime atmosphere.* See whether the food looks appetizing and if residents are rushed or given the time they need to eat. Check the amount of attention received by residents who need help. Ask what happens if a resident has to miss a meal. Malnutrition is a serious problem for the elderly, and there should be alternative arrangements for those who occasionally cannot make it to the dining room.

4. **Ask to see a variety of rooms.** Don't confine your tour to the private rooms, even if your family member will be in one. Ask to see rooms with two or more residents as well.

5. **Visit areas for patients with dementia.** Units where residents with dementia are cared for should be specially designed to accommodate them comfortably and safely. The layout should be simple, perhaps circular, to allow for safe wandering. The unit should have a special recreation program, separate from that of the rest of the facility.

6. **Check outdoor areas.** There should be a pleasant, enclosed outdoor area easily accessible by all residents, including those in wheelchairs. If the facility is in a large city, it may substitute an atrium filled with plants, where residents can feel as though they're in a relaxing park.

7. **Ask to see the most recent state inspection report.** This should be prominently posted in a public area. Ask about any violations that are noted on the report. Violations may not pose an immediate threat to

patient well-being, but if any violations were noted, even minor ones, the facility should already have taken steps to address them. Ask for details.

8. **Have a discussion.** Before leaving, sit down with the guide, the admissions director, or the administrator to get a feel for the overall philosophy of the place. You might initiate the conversation by asking what makes this facility special. If the response is generic, be wary. If, however, the staff member lights up and talks about employees' length of tenure, changes made in response to a residents' council, or about how the place has made special efforts to accommodate the preferences of individual residents, take this as a very positive sign. Ask about any concerns you have. You might, for instance, want to know about resident autonomy. Some facilities provide a great deal of independence when it comes to areas such as special recreational and therapeutic programs. Some have small kitchen facilities where residents can prepare their own snacks. Ask if pet therapy, such as visits by specially certified dogs, is part of the facility's program. It has been well documented that all patients, including those suffering from dementia, can benefit profoundly from contact with animals.

9. **Come back to see more.** If you like what you see at a facility, visit at least twice more before you make a final decision. Stop by in the evening and on a weekend. These are the times when staffing levels may fall. Make sure residents still receive all the care they need, that no one waits too long for help, and that the staff is not too busy to keep a careful watch on all residents.

10. **Check the Web.** There is a wealth of information about nursing homes on the Internet. Start your search at Nursing Home Compare (*www .medicare.gov/NHCompare/home.asp*), a Website maintained by the federal government's Center for Medicare and Medicaid Services. This site offers detailed information, arranged by location, about nursing home facilities. It includes details about the latest state inspections, staffing levels, and six quality measures. Although it may be difficult to evaluate some of the information—staffing levels, for instance, may include administrative personnel—the site can be quite useful for comparing data on the facilities you're seriously considering. It will enable you to see how your candidate facilities stack up against each other and against the state and national averages. Other useful sites are hosted by Member of the Family (*www.memberofthefamily.net*) and the National Citizens' Coalition for Nursing Home Reform (*www.nursinghomeaction.org*).

QUESTIONS TO ASK

General

Does staff appear competent, engaged, and friendly?

Are residents well groomed?

Are they out of bed?

Are they out of their rooms?

Are calls for assistance answered promptly?

Rooms

Are rooms attractive, comfortable, and clean?

Do bedrooms have windows and natural light?

Have residents personalized their rooms?

Lounge Areas

Are they comfortable, with sufficient seating?

Is there a place for private visits?

Is there a place where residents can watch TV together?

Activity Programs

Is there a schedule of daily events posted where residents can see it easily?

Is there a wide variety of activities?

Are there activities for residents confined to their rooms?

Is there a library and are books distributed on carts to individuals who can't leave their rooms?

Is there a regular coffee or social hour?

Do residents participate in planning activities, or can they suggest new ones?

Is there an active volunteer program that includes regular visits from people who can entertain or offer classes or lead discussion groups?

Dining Area and Food

Is the menu appetizing? Does the food taste good? (Try it.)

Are substitute items available on every menu?

Do residents who need assistance receive it and are they given adequate time to eat?

Do residents finish at least half their meals?

Are residents satisfied with the food?

Bathrooms and Showers

Is there a call button near the toilet?

Does the bathroom accommodate wheelchairs easily?

Are there grab bars?

How often are residents offered baths or showers?

Choose a Nursing Home Alternative

◆◆◆

There are a variety of choices available for seniors who can no longer live
alone but aren't yet ready for a traditional nursing home. Before you can determine the best option for your family member, you will need to evaluate
three elements: physical requirements; lifestyle preferences; and financial resources, including governmental assistance, such as Medicare (see "How
Medicare May Help," page 378). Above all, your goal should be to allow as
much independence as possible, while assuring a safe, full, and satisfying life.

1. **Assess physical needs.** Safety should be the first consideration in deciding what type of assistance an older person may need. Both physical
   and mental faculties come into play in making this assessment. Consult a
   physician, preferably one who has treated your family member in the
   past. Often the right diagnosis and treatment plan can remedy physical
   problems so that living independently remains an option. For example,
   strength and balance training may be able to counter physical debilities
   that might otherwise lead to falls. Loss of short-term memory may indicate metabolic or other physiologic disturbances amenable to medical
   treatment. Total Living Choices, a Seattle-based company, offers a free

needs-assessment tool, called Care Interpreter™, on its Website at *www.tlchoices.com*.

2. **Consider lifestyle preferences.** Although many people prefer to remain in their own homes, there are times when doing so isn't the most attractive alternative. If a mate dies and there are no other family members at home, isolation can be a real problem. In this case, moving closer to children or other family and friends may be the ideal choice. Other considerations may include climate, size and type of community (urban, suburban, or rural), access to favorite activities (golf or other sports, theater, music, academic or scholarly pursuits), and ease of connections with fraternal or religious organizations.

3. **Determine resources.** Personal resources include savings, the profit from selling a home, investments, and reverse mortgages (see "Refinance Your Mortgage," page 322). Government and private resources include Medicare (see "How Medicare May Help," page 378), Medicaid (certain states offer assistance with home and community care), long-term care insurance (see "Buy Long-Term Care Insurance," page 356), veterans' benefits, and possibly help from union, professional, or fraternal organizations.

Options for Care

After you have assessed the physical, emotional, and financial needs of your loved one, you can begin to discuss your options. Here are some of the basic choices.

1. **Staying put.** Most people find this the most attractive choice, especially when they're physically and mentally sound. Staying home can become a realistic choice, even for those with physical limitations, by making certain alterations to the house. A good source for what's locally available is *www.improvenet.com*. There are also many community-based services to help at-home seniors, including Meals-on-Wheels, volunteer visits, help with grocery shopping, and congregate meal sites, where seniors get together for prepared, well-balanced meals. To find local providers for a host of services, check the resources section of Elder Locater at *www.eldercare.gov*.

2. **Continuing-care retirement communities.** These offer graduated levels of care, from totally independent living in apartments or houses to skilled

nursing care in an affiliated nursing home. Typically, these communities require a substantial entrance fee—the equivalent of buying a house or condominium—as well as a monthly fee. Some facilities offer a choice of comprehensive or limited plans. In comprehensive plans, the monthly fee may cover unlimited nursing care if that becomes necessary. Other plans may offer a restricted or modified contract stipulating a certain level of care, beyond which additional fees would be charged. Residents move from one stage to another, as needed, so one might begin in a separate house or apartment, move to a communal arrangement, and, if necessary, wind up in the affiliated nursing home. Continuing-care retirement homes offer the assurance that residents will remain within the community for the rest of their lives. These facilities are not federally regulated, but they should have accreditation from the Continuing Care Accreditation Commission. To find a facility in your area, log on to its Website at *www.carf.org.*

3. **Assisted-living facilities.** These are similar to continuing-care retirement communities, although they often provide a more narrow range of services. Usually, these facilities are restricted to residents who need at least a limited amount of assistance, either with meals or with personal care. When residents need more advanced skilled nursing care, they might have to transfer to a regular nursing home. To find an assisted-living facility in your area log on to Assisted Living Info at *www.assistedlivinginfo.com.*

4. **Congregate senior housing.** These generally provide private living quarters with centralized dining services, shared communal spaces, and access to and some direction for recreational and social activities. Many of these facilities also provide transportation services as well as personal-care and rehabilitative services. They may overlap assisted-living facilities. Frequently, states or cities subsidize rents in apartment complexes for seniors.

5. **Group homes.** These are essentially boardinghouses for seniors. They're usually in private homes, and each senior has a private bedroom. Meals are shared, provided by the owner of the home. Seniors who own their own homes may consider starting their own group homes to share costs and again have companionship that the death of their partners may have deprived them of.

HOW MEDICARE MAY HELP

Medicare offers two limited programs that may help seniors pay for housing as an alternative to skilled nursing home care. The Program of All-Inclusive Care for the Elderly (PACE) is an optional benefit under both Medicare and Medicaid that features comprehensive medical and social services, provided at an adult day health center or in a person's home. The program, however, is available only in certain states. For complete eligibility requirements and to find out whether a program is available in your state, check *www.medicare .gov/Nursing/Alternatives/Pace.asp*.

Medicare also offers its Social Managed Care Plan in four communities, Portland, Oregon; Long Beach, California; Brooklyn, New York; and Las Vegas, Nevada. The plan provides the full range of Medicare benefits offered by its standard Managed Care Plan, plus additional services, which include care coordination, prescription drug benefits, chronic care benefits covering short-term nursing home care, and a full range of home- and community-based services such as homemaker, personal-care services, adult day care, respite care, and medical transportation. For eligibility details, check online at *www.medicare.gov/Nursing/Alternatives/SHMO.asp*.

TIP: Various respite programs are available for family members who provide full-time home care for elderly relatives. These programs offer a break to caregivers by providing temporary housing for the senior in a variety of facilities, ranging from nursing and group homes to hotels. These longer-term respites are generally for a maximum of two weeks. Respite care can also provide just a few hours of free time through adult day-care programs for the older person. To find respite resources in your area, log on to *www.archrespite.org*.

Find Help for Seniors

There is an abundance of services designed specifically to meet the needs of older citizens. The Administration on Aging, a part of the federal Department of Health and Human Services, maintains a helpful Website, Eldercare Locator (*www.eldercare.gov*). This site is an excellent starting point for anyone researching resources for seniors on both state and federal levels. Use this list to refine and expand your search for senior-targeted services.

1. **Benefits Checkup** (*www.benefitscheckup.org*). The National Council on the Aging created this comprehensive Website to help seniors connect to government programs in health, utilities, housing, and other needs. No registration is required. Just complete a simple questionnaire to be directed to programs for which you or your family member may qualify. It includes complete contact information and instructions on how to apply. The site is completely confidential and does not require a name or Social Security number.

2. **State resources.** Every state has an office that coordinates information about programs for senior citizens. The Mid-Florida Area Agency on Aging has a Website that lists the contact information, by state, for each of these offices. The address is *www.mfaaa.org/statesaging.aspx*.

3. **General Websites.** The American Association of Retired People (AARP) offers a host of services and information for seniors. You don't have to be a member to access its Website at *www.aarp.org*. Seniors-Site (*www.seniors-site.com*) offers information about everything from health and money issues to travel ideas, and the National Council on the Aging (*www.ncoa.org*) has links to other sites as well as an on-line monthly magazine, *Seniors' Corner*, with articles on many subjects of interest to seniors.

4. **Housing information.** The Department of Housing and Urban Development maintains a Website devoted to senior issues at *www.hud.gov/groups/seniors.cfm*. The site offers information on remaining at home (including an explanation of reverse mortgages), renting an affordable apartment, various loans seniors can qualify for, and how to protect against housing discrimination and various frauds.

5. **Home-based physical therapy.** Medicare will pay for a certain number of visits by a physical therapist if a doctor has provided a written prescription and the therapist is from a Medicare-certified agency. Because home-based therapy can be expensive, this is an important distinction. After an initial evaluation, the agency will tell you how many sessions Medicare will cover.

6. **Social Security.** The Social Security Administration's site (*www.ssa.gov*) provides comprehensive information on Social Security, disability, and Supplemental Security Income (SSI).

7. **Medicaid.** For general information on Medicaid, see the Centers for Medicare and Medicaid Services site at *www.cms.hhs.gov/medicaidgeninfo*. Medicare requirements vary from one state to another; contact your state's specific Medicaid site for complete information.

8. **Food Stamps.** Complete information about the Food Stamp program is available from the Department of Agriculture at *www.fns.usda.gov/fsp*.

Elder-Proof a Home

◆◆◆

Elder-proofing a home is really just an exercise in common sense. Although older people are often less agile than young people, the causes of accidents and mishaps are pretty much the same for both. It's just that older people are more likely to have balance and vision problems, and accidents tend to have more serious consequences. When elder-proofing a home, pay particular attention to issues of light, unobstructed surfaces, and predictability.

1. **Create level surfaces.** Falls are particularly dangerous, because healing can be much slower in older people and sedentary rest can, in itself, cause serious cardiovascular problems. It's essential, then, to create level surfaces by eliminating scatter rugs. Deep-pile carpet can be a problem, especially for people who use walkers or canes. Wall-to-wall low- or no-pile carpet is better, and it should be well installed, with low edges and a thin pad.

2. **Remove loose objects from the floor.** That includes wires and extension cords, pet and children's toys, and pet bowls (keep them under the kitchen table).

3. **Keep all floors slip-free.** Wooden floors should never be highly polished and should be coated with a nonskid finish. Kitchen and bathroom floors should also be made of nonskid material.

4. **Keep the house well lit.** The house needn't be lit up like a Christmas tree, but there should always be enough light to see well, even if the resident has cataracts. There should be a light switch at the top and bottom of stairs and at the entrance to all rooms. Keep automatic night-lights in every room, and make sure the path to the bathroom is well lit at night. There should always be a flashlight next to the bed, and automatic power-failure lights, the kind that go on when the power fails, in every room. Don't forget outdoor lights; the path from the car to the front door should be well lit.

5. **Maintain a holding pattern.** If an older person does not use a cane or walker, watch how he navigates a room. He may grab hold of familiar objects in order to go from one place to another. Make sure these are sturdy pieces of furniture that aren't easily tipped over. If necessary, install railings in rooms where substantial furniture is impractical, as in the bathroom.

6. **Keep hot water below scalding.** Make sure the hot water heater is set to maintain water no hotter than 120°F; scalding is an entirely preventable accident.

7. **Make sure bath and showers are nonslip.** If the bathtub surface isn't already nonslip, install nonslip adhesive strips. If the entrance to the shower is a step up, consider replacing it with a flat entrance. If the bath has sliding doors, consider replacing them with a shower curtain, and install secure railings in the bath and next to the toilet.

8. **Avoid surprises.** A dog that jumps up for sheer joy or a cat that suddenly appears behind a half-closed door can startle anyone; joyful events like these can precipitate a fall in a frail person. Be aware that if you bring an older person into your home, you need to accommodate someone who may not acclimate easily to your lifestyle. It may be annoying to see grandma's false teeth on the table beside her bed, but she needs to know where they are, and if that's where she's used to keeping them, that's where they belong when they're not in her mouth.

Manage Elder-Specific Health Care

◆◆◆

Broadly speaking, seniors need to take the same steps as younger people to stay healthy: eat right, exercise, and get regular health checkups. However, as the body ages, the practices that used to fulfill the requirements for healthy living may no longer suffice. Here are tips to help seniors stay healthy.

1. **Consider a geriatrician.** If a person over fifty has a well-established and satisfying relationship with an internist or family practitioner, there's probably no reason to switch primary-care doctors. Seniors over sixty-five who need to find a new doctor, however, are well advised to focus their search on geriatricians, physicians who have been board-certified in the health needs of the elderly. Geriatricians are more likely to be aware of the physiological alterations that come with age, such as the efficiency with which drugs are metabolized and other changes that can make an important difference in the way an illness is treated. Just as a pediatrician is the most appropriate choice of physicians for children, geriatricians are the first choice for patients sixty-five and older.

2. **Get regular checkups.** Regular visits with your physician become more important as you age. A good physical exam includes blood and urine tests and time for the patient to ask questions. Here's what the American Geriatrics Society recommends:

- Blood pressure check at least yearly

- Height and weight yearly

- Annual influenza vaccine

- Lipid (blood fat) screening every five years, and more often if there is any indication of coronary artery disease, diabetes, prior stroke, or peripheral artery disease

- Pneumonia immunization, once at age sixty-five

- Bone density test for women at least once at age sixty-five, or age fifty if a woman has risk factors such as a thin frame or history of smoking or heavy drinking

- Tetanus immunization every ten years

- Smoking cessation consultation at every office visit, if appropriate

- Alcohol abuse screening
- Depression screening
- Diabetes screening
- Fecal occult blood test yearly and/or sigmoidoscopy every three to five years, and/or colonoscopy every ten years
- Mammography annually for women and clinical breast exam for all patients (including men) every one to two years
- Eye exam every year, including the test for glaucoma
- Skin exam yearly
- Cognitive impairment screening yearly
- PSA (prostate specific antigen) and digital rectal exam for men (The need for this test is controversial. Discuss the test with physician first.)
- Thyroid-stimulating hormone test yearly for women

3. **Keep physician abreast of all medications and dosages.** Even if a patient has been taking the same drug for years, the doctor should be made aware of the current dosage so that it can be adjusted if necessary. An appropriate dose at age seventy is different from the appropriate dose at age fifty. The same is true for over-the-counter drugs.

4. **Use special pillboxes to keep track of medicine.** Seniors typically take more drugs than younger people, and remembering which drug to take and when can be confounding. Special pill containers, marked by day and even by time of day, can be purchased at any drugstore. Fill the containers once a week, referring to a written schedule.

5. **Maintain a healthy diet.** Appetite often diminishes with age. Sometimes this is an indication of illness or of changes in metabolic function that should be brought to the attention of a doctor. At other times it is the result of a diminishing sense of smell brought on by age or of a slowing metabolism. Buying and preparing food can seem more of a chore as people age. Because the need to maintain a healthy diet doesn't change, extra care must be taken to ensure that seniors remain well nourished. In addition, kidney function diminishes with age, so the elderly may need to be more conscious of drinking sufficient quantities of water. Adequate hydration becomes even more vital for people taking diuretics.

6. **Physical exercise.** No one should start an exercise program without consulting a physician, but seniors who have been exercising should make

a point of continuing, and those who haven't should know that it's never too late to start. Workouts for seniors should focus on flexibility (stretching), endurance (walking, cycling, or swimming), strength (weight training), and balance (tai chi, dance, yoga, or postural awareness).

7. **Mental exercise.** Although keeping the mind active may not prevent dementia, stimulating mental activity can dramatically improve the quality of life. Reading, working crossword puzzles, learning a new language, or simply studying a new subject all qualify as mental exercise. If this mental stretching can be done in a social setting, such as a book club, so much the better.

Be Aware of Scams Aimed at Seniors

Seniors account for a disproportionate number of fraud victims—well over half, according to the American Association of Retired People (AARP). Studies by AARP show that people sixty and older are more likely to assume the friendly voice on the telephone is a nice young person just trying to earn a living. Because crooks can be just as persuasive as good salespeople, it can be difficult to distinguish between the two. Here are some of the most common scams aimed at seniors and a general guide on how to minimize the chance of becoming a fraud victim.

1. **Bank examiner scam.** In this scam, someone posing as an FBI agent, police officer, or detective asks for assistance in an ongoing investigation. The caller describes an elaborate crime scheme and asks you to pose as a victim, withdraw a sum of money, and hand it over to the "investigator," who will then redeposit it to your account. Needless to say, you never see the money again.

2. **Charity look-alikes.** Here, a phony organization uses a name similar to that of a legitimate charity to solicit donations. Before donating to any charity, check it out (see "Choose a Charity," page 338).

3. **Work at home, easy-money schemes.** These are often advertised in local newspapers and in spam messages. They promise good money for

doing simple work at home, such as stuffing envelopes, and ask for an initial investment to cover the costs of "training" materials. In return, either nothing arrives or you receive instructions on how to con someone else in the same way.

4. **Nigerian e-mail fraud.** This scam is so old that it used to be called "letter fraud." Now the swindle generally arrives as an e-mail from someone posing as a Nigerian government official, doctor, or prince. The message asks to use your bank account for the transfer of a large sum of money the scammer claims he is trying to get out of Nigeria (there are now variations involving countries other than Nigeria). The victim is offered a large share of the money in return. The perpetrator asks for personal and banking information, blank letterhead, and deposit slips, all of which help the scammer steal your identity and tap your bank account. Sometimes, money is requested to help pay for bribes necessary to get the money out of the scammer's country. In some cases, the scammer appeals to the victim's larcenous side to share in a clearly illegal scheme. In other cases, the appeal is to sympathy or sense of justice.

5. **Lotteries.** This is frequently a phone-based scam. The caller may offer a chance to win a Canadian, Australian, or other foreign lottery not otherwise available in the United States. The caller usually asks for a credit-card or bank account number from which to debit the price of the lottery tickets.

6. **Home improvement scams.** If anyone offers to work on your home or lawn at a deep discount, especially if you haven't solicited bids, you've probably been targeted for a scam. Occasionally a certain amount of low-quality work is done; more often, the "workers" simply skip out with the up-front payment. Among the signs of a likely scam: itinerant workers with no local connections, the offer to do work with supplies left over from another job, and the demand for cash payment.

7. **"You've won!" calls.** An excited caller says you've won something wonderful, a cash prize, a vacation, or a car. This is the time to hang up. The next words are likely to be a request for your social security number "just to verify your identity," or the stipulation that you have to buy a magazine subscription or some other relatively small item, for which you'll have to furnish your credit-card or bank account number.

8. **Investment fraud.** This often comes in the form of an offer to increase the return on your fixed income. The promised rate is always extraordi-

nary, usually from 12 to 20 percent annually. The business selling the investment opportunity is often located in another state, and the caller frequently offers to provide overnight delivery services for the transport of the potential victim's blank checks, deposit slips, or a lump sum payment. The damage is compounded if the victim supplies personal information in addition to a lump sum payment.

9. **Medical equipment.** Medical equipment scams take a variety of forms. Sometimes equipment is offered free and then billed to Medicare or private insurance. Sometimes there is no equipment at all, just a phony offer. Warning signs of this scam are that the product is available "today only" or that it's a "stupendous breakthrough." Never consider medical equipment or devices unless you've talked to your doctor about them first.

10. **Living trusts.** Scam artists play on the fact that most people are not particularly sophisticated when it comes to complex financial matters, such as the structure of trusts and estates. Frequently the scammer claims that a trust will protect assets from inheritance taxes or can serve to shelter assets, should the individual ever need to apply for Medicaid. Sometimes, the scammer simply charges outrageous sums for boilerplate forms.

11. **Medicare fraud.** Never give in to pressure or scare tactics from anyone claiming your Medicare coverage is in jeopardy. When in doubt, call 1–800-MEDICARE (633–4227) to authenticate any information.

Talk with Aging Parents

◆◆◆

The evening before major surgery is not the best time to ask your mother what kind of burial arrangements she would prefer. Similarly, it's infinitely better to approach your father on the question of heroic life-support measures when he is healthy, long before the topic is painfully relevant. Unfortunately, death and money often rank with sex and politics on that list of topics family members tacitly agree not to discuss. Also, adult children may hesitate to pose questions as crucial—and simple—as the whereabouts of wills and insurance policies, for fear of appearing greedy or calculating.

HOW TO AVOID SCAMS

Never reveal your Social Security, credit-card, or checking account number to anyone you don't know.

Never do business over the phone with anyone who calls you to initiate a purchase or any other transaction.

Beware of "too good to be true" offers. If it sounds that way, it probably is.

Ask for written materials before you commit yourself to any offer or request for a donation.

Check out companies with the Better Business Bureau.

Hang up, close the door, or simply walk away if anyone pressures you to make an immediate decision involving your money.

The organizations listed below are dedicated to preventing fraud against elderly people.

National Fraud Information Center (NFIC)
1701 K Street NW, Suite 1200
Washington, DC 20006
Hotline: 800–867–7060
www.Fraud.org

National Center on Elder Abuse (NCEA)
120 15th Street NW, Suite 350
Washington, DC 20005–2800
202–898–2586
www.ElderAbuseCenter.org

National Academy of Elder Law Attorneys
1604 North Country Club Road
Tucson, AZ 85716
520–881–4005
www.nela.org

The truth is, children of aging parents *must* ask about these delicate topics. Here are some ideas to keep in mind when broaching them.

1. **Pick the right time and place.** Don't try to discuss emotional or delicate issues around the Thanksgiving table. Choose a time away from holidays or large family get-togethers, when everyone is likely to be as free from stress as possible. Don't have the talk via long distance; these conversations should take place face-to-face and sometimes hand-in-hand.

2. **Accept the discomfort.** Death is rarely a popular discussion topic, and talking to your parents about their eventual death can stir up feelings everyone would rather avoid, including sadness, grief, betrayal, and fear on both sides. Discussing money is not much easier, because this issue may bring up old resentments, guilt, and the fear—again, on both sides—of appearing grasping or selfish. But waiting until these questions are of critical significance will cause more discomfort and difficulty in the long run.

3. **Ease into it.** Choose a relatively nonthreatening topic sentence. For instance, "I was just reading that it's important for families to know where certain documents are, in case something happens." Or you might ask if your parents would like to seek legal advice to ensure that their estate will be handled according to their wishes. The answer might be, "I don't want to deal with that now," in which case you might ask if they would be willing to schedule a time to talk, gently pointing out that these issues will ultimately affect everyone in the family. Mention that when financial plans aren't spelled out clearly the state often steps in and ignores everyone's wishes.

4. **Make it clear that your parents are in charge.** Sometimes parents are reluctant to engage the issues of finances and long-term health plans because they fear the discussion itself may be a first step toward limiting their independence or relinquishing power over their future. Emphasize that the purpose of these discussions is to understand your parents' wishes so that they can be honored.

5. **Set realistic goals.** Don't approach the discussion hoping to get the whole thing over with at once. Make a list of the topics you need to cover and plan to broach just one at a time. If you and your parents have a relatively comfortable and productive conversation, you may cover a lot of ground in one sitting, but let your parents' reaction be your guide.

HEALTH TOPICS FOR DISCUSSION

Advanced health-care directives. There are basically two kinds: a living will, in which the person spells out the kind of care he wants or does not want under certain circumstances, and a health-care proxy (or durable health-care power of attorney), in which she names someone to make decisions about her health care if she should become incapacitated. They are not mutually exclusive, and many people have both. Many Websites offer samples of living wills and health-care proxies, with details tailored to the regulations of each state. Go to *www.uslivingwillregistry.com* or *www.leagldocs.com*.

Assisted living, nursing homes, and alternatives. The more involved everyone is, including parents, in decisions about what to do when parents can no longer take care of themselves, the better. These can be complicated issues, involving money, autonomy, and personal dignity, so they're best handled when everyone is well and can think clearly about them, without the terrible pressure of having to make immediate decisions (see "Choose a Nursing Home ," page 370 and "Choose a Nursing Home Alternative," page 375).

Quality-of-life issues. These can be difficult to deal with in the abstract, but, again, the earlier the topic is broached the better. While parents are healthy the discussion will, by definition, be general, and you can include yourself in it. Raise questions about what "quality of life" means. Is it freedom from pain or discomfort? The preservation of independence? The ability to continue to function, mentally or physically, at a certain level? In the event of life-threatening illness, the discussion becomes much more concrete. Is the possibility of a few more months worth the intense suffering that certain treatments entail? Would one rather stay at home, even if it meant a slightly shorter life, than spend the final weeks in a hospital? The answers to these and other questions related to end-of-life issues may well change as the end approaches, but it helps to have considered them before that point.

Organ donation. Know ahead of time how your parents feel about donating their organs or tissues after they die. For some, religious issues might preclude organ donation; others may be willing to donate tissue, such as knee cartilage, even if they're uncomfortable with the idea of donating a heart or kidney. The time to discuss these things is well before any decision needs to be made.

FINANCIAL TOPICS FOR DISCUSSION

Important papers. If you are to be responsible for the well-being and the estate of your aging parents, you need to know where certain documents are. These include wills, insurance policies, advanced directives, durable power of attorney documents, deeds to property and cemetery plots, instructions on funeral arrangements and burial, and anything having to do with your parents' estate. Asking where these papers are, of course, raises the issue of whether an up-to-date will and other critical documents exist. If they don't, it's time to begin.

Items of sentimental value. Family relationships have been torn asunder for decades over matters as mundane as Grandma's soup tureen or Grandpa's retirement watch. A sentimental object may not have much monetary value, but it can have the power to destroy family relationships. Discuss the disbursement of these items while a parent is still around to participate.

Burial arrangements. Do your parents want to be buried or cremated? Do they want a religious funeral or a celebration of their lives? Have they already made plans? It's much easier to answer these questions well before the need arises. The financial, religious, and social plans can be made without the intense emotions that accompany death.

6. **Keep old issues off the table.** Focus on the future, on what decisions need to be made, and on what you need to know. Avoid any temptation to air old grievances.

7. **In a crisis, deal with one item at a time.** If a parent falls ill before you've had the opportunity to talk about any of these matters, focus on one issue at a time. Confine your questions to those that require immediate action to avoid overwhelming your parent. For example, if you need to ask your father about his wishes for a health-care directive (see "Health Topics for Discussion," page 389), don't seize the moment to work his will into the discussion.

[Death and Grieving]

Help a Grieving Friend

It's the most natural thing in the world: Someone close to you is mourning a loved one, and you would like to offer comfort. In our society, where death is the last taboo, you may feel helpless, uncertain, even embarrassed, in the face of grief. Grief experts point out that feelings of helplessness may stem from wanting to be and do more than is possible. Grief is real, and the role of a friend is to be a companion, not a savior.

1. **Deal with your own emotions first.** Your goal is to help and support your friend. The last thing you want to do is project your own fears of death and loss, but that can happen if you haven't taken the time to calm yourself before trying to comfort your friend.

2. **Understand your role.** You're a friend, not a teacher. Be careful not to set expectations or instruct on the art of grieving. A grieving friend isn't looking for advice or even understanding. One of the least helpful things you can say is "I know just how you feel." You don't. Each person's grief is unique, and in this case comparisons are truly odious.

3. **Listen carefully.** Your first job is to listen. Make it clear you're paying special attention by maintaining eye contact. Sit in a relaxed posture by uncrossing your arms and legs and facing your friend. Don't interrupt and don't rush to respond. It's absolutely fine to have pauses and moments of silence. These quiet moments allow your friend room to cry or to initiate talk when he's ready.

4. **Don't smother.** Physical touching can be a part of active listening. A hand on an arm, for example, can be enormously supportive. But don't rush to hug a friend who starts to cry, because you may stop the tears in their tracks. It's okay to embrace someone who's crying, of course; just don't rush in too quickly and cut off the feelings you're trying to support.

5. **Keep the focus on your friend.** Allow your friend to express any emotions he feels. When a friend expresses pain, your instinct may be to try to cheer him up or distract him by changing the subject, but even if you are uncomfortable with the feelings he is expressing, focus on him and keep listening. He may repeat the story of the death. Listen each time and pay renewed attention. Your friend isn't so much conveying facts, as

he is trying to share overwhelming feelings. Don't try to deflect the pain; just keep listening.

6. **Don't talk about yourself.** Remember, there are no analogies to your friend's grief, so don't talk about how you felt when your father died. That can come later, but in the raw intensity of recent loss, even the best-intentioned comparison can have the unintended consequence of actually dismissing the grieving person's present pain.

7. **Avoid clichés.** Clichés are shorthand, quick-fix replacements for thoughtful remarks. Expressions like "you're holding up well" or "think of all the wonderful memories," translate into "get a grip on yourself" or "I don't really want to see how much pain you're in." Silence is fine if you are at a loss for words at a particular moment. If you try to fill a quiet moment with a platitude, you may be conveying the opposite of what you mean.

8. **Don't disappear.** Holidays and special anniversaries may be acutely painful times to someone mourning a loved one. Your acknowledgment of those occasions and your presence can be as important as when the grief was new. If you're not physically present for a birthday, holiday, or anniversary, you can still reach out with a phone call or a note. Mention the loved one by name. It's another chance to tell your friend that you honor his loss and his feelings, that there is never shame in grief, and that the only remedy for pain is to bear witness to it.

9. **Watch for physical reactions.** This is especially important when older people are grieving. Watch for weight loss or other signs that depression may be sapping your friend's health or strength.

10. **Bring comfort food.** Especially in the first weeks after a death or other great shock, your friend may not even think of eating or may not have the energy to provide food for himself or the family. Deliver hot soups, casseroles, or anything else that is nourishing and you know your friend would enjoy. Anything that freezes well is a big plus.

11. **Locate resources for your friend.** Find the names and numbers of local bereavement support groups or therapists who specialize in grief counseling. Make them available to your friend if it seems appropriate.

12. **Don't cross the street.** If you're casually acquainted with someone who has suffered an especially grievous loss, you may be tempted to avoid her

because you don't know what to say. "Hello, how are you?" or "I've been thinking of you; it's good to see you" are low-key but important ways of being present for those who may feel isolated in their pain.

13. **Take the initiative.** Weekends, evenings, and holidays are going to be the most difficult times for a grieving person. Reaching out socially—by offering anything from a family dinner invitation to a chance to walk in the park—can make a big difference.

14. **Don't expect reciprocation.** The social overtures you make to your friend may not be reciprocated in the conventional way. Don't keep score or expect a grieving friend to call you just because you picked up the phone the last time.

15. **Discourage major life changes for at least a year.** Sometimes a grieving person thinks that undertaking a major endeavor will be helpful. Moving, changing jobs, or making other life changes under the influence of great sadness and pain can turn out to be a mistake. If you have a close friend who's contemplating rash decisions, listen and talk it through, or encourage him to see a counselor.

16. **Be practical.** In addition to bringing comfort food, you might also volunteer to do laundry, simple cleaning, grocery shopping, cat box scooping, or other chores that can take a burden from your friend's daily life.

Talk with a Friend Diagnosed with a Serious Illness

◆◆◆

Friends share, and they don't share just the good times. When a friend is diagnosed with a serious illness, the news triggers contradictory feelings, including fear, pain, and anger, as well as deep concern and sympathy. How we respond can be both a measure and a test of our friendship. Many of the rules for talking to a grieving friend (see "Help a Grieving Friend," page 393) apply to talking to a friend about illness. Thus, it's important to acknowledge the less noble feelings, but it's critical to keep them at bay for the

LOSING A BELOVED ANIMAL

Many people develop deep bonds with their pets, and when a pet dies they expect their close friends and family to acknowledge their pain. Too often, people who haven't formed this kind of deep bond with an animal don't appreciate how intense the grief can be. If a friend loses a beloved animal, the same rules apply as when a beloved person dies. Listen. Never judge. Pay close attention. Just be there. Above all, don't make the mistake of comparing the death to any other. The relationship that has been lost was unique. Just as you would never tell a new widow to cheer up and find another husband, don't tell a friend who's grieving for an animal to get another pet. Don't say, "You'll get over it." Grief can't be cured, but grief for an animal, like grief for a person, can be acknowledged and even shared, whether or not you're an animal lover yourself. It's just a matter of empathy. Or, to put it another way, it's just a matter of friendship and love.

sake of the friend and the long-term prospects for the friendship. Put the fear aside and focus on the friend.

1. **First, listen.** People deal with the diagnosis of a serious illness in different ways. Some treat it with seeming indifference, which may signal denial, while others panic. Some regard it as a challenge, some as an occasion for profound self-pity. How you react will depend on how your friend faces the diagnosis, but you won't know that unless you listen to how she conveys the news to you. Don't interrupt, and don't express your own shock at the news. Your friend may want to express fear, anger, resentment, or anxiety; she may not want to talk about the illness at all. Take your cue from her. She may simply value the chance to get away from thoughts of illness and want to talk as though nothing were different. The first job of a friend is to listen, to be there, and to be sensitive to the cues your friend is giving.

2. **Validate feelings.** Serious illness can provoke many contradictory emotions, including guilt, self-pity, fear, courage, depression, and every

other feeling flesh is heir to. Sometimes, it's impossible to share those feelings with a spouse or child, because they may themselves be the object of those feelings. A friend may be the only release. As you listen, don't make judgments and restrain yourself from giving advice. Your most important task is to make it clear that you empathize with the feelings being expressed.

3. **Don't confuse acceptance with defeat.** If the illness is particularly serious or ultimately fatal, people tend to expect others to react with defiance. Acceptance, however, can bring a sense of control and doesn't necessarily mean your friend has given up hope. If your reaction is resistance, if you reject your friend's acceptance of his situation, it denies him your participation in realistic plans and strategies for coping and effectively denies him your emotional support.

4. **Don't play doctor.** Short of making sure your friend has appropriate medical care, don't take on the role of caregiver, even if in fact you are a health professional. Your role as friend is irreplaceable; others can fulfill the role of physician.

5. **Be specific when you offer help.** Vague statements like "just ask if you need anything" aren't helpful. If there's something you know would be helpful, such as going shopping or preparing a meal, offer to do it. Be creative. If your friend's been shut in, offer to take him for a drive. If he's bored, offer to rent a movie or play a game, or read to him. Don't be afraid of offering something foolish; sometimes the seemingly silly thing, like offering to read a story out loud, is just the thing to break through depression.

6. **Don't lie.** If your friend looks terrible, don't tell her how good she looks. That doesn't mean you have to say she's now a poster child for the seven plagues, but it doesn't help to deny the obvious. If the illness is apparently worse, don't say he seems to be getting better. Illness can be isolating; lying makes the isolation that much more profound.

Steps to Take When Someone Dies

◆◆◆

Most people have little first-hand experience dealing with the details of death. Close family members often die in a hospital, where trained medical professionals take care of many basic tasks. If someone dies at home, you are very likely to be in shock in addition to being at a loss about what to do. Here are the steps to take in case this ever happens to you.

1. **Don't move or disturb the body.** No matter what the cause of death, leave the body undisturbed unless you have specific authorization or a permit to move it.

2. **Call the proper authorities.** If the death was expected and the patient was under the care of a doctor or hospice organization, call either of them. If the death was unexpected, or if you don't know the physician or hospice phone number, dial 911. The police will determine whether to conduct an investigation or to release the body to the funeral home you choose.

3. **Obtain a death certificate.** No matter what the circumstance or cause of the death, you will need a death certificate signed by an attending physician or other medical authority.

4. **Call a friend or relative for support.** Don't try to cope with death, expected or not, by yourself. You can benefit enormously from both the emotional and practical support of a friend.

5. **Determine if the person wanted to donate organs or tissue.** If the death occurs in a hospital, make sure you honor the deceased's wishes about donating organs or tissue. If you're not certain what those wishes were, check the person's driver's license; it may indicate that he or she wanted to be an organ donor.

6. **Call family and friends.** Call the people you feel closest to and ask each one to call a few others, so no one has the burden of making all of the calls.

7. **Find out if any arrangements have already been made.** If you're a spouse or next of kin, you probably know what provisions have been made. Otherwise, ask close friends or relatives whether the person belonged to a burial society or had prepaid funeral arrangements. Be sure

to find out whether or not a burial plot or other resting place has already been chosen and paid for.

8. **Deal with the remains.** If you've already chosen a funeral home, call and tell them where to pick up the body. If there are no arrangements in place, you can ask any funeral home or ambulance service to pick up the body and take it to a mortuary for temporary storage. You are under no obligation to use this institution for further services; just make it clear that you are only asking for transport and temporary storage. Depending on the weather, a body can be left at home for as long as seventy-two hours, so don't feel you must make a hasty decision if you are unsure of what you'd like to do next.

9. **Determine place and other details for a service.** Make plans, or ask family members about their plans, for a funeral, burial, cremation, memorial service, or other arrangements.

10. **Place an obituary.** The funeral home will usually take care of this for a small fee, but you might also want to notify alumni or professional organizations. If the deceased was well-known, you may want to call a member of the press or ask a colleague to write and place an appropriate obituary. If the family would like, include details about funeral services.

11. **Call the employer.** If the person was still working, call her employer and ask about any benefits that might be due, including pay or disability benefits. Ask about any pension or life insurance that might have been carried through the employer. Also check on continuation of medical benefits for immediate family members.

12. **Call the Social Security Administration.** If relevant, also contact state agencies or the Veterans Administration, and notify any union or professional organizations of the death and ask if the deceased held life insurance policies with them.

Learn about the Death-Care Business

◆◆◆

Few consumers would deliberately spend thousands of dollars on a product they chose hastily while they were emotionally distraught, yet that's exactly what many people do when they're confronted with making funeral arrangements for a family member. The best way to avoid spending more than you would like—or can afford—is to learn your options and your rights ahead of time. This list will help you to be a more rational consumer when the need to make funeral arrangements arises.

1. **Know what funerals can cost.** According to the Federal Trade Commission, which regulates the funeral industry, a traditional funeral, including casket and vault, costs about $6,000. But that figure does not include "extras" such as flowers, obituary notices, acknowledgment cards, and limousines. Such trappings can quickly bring the bill to $10,000. The cost of renting a viewing room in a funeral home can be higher than the daily rate for a suite in one of the finest hotels in the world.

2. **Plan ahead to make rational decisions.** Making funeral arrangements in the midst of grief can amount to throwing yourself on the kindness of strangers, strangers whose living depends on selling sometimes costly products and services to grieving relatives. Although most professionals in the funeral industry are honest, you are likely to save a considerable sum by doing your research well before you need the information. You can even make complete arrangements ahead of time. The Website *www.finalarrangementsnetwork.com* offers comprehensive information about funerals, cemetery plots, and cremation services, and it includes links to individual funeral homes and cemetery plots for sale by owners. The site can walk you through planning for just about any kind of arrangements you'd like. Another useful site is *www.funeraldirectory.com*, which has a special "planityourway" section.

3. **Consider the prepayment option with caution.** Prepaying for funeral services can save money, but such arrangements are governed by the laws of individual states, and protections vary from one state to another. If you're considering prepaying for funeral goods and services, keep the following in mind and make sure you ask the right questions. Also, make sure your family knows about any arrangements you've made. Know ex-

actly what you're paying for. Are you buying just a casket or paying for a complete service as well? Are you protected if the firm goes out of business? Can you cancel the contract and get a complete refund if you change your mind? What happens if you move to another part of the country or die while you're abroad? Can you transfer the services to another funeral home and, if so, will that entail an additional cost?

4. **Know your rights under the Funeral Rule.** According to the Federal Trade Commission's Funeral Rule, a provider must make it clear that you have a right to choose only the goods and services you want (with some exceptions, such as embalming if the burial or cremation is delayed). He must provide a written price list for every item and show you the list before you are shown the goods. He may not refuse to handle, nor charge a fee for handling, a casket purchased somewhere else. If you opt for cremation, the funeral director must make available low-cost alternative containers (made of heavy cardboard or plastic and sometimes labeled "temporary"). The Funeral Rule also requires funeral directors to give their prices over the phone.

5. **Save money by buying a casket or urn directly.** You can usually save a considerable amount of money by purchasing products from the manufacturer. There are dozens of sites to choose from and most will ship overnight, usually for a fee. To see what's available, compare prices and terms on several sites that sell caskets directly, including *www.americancaskets.com*, *www.casketsonline.com*, *www.casketsdirect*, and *www.casketsexpress.com*. You will also find links to casket sales at both of the sites mentioned in number two, above.

6. **Know what costs you can't avoid.** Funeral homes have what's known as a nondeclinable charge. This basic fee includes costs that are common to all funeral arrangements, such as planning, securing copies of death certificates, sheltering the remains, and coordinating the arrangements with the cemetery or other third parties. It does not include any extras, such as a casket, embalming, and renting a room for a viewing or religious service.

7. **Understand what constitutes a full-service, traditional funeral.** Beyond the nondeclinable services, the traditional full-service funeral would include a viewing or visitation at the funeral home, a formal funeral service, use of a hearse to transport the body to the funeral home and burial site, the use of limousines from the funeral home to the burial site, and burial, entombment, or cremation of the body. You'll also be

ORGANIZATIONS THAT CAN HELP

American Association of Retired People Fulfillment

601 E Street, NW
Washington, DC 20049
800–424–3410
www.aarp.org

AARP is a nonprofit, nonpartisan organization dedicated to helping older Americans achieve lives of independence, dignity, and purpose. Its publications, "Funeral Goods and Services" and "Pre-Paying for Your Funeral," are available free by writing to the above address. This and other funeral-related information is posted on the AARP Website.

Council of Better Business Bureaus, Inc.

4200 Wilson Blvd., Suite 800
Arlington, VA 22203–1838
www.bbb.org

Better Business Bureaus are private, nonprofit organizations that promote ethical business standards and voluntary self-regulation of business practices.

Funeral Consumers Alliance

33 Patchen Road
South Burlington, VT 05403
800–765–0107
www.funerals.org

FCA, a nonprofit educational organization that supports increased funeral consumer protection, is affiliated with the Funeral and Memorial Society of America (FAMSA).

Cremation Association of North America

401 North Michigan Avenue
Chicago, IL 60611
312–644–6610
www.cremationassociation.org

CANA is an association of crematories, cemeteries, and funeral homes that offer cremation.

International Cemetery and Funeral Association (ICFA)

1895 Preston White Drive, Suite 220
Reston, VA 20191
800–645–7700
www.icfa.org

ICFA is a nonprofit association of cemeteries, funeral homes, crematories, and monument retailers that offers informal mediation of consumer complaints through its Cemetery Consumer Service Council. Its Website provides information and advice under "Consumer Resources."

charged for embalming and dressing the body. In addition, you will pay separately for the casket, flowers, and the cemetery plot or crypt.

8. **Decline the optional services you don't want.** No state requires embalming the body, and it's illegal for a funeral director to tell you otherwise. Nor need you pay for dressing the body or cosmetics, especially if you choose not to have a public viewing. Limousines are optional, and you're free to supply whatever flowers you choose, or none at all. Expensive caskets are not required, and beware of any funeral director who tries to manipulate you into "honoring" your loved one with a pricey coffin. It's legal to bury a body in something other than a traditional casket. In fact, some religious groups require that a body be interred in a burial shroud or a plain pine box. It is illegal under the FTC's Funeral Rule for a funeral director to suggest that you're not paying proper respect to the deceased if you choose not to buy these extras. If you feel any pressure to do so, report the funeral home to the Federal Trade Commission.

9. **Opt for direct burial or direct cremation for maximum savings.** Many families now choose "direct burial" or "direct cremation," in which the body is buried or cremated shortly after death, with no formal service at the funeral home. A memorial service can be held later. In cases such as these, the only costs would be the basic (nondeclinable) fee, the cost of a container for the remains, a fee to transport the body to the cemetery or crematorium, and the cost of a burial plot.

Conclusion

Well, there you have it. Squillions of tips, tricks, and solutions to guide you through the complexities of life. *Keep It Together* features topics as wildly diverse as life itself, so you probably haven't read it from cover to cover, but I hope you will continue to pick it up whenever you feel the need for advice, whether that might be guidance on handling a delicate predicament, instructions for a basic how-to, or maybe just the reassurance that you've got the right idea or covered all your bases as you go about the business of life.

Whatever your particular need in the moment, I hope you find what you're looking for whenever you turn to these pages. Above all, I'd like you to gain the feeling of empowerment that comes from taking charge of your day and your life. Even if you've only skimmed the book so far, I hope *Keep It Together* already has you feeling more efficient, informed, prepared, and, best of all, confident.

Kirsten M. Lagatree

Index